ROB RILEY

The story of our mate is incredibly sad. The challenge for Quentin Beresford has been to tell the chapter of that story that is our mate's alone. There will be those that feel betrayed and those whose hearts will be forever broken but our mate would have demanded honesty. The life portrayed in these pages will above all else challenge our capacity to look into this blighted page of our history and to deal with and understand the nature of our national racist cancer.

Patrick Dodson
Broome

As a baby, Rob Riley was separated from his family and taken to the 'half caste' home, Sister Kate's, whose purpose was to strip him of his indigenous identity. As an adolescent, he lived in the squalor of the Pingelly Reserve and in the slums of East Perth. And yet, despite all this, he grew up to become one of the most effective and most loved Aboriginal political leaders of Australia's modern political history. Rob Riley was intimately associated with all the great causes of his people—the struggles for land rights, self-determination, the signing of a treaty, the search for truth about Aboriginal deaths in custody and the stolen generations. Yet his final years were overtaken by intertwined public and private suffering, as he fought the inexorable rise of the reactionary forces in society and as the traumas of his early life slowly overcame him. In this detailed and delicate biography, Quentin Beresford tells a story of triumph and of tragedy. I cannot think of a finer introduction to Aboriginal politics in the contemporary era. I urge all Australian citizens who care about reconciliation to read it.

Robert Manne
Professor of Politics
La Trobe University

ROB RILEY
AN ABORIGINAL LEADER'S QUEST FOR JUSTICE

Quentin Beresford

Aboriginal Studies Press

First published in 2006
Reprinted 2007, 2008
by Aboriginal Studies Press

© Quentin Beresford 2006

All rights reserved. No part of this book may be reproduced or transmitted in any form or by any means, electronic or mechanical, including photocopying, recording or by any information storage and retrieval system, without prior permission in writing from the publisher. The *Australian Copyright Act 1968* (the Act) allows a maximum of one chapter or 10 per cent of this book, whichever is the greater, to be photocopied by any educational institution for its education purposes provided that the educational institution (or body that administers it) has given a remuneration notice to Copyright Agency Limited (CAL) under the Act.

Aboriginal Studies Press
is the publishing arm of the
Australian Institute of Aboriginal
and Torres Strait Islander Studies.
GPO Box 553, Canberra, ACT 2601
Phone: (61 2) 6246 1183
Fax: (61 2) 6261 4288
Email: asp@aiatsis.gov.au
Web: www.aiatsis.gov.au/asp/

National Library of Australia
Cataloguing-In-Publication data:

Beresford, Quentin, 1954– .

    Rob Riley: an Aboriginal leader's quest for justice.

    Bibliography.
    Includes index.
    ISBN 0 85575 502 4.

    1. Riley, Rob, 1954–1996. 2. Aboriginal Australians—Biography. 3. Political activists—Australia—Biography. 4. Stolen generations (Australia)—Biography. I. Title.

305.89915092

Front cover illustration: Rob Riley, *West Australian Newspapers Ltd*
Index compiled by Michael Harrington
Designed and typeset by Sprout Design
Printed in Australia by Ligare Pty Ltd

Contents

Illustrations		vii
Acknowledgements		xi
Abbreviations		xv
Publisher's Note		xvi
Introduction		1
ONE	Prisoners of Racism: The History of Rob Riley's Family	9
TWO	Bound for Assimilation: A Childhood at Sister Kate's	33
THREE	Life at the Margins: Growing up Aboriginal	57
FOUR	Apprenticeship: Joining the Aboriginal Legal Service	76
FIVE	Noonkanbah: The Struggle for Heritage	100
SIX	A Bigger Stage: The National Aboriginal Conference	121
SEVEN	Betrayal: The Demise of National Land Rights	166
EIGHT	Enemies Within: The End of the National Aboriginal Conference	197
NINE	At the Cutting Edge: Political Battles in Canberra	211
TEN	War on All Fronts: Return to the Aboriginal Legal Service	242
ELEVEN	Mounting Despair: The Final Campaigns	279
Legacy		329
Notes		337
Bibliography		354
Index		363

Illustrations

following page 32

Anna Dinah (née Miller), Rob Riley's maternal grandmother, Moore River Settlement.
South Australian Museum, no. N2100

The church at Moore River Settlement.
Photograph courtesy Battye Library, State Library of Western Australia.

Camp at Moore River Settlement.
Photograph courtesy Battye Library, State Library of Western Australia.

Sam Dinah revisiting Moore River Settlement.
Photograph Quentin Beresford.

Sam Dinah at the Commemoration Wall in the Cemetery, Moore River Settlement.
Photograph Quentin Beresford.

Sister Kate Clutterbuck.
Photograph courtesy Battye Library, State Library of Western Australia.

The last cottage Rob lived in at Sister Kate's.
Photograph Quentin Beresford.

following page 64

Robert Dinah (later Rob Riley), aged about five, at Sister Kate's Children's Home.
Photograph courtesy Riley family.

Rob Riley with friend from Sister Kate's.
Photograph courtesy Riley family.

Rob Riley and his mother Violet, early 1990s.
Photograph courtesy Riley family. Copyright West Australian Newspapers Ltd.

Dennis Daebritz, Rob Riley, Beth Daebritz, Megan Riley, Jeannie Riley and Emma Riley.
Photograph courtesy Riley family.

Lila Riley, Rob's grandmother on his stepfather's side.
Photograph courtesy Riley family.

Rob Riley and his stepfather, Bill Riley.
Photograph courtesy Riley family.

Rob Riley, Jeannie Morrison and friends, 1974.
Photograph courtesy Riley family.

following page 80

Rob Riley and Jim Morrison at a land rights rally, late 1970s.
Photograph courtesy Riley family.

Brian Wyatt at Black Action Rally.
Photograph courtesy Riley family.

Protest against Western Australian government changes to the Electoral Act to remove Aborigines from the rolls, c. 1978.
Photograph courtesy Michael Gallagher.

following page 112

Dicky Skinner at Noonkanbah, August 1980.
Photograph courtesy Western Australian Newspaper.

The Blockade, Micky's Pool, Noonkanbah, August 1980.
Photograph courtesy Michael Gallagher.

The Blockade, Micky's Pool, Noonkanbah, August 1980.
Photograph courtesy Michael Gallagher.

following page 144

NAC WA delegates: Rob Riley, Margaret Mallard and Peter Yu, early 1980s.
Photograph courtesy Riley family.

Robert Riley in his late twenties, early 1980s.
Photograph courtesy Riley family. West Australian Newspapers Ltd.

Rob Riley and Peter Yu in Broome, c. 1983.
Photograph courtesy Riley family.

John Pat rally, 1983.
Photograph courtesy Riley family.

following page 176

Rob Riley and Roger Shipton, national land rights rally, Canberra, May 1985.
Photograph courtesy Riley family.

Rob Riley addressing national land rights rally, Canberra, May 1985.
Photograph courtesy Riley family.

Rob Riley with Prime Minister Bob Hawke, Hazel Hawke and 'Sugar' Ray Robinson, c. 1984.
Photograph courtesy Riley family.

Handing over Uluru in October 1985, Rob Riley taking the photos.
Photograph courtesy Riley family.

Rob Riley and Aboriginal Affairs Minister Clyde Holding, c. 1985.
Photograph courtesy Riley family.

following page 240

Rob Riley and Jack Ah Kit, Uluru, late 1980s.
Photograph courtesy Riley family.

Dean Collard and Ted Wilkes with Rob Riley at the Bicentennial, 1988.
Photograph courtesy Riley family. Photo by Sheryl Osborne.

Male dancers, Barunga Festival, 1988.
Photograph courtesy Riley family.

Gerry Hand and Bob Hawke, Barunga Festival, 1988.
Photograph courtesy Riley family.

Women dancers, Barunga Festival, 1988.
Photograph courtesy Riley family.

following page 272

Royal Commission into Aboriginal Deaths in Custody (Underlying Causes) Travelling Investigative Party, c. 1990.
The photographer was Pat Dodson.
Photograph courtesy Riley family.

The Dalai Lama in Perth, 1992.
Photograph courtesy Riley family.

On the airwaves, early 1990s.
Photograph courtesy Sam Dinah.

Rob Riley addressing rally to protest Western Australia's controversial juvenile justice legislation, February 1992.
Photograph courtesy Riley family.

Rob Riley with Aboriginal Affairs Minister Robert Tickner, Aboriginal Legal Service offices, mid-1990s.
Photograph courtesy Sam Dinah.

following page 320

On holidays: Lydia Collard, Rob Riley, Emma, Megan and Jaymea.
Photograph courtesy Riley family.

Rob and his daughter Megan.
Photograph courtesy Riley family.

Rob and Jeannie's children: Emma, Megan and Jaymea, on holiday in Pemberton, WA.
Photograph courtesy Riley family.

Ted Wilkes opening Rob Riley Walk, Curtin University.
Photograph courtesy Riley family.

Gough Whitlam and Violet Riley on the occasion of Rob's posthumous award of Human Right and Equal Opportunity Commission, Human Rights Award, Sydney 1996.
Photograph courtesy Riley family.

Rob Riley's grandchildren at his grave in Pingelly: Izayoh Riley, Jaxon Mallard and Caitlyn Mallard.
Photograph courtesy Riley family.

Acknowledgements

In writing this book I was generously supported by many people.

The idea for a biography of Rob Riley came from Jeannie Morrison and from Rob and Jeannie's daughters, Meagan, Jaymea and Emma. Together they showed great strength in believing Rob's story needed to be told. The book reflects so much of their input. They made themselves repeatedly available to provide background information, discuss approaches and provide feedback while at all times allowing me the independence to develop the manuscript.

Rob's uncle, Sam Dinah, was immensely helpful in reconstructing the family's background. His kind permission to use his mother's personal material greatly added to the scope and depth of the book. The tours he arranged of Moore River Settlement and Sister Kate's added major insights into Rob's background.

Maxine Chi also provided valuable assistance to the project. She made available Rob's extensive personal archive as well as her own insights and recollections about Rob. Her constructive feedback on the penultimate draft is appreciated. I thank her for her courage in reopening such a painful period in her life.

Without the willingness of the following people to be interviewed — some of them several times — about their memories of Rob, I would not have been able to piece together the threads of his life. Some offered many hours of recollections. I would like to thank them all for their patience and generosity. In alphabetical order they are: Jill Abdullah, Geoff Adlide, John Ah Kit, Malcolm Allbrook, Robyn Ayres, Les

Ayton, Richard Bartlett, Jenny Bedford, Greg Benn, Min Bradley, Tony Buti, Christabel Chamarette, Alan Carpenter, Dawn Casey, Maxine Chi, Chris Coomer, Dean Collard, Catherine Crawford, Stuart Crowe, Beth Daebritz, Sam Dinah, Pat Dodson, Mick Dodson, Peter Dowding, Pat Dudgeon, Dennis Eggington, Michael Gallagher, Stephen Goodall, Sue Gordon, Anna Haebich, Gerry Hand, Steve Hawke, Ian Horrocks, Darryl Kickett, Graham McDonald, Les Malezer, Megan Mallard, Michael Mansell, Carol Martin, Steve Mickler, Jeannie Morrison, Peter O'Brien, Sharon O'Neil, Jackie Oakley, Howard Pedersen, Jeannine Purdy, Fred Reibling, Violet Riley, Emma Riley, Jaymea Riley, Paul Seaman, Heather Skullthorpe, Robert Tickner, Philip Vincent, Cathcarte Weatherly, Sir Ronald Wilson, Joan Winch, Brian Wyatt, Cedric Wyatt, Ted Wilkes, Peter Yu.

For professional advice and support on the many sensitive issues involved in this project, I thank Tracey Westerman and staff at Indigenous Psychological Services and Professor Graham Martin, Director of Child and Adolescent Psychiatry, Department of Psychiatry, University of Queensland.

Several people took time out of their busy schedules to read the various drafts of the manuscript. I am particularly indebted to Howard Pederson, Tim Muirhead, Steve Mickler and Ted Wilkes for their comments on the penultimate draft. In accessing their respective professional backgrounds in Indigenous affairs, I was given insights and details which improved the book. Chris Sheil provided constructive dialogue and feedback throughout the project, while other people offered valuable help with parts of the manuscript. Pauline Carroll provided access to the literature on biography, and her comments on the Introduction were especially helpful. Steve Hawke, Richard Bartlett and Gerry Hand provided feedback on one or more of the chapters which greatly helped in clarifying matters of historical detail.

While all the people who were interviewed or who offered advice will readily see the contributions they have made, the author naturally takes full responsibility for the finished product. I respect the fact that not everyone agreed with all of my interpretations and conclusions.

Michael Gallagher has my appreciation for making available his unique photographic record of the Aboriginal protest movement of the 1970s and 1980s, and I was especially fortunate in having access to Steve Mickler's extensive resources in contemporary Aboriginal politics.

I acknowledge the generous grant from the Institute of Aboriginal and Torres Strait Islander Studies (AIATSIS) in Canberra. The willingness of this organisation to support the project enabled the fullest possible collection of research materials and interviews.

I could not have asked for a better publisher. Aboriginal Studies Press, the publishing arm of AIATSIS, and its Director Rhonda Black and Deputy Director Gabrielle Lhuede provided the best possible editorial advice and assistance. I greatly enjoyed working with both of them. I also greatly benefited from the feedback of several anonymous reviewers arranged by the Press. Caroline Williamson made an important contribution with her rigorous editing of the final draft.

Working on the project with me were two excellent research assistants. Bianca Blake and Fay Davidson brought commitment and great professional skills to the project. Together they unearthed a wealth of materials upon which much of this book is based.

I am grateful to a number of people at Edith Cowan University for the support and specialist advice offered to this project: Professor Patrick Garnett, Professor Bill Louden, Associate Professor Peter Bedford, Julie Harris and Richard Goodwin. The granting of study leave greatly expedited completion of the book. The administrative assistance of Janice Bryant and Bill Noble is appreciated.

The transcribing of many hours of tape recordings was expertly handled by Aimee Benson.

The book benefited greatly from a Research Fellowship at the Center for Humanities at Wesleyan University in Connecticut during the spring semester, 2005. I am grateful to its Director, Professor Henry Abelove, for this invitation and for his dedication in creating such a collegial, stimulating and supportive environment for scholarly work. I would like to thank the Spring 2005 Fellows for their friendliness and interest. The secretarial assistance at the Center provided by Ms Brenda Keating and Ms Susan Ferris is especially appreciated.

Authors have so much to thank their families for. My son William and my daughter Michelle provide cheerful diversions in Perth during the writing of the book, and their patience and support when I was rather too preoccupied was greatly appreciated. William came to the rescue when long distance research assistance was required.

To my friends, a heartfelt thank you for listening and interacting with the issues behind Rob's story.

The greatest debt I owe is reserved for last. My wife Marilyn had a profound impact on this work. She shared the entire journey of this challenging project, providing a constant sounding board and source of encouragement. She generously devoted most of her time during our six-month stay in Connecticut to sharing her insights about Rob's background, the art of writing biography and the approaches needed to underpin the work. In addition she brought her incisive editorial skills to correcting and commenting upon each stage of the manuscript. I will be forever grateful for her contribution.

Quentin Beresford
Perth, December 2005

Abbreviations

AIATSIS	Australian Institute of Aboriginal and Torres Strait Islander Studies
ALS	Aboriginal Legal Service (WA)
AMIC	Australian Mining Industry Council
ATSIC	Aboriginal and Torres Strait Islander Commission
CLAC	Civil Liberties Action Committee
CLC	Central Land Council
KLC	Kimberley Land Council
NAC	National Aboriginal Conference
NACC	National Aboriginal Consultative Committee
NAIDOC	National Aborigines and Islanders Day Observance Committee
NLC	Northern Land Council
PD	Parliamentary Debates
PLO	Principal Legal Officer
RCIADC	Royal Commission into Aboriginal Deaths in Custody
TRG	Tactical Response Group
VP	Votes and Proceedings
LA	Legislative Assembly

Publisher's Note

Readers are advised that this book contains images of people who have passed away. Every effort has been made to contact copyright owners. If a photograph appears in this book without due acknowledgement, please contact Aboriginal Studies Press.

Introduction

On 30 April 1996 Aboriginal activist and leader Robert Riley — born Robert Dinah, and universally known as Rob — drove into a plain, besser-block motel on a busy highway in a light-industrial part of Perth's southern suburbs. He paid cash for room 24, carried in a few personal belongings and shut the door. Alone in the crammed and sparsely furnished room, he penned his final thoughts. The next day, staff found him dead, hanging from the shower fixture. He was forty-one.

The note he left was intended as much for the nation as it was for his family and friends. It was written as his mind was being dulled by sedatives and in handwriting that tumbled erratically across the page. Yet what he wrote retained a clear and incisive thread. He said he had experienced and witnessed 'so much trauma, shame and guilt that I can't make peace with myself'. To his family and friends he expressed his love and sought their forgiveness. His three daughters were uppermost in his mind. Then, in an outpouring against the society he had fought so relentlessly to change, Rob wrote: 'Understand white Australia that you have so much to answer for. Your greed, your massacres, your sanitised history in the name of might and right'. Finally, he made a political statement on the experience that had shaped his life — his childhood removal from his family under the policy of assimilation. He pleaded to the nation: 'Don't let the national inquiry into the removal of Aboriginal children be swept under the carpet'.

Following his death, obituaries gave an instant measure of the impact of his life. Writing in *The Canberra Times*, Jan Mayman described Riley as 'brilliant and charismatic', and a speaker of hard truths.[1] Gerry Hand, federal Minister for Aboriginal Affairs in the late 1980s, who had employed Rob as his senior advisor, praised his contribution. 'I rate him as something very, very special, and when history records that period of the seventies and eighties ... the name Rob Riley is going to figure very prominently'.[2] Aboriginal leader Noel Pearson paid a similar tribute: 'He goes down as one of the great Aboriginal leaders of all time'.[3]

The list of Rob's involvements confirms his status as a major Aboriginal political figure. He was Executive Officer of the Western Australian Aboriginal Legal Service (ALS) in the late 1970s; he participated in the pivotal Noonkanbah sacred sites dispute of the late 1970s; he led the National Aboriginal Conference — the main political voice for Aboriginal people — in the early to mid 1980s; he was a leader in the campaign for national land rights in the mid 1980s. He was senior ministerial advisor to federal Aboriginal Affairs Minister Gerry Hand in the late 1980s during the negotiations over the proposed Treaty between the federal government and Aboriginal people, the establishment of the Aboriginal and Torres Strait Islander Commission (ATSIC) and the appointment of the Royal Commission into Aboriginal Deaths in Custody. He headed the Western Australian Issues Unit for the Royal Commission and then returned to the ALS in Western Australia, in which he served again as Executive Officer between 1990 and 1995. During this intense period, Rob was an active participant in the negotiations and debate over native title following the High Court decision in the Mabo case. He also lobbied extensively for the establishment of an inquiry into the Stolen Generations.

After the announcement of his death, *The West Australian* was crammed with heartfelt testimonials for weeks on end. His funeral service overflowed with people from all parts of the community united in shock and grief. There was a sense of loss not only of a leader but of a unique individual. Rob commanded not just respect, but widespread affection. Those who knew him only as a public figure admired his commitment, his articulate command of the issues and his willingness to reach out into the white community for support. Those close to him loved him also for his fearlessness, his irreverence and his capacity for friendship.

~~~~~~

When his family invited me to write his biography, it was clear that the task presented a number of challenges. The first was to balance out my sympathy for the role he played in Aboriginal politics, at least as I had observed it as an interested member of the public during the 1990s, with the appropriate detachment needed by a biographer. While neither a friend nor a colleague of Rob's, I did meet him a number of times in the mid-1990s. I was researching a book into the over representation of Western Australia's Aboriginal youth in detention;[4] and in his capacity as Executive Officer of the Aboriginal Legal Service Rob had enthusiastically supported the project. My colleague and I periodically briefed him on our findings. We were able to report, for instance, that youth with the most serious criminal records often came from family backgrounds where one or both parents had been removed in childhood under the policy of assimilation. The depth of his interest in our project was impressive. He asked questions about our data and offered his own insights into the pressing social problems behind the disproportionate number of incarcerated Aboriginal youth.

It was no idle commitment for him to meet with us. The state of his office highlighted the dynamism of his existence. From the reports piled high in every corner and the papers haphazardly strewn across his desk, it appeared that Rob faced a daily struggle to keep on top of the tide of issues swamping the Aboriginal Legal Service. He was keen to talk with us, but we were never left alone with him for long; aides would appear to remind him of some appointment or other. The flow of energy seemed constant, the work life chaotic.

Those encounters were in the first half of 1995. In the second half of that year, along with many other Western Australians, I watched with concern and disbelief as Rob's emotional decline played out in the media. He was photographed by the press in front of the sign directing people to Royal Perth Hospital's 'Block D': the Department of Psychiatry. His face appeared expressionless, emptied of life. The editor's headline to the accompanying story read: 'Riley tells of life in tatters'.[5] Like many observers, I wondered how his life had reached this point.

However, I commenced the project with few preconceived ideas about his personality and life. I knew almost nothing about his background and little of his political career before the early 1990s. I had been actively encouraged by his family to explore every line of inquiry I thought might usefully shed light on his drive, his ideals, his achievements and his death.

The second challenge in writing about Rob was the sheer scale of his involvements. Would it be possible to do justice to all of them? This problem merged into a third challenge: how to write about Rob as an individual, as well as in the context of the tumultuous history of modern race relations.

Rob's life was woven into the fabric of the struggle to secure justice for Aboriginal people. This struggle was conducted by a broad coalition of Aboriginal leaders and organisations which I refer to as the Aboriginal rights movement.

The increased assertiveness of the rights movement during the 1970s helped fuel a backlash in Australia's relationship with its racial history. Rob's political development is inseparable from these debates. He became caught up in the fight to control the national story on race relations with Aboriginal people.

Aborigines were largely written out of the national story by Australia's first historians. However, from the late 1960s a wave of pioneering history documented Aboriginal experiences of resistance to frontier violence, repressive government policies and institutional racism. This view of the national story on race increasingly enraged a range of conservatives — business leaders in the resource industries, sections of the Liberal/National parties and some public intellectuals — who saw such Aboriginal history 'as romanticising the "noble savage", blackening the national reputation, encouraging present-day Aborigines in futile separatism and fostering the break-up of Australia'.[6]

The 'war' over Aboriginal history began in the mid-1980s as a series of pre-emptive strikes by influential conservative figures, reacting to the intensification of the land rights debate. Within a few years the entire Aboriginal rights agenda was subject to a conservative re-interpretation: land rights was about guilt; genocide was a fiction; and policies of assimilation came from the best intentions.

As early as 1984, Rob argued that it was not possible for Aboriginal people to forget the history of dispossession and marginalisation: 'It is dishonest for others to argue that we should start now from a basis of "equality". As with all other peoples, our past shapes our present and our future'.[7] Rob developed a keen understanding of Australia's racial history. His many public talks were infused with the history of Aboriginal oppression and injustice. In particular, he understood the painful legacy of Australia's racial past. In a 1994 address, he argued:

> Historically, the truth is that the Indigenous people of Australia have been subjected to more intense social engineering, and social and cultural genocide, than people from any other former British colony. The legacy of the policies of indentured labour, assimilation and integration will continue to manifest itself for many years to come.[8]

Thus, a biography of Rob Riley takes us deeper into the history 'wars', beyond the rhetoric of the attacks from the so-called 'New Right' and the cut and thrust of the media comment they generated, into the Aboriginal experience of Australian racism.

Rob was fearless in depicting as racists some of Australia's state and federal politicians, talkback radio presenters and captains of industry. His public statements are littered with robust accusations that those in influential positions who denied Aborigines rights were racists. Rob's accusations of racism were not personally vengeful. For him, racism was a multilayered system of control. He knew from his own personal experience that racism encompassed discrimination against individuals, the origins of which lay in white prejudice. But when he lashed out at selected political, media and industry leaders he was referring to a much more complex dimension of race involving a system of institutional power: a means to deny to Aborigines as a race acknowledgement of past injustices, access to the nation's resources and control over their own future.

While I have been mindful to keep Rob at centre stage, there has been an inevitable blurring between his life and the dramatic events which surrounded it. He was, after all, one of a relatively small group of prominent activists at the centre of an epic historical struggle.

A fourth challenge in undertaking a biography of Rob relates directly to the nature of biography itself. Biography is sometimes said to fall short of its claims to be able to capture the essence of an individual's life and link this to their achievements.[9] Human personality, it is claimed, and its interaction with the world, is elusive. As Rob's battle with mental illness testifies, his was a multilayered and intense emotional life. His friends and colleagues knew the outlines of his institutional background, but they rarely received more than superficial accounts from him. Rob's troubled life was mostly well concealed behind his persona of a fearless Aboriginal rights campaigner. His descent into despair and eventual suicide shocked most of his friends and colleagues. Many were jolted into a realisation of how little they knew about his past and his inner life. Their reactions highlight the larger problem of the elusiveness of human personality: how much do we ever really understand about the emotional makeup of another individual?

A number of avenues opened up to trace the evolution of Rob's character. Foremost were his writings and published interviews. Rob wrote several revealing pieces about his childhood and he was interviewed at length in the mid-1980s by the State Library of Western Australia and again in the mid-1990s for the ALS's project on the Stolen Generations. This material contains many deep insights into how Rob had been shaped by his tumultuous past and how he had internalised these experiences.

Rob's friends and colleagues also offered innumerable insights. I interviewed at length more than sixty people from all parts of his life, a number of them several times over. Many have reflected on their experiences with him in the years since his death. These taped interviews comprised over 1200 pages of material.

In light of the personal and sensitive nature of much of the material given in interviews, and the request by a few people to remain anonymous, I decided not to identify individuals in the endnotes of this book unless the contents of a particular quotation required the identification of an individual. All people interviewed are listed in the Acknowledgments.

As a public figure, and one who was adept at using the media, Rob also left a rich trail of his thoughts on the public issues he campaigned for. Often he couched his statements in a reflective mode, leaving clear insights into his thinking.

Lastly, Rob had an extensive collection of private papers relating to his public career. These mainly concerned his period with the National Aboriginal Conference in the early to mid 1980s and consist of letters written to, and received from, a range of political and public figures. Also contained in his papers are important materials relating to his mental illness and the circumstances surrounding his departure from the ALS. Thus, as much as the genre of biography will allow, it is possible to understand much of his make-up and the course his life took.

However, there can never be a definitive biography, only a version of an individual's life. Rob touched many people through his convictions, his humour and his empathy. He infuriated his opponents with his uncompromising approach to politics, and he exasperated some of those with whom he worked because of his unconventional style of management. Not surprisingly, there were differences of opinion among the people I interviewed as to who the 'real' Rob was. Virginia Woolf's reminder to biographers many years ago, that they must 'be prepared to admit contradictory versions of the same face', is applicable here.[10]

In the case of Rob, as with most other multifaceted characters, much depended on the level at which people interacted with him and, of course, how they as individuals responded to him. Yet the core of Rob's being was his commitment to political struggle, and it is this dimension of his life which is central in the book, even though I have sought the broadest possible understanding of how this related to other aspects of his life.

The final challenge of writing a biography about Rob related directly to his suicide. There was a risk that his tragic end would overshadow the achievements of his life. Yet it was impossible to ignore the powerful psychological forces governing his life: trauma, loss, betrayal and an underlying search for belonging. I have attempted to explore and explain the impact of each phase of his life on his emotional contours and their connections to his political struggles and to his death. Applied to Rob's life, the 1970s phrase that the personal is political is apt. At the same time, I wanted to avoid the book being infused with a single-minded attempt to explain his suicide. This risked downplaying his achievements. The result is, I hope, a balance.

Rob had a complex and intense make-up. Most of the underlying influences on his personality were largely hidden from view until the last years of his life. But the personality he showed to the world was a curious and contradictory mix of impatient idealism and underlying vulnerability. This mix was manifest in a temperament which combined anger, passion and competitiveness, uncertainty over self, and empathy for others. Serious-minded, he was also a noted joke-teller and mimic, blessed with the innate ability to 'take the piss' out of people. Conventional in most aspects of his dress, he delighted in amusing colleagues by wearing loudly coloured and, at times, oddly matching socks, often sporting them on formal occasions. He liked to show his disdain for formalities. A long-time opponent of police violence towards Aborigines, he developed a close collegial relationship with a senior executive of the Western Australian police force. Though he was mostly indifferent to the material aspects of life, his prized possession during the 1990s was a red Aboriginal Legal Service executive car with the number plate ALS 007. This choice of vehicle polarised views about Rob. Some saw it as manifestation of ego: his love of public notoriety. Others interpreted it as an expression of Rob's humour. In identifying himself with the character of James Bond, Rob was simply sending himself up. Likely, it was a combination of both.

His high media profile also irritated some of his detractors, further feeding an impression among a few that Rob was ego-driven. Yet many more people regarded this public profile as instrumental in challenging and changing political and community perceptions of Aboriginal issues.

Rob's story has much to offer contemporary Australia. It sheds light on the still unresolved intergenerational impact of past racial policy, while opening up to closer scrutiny Australia's response to Aboriginal demands for political change. The life Rob chose in confronting white Australia with the demand for understanding and justice provides many insights into the challenges faced by Aboriginal activists of this era. Despite the tragedy of his death, his life is a story of survival against great odds. Rob triumphed against a childhood ravaged by emotional and material deprivation. Forged by the history of racial oppression, he sought to change the course of history so others would have opportunities historically denied Aboriginal people.

CHAPTER ONE

Prisoners of Racism: The History of Rob Riley's Family

'I can picture exactly the way it was', Rob's uncle, Sam Dinah, exclaims. Time and desecration have taken their toll on Moore River Settlement; only a few of the original structures survive at the once notorious prison for dispossessed Aborigines. Sam sees past the crumbled foundations and the scattered bits of fallen buildings, and reels off where the bakery, Superintendent's house, dormitory, staff quarters and other sundry parts of the once expansive and crowded Settlement were in the 1940s when he lived there as a small boy along with his mother (Rob's maternal grandmother), sister (Rob's mother) and other siblings.

Set on two imposing sandhills which rise sharply out of an isolated part of Perth's dry but environmentally unique coastal plain, the Settlement today is ghostly quiet. Only the occasional screeches of birds and the breeze rustling the tops of the imposing stands of pine disturb the silence. This is a place where hundreds of Aboriginal people suffered and where their sorrow can be felt to this day. It is where Rob's story begins.

Even before this visit to the Settlement, Sam had given me a raw insight into its lasting impact. From the start of the project, he had been helping me piece together the family's history. One day, when I was in his office at the Aboriginal Legal Service, he unexpectedly asked me: 'Do you want to see my mother's Native Welfare file?' Sam thrust his arm into a huge cardboard box sitting in the corner of his office. After rummaging around in a metre-deep bundle of papers, he pulled out a file, 5 centimetres thick. It was the 'Native Welfare' file belonging to his mother, Anna Dinah (née Miller), a documentation of her life maintained by officers of the Department of Native Affairs. 'Here,' he said, 'have this. I've never read it. It's too painful'.

Sam's periodic visits to the Settlement are emotional occasions. This was his childhood home. His memories are bitter-sweet. Our visit turned up some unexpected reminders of how embedded is his family's history in this place. We toured the dingy prison known as the boob. As Sam read through the names etched into the wall he came across the name 'Dinah', and concluded that his father must have scratched his name into the wall during a period of incarceration for infringing the authority's draconian rules. We moved over to the resource centre set up in recent years for former residents and visitors. Sam rifled through the five thick photograph albums and was struck by an image of himself as a grinning five-year-old. He does not possess photographs from this part of his childhood and did not know this one existed. It was a moment of pleasure for him as he examined all the cheeky-looking faces around him.

Meanwhile, as I flicked through a visitors book, my eye caught an unexpected entry. On 2 September 1990, Rob Riley visited Moore River (by then renamed Mogumber) with his mother. He had come to pay homage to the place that had shaped the destiny of his family. Next to his name, the small space allowed for visitors' comments was left blank.

Sam and I moved to the cemetery. Here, scattered through a large area of scrub, were small, rusting, mass-issue iron crosses with nothing more than RIP inscribed on them. The scene resembled a war-grave site, only without the reverential small white crosses and neat landscaping that marks such symbolic places. For Moore River internees, the final indignity was to be buried in an unmarked grave. These people's bodies had simply been dumped, disposed of haphazardly in the least costly manner and with the least possible respect. Even though the authorities had kept copious files on their lives and had issued many with anglicised names, they were buried nameless in an unfenced grave site. There are many of these small, rusting crosses dotting the bush surrounding the far end of the second sandhill. 'Mum's buried somewhere around here,' Sam said, 'but you'd never know where'.

Of the vast, coercive powers the white authorities had to control the lives of Aboriginal people, the power to remove children from their families was the most feared. And this job usually fell to local police officers. The sight of parents wailing as black police cars sped away down dusty roads carrying traumatised children bound for institutions was common throughout Australia in the 1930s and 1940s, especially in the west. While not all Aboriginal children entered institutions by such coercive means, it is most likely Anna Miller did. When taken to Moore River Settlement in 1922 she was a feisty fourteen-year-old with a father who loved her. She was bright, spirited and literate. It is unlikely she would have gone willingly. Force would have been required. But we cannot confirm the manner of her departure, which, in itself, is a chilling testimony to the power exercised by the state over the lives of Aborigines. The book-length file on Anna developed by the Native Welfare Department is silent on the circumstances of her removal; a child could be taken and no-one had to account for their actions.

At the time of her removal, Anna was living with her father, Sam Miller, at Mount Barker. Nothing is known about her mother. Sam, like many male Aborigines in the south-west in the 1920s and 1930s, was an itinerant farm worker. He lived through the dispossession and economic marginalisation which the Noongars of the south-west of Western Australia suffered from the time of settlement in 1829. While maintaining on-going links with their traditional lifestyle for much of the nineteenth century, Noongars had, by the early decades of the twentieth century, been largely reduced to an itinerant rural labour force. Though impoverished, Sam wanted to care for his daughter. In the several letters he wrote to authorities over a number of years, he pleaded for her return, stressing his ability to provide for her.

In the years following Anna's arrival, occasional reports surfaced in the press that Moore River functioned more as a prison or a concentration camp than a 'settlement'. But few objections were raised to the infringement of the basic rights of the people forced to live there or their mistreatment.[1] Not only was suffering inside its boundaries well hidden from view, but prevailing attitudes towards Aborigines did not allow a humanitarian response to their plight. Anna Miller grew into an adult in this austere and isolated world. A loving and maternal person by nature, her confinement sharpened her defiant and tenacious side as she became trapped in the web of racial thinking that kept her a prisoner.

This settlement — like several others — was the brainchild of A.O. Neville, the Commissioner of Native Affairs in Western Australia from 1914. The Settlement was originally planned as a small, self-supporting farming settlement of some 10,000 acres, which would also provide education and training for children. However, the poor soils and harsh, bone-dry summers quickly soured Neville's dream of European agriculture. Within a few years Moore River Settlement functioned as a multi-purpose institution for Aboriginal people but mainly housed those rounded up by government under Ministerial warrant.

Anna Miller came to the attention of the authorities under Neville's policy of enforcing a stricter regime of control over the state's 'half-caste' population of children — in the racist language of the first half of the twentieth century. Like most of the Aborigines sent to Moore River, Anna was brought in under the powers of the infamous *Aborigines Act 1905 (WA)*, which, in conferring on the Commissioner of Native Affairs dictatorial powers over Aborigines, marked the beginning of Western Australia's adoption of racism as state policy. The Commissioner was empowered to remove Aboriginal children from their families by virtue of his role as guardian of all Aboriginal children until the age of sixteen. The Act also gave authority to direct, under ministerial warrant, Aboriginal people to any reserve or settlement the Commissioner thought fit.

The Act paved the way for the establishment of reserves to which Aborigines could forcibly be removed. It outlawed 'miscegenation' — procreative sexual union between the races — and banned Aborigines from owning guns. Any Aboriginal camped outside a reserve could be removed at will by the authorities, and Aborigines were not allowed to wander in towns without a permit or to enter prohibited areas — which could be created any time the government deemed it 'necessary'. It was an Act for the subjugation of a group of people because of their race, and ranks among the most oppressive pieces of such legislation anywhere in the Western world during the twentieth century.

The extraordinary set of controls contained within the Act emerged out of the Royal Commission 'On the Condition of the Natives'. Headed by Queenslander Dr E.W. Roth, the Commission was notable for drawing attention to the emergence of the 'half-caste' problem and especially the rising number of such children. Roth foreshadowed the need both for increased powers to deal with them and for government institutions to house them. His ideas were the product of a centuries-old ideology of the inferiority of Indigenous races: views which had been given added impetus from the 1870s by the popular adaptation of Darwin's theories of 'survival of the fittest' to the world's 'primitive' cultures. Thus 'full-blood' Aborigines were widely thought to be a 'dying' race, with public concern fixed on the 'problem' of the rising number of 'half-castes'.

Roth's recommendations were embodied in the Aborigines Act 1905, which was rushed through the state's Legislative Assembly with little more than an hour's debate.[2] However, the Act's vast powers languished for want of an able administrator to give full effect to them. Nearly a decade later such an administrator came forth in the person of A.O. Neville. In 1914, Neville was appointed to the position of Commissioner of Native Affairs, and he quickly demonstrated the zeal, organisational capability and ambition to use the powers granted to him to address the 'Aboriginal problem' in Western Australia.

From the time Anna Miller entered Moore River Settlement, she became subject to Neville's evolving racial vision, firstly of the segregation of the races and later of the biological absorption of the 'half-caste' population into the white community. This controversial plan, which he developed during the 1930s, involved taking full control over the lives of 'half-caste' children. Such planning placed Neville at the forefront of racial thinking in Australia, and ranks him as one of the most articulate spokespersons for 'racial science' in the English-speaking world during its 1930s heyday.

Anna's Native Welfare file is silent about her early life in the Settlement. But the life of the institution is well documented. Three distinct groups lived there. The whites ran the place and lived (and often behaved) like feudal lords. The Aboriginal children and young people lived in the Compound, which comprised rudimentary boys' and girls' dormitories, school building, kitchen and ablution block. Adult Aborigines lived in a decrepit camp of army-built huts some distance down from the Compound. As a teenage girl it is likely that Anna lived in the Compound before moving to the camp.

Possessed of an innately defiant spirit, she was acutely aware of the injustice of her confinement, and she waged a long-term campaign of correspondence with 'Mister Neville' protesting at the denial of her freedom. Her letters — written in a careful hand and expressing her longings and fears — stand today as an intimate testimony to Neville's calculating control over Aboriginal people.

A.O. Neville has remained an enigma.[3] How could an urbane, serious-minded and, in some ways, compassionate bureaucrat, aware of the historical suffering of Aboriginal people and a keen student of their customs and lifestyle, devise such an audacious plan to wipe them out?

Possessed throughout his life by a love of adventure, the young Auber Octavius Neville arrived in Western Australia from England in March 1897, to join his brother and to search for opportunities in life. The son of a Church of England minister, he imbibed the values of Christianity and Empire, which intertwined into an elitist view that Englishmen had a moral and a civilising duty towards the Empire's 'subject races'.

In Perth, he found a society suited to his outlook and receptive to his ambitions for advancement. At the turn of the century, Australia's most remote city was a class-conscious and conservative colonial outpost, dominated by a ruling clique of 'old' families who 'clung tenaciously to the manners and codes of behaviours of a British society many of them ... had never seen'.[4]

Beginning as a clerk in the Works Department, Neville rose quickly through the ranks, earning a reputation for administrative efficiency. Impeccably mannered and dressed, his characteristic oiled-down hair, parted just to the side of centre, gave him the appearance of the city banker or Treasury official that he might have aspired to become. But fate played its hand. In 1914, the Minister for Aboriginal Affairs, the knockabout Rufus Underwood, persuaded Neville to take over the troubled Aboriginal Affairs Department. Apprised of his excellent reputation within the tight circle of Western Australian public servants, Underwood wanted Neville to sort out the Department. At forty years of age, Neville embarked on a career that not only consumed him, but guaranteed he would be a contentious figure in his lifetime and afterwards.

Although it was widely regarded as an administrative backwater, Neville's fledgling new Department thrust him into an issue which was quickly emerging as a preoccupation for the aspiring population of Western Australia: what to do about the Indigenous population it had dispossessed and marginalised. Within this population was an especially worrying group: the products of mixed parentage — the much vilified 'half-castes'. Where would they fit in this developing society? Where would their true allegiance lie — with the whites or with their Aboriginal kin? And could such a people be trusted? Surely, contemporaries thought, 'half-castes' must be the product of 'bad elements' in both groups: promiscuous Aboriginal women and white men of bad character who were prepared to flout the taboo on sexual union between the races.[5] These became the issues that consumed Neville.

When Neville interned Anna Miller in Moore River in 1922, his thinking on solving Western Australia's race problem was slowly taking shape. Only months after taking control of the Department, he embarked on his first tour of inspection. In the vast and sparsely populated hinterlands of Western Australia, Neville encountered a derelict and dispossessed Indigenous population. He came into contact with the large number of 'half-caste' children in Aboriginal camps. Such children, he thought, had no future unless he took full charge of his responsibilities for them as their legal guardian under the Act.

The tour shocked him deeply, propelling him on his search for a solution to the problems he witnessed.

His starting point came naturally to someone of his background. The concept of race — the widely perceived existence of superior and inferior peoples — was in its ascendancy in the English-speaking world and Neville was a firm advocate of its importance in the affairs of humankind. In the early 1920s, for example, he claimed that the White Australia policy would 'ultimately achieve success' and that it involved 'an idealism of a very lofty kind'.[6]

While Neville began mulling over the relationship of the concept of race to policy in Aboriginal affairs, Anna Miller came to his attention in the institution he had created. At some point in her early years in the Settlement, she ran away, and when recaptured she had her shoulder-length hair completely shaved off as a punishment.[7]

In 1928 Neville received a request from a Mrs R.G. Thomas of Green Hills for the services of an Aboriginal girl as a domestic, and especially to help look after her two children. On 14 February 1929, Neville wrote to Mrs Thomas advising her that 'there is a half-caste girl who could be sent to your service'. He stipulated that she receive a wage of 10 shillings per week, of which Anna was to receive a quarter 'as pocket money'; the rest to be held in trust by the Department.

In early March, Neville reported that Mrs Thomas rang him complaining that Anna had been 'most unsatisfactory' since her arrival. She had been 'sulky' and was continually sending notes 'per medium of the children saying she is sick'. More defiant behaviour followed: 'One day during the weekend she absconded and Mr Thomas had to go in search of her and when he found her heading for York, had to pick her up bodily and put her in the car'. Mr Thomas told his wife it would be best to send her back. On her return to the Settlement in March 1929, she was pregnant with her first child, Ivor.

By the time Mr Thomas sent Anna back to Moore River, Neville was close to having formulated his plan for solving the Aboriginal 'problem' in Western Australia. Challenging the prevailing policy of banning interracial marriage — one of the fundamental restrictions placed by governments on the relationship between whites and Blacks — he disclosed his ideas on biological absorption in 1930 in a series of articles he wrote anonymously for *The West Australian* under the initials AON, conscious of the controversy his ideas might stir. A dedicated advocate of the 'rational' ideas of modern science, he had assembled his plan from an amalgam of 'racial science', Social Darwinism, eugenics, and the emerging science of genetics.

The racial 'science' behind Social Darwinism reflected the widespread belief that the culturally inferior 'full-blood' Aboriginal would die out, just as naturalist Charles Darwin had theorised occurred in the process of natural selection in the animal world. Neville believed this group would die out of its own accord. The emerging 'science' of eugenics which, by the 1930s, had grown into an intellectual movement aimed at improving the quality of human populations by manipulation of the fertility of different categories, influenced Neville's call for the 'half-castes' to be married off into the white community, while the emerging science of genetics dictated to him that through successive intermarriage they would become steadily lighter in colour. Neville argued: 'Eliminate the full-blood and permit the white admixture [to "half-castes"] and eventually the race will become white'.[8] Neville also appropriated genetic principles to reassure the public that 'throwbacks' to Aboriginality would not occur in unions between 'half-castes' and whites.

The success of such a policy would require the strong hand of government. The state would have to rigorously control the lives of Aboriginal children and young adults so that they could be trained up and married off into the white community. The policy of biological absorption is now often forgotten. In the contemporary popular imagination it has largely been incorporated into the policy of cultural assimilation, which replaced it after the Second World War, in response to its connections to the rampant racism of the Nazis.[9]

While there were elements of paternalism in Neville's relations with Aboriginal people, he makes abundantly clear in all his writings his commitment to the precepts of racial thinking: the inevitability of 'full-bloods' as a 'doomed race' and the undesirability of 'half-castes' emerging as a potential new race. His dealings with Anna Miller — and her children — were set within this framework.

As Neville dabbled in his social sciences reading in the early 1930s, the position of young women in the Settlement was especially grim. With little real work to do, and no opportunities for outside contact, most suffered grinding boredom. Having children out of wedlock was common. Anna Miller's children were born to two men with whom she enjoyed long-standing relationships.

Twelve months after Anna Miller's return from the Thomas family, Neville again had cause to deal with her. By 1930 she had formed a relationship in the settlement with a young man named Albert Dinah, and Neville wrote to Sam Miller asking whether he had any objection to his daughter marrying Albert — someone he had most likely never met. There is no record of Sam Miller's reply, but Neville had no intention of relinquishing ultimate control over Anna's life. As he informed her father: 'I agreed that if the parents consented Dinah should go out and find a job before the marriage could take place. Then the two could go out together, but Ivan... Anna's child, is to remain at the settlement'.

It was the first of many refusals to allow Anna's children to leave Moore River. Neville and the Moore River Superintendent — the tyrannical Arthur J. Neale — alternated between denying requests by Anna to leave Moore River, and denying the right of her children to leave when agreeing to consider that she be allowed to move on. The effect was the same: she was condemned to life in the institution for all but a precious few years.

For those without children, escapes were common. In her book *Follow the Rabbit-Proof Fence* (subsequently filmed), Doris Pilkington immortalised the story of the three young girls who, in 1931, fled the Settlement and journeyed 1600 kilometres back home to their community. The feat of these girls was emulated — albeit on a lesser scale — by others. In 1939, for example, Neville was informed by police that 'Edith Morrison, a 13 year old native girl, who escaped from Moore River Settlement on March 13', had been discovered at Katanning. She had apparently travelled most of the way on foot.[10] The girl had travelled over 300 kilometres, managing to evade the mounted troopers stationed at the Settlement to track and capture runaways.

As Neville thwarted Anna's return to her father by refusing to let Ivan accompany her, he was becoming ever more alarmed about the growth of the 'half-caste' population in the state. Neville believed they lacked a future, being separated from their traditional ways and marginalised and unwanted by white society. In his mind all 'half-castes' shared the same predetermined and unattractive manner, their culture and biology creating the need for an authority figure to keep them under control. He judged the 'half-castes' 'difficult to handle'. In his eyes, they were without gratitude, callously self-interested, and moody. His steely observations had created the perfect rationalisation for dictatorial control over their lives; they needed to be 'protected and disciplined to some extent in spite of themselves for their sakes and ours'.[11]

Meanwhile, in Moore River, Anna's life ground on: a slow, numbing, unrelieved existence that gnawed at her spirit. She was forced to play by Neville's rules. In May 1930 she wrote to Neville requesting permission to marry Albert, but indicated that there was trouble in the relationship. In June Neville placed the same qualification on the marriage: so long as Albert could obtain satisfactory work, he would have no objection.

In 1932, Neville received a heart-felt plea from Sam Miller asking for the return of his daughter:

> I cannot see why you should refuse me to have her back. I am always on work and never beg for work. I get my contract whenever I roam so I am sure enough to keep her and her children. Please Mr Neville let her come back and I'll send the money for them whatever it costs ... I think it is fair for you to let me have her back.

Neville sought advice from Superintendent Neale who insisted to Neville that 'Anna Miller should not go back to her father', because she 'will not do any good out at [domestic] service'. Neville was reluctant to let Ivan, now four years old, leave the settlement, and to compound matters for the Superintendent, Anna was expecting another baby to Albert Dinah. Neville told Sam Miller that if he consented to Anna returning to him it would only be on the basis that the children stay at the Settlement.

Details are scanty on what happened to Anna over the next few years. But it is clear that she lived in appalling conditions in Moore River. In 1934, H.D. Moseley, the Royal Commissioner inquiring into Aboriginal affairs, visited the settlement. He was shocked. In the Compound he found the dormitories had 'a dilapidated appearance' and were 'far too crowded'. They were also 'vermin ridden to an extent which ... makes eradication impossible'. There was no accommodation for the children other than the dormitories. Moseley found that the educational facilities were inadequate, consisting in summer of a 'bough shed'. In one of his few understatements, he described the children's diet as leaving 'much room for improvement'. In fact, it could hardly have been more deficient in essential nutrients. Fresh milk, fruit, and vegetables were rare and there was 'an insufficiency of meat'. The poor diet, Moseley found, resulted in many children visiting the Settlement hospital.

Moseley reserved his harshest criticisms for the way the 'inmates' were punished. Shown a place of detention called 'the boob', he described a small detached 'room' made of posts driven into the ground, the floor consisting only of sand, with scarcely a gleam of light, and with little ventilation. Despite his inbuilt attitude of racial superiority, Moseley was appalled at the 'barbarous treatment' of inmates, who might be incarcerated in the place for as long as fourteen days. He called for it to be pulled down.[12]

Moseley believed that children and adults should be completely separated in the Settlement because he had found the children 'living within a few hundred yards of a collection of useless, loafing natives' who enticed the compound girls to the camp.

The proceedings of the Moseley inquiry were widely covered in *The West Australian* prompting continued public interest — and in some quarters, concern — about the institution and its unfortunate 'inmates'.

Meanwhile, Albert Dinah had been imprisoned in Fremantle Gaol, and a request by Anna to marry another man was again turned down by Neville. During this period, Superintendent Neale described her to Neville as a 'hopeless case'. Fully two years after Sam Miller wrote asking for his daughter back, Neville and the Superintendent were still debating the merits of the case. The Superintendent's assessment was blunt: 'if she goes to her father, can he keep her, or will she be on rations? If the latter she may as well stay here'.

While immersing himself in the minutiae of cases like Anna's, Neville continued on his grandiose quest to shape racial policy. In 1936 his powers were increased through the *Native Administration Act 1936 (WA)*, which 'revealed intense official concentration on the control of individual Aborigines'.[13] Its major implication as far as Anna Miller was concerned was to strengthen Neville's powers to control children (increased to the age of twenty-one) and to control marriages entered into by Aborigines. Neville could now meddle in the personal lives of Aboriginal people — waiting upon and screening their marriage proposals — with almost total power.

Clearly growing more distressed at her continued confinement, Anna Miller decided to change tack in her dealings with Neville and asked only to be allowed to go on a holiday to see her father. She also expressed some interest in marrying Albert upon his release from Fremantle Gaol. Of her wish to marry, Neville wrote to Superintendent Neale with the familiar, well-rehearsed and ultimate threat: 'Whether the children will leave the Settlement with the mother remains yet to be determined'. Neville simply ignored the request for a holiday, forcing Anna to write again more than twelve months later. This time she was defiant: if her request for a two-month holiday was turned down, she would run away.

She let Neville know exactly how she was feeling. 'I am sick and tired of staying', she wrote. 'I am sure I never murdered anybody to stay here you know Mr Neville.'

Anna was trapped in a dilemma she could not resolve: without a Neville-approved partner in marriage she would not be allowed to leave — and even with a partner Neville would not let her children out of the Settlement. She was his prisoner. She took what little control she could over her life, informing Neville that she no longer wanted to marry Dinah: 'still and all Mr Neville if I got to get married to go away from here, I'd rather stay here'. She signed off her 20 January letter with obvious sarcasm: 'Well Mr Neville, you know best'.

Her application for a holiday dragged on into 1936 with no approval forthcoming from Neville. She wrote two more letters to him pleading her case. In February she explained to him why she had abandoned plans to leave the Settlement — 'because you wouldn't let me take Ivan' — and 'you know Mr Neville no one will take a Mother's place'. This was especially concerning to Anna because, as she informs Neville, none of the staff at the Settlement cared much about the children, and usually 'only when it's too late'. But she renewed the plea to be allowed to go on holiday. 'Please Mr Neville can you let me go as soon as you can. I will be satisfied if you will let me go for a holiday.'

A month later she had grown desperate:

> I have been waiting to hear from you about my holiday — you are a long time letting me know true Mr Neville you can't imagine how this place worries me I have been here such long time and I know I can't get away. Any other ways only you can help me. So I depends on you for a help. True Mr Neville I rather be dead than live here any longer.

Another month passed without a word from Neville. The silence forced Anna to rethink the situation. She made up her mind to marry Dinah, and she was clear about why she had to. In a letter written in April 1936 she explained to Neville: 'to me it seems as long as I am single I will stay here all my life'. She threatened to run away with Dinah, hoping 'some day good things will come' out of the marriage and expressed her sorrow that her father's wish to have her returned had petered out after he had battled years of official obstruction. She ends her letter: 'This place sent [sic] anyone mad'.

Predictably, Neville threw the same old spanner in the works in response to her new request. He didn't oppose the marriage but was undecided on the fate of her four children, two of whom were Dinah's. Finally, after fourteen years of internment, Anna's campaign to take control of her own life was rewarded: she and Albert were married at Moora and given a ticket to Mount Barker. Three of the children were allowed to accompany them, but eight-year-old Ivan was forced to stay behind, in a move which Sam Dinah explains today as 'a ransom'.

Her freedom was short-lived. Shortly after their marriage Dinah was sent back to gaol, although the circumstances are not known. Anna nevertheless moved back with her father, obtained a job and, as her youngest son, Sam remembers of this time, 'things started to look up'. However, in September 1937, Neville, acting on hearsay that Dinah might wish to harm Anna on his release from prison, removed her back to Moore River under ministerial warrant. A few years later it was revealed that Neville took the decision because she 'was found living with another native and consequently removed because *it was thought* [author's italics] Dinah would cause trouble if he found her living with another native on his discharge from prison'.

Anna's return under warrant in 1937 coincided with Neville's return from the inaugural Commonwealth–State Conference on Aboriginal Affairs. Here he had found the stage to launch his attempt to influence national policy on race. Forceful, articulate and visionary, he laid out before Conference delegates the finely-tuned plan for biological absorption he had been wrestling with for over ten years. In sponsoring the Conference motion for biological absorption, Neville explained that Western Australia had gone further in the development of a 'long range plan' than any other state 'by accepting the view that ultimately the natives must be absorbed into the white population of Australia'. Neville reassured delegates that 'the aborigines of Australia sprang from the same stock as we did ourselves; that is to say they are not negroid, but give evidence of Caucasian origin'.

Having thus placated any concerns about the 'science' of merging the two populations, Neville explained that the new law over marriages had a racial purpose: 'to prevent the return of those half-castes who are nearly white to the black'. He made it clear: 'Under this law no half-caste need be allowed to marry a full-blood aboriginal if it is possible to avoid it'.[14]

Neville told delegates that he had overcome the one problem that had stood in his way of achieving the ultimate goal of a racially pure society: the reluctance of missions to enact the new laws over marriage. This, he further explained, was being overcome in Western Australia with the establishment of government institutions to receive 'half-caste' children taken from their mothers. It was to one of these institutions established by Neville — Sister Kate's Children's Home — that Rob Riley would later be sent.

The most chilling aspect of Neville's plan was his calculated understanding of its devastating impact on Aboriginal people. 'It is well known', he told delegates, 'that coloured races all over the world detest institutionalisation. They have tremendous affection for their children'. In concluding his pitch to delegates for support to pass his motion, he let them contemplate the ultimate goal: with the merger, over time, of the entire Aboriginal race into the white community, it would be 'possible to imagine that there were ever any Aborigines in Australia'.[15]

For Anna, her return in 1937 brought the distress of losing control over her children in the Settlement. Between 1937 and 1944, she gave birth to two more children, bringing to six the number of children with her in the Settlement: Ivan, Lois, Walter, Violet (Rob's mother), Samuel and Janet. She lost control of all of them.

The children lived in the Compound and only saw their mother on occasional weekends. Violet remembers the Settlement as a place of extremes. There were happy times such as sports days and dances at which her mother played the accordion. Yet at other times 'there would be tension and fear in the air at the camp. Fighting would break out and people would be afraid to come out and mix'.[16]

A feeling of being deprived is Sam's dominant memory of the place. It was equivalent to 'being brought up on the streets'; children had to quickly learn how to survive. The boys' dormitory housed a hundred boys and contained little more than wrought-iron beds and horse-hair mattresses. Bathing and provision of clean clothes happened only once a week. The dormitory was rodent-infested and the food was 'an off-shoot of army rations', cooked by 'a rough and ready sort of bloke' whose staple was boiled puddings. But the worst thing for Sam — still only three or four years old — was being locked in the dormitory from 6 p.m. until morning. All the boys were locked in on their own, unable to get a drink of water or even to go to the toilet. For Sam it remains a vivid memory, 'a frightening experience'. When they wanted to go to the toilet, the younger boys quietly sobbed until one of the older boys heard their cries and carried them to the back of the dormitory where there was a rusting bathtub for emergencies.

Even as the authorities followed this practice of locking the children in overnight, they recognised the damage it would likely cause. In 1943 the Deputy Commissioner for Native Affairs wrote: 'If we attempted to apply the same conditions to children in our own homes, the outcome would be disastrous and result in the rearing of children with a generally depressed outlook'.[17]

One small step towards improved conditions for children at Moore River was made in the early 1940s.[18] A kindergarten for the thirty youngest children was opened to the acclaim of authorities. Located some distance from the camp proper, the kindergarten was strictly segregated: children were rarely allowed to see their parents, living in 'an institution within an institution'. The segregation from camp and parents was critical to the intended purpose of the kindergarten. It was, one of the historians of Moore River has written, a 'daring and quite blatant experiment in total social engineering ... designed to function as a kind of hatchery for European culture'.[19] As Sam recalls, his mother 'had no maternal dealings with me after I was taken away and put in the kindergarten'. It was also the first of several separations from his older sister Violet, separations which would have deep emotional impacts on their sibling relationship. He only saw Violet around the camp compound and on school holidays. Two or three teachers catered for the children sent there, and little thought was given to what would happen to the children once they left the kindergarten; their only option seemed to be to return to the hopelessness of the compound.

With her children taken from her, Anna Miller survived Moore River during the late 1930s and early 1940s mostly without protest. Her nemesis A.O. Neville had retired, feted in the press for his work as 'The Natives' Friend'.[20]

By 1941, Anna's father was no longer able to get work, existing 'on rations' at Mount Barker, and becoming increasingly frail. But he did not give up on the struggle to be reunited with his daughter. He wrote to Neville's replacement, Commissioner Bray, asking that Anna and the children be returned to him. He would send the fare 'as soon as you say yes'. Bray, seemingly showing as little compassion as Neville, turned down his request. He told Anna's father, 'She has her children with her and, as they are being educated and trained, I think she is serving a good purpose by staying with them at the Settlement'.

Two years later, weary, debilitated and in uncertain emotional health, Anna wrote to Commissioner Bray and posed the ultimate question: 'I am only asking you whether I am here for life'. When, at the beginning of 1944, she gave birth to her last child, Janet, she experienced another fruitless encounter with officialdom. She made a claim for maternity allowance, which had been introduced by the Commonwealth government the previous year, but was not available to all Aboriginal people. Her claim was rejected by the Maternity Allowance Office in Perth on advice from Commissioner Bray and on clear racial grounds. As he explained: 'I have to advise that this woman is a three-quarter caste native and, therefore, possesses a preponderance of native blood. She is not exempt from the Native Administration Act'.

Without warning, events took an unexpected turn for the better in 1945. After over twenty years of being confined by the authorities to Moore River, Anna's application to take her children to Mount Barker to be with her family was granted for only the second time — the first in nearly a decade. She was granted temporary leave. Her brother Clem and her father helped her look after her children. She enrolled the children in school, with the exception of sixteen-year-old Ivan, who obtained employment. Her life became stable and she relished the experience. She wrote to the new Commissioner for Native Affairs, Mr McBeath, in January 1947, buoyed by her new life of freedom and pleading not to be taken in again. In a recognisably desperate voice, she wrote:

> I stayed in the settlement all those years with my children… I stayed and spent the best of life with children, as you know I getting old now, and I would like to stay with brother and Dad… I will never make troubles of any sort; I will truthfully say when I'm sick of being down here I will gladly come back to Settlement… But Mr McBeath,

> you will understand a few month away from the settlement make you satisfied of being out.

However, some time after writing this letter, she had relocated herself to a camp on a private property three miles outside of Mount Barker with her family and also with a new partner, Joe Ryder. Their camp was a 'bough lean-to' and became a haven for other Aboriginal people visiting the District. Inevitably, the authorities caught up with them for camping illegally on private property. In February 1947, the camp was visited by Constable Wrigley to inform them they must remove their camp and transfer immediately to the designated newly gazetted Mount Barker reserve.

When Commissioner McBeath heard about Wrigley's visit he dispatched a tersely worded memo confirming that the authorities had no intention of relinquishing their control over Anna's movements:

> I am completely unfavourable to Mrs Dinah's request for permission to remain in the Mount Barker District, therefore I would be glad if you could kindly inform her that she is required to report immediately to either Moore River or Carrolup Native Settlement. When Mrs Dinah was given permission to visit Mount Barker it was upon the understanding that she returned to Moore River. I anticipated that she would endeavour to remain away after leaving, and I am not prepared to agree. If Mrs Dinah is not prepared to go to either Moore River or Carrolup Native Settlement voluntarily, then I will arrange to secure the issue of a warrant for her return under escort.

The obsession the Native Affairs Department had with Anna Miller (now Dinah) is deeply puzzling. Why would it send out the long tentacles of its administrative arm to drag her back yet again? Was it because of the ever-present fears about losing control over her children? Or was it the issue of her status as a 'three-quarter caste' and the threat this posed to authorities if she cohabited with other Aborigines? Both are likely to have played a part, in light of Neville's — and his successor's — stated policies.

Back in Moore River, Anna was resigned to her fate. 'I must be in here for a life sentence', she told the Acting Commissioner for Native Affairs in April 1947, 'but never mind'. She complained that she had been forced to end her new life with Joe. However, with characteristic resilience, she began a new campaign to be able to rejoin him. She issued a request to this effect and to be able to take Janet with her: 'I should be able to have a baby one with me. Joe is the father of Janet and he is willing to keep her ... Spare me one please'. But the infant Janet was removed from Anna by the Department and sent to New Norcia Catholic Mission, where she grew up without any contact with her siblings.

In August 1947 Anna again grew desperate, writing to McBeath that she was: 'really fed up to my neck staying here from one year to another. I been here since 1922 and still here'. She told McBeath that she knew why this had happened: she wouldn't leave the Settlement while her children were there. 'I always stay with them', she proudly acknowledged.

Not long after writing this letter, Anna Dinah passed away. Her life had been unimaginably hard, and the denial of natural justice dispensed by Neville, Bray and McBeath was typical of the wider oppression of most Aborigines. Her commitment to her children was her life's achievement, attained at the expense of her independence. She died at barely thirty-nine years of age, of causes unknown. Sam believes that it was 'from a broken heart'. In a cruel irony, Anna died only a few years before Moore River Settlement was abandoned. As Sam explains of the mother he barely knew: 'Had she hung on for a few years she might have been able to get out'.

Anna's life-long incarceration was, of course, made lawful under the Aborigines Act 1905, which included provisions for the infamous 'Ministerial Warrant'. If Anna Miller had survived to the age of forty-six, she would have seen the abolition of this most odious part of Western Australia's racial laws. S.G. Middleton, a more enlightened administrator of Aboriginal affairs, found the use of warrants to be repugnant. Lamenting the practice of using this devise to incarcerate hundreds of Aborigines 'in primitively equipped settlements for indefinite periods', warrants had, under his leadership, 'become utterly discredited'. But the damage was done, and Middleton was aware of its extent. He wrote:

> the psychological aspect of the 'Warrant' system was forcibly brought home to me some time ago, when I read the Department file of a middle-aged aboriginal charged with murder, and subsequently convicted of manslaughter. This man's life had been warped by repeated and morally unjustifiable detentions, and his eventual serious crime may, in no small measure, have been due to a bitter and rankling sense of injustice. If a trained psychiatrist were to check through the official sheaves of paper recording the lives of these unfortunate people it would be surprising if he did not marvel that so much injustice could result in so little violent reaction.[21]

Anna Dinah, of course, was one of 'these unfortunate people' and Middleton's comments provide another layer of insight into the anguish she suffered during her quarter-century incarceration in Moore River.

She is remembered by Violet as 'delicate but strong in character':

> Though mum was strong and defiant against the authorities that had imprisoned her and her children at Moore River through no wrong doing or fault of her own, other than she was aboriginal, she was a gentle person, good humoured, kind and loving. She had such a lovely, pleasant nature. She was so kind, always willing to help. She would give the last of what she had to help another.[22]

Anna's death in 1947 brought new uncertainties to her children. Over the next ten years they were scattered across the far-flung Western Australian mission system.

The moves began without warning. A group including Sam and Violet were told they were going to be taken away from the Moore River Settlement. In the darkness of early morning, they were all put on the back of a truck, driven down to Mogumber Station and then brought down to Perth, where they were billeted out before the long drive out to Carrolup Settlement.

Carrolup was another of the institutions which Neville had established as part of his long-term vision for segregation and, ultimately, biological absorption. However, with the latter idea on the wane by the time Violet and Sam arrived, Carrolup was just another decrepit institution in Western Australia's racial 'gulag': its network of government and church institutions which denied Aboriginal people their liberty and self-determination.

Happily for Violet and Sam, Carrolup provided a welcome, two-year interlude in their institutionalised existence. Founded on a site outside of the wheatbelt town of Katanning in 1915 during Neville's first year as Commissioner, Carrolup was opened due to the mounting pressure for segregation coming from the local white community. By the time Sam and Violet arrived, the institution was known by officials to carry a stigma among Noongars as a 'penal settlement' 'because many of the former inmates were sent there against their or their parents, will'.[23]

Yet in comparison to Moore River, Carrolup offered a better life for Violet and Sam. Their lives were brightened by the provision of clean clothes every two or three days and a bath every night. The food was better, although still issued by 'an old army cook'. There were even sheets on the bed, and Violet and Sam both went to school.

In December 1949, a new Superintendent, V.H. Sully, took up duties at Carrolup. In his inaugural Annual Report to Parliament for 1951, he exposed the shameful conditions at the institution. Previous reports, he complained, had been 'flowery', showing that all was well when, in fact, it was not. The dormitories, he said, 'were enough to make anyone sick ... they were filthy and a disgrace'. Not only did they stink 'with the dirt, grime and ill-use of years', but outside the dormitories conditions were dangerously unhygienic: 'There were no external drains leading away from the bath section. Internal drains reeked of excreta and rabbit entrails. They were generally polluted and there appeared to be no hope of rehabilitation'.[24] To his credit, Sully embarked on a clean-up and make-over: scrubbing with disinfectants, painting, and provision of new bedding and curtains. By the middle of 1950, he was able to boast that his institution had a fresh, almost 'sweet' appearance. By this time, however, Sam and Violet had been moved again — in the back of an old Austin truck — to Roelands Mission, outside Collie.

Roelands was founded in the late 1930s by a prominent member of the Church of Christ. Few institutions so starkly illustrate the gap between the official version of success and the Aboriginal experience of profound suffering and, often, life-long scarring. Rob's life was indirectly shaped by the experience of his mother and uncle in this institution.

As at Carrolup, a sharp distinction existed between the official version of Roelands and the truth. In the Annual Report to the Commissioner of Native Affairs, Superintendent K.C. Cross extolled the efforts of his staff in providing induction to Christian life and practical training in domestic service and farm work. These had earned the praise of both employers and of the Aboriginal young people in its care. The work with these young people, he went on, 'proved an inspiration and a sense of accomplishment'.

Beyond these bland statements, Roelands had a darker side: vindictive punishment, dehumanising regimentation, and zealous evangelicalism. 'If we stepped out of line, we got the cuts, they regularly laid into us', Sam explains. 'You had to be clean in thought and deed and we lived by the bell — school, lunch and tea'. The 200-odd children also laboured long and hard in the Mission's farming business: in the orchards, making wooden fruit cases, and milking cows — all unpaid labour.

Sam can now put into some perspective the damage that his and Violet's years of institutionalisation caused. First was the 'superiority of officialdom':

> That made us feel inferior. Growing up in the institutions we were made to believe that we were inferior to white people in particular and we were made to believe that we were co-dependent on their thoughts and attitudes to us; we were just recruited to do what we were told, when we were told, without question. We had to conform in a way that wasn't questioned, because if we didn't it was taken as a form of rebellion and we were punished severely.

In a few years' time — when Violet gave birth to baby Robert — this sense of inferiority and conformity would have tragic consequences for her, for Robert and for their wider family.

Another tragic consequence of the mission experience was the loss of the sibling relationship between Violet and Sam. Like Moore River, Roelands had segregated dormitories for boys and girls. Although brothers and sisters tried to look out for each other, they had little time to speak let alone engage in extended interaction: 'Even when I came out, I had an apprehensive relationship with Violet'. Sam wasn't even told about Violet's release from the institution to go out to work at age fourteen. As he explains: 'You didn't even know at times somebody had left, until it became obvious they were missing ... I didn't know Violet had gone. Somewhere along the line somebody told me'.

When Sam heard that his sister had left, 'it didn't affect me at all'. Sam now believes this indifference was another consequence of his institutionalisation: 'events just happened without question. That was the norm'. This mental attitude, and the emotional separation from his sister, would also be played out in the tragic events to follow. When Violet gave birth to Rob, there was no close family to help her, and for years she would not tell Sam of Rob's birth and removal, even when they were reunited after years of separation.

Upon release, Violet was sent to Capel in the south-west to work as a domestic. This placement followed official thinking that 'native domestics ... seem to be better placed on farms or stations'.[25]

When young girls like Violet left a mission they were offered no support. No-one took responsibility for them. Unskilled and untrained, and often unable to locate any surviving family members, they found it difficult to get jobs, and many were forced to return to Aboriginal camps. Racism was an ever-present reality, limiting the availability of accommodation and exposing them to exploitation, including rape and prostitution.[26]

They entered a society deeply fixated with race. The most obvious manifestation of this was the system of racial classification which, as the Commissioner of Native Affairs explained in 1953, was rigidly enforced: if an Aborigines' 'caste record shows that he possesses, e.g. one sixtyfourth of aboriginal blood, i.e. one-sixtyfourth of aboriginal blood above that of a quarter-caste, then he is classified as a "native" and is subject to the discriminatory clauses of all legislation that make special reference to natives'.[27] Among the raft of discriminatory measures was one that ignored one of the most fundamental tenets of democracy: namely, that while they were subject to taxation laws, Aborigines were denied the right to vote in both state and Commonwealth elections. Equally importantly, they were exempt from certain Commonwealth Social Security benefits because, under the Commonwealth's Social Security legislation, 'persons with a preponderance of aboriginal blood over that of the half-blood are not eligible for the maternity allowance, old age, invalid or widow's pensions unless they are exempt from the state's welfare act'.[28] Lack of access to welfare payments further impoverished many Aborigines and their families, already hard hit by the contraction of their employment opportunities due to competition from the rising numbers of post-war immigrants.

The loss of employment opportunities meant a slow decline in living standards for most Aborigines living in the south of the state. Segregation on reserves only served to deepen their impoverishment. Segregation remained a key pillar of Aboriginal policy, as the Commissioner for Native Affairs in his Annual Report for 1958 explained. In a stinging attack on community attitudes, he claimed that the 'inescapable conclusion' was that natives were not wanted in the metropolitan area any more in the late 1950s than at the turn of the century.[29]

Conditions on the reserves were nothing short of abysmal; they were rural ghettoes in a rising sea of prosperity. In perpetuating segregation, Western Australia was storing up a social problem of dangerous proportions. Commissioner Middleton knew as much. The grimy tents and tin humpies of the reserves were, he wrote, 'the breeding ground of discontent and apathy'. With no standards to live up to and no hope of anything better in the near future, 'the occupants of such camps are left without any incentive to strive for better things'.[30] Succeeding generations, Middleton warned, 'may live to regret' the anti-social attitudes festering on the reserves.

This was the world Violet encountered when she was released in the early 1950s. Young, inexperienced, and unworldly, she had no family to which she could return and few job prospects.

Rob Riley would soon come into this world. It would not change a great deal in the first twelve years of his life, and during this time he too would experience the state's historical obsession with the meaning of race, the power of its legislative controls over Aboriginal families, the prejudice of its people, and the hopelessness of its segregated reserves. Rob Riley's political career is fused to the struggles of his family and to those of the wider Noongar community. Created by history, he would turn his anger towards the struggle to change Australia's race relations. He had, according to Violet, inherited from his grandmother Anna Miller the same spirited compulsion to challenge injustice.[31]

Anna Dinah (née Miller), Rob Riley's maternal grandmother, Moore River Settlement. Note the identification number.

The church at Moore River Settlement.

Camp at Moore River Settlement, where Anna Dinah lived. She was separated from her children, who lived in the compound on the other side of the settlement.

Sam Dinah revisiting Moore River Settlement. This infamous institution was the home of Rob's maternal grandmother, Anna Dinah (née Miller), his mother, Violet, his uncle Sam and their other siblings.

Sam Dinah at the Commemoration Wall in the Cemetery, Moore River Settlement. Anna Dinah is buried here in an unmarked grave, as were hundreds of others.

Sister Kate Clutterbuck, founder of Sister Kate's Children's Home. Although Sister Kate had departed by the time of Rob Riley's arrival there, her 'cottage model' lived on, as did the purpose of the institution: to assimilate Aboriginal children.

The last cottage Rob lived in at Sister Kate's. He moved there aged seven following the departure of his cottage 'mother', Min, with whom he was close.

CHAPTER TWO

Bound for Assimilation: A Childhood at Sister Kate's

Speaking to the press in 1995, a visibly upset Rob Riley finally found the courage to express his feelings about his life in Sister Kate's Children's Home. It had taken him a lifetime of struggle to do so. He spoke about the time he received his first visit from his parents, when he was ten years old. His step-father (he described him as his father) Bill Riley gave him two small coins as a present, and young Rob was overwhelmed by this assurance that he actually belonged to somebody. He told the interviewer that he treasured the gift so much it was still in his possession. His memories conjured a tragic irony. In its day, Sister Kate's was a pioneer in offering 'orphaned' children richer lives than the drab, loveless dormitory. Yet the institution was deeply entwined with the racial policy of assimilation.

Established in 1932 on an expanse of picturesque grounds in what was then Perth's outer fringe, Sister Kate's Children's Home quickly became the showpiece for Western Australia's evolving policy of assimilation. Dotted with seven small cottages, with dairy cattle grazing nearby, it owed its origins to Sister Kate Clutterbuck, who was known in Perth society for her decades of selfless work with disadvantaged children. However, she died in 1946, and by the time Robert Dinah was placed in the Home in 1955, the kindly face she put on children's experience of assimilation had been replaced by a stricter regime.

Not surprisingly, Rob's journey through Sister Kate's from babyhood to early adolescence was to shape his life. His isolation from his natural family for the first twelve years of his life formed him. It produced life-long struggles over his identity; led to a deep uncertainty about his bonds with his natural family; and fed the anger that drove him into political activism. As the story he told about the visit of his stepfather revealed, Rob's memory of Sister Kate's was inseparable from his childhood anxiety and his need for a sense of belonging. Rob had to shift cottages, change 'mums', skirt around the unpredictable temperament of the Home's managers — Mr and Mrs Daniels — and face the additional trauma of sexual abuse.

Despite these swirling currents of unhappiness, Rob retained deep emotional bonds with those with whom he grew up in the Home. He maintained close contact with some of these people. He also visited the place as a young adult, and chose to be married in its church. This dual response is not surprising. Sister Kate's was a world of live-in 'mums', 'brothers' and 'sisters', who played in the expansive garden and had outings on special occasions. It is where he had his birthdays and Christmases, and learnt the skills of navigating the world. Through its cottage system ran some of the warm, affectionate feelings of a conventional home. There were always other children to play with, and the communal structure of the place brought a sense of collective bonding which existed in spite of the Home's management. In short, Sister Kate's fostered the competing sides of Rob's personality: the happy, bright, personable side and the angry, sad, and troubled one.

That Sister Kate's could produce such emotional extremes is linked to the very reasons for its foundation. Underneath the world of 'mums', children at play and inviting gardens lay the real purpose of the Home: it was established to assimilate part-Aboriginal children, receiving the active support of A.O. Neville as part of his grand vision for biological absorption. This aim was shared by Sister Kate.

Sister Kate Clutterbuck was a devout Anglican, who had spent her early missionary days in the slums of London before arriving in Perth in 1901. She established a home for orphans — Parkerville Children's Home — which she operated for many years to wide acclaim. In the early 1930s, unwilling to accept retirement, she visited the Moore River Settlement, and wrote to Neville offering to establish a Home for its children. Her letter coincided with Neville's own plans for biological absorption.[1] These plans were to govern the Home in succeeding decades. In 1951, Miss Lefroy, Sister Kate's close colleague and successor, wrote to the Commissioner of Native Affairs reminding him of the Home's history: 'About 19 years ago Sister Kate approached Mr Neville ... and offered to open a home for quarter-caste children with my assistance, in which they would be brought up as white children and from which they would enter the white community'.[2]

Sister Kate's relationship with Neville has raised sensitive issues in light of the recent investigations into the sufferings of the 'Stolen Generations'. Her biographer, Vera Whittington, felt compelled to tackle the issue head on: 'Let it be clearly said: Sister Kate had no hand in separating mothers and children. She saw the depredation of children's life at the Moore River Settlement and responded to their need'.[3] This is true to the extent that, as Miss Lefroy set out in the above letter to the Commissioner in 1951, '[I]t was agreed that he [Neville] should select the children'.

Letters written by Neville[4] indicate that Sister Kate willingly placed her institution within the objectives of biological absorption. In one such letter, dated 1944, Neville explained: 'Children placed with Sister Kate are never released to their parents. This would be a direct contradiction of the principle of their segregation from native persons, as they are placed with Sister Kate for this very reason'. In another letter, dated 1947, Neville suggested that Sister Kate's racial views were even more strictly adhered to than his own: 'I cannot see any objection to the marriage of two quadroons. Evidently Sister Kate believes in the marriage of quadroon girls to white men, to [breed out the colour.]'

Whittington paints Sister Kate's 'system of care' for the children she 'rescued' as being a humane departure from the prevailing regimental, institutional model. Based on the cottage system — complete with 'cottage parents' and 'cottage siblings' — it offered children 'the love and the care to be found within the ideal family'.[5] Many Aboriginal people who went through the Home during her era have testified to her kindness and to the encouragement she gave to children. Many felt she made a positive difference in their lives and remained grateful for the opportunities she provided. She was universally known as 'Gran' in the Home.[6] The system was flawed, however, and its deficiencies became apparent after Sister Kate had retired.

The cottage system, so approvingly described by Sister Kate's contemporaries and by her biographer, gave control to individual cottage mothers. Sister Kate may have been able to replicate the model by example among others, but it languished following her departure, and especially after the Presbyterian Home took over the running of the institution in 1953, two years before Rob arrived. From this time, the cottage model represented a parental lottery and Rob himself experienced both its benefits and shortcomings.

How children arrived at Sister Kate's is complex. Sister Kate herself propagated the largely fictitious explanation that 'orphans and fatherless children sent to us by the Aborigines Department' formed the basis of children coming into the Home. This view has been countered by recent extensive research on the institution which has found that: 'Children were sent to the Home on the basis of colour, not need. "Nearly white" children, orphaned or not, were chosen by the Department [Native Welfare] to further... [its] social engineering experiment'.[7]

There were other cases as well. Single Aboriginal mothers were particularly vulnerable to losing their children, because most could not find employment, and until the early 1960s they were denied access to social security. Children from this background were in Sister Kate's during Rob's era.[8]

In other cases, parents were motivated by their desire to offer their children opportunities. Sue Gordon, now a prominent Children's Court magistrate who grew up in Sister Kate's during the 1950s and 1960s, explains:

There are some Aboriginal parents around Perth who ... actually put them [their children] there who want to be called Stolen Generation but they weren't stolen. Their parents put them there for one reason or another. In my era, there was a large Noongar family from the South West whose mother made a tremendous decision to put all her children in Sister Kate's but she used to come and visit them. She knew the reputation of Sister Kate's so she did that to give the kids a chance and she would come and visit them ... [she had] six or seven children and no husband and no job.[9]

~~~~~~

Violet's circumstances were different. Following a short period as a domestic at Capel, and after falling pregnant, Violet returned to Moore River Settlement, which had been taken over as a Methodist Mission. It may have been the only place to which she felt she could return. It was from here that Robert was removed. No documentation exists from either the Child Welfare or Native Welfare Departments explaining Rob's removal from his mother. Although Violet has made definitive statements about these circumstances, these are very brief. Understandably, the matter remains an extremely painful one for her.

As she explained to the award-winning *Four Corners* documentary on Rob's life made in 1996: 'I'd just like to say that when I was at the Home, there was another couple of girls who had young children and this one particular morning the welfare lady just come and said she was going to take the babies to a home'.[10] In a recent interview she made a similar explanation: 'I don't know what year, but he was a very small baby when they took him from me — about six months old'. The name of Rob's father has not been disclosed for this project, although it is acknowledged he was white. Rob had few details about him and the two never met.

There would be no reason to revisit Violet's account had not officials from the Child Welfare Department and the management of Sister Kate's made written comments in the mid-1960s — ten years after Rob's arrival at the Home — that he had been abandoned by his mother. This communication, which forms part of Rob's Native Welfare file, also includes a letter written in 1965, by the Secretary of Sister Kate's, to the Minister for Child Welfare, that he was 'left at this Home, by his mother Violet Ethal Dinah on the 3rd of August, 1955'. In June 1958, a Welfare Officer claimed that Violet showed no interest at all in Rob, a claim repeatedly made both by Child Welfare and by the staff at Sister Kate's.

In many of the cases involving the Stolen Generations, a complex web of circumstances lay behind a child's removal, notably pressure from authorities leading to lack of informed consent, and personal circumstances arising from past institutionalisation including lack of family support networks and lack of a reasonable income. In the 1950s, the removal of children from young, unmarried mothers — black or white — was common practice. At the time, a young, unmarried, black mother probably had little chance of keeping her baby if she came to the notice of authorities in the metropolitan area. In spite of these ambiguities, the testimony of Rob's mother is clear and consistent.

Violet told the *Four Corners* documentary that she was not allowed to visit him in Sister Kate's, but 'sometimes I used to go with the girls and I used to get a glimpse of him in the nursery ... but in them days it was very hard because we were told not to go near any of the children'. This account by Violet suggests that Sister Kate's and the Child Welfare authorities may well have devised their own version of the reasons for Rob's placement in the institution. This possibility has a broader context. Today, some with close dealings to the Home in the 1950s and 1960s maintain that management routinely lied to the children about their backgrounds. Rob certainly believed this happened to him, as will be discussed later. Obviously, no documentation exists to prove such an accusation. If true, we can only speculate about the motivation: a desire to 'save' or 'protect' children from harsh realities, or a commitment to the ideals of assimilation. In any event, if information was falsified, the flow-on impact on children would have been profound in some cases.

One thing which authorities did not attempt to hide was their interest in the racial make-up of the children. Rob's Native Welfare file is scattered with comments about his race, confirming the authorities' underlying motivations in raising the children. A hand-written memo on his file classified him as '7/16th Aboriginal; the son of Violet who was 7/8th'. This classification gave Rob the status of 'native in law', and subject to the jurisdiction of the Native Welfare Department. Interest in Rob's colour continued over the next few years. In 1958 an officer from Child Welfare described him as 'a nice little boy — shows little colour'.

~~~~~~~~

Following the death of Sister Kate in 1946 the Home passed into the temporary management of the ageing Miss Lefroy, who maintained Sister Kate's attitude to race: 'we never mention colour to the children'.[11] Longer-term, the institution was managed by Mr and Mrs Miner, who attempted to carry on Sister Kate's charitable approach and her emphasis on the children obtaining an education. The Miners also encouraged children's contact with the outside world through picnics, monthly movies and placement in casual employment. Children sent out were given full board and money earned was sent back to Sister Kate's.

However, the year before Rob arrived, the Miners were replaced by a Presbyterian couple, Mr and Mrs Daniels, ushering in a new era in the life of the Home. Few remember them with affection. Mrs Daniels is remembered by some as being especially forbidding. Joan Winch, who worked at Sister Kate's under the Daniels, recalls her as 'very strict with a tendency towards religious fanaticism'. She was 'not at all motherly'. Matronly in appearance, she had the demeanour of the stern headmistress of an English private girls' school. Steve Goodall, who grew up with Rob in Sister Kate's, recalls being frightened as a young child by the couple, but he was lucky enough to have a strong cottage mother who would try to protect him and Rob from them. He recalls fearing the departure of his cottage mother for a ten-week holiday. She was his 'protector' and her absence left him 'exposed to the wrath of the superintendents'. To the children they were a formidable couple. Mr Daniels had a formal, official-looking demeanour and a great fondness for driving his black Riley motor car. He regularly spanked children. To some of the children, Mrs Daniels was simply 'a tyrant': her way of interacting with the children 'was always with a finger pointing. She would be 100 metres from you and she'd be at full gallop, pointing'.

Rob commenced life in Sister Kate's in Aunty Vi's [Bennett] babies room — where all young ones were given her undivided attention. Although not Aboriginal herself, she was one of the few staff who sacrificed her own life and motherhood for work at Sister Kate's. Sue Gordon recalls happy visits to Aunty Vi's nursery: 'I was always happy to visit her and the little kids and a lot of us used to visit Aunty Vi because she had all the babies and we wanted to see them'. It was these visits that forged bonds between older and younger children in the Home and specifically between Sue and a young Rob Dinah.

At age three or four, children were required to move from the care of Aunty Vi and live in another cottage. There was no formal handover, as Joan Winch explains: 'As a cottage mother you didn't know where the kids came from, you didn't get information about their backgrounds or dispositions ... you just got a child'. In his move away from the nursery, Rob was lucky in the parenting lottery. He was placed in the cottage of Min Lockyear (now Bradley), located at the farthest end of the Home's grounds. It was near what was called the Meadow, which was actually a swamp. At this end of the Home's grounds, the cows were kept and the milking shed was located. It was an appealing place for the children. There was a big pond with lilies where kids would catch marron. Min's house was a retreat for many of the children. Min is remembered by all the children as someone special. Not only was she 'always just there', she made a point of being able to offer a biscuit or a lolly or a bit of bread and jam or bread and dripping.

If anyone could take the role of replacement mother, it was Min. One of Sister Kate's 'originals', she had been placed in the Home following the death of her parents and with the full consent of her relatives. Unlike some of the other cottage mothers, Min offered Rob and the other twelve children in her cottage love, support, stability and homely values. She devoted her life to the children. Her cottage was a warm, loving, cosy household, a 'real family'. She would play country and western on her guitar and sing with the children. She read a story to the children every night and took great pride in dressing them neatly, no mean feat given that the Home did not provide new clothes for the children. They were allocated secondhand clothes donated to the institution. Min was strong on developing good habits: 'It is manners and cleanliness that counts', Min would tell the children. Saturday was always the day for the children to help with house cleaning, and afterwards they often went out on picnics where they still asked if they could leave the table, even though they were sitting on the ground. To complement the 'normal' family atmosphere, Min gave the children birthday parties, presents and also regularly took them to the football.

The key to her success with the children lay in her own background. She could relate to the kids because she was a 'Homie' [as the children were universally known].

Rob bonded closely with Min. Although she would not likely admit to having any favourites, Min 'absolutely loved Robert'.[12] In his writings and published interviews on his childhood, Rob does not describe his relationship with Min. He probably felt to do so would be an affront to his natural family. Yet privately, Rob confided to his close friends his childhood emotional ties to Min and the debt he owed her. One of his oldest friends and colleagues, Peter O'Brien, explains that Rob 'absolutely adored Min': 'She was Mum in a mumless situation. She was caring ... he desperately needed to be loved and she was there to give him what love she could ... he was always very grateful to her for the unconditional love that she bestowed on so many of them'.[13]

Min recognised Rob's emotional vulnerability and paid him special attention. But, as a small boy, he was unhappy. The one surviving photograph of Rob as a four- or five-year-old depicts an angelic-looking child with big, dark, doe-like eyes and a sweet but vulnerable expression. He has an unmistakable look of sadness. Joan Winch observed a very young Rob's relationship with Min: 'As a young boy of four or five, Rob was quite unhappy. He always looked like he wanted to be with Minnie all the time. He was insecure, clinging'.

Whilst he lived in Min's cottage, Rob formed a caring relationship with a young woman and her boyfriend as part of the Daniels' increased efforts to link children to the outside world. When people wanted to offer an outing or weekend stay-over to a child from Sister Kate's, they needed only to ring the management and a child would be allocated. It was in this casual manner that eighteen-year-old Beth Daebritz and her young partner — later husband — formed a close relationship with the young Robert Dinah.

In 1957 they both worked at West Australian Newspapers Ltd. Each year the company's social club organised a huge Christmas party for the workforce and their children. As the young couple didn't have any children, 'we thought we would ring an orphanage'. They rang Sister Kate's and asked if they could take four children. One of them was four-year-old Robert. 'Now I look back on it,' explains Beth, 'it was strange we were not interviewed beforehand'. When they first went to the Home, Beth and her partner asked questions about how the children came to be there. In what appears almost certainly a fabricated story, they were told that 'Robert was brought to Sister Kate's in an appalling and emaciated state; they burned his clothes and had to set him right again'. It is extremely unlikely that the Mogumber Home (Moore River, recently renamed) would have allowed a child to leave in this state.

Beth and her partner enjoyed the experience with the children so much that they rang back the next week and asked if they could take just two, one of them being Rob. It was the beginning of a long and meaningful relationship which involved taking the two boys out of Sister Kate's — usually for the weekend — until Rob was about eleven years old. Beth remembers the times she would walk up to Rob's cottage, and greet a shy but welcoming Min. The same routine happened when they returned Robert and his friend. 'The kids loved her … they would rush in and hug her legs'.

Beth was able to observe Rob closely as he was growing up and she, too, was aware of his emotional vulnerability: 'I remember him being very easily hurt. Quite shy, not an outgoing child. Deep thinking. Intelligent, but quite emotional. Fragile in a way. He would get upset at the slightest rebuke'. Beth found Rob loved to be read to and he was very easy to have around. The family had a beach house at Quinn's Rocks and they would take Robert there for the weekends. Beth lost contact with Rob after he left Sister Kate's to rejoin his family, but she followed his career and met up with him several times during his adulthood.

Another positive influence in Min's cottage was the cricketer, and later Australian captain, Bobby Simpson and his wife Meg. As Min recalls, he lived in Western Australia for a time and he'd take kids out for weekends. Even after he left the state he would still return to the Home when playing in Perth. He would drop in to see Min and the kids and teach them to play cricket.

Over time, Min developed a relationship with a man which gradually grew stronger. Eventually — when Rob was about seven years old — Min faced a difficult life decision. She wanted to get married but, with rare exceptions, the cottage system did not allow husbands to live in. Consequently, Min left Sister Kate's.

Reflecting on these events of more than forty years ago in her homely kitchen in a seaside town south of Perth, Min said it was hard to leave. She paused before poignantly acknowledging: 'Sometimes I think that me leaving upset a lot of their lives'. Steve Goodall agrees, but he doesn't blame Min; she had her own life to lead, and it was the management's policy not to allow husbands to join the cottage system.

~~~~~~

It does not take much to imagine how Min's departure would have affected a child like Rob. The small, shy boy's ties to an affectionate mother-figure were broken, and it's unlikely that there would have been a sympathetic response from the Home's management to the difficulties this caused for Rob and the other children. Certainly, Min's departure ushered in a more troubled period in his life.

According to Sue Gordon, Rob did not cope with the sudden and dramatic change of domestic environment: 'Well I know he didn't like the movement. If you're feeling safe in a place, that's where you want to be'. She elaborates further saying that it would have been 'horrific' to suddenly move from a 'motherly environment' where the one person was 'devoted to them' to a new cottage with a completely different environment, and one where the children were given much less attention and affection.

Rob's move exposed him for the first time to the defects in the cottage system. It was only ever going to be as good as the cottage mothers who looked after the children. As the wages were low and the working conditions poor, only the committed or the desperate would seek employment at Sister Kate's. Tragically for the children, there were too many who fitted into the latter category. It was an era when employment opportunities for women were limited, and especially for those who were unskilled, single mothers or recent divorcees. For many of the staff, Sister Kate's was a stopping off place until something else came along, and for some it was a job of last resort. Most did not stay long: some as little as a few months, others a maximum of a few years. Min recalls that some of the other cottage mothers were 'strange people'. One was Italian and couldn't speak much English. Another had two older boys of her own who bossed the kids around. Some of them lived there for the free board and lodgings and didn't know how to relate to the children.

There were other bizarre characters. One woman arrived as a cottage mother, together with her daughter, in a yellow Jaguar car complete with running boards. To the children she seemed to be from another world, so resplendent was she in fur coat, peroxide blond hair, high-back leather patent shoes and bright red nail polish. She didn't stay long, but she used to take the children for rides at weekends in the Jaguar.

Another of the cottage mothers was a woman who used to play the piano and claim that she had an operatic voice. She would sit at the piano in the nude, and ask the boys to come and brush her long hair while she played. As this example shows, oversight of the character of some of the cottage mothers was lax, exposing the children to various forms of potential abuse.

Some of the cottage parents who blew in and out of the place were cruel in their dealings with the children. As each cottage mother had her own autonomy to establish routines and relationships, it was a system which allowed cruelty in some of the homes, while not in others.[14] There were instances where children as young as four were required to scrub large floors. At one point Joan Winch, who ran the cottage next door to Min, complained to Mr and Mrs Daniels and asked that a stop be put to the harsh treatment meted out to some children. She even threatened to inform Child Welfare about some of the practices.

There were less direct — but no less damaging — forms of cruelty. Sue Gordon recalls 'the absolute power' that she believes both the Miners and the Daniels's exercised over the children. This power extended to sending 'naughty' children to an even more repressive Catholic institution where children were under constant supervision, where they undertook washing and ironing for the public schools and hospitals. One girl went there for three years without the other children being told where she had gone.

There were other damaging practices. Siblings brought into the Home — some as young as three years old — were separated and placed in different cottages. Children were compelled to hang out any sheets and pyjamas they had wet or soiled the night before, in full view of their friends. Bedwetting, even among the older children, was not uncommon. In itself this was an indicator of the emotional stress some of the children were under. Such practices confirmed an opinion that many of the cottage mothers — and certainly the Home's management — had little instinctive understanding of the emotional needs of children. In a few cases, a pervasive dislike of children was evident. Steve Goodall also has vivid memories of one adult who took delight in putting 'you under all the cows that kicked'.

As part of its self-appointed mission of assimilation, there is evidence to suggest that the management at Sister Kate's persistently denied children knowledge of their family backgrounds. As previously mentioned, there are strong claims that it openly lied about them. For Rob, this reinforced his insecurity; he could never fully believe what he was being told. Joan Winch has publicly detailed the extent of the cover-up perpetrated by the Home's managers and at least some of its staff: 'a lot of the kids were told, "you were abandoned by your parents. We found you on a bush track" or "Your parents didn't want you"; "you have no home".'[15]

There was a profoundly damaging lack of warmth in the relationship between many of the staff and the children. There were exceptions — Min, Aunty Vi and Joan among them. Others are remembered by some as being emotionally distant from the children. Sue Gordon recalls:

> There was always the kids to play with but nobody to talk to about your problems. Nobody to ask questions of ... So you just went through life. I mean funny things like girls with periods, you found that out by yourself. Found out about sex later in life, because no-one told you those things. So, it was quite a sterile environment ... There was no love or affection from any of the people who looked after us.[16]

In one cottage the children were packed off to bed at 4.30 in the afternoon[17] while in others there was no-one to greet the children when they came home from school. As Joan Winch recalls, few of the adults played games with the children. Rob's lifelong struggle to come to terms with his institutionalisation may have had its roots in this lack of affectionate relationship with adults, especially after Min left. He had to struggle to understand and express his inner feelings.

The harsh life in the Home had one positive benefit. It further strengthened the already close bonds between the children forged by their communal cottage life. Rob described the relationships as being like brothers and sisters.[18] Min said that all the children in her cottage 'stuck together'. Steve Goodall talks today about the special bond that exists between the 'Homies'; he says that it was not possible to grow up in a house all together for years on end 'without developing a relationship like growing up as your brother'.

Such affectionate relationships created the most enduring positive memories for the children. The grounds at Sister Kate's were a child's paradise — expansive and containing many and varied adventures. Full use of them was made on Sunday afternoons, the one time in the week the children were given their collective freedom. They invented their own games like 'kick the can, games hiding all around the Home, and rounders'. A particular favourite was a game called 'hip', an adaptation of 'hide and seek' played with a thin branch of a tree, the object being to try to find a playmate and touch him/her on the hip with the branch. On Sunday afternoons, after all their chores were done, the children had four hours of uninterrupted play.

Young Robert Dinah had one natural advantage at such games. He was a fast runner. He could always be seen running around the Home, his little legs going flat out.

There were hilarious moments as well. Rob fondly remembered the antics of the two bulls usually locked up in their pen at the back of the milking shed. One day, 'we were playing in the cow paddock ... about forty kids, all playing and we let the bulls out of the cow paddock and they went charging off into the distance with all these kids'.[19] It was times like this, with all the children mixing in together, that helped him remember into his adulthood the positive side of Sister Kate's, 'as if it was one big happy family'.[20]

The bonds between the children were strengthened by the experience of school. Interviewed in 1984 at the time of his emergence as a national leader, Rob explained the 'us against the world' spirit between the children: 'growing up in an institution with other kids, you had a relationship with them that was very special and you treated them as your family. Going to a school environment [Queens Park Primary School was just across the road from the Home] where it was all the Homie kids as opposed to all the non-Homie kids'.[21]

Sue Gordon experienced the same collective identity forged by the racism at the school: 'We weren't Aborigines in the Home, but when we went across the road to school we were Aborigines. We were natives and darkies and all that sort of thing'.[22] The racial attitudes of the school children were in part shaped by the school curriculum. Just before Rob's arrival, Miss Lefroy, the then Principal of the Home, complained to the Commissioner for Native Affairs about this matter. She wrote: 'If the Education Department would delete from their School Books all passages referring to the Natives as the lowest and most degraded of human beings, it would greatly help these near white children to overcome their inferiority complex'.[23]

Rob also recalled the racist atmosphere at the school. His memory centred around the school uniform — khaki shorts and khaki shirts. The 'Homies' were often late for school because every morning they had to go to church and say their prayers. As all the other children were lining up in the quadrangle, the 'Homies' came running around the corner en masse to be met by a chorus 'Ahki Khakis for the little darkies'. It didn't seem to Rob an overtly racist jibe, just a form of teasing. But the children felt sensitive enough about it to ask the school management to change the colour of the uniform, which they did.[24] Yet was the decision taken out of sensitivity for the children's self-esteem, or to remove unwanted attention from their racial backgrounds?

Rob remembered that the collective strength of the 'Homies' kept them out of too much trouble: 'There were so many "Homies" that if there was any trouble that got out of hand ... the "Homies" would all stick together, as a family within the whole group.' This group strength 'was a sort of intimidation for the rest of the school ... they had protection within that sort of clique'.[25]

The group bonds were shattered for Rob Riley, however, in one dramatic incident. He was sexually assaulted as a nine-year-old by three of the Home's boys.

Up until the early 1990s, Rob disclosed to very few people his memories of this assault. The sense of betrayal must have been profound, because he knew the boys in a close 'family' setting. Longer term, his sexual assault at Sister Kate's vied with his feelings of loss over his natural family in creating the underlying disturbances in his personality.

From an early age Rob harboured the feeling that he belonged to someone. Interviewed in 1995 for the Aboriginal Legal Service publication about the Stolen Generations, *Telling Our Story*, Rob outlined how he would often ask the staff at the Home why he wasn't visited by his family or parents. They told him that he 'did not have a family and that he was an orphan'. He went on to explain how he 'used to get into trouble for incessantly asking questions about his family'. On some occasions, 'he was punished by having to bend over and being hit on the backside with a leather thong by the superintendent'. Rob told the interviewer that his punishments made him 'very confused and he could not understand what was wrong with asking about his family'. He was sure in his own mind as a boy 'he belonged to someone'.[26]

Successive managements at the Home actively discouraged visits from relatives. There was a misguided belief that the children should be allowed to make their own way in the wider community without the influence of their Aboriginal culture. Confusion arose for some children because, despite the reluctance to grant visits, some parents did make it inside the Home. Some made their own individual arrangements with cottage mothers.

Steve Goodall was only ever given the most fleeting glimpses into his background:

> There was no truth ... the only person who ever told me the truth about my family was Min because every show day ... we would all go in a bus down to the Royal Show, and from the age of four I can remember this black woman coming up to Aunty Vi and to Min and I'd be holding onto one of their skirts ... [and] this black woman would bend down and kiss me and cuddle me and exchange some money with either Min or Aunty Vi, and when I was old enough they told me that that was my grandmother, and they were the only ones who ever told me the truth, that there was this woman who was denied seeing me; the only time she could see me was to sneak a cuddle and a kiss at the Royal Show and I would say that for the majority of kids, that was the way it was.

Unfortunately for Rob, Min says she knew nothing about his family background to pass on to him.

Likewise, children's racial backgrounds were hidden. Sue Gordon explains: 'We were told we weren't Aboriginals'. She recalls how this denial created anxiety about other Aborigines because they were given 'a fear of dark people'. One can only imagine the confusion arising for children who were also the butt of racial jibes at school. Certainly as a young boy Rob had no awareness of his racial background. Beth Daebritz tells the story of the day Rob was in the bath at her place washing himself after a day's active play. He started scrubbing his knee and called out to Beth: 'Bef [as he pronounced her name], 'it's not dirt; it's just brown'.

The impact of this denial of family on many of the children was severe. Much of Rob's later anger would come from the full realisation of these lies and the broken trust they entailed for him. It fuelled his uncompromising approach to politics and it underpinned his later abhorrence for broken political deals.

At ten years of age, having spent almost his entire life in the institution, Rob faced a dramatic change in his circumstances, which in a few years propelled him into a starkly different life with new challenges to overcome. Each without knowing what the other was doing, Violet and Sam reconnected with Rob inside Sister Kate's.

The records show that on 26 March 1964 Violet visited Sister Kate's with her husband, Bill Riley. It was only at this time that Violet felt her life was stable enough to attempt to try to get Rob back. The circumstances which brought her to this visit, and the accompanying determination to seek Rob's return to her, illustrate parts of her own harsh journey as an Aboriginal woman in Western Australia.

Violet met Bill in 1955, but her early relationship with him had been unstable. For some years they lived together at Allawah Grove, a collection of fifty 'huts' on the outer metropolitan fringe of Perth offered by the Housing Commission to the Department of Native Welfare. Native Welfare operated the site as a reserve in response to pressure from local whites concerned about Aboriginal camps in the area. It was a dismal place. The aim of the Native Welfare Department in running Allawah Grove was to 'provide accommodation for the increasing number of Aborigines who were then attempting to make their home in the metropolitan area'. Ultimately, it was hoped 'to assist families to progress socially to the stage where they could be assisted to obtain better housing within the general community'.[27]

Thus, Allawah Grove was originally intended for 'only the higher status families'; the others were to be sent to a reserve. However, the aims of the Department were thwarted by public pressure against the establishment of a reserve for this purpose, and because 'many of the more socially and economically adjusted Aborigines had moved ... [mainly to East Perth], Allawah Grove was left with the less sophisticated ones'. This is the language of assimilation again — 'less sophisticated' would likely have included people like Violet from highly disrupted backgrounds, with few relatives able to provide support and with few employment opportunities. Most of the population at the settlement were unemployed and most showed 'no desire for assimilation'. According to one contemporary, Allawah Grove was 'a society fast becoming a subculture'.[28]

At some point in the early 1960s, Violet and Bill headed off to the old Moore River Settlement, renamed Mogumber Mission, where Bill obtained employment. Opportunities for either visiting Robert or seeking his return ceased. Several years later, the couple returned to Perth and set up house in inner-city West Perth, which had links to East Perth, the main Aboriginal 'ghetto'.

Later in life Rob described his visit from his mother as 'the happiest and saddest day of my life'. It was the happiest day of his life because it vindicated what he had always believed, that he belonged to someone. Seeing his parents was final proof that he did belong. He also found out he had brothers and sisters. However, the visit was bittersweet because of 'the trauma of being punished' for asking questions about who he belonged to. He also felt sad that day because the reunion with his parents made him realise that he had been 'robbed' of part of his life.[29]

It is almost impossible to imagine how he internalised such conflicting emotions. According to the Superintendent, Mr Daniels, Rob became emotionally disturbed by his parents' visit, with the result that he wetted his bed. Mr Daniels 'had advised Mrs Riley that she could best serve Rob's interests by keeping away from him'.[30] However, by this time Violet was determined to have Robert returned to her, and she began calling at the Child Welfare Department for permission to take him home.

Meanwhile, Violet's brother Sam had an unexpected encounter with ten-year-old Rob on a chance visit he made to the Home. Sam had only just found Violet after years of separation, following her much earlier release from the mission at Roelands. Although he had stayed with her a few times at Allawah Grove, Violet did not mention Rob. As Sam explains, until he visited Sister Kate's for a fete with his girlfriend, he didn't know Rob existed. At the fete somebody called out the name 'Dinah' and gestured, 'Here, Dinah, over here'. Sam thought someone was talking to him. He looked around and was surprised by a child's voice calling out to another child a little way off into the distance. He turned to the young boy and asked who he was calling out to, and the reply came that he was talking to Robert:

> 'Robert who?' I asked. 'Robert Dinah.' That is when I called Rob over and asked his name. He sort of looked at me shyly, head down and he said 'Robert Dinah'. He told me his Mum was called Violet [which, presumably he had only learnt from her recent visit]. 'Violet is my sister,' I told him. 'I will be your uncle then.' I gave him some money and let him go and play, he was a little bit embarrassed. Then on leaving we went up and told him we'd come back to visit.[31]

Sam returned a few times and took Rob out, but he was not in regular contact with Violet during this period. His life in the mission had trained him to accept whatever was put in his path, and this meant he felt no urgency to contact her about his discovery of Rob.

Simultaneously, Violet's campaign to have Rob released was protracted and painful. Sister Kate's and the Child Welfare Department placed major obstacles in the way of Rob's return. Both agencies found it hard to shake off their stereotypical attitudes of Aboriginal people as inherently bad parents and their corresponding faith in the benefits of assimilation. As the documentation shows, the Superintendent of Sister Kate's, Mr Daniels, tried to obstruct Rob's return by using highly questionable methods. Violet sums up her struggle with officialdom: 'I had a lot of problems trying to get him out. They rejected me two or three times. They said the place wasn't good enough for him. So I had to prove myself in my living standards, which I made the effort to do'.

Several months after Violet visited Rob, the Secretary of Sister Kate's wrote to the Minister for Child Welfare applying to have Rob committed as a ward of the state. A few weeks later, in August 1965, a Superintendent with Child Welfare wrote to the Commissioner of Native Welfare informing him that Violet's visit had indeed motivated the Superintendent of Sister Kate's 'to seek the prevention of his removal by his mother'. The Child Welfare Superintendent then raised with Native Welfare the possible need for 'legal control by committal' if it was considered that he should remain at Sister Kate's. There is a strong inference in the correspondence to and from senior officials in the Child Welfare and Native Welfare Departments that they were fed information about the reasons for Rob's original placement in Sister Kate's — that he 'was virtually an institutional orphan' — by the management of Sister Kate's.

The application by Sister Kate's for the authority to make Rob a ward of the state set in motion the cumbersome process of investigation by the Child Welfare Department into Violet's suitability as a parent. In its initial phase this was based solely on interviews with her and began for the first time in December 1965 when she was interviewed by the Department. In the record of that interview Violet supported her application for Rob's return by stating that she lived in a self-contained flat, comprising half a house ... three bedrooms, lounge and kitchen. Her husband was in regular employment at Federal Tinware, where he earned about £18 per week. She further explained that she had six children under the age of nine years in her care, all of whom were the children of her present marriage. She said that she had her own furniture including bedding which would be adequate should Rob return home. Violet was recorded as making one last emphatic statement. She wanted Rob in her care 'as she at last feels she could adequately provide for him, and her other children, who have met Robert when he visited relatives of hers, would also like him home. She stated her husband is perfectly agreeable to Robert's coming to live with them'.[32]

In the next two months Violet was interviewed several more times by the Department regarding Rob's return. Clearly, they were unconvinced by her responses, because in a letter to Mr Daniels an officer from the Department stated that it was 'contemplating ministerial committal of Robert'. In response to this communication, Daniels wrote a letter about Violet to the Director of Child Welfare in which he confirmed that Mrs Riley had come to the Home to discuss Robert's future. But according to Daniels, she was 'very vague' about her future plans for him such that they only 'gathered' that she wished to take him away. Daniels proceeded to outline key parts of the conversation with Violet which appeared designed to continue building the case for committal. He claimed that she 'admitted that her husband drinks' and that they had six other children and just two bedrooms (a clear distortion — see Violet's comments above) in the house in which they lived. Daniels' unfavourable views about Violet were revealed in the letter:

> She [Violet] has promised Robert a wrist watch and a camera, a promise obviously without means of fulfilment and equally obviously made with the motive of purchasing his favours ... it would not appear, therefore, that her present interest in Robert is motivated by any degree of affection or sense of responsibility. The only reason I can see for wishing to take Robert is that she may have to pay for his maintenance which is obviously impossible.

While Daniels kept up his campaign for committal he also continued to block Violet from visiting Rob. A handwritten note on Rob's file — containing an indecipherable signature and no letterhead, but most likely from a Child Welfare officer — dated May 1966 stated:

> Mrs Riley called 3/5/66 and told me that she and her husband were quite prepared to have Robert home. They have, according to Mrs Riley, been told by Mr Brennan DNW [Department of Native Welfare] to visit Robert in order to re-establish a relationship and then take him home. They have been doing this but have been discouraged in their desire to take Robert home by Mr and Mrs Daniels.

Surprisingly, the unidentified Child Welfare officer was the first to raise the obvious point about any properly constructed due process in a matter involving the return of a child to its parents: 'I feel that an inspection of the home should be made'. This was an extraordinary point to raise at this stage in proceedings. Why had it taken nearly two years from the point of Violet's first visit which signalled her intentions for Robert, to raise such a basic procedure? After all, the Department, acting at least in part on advice from Sister Kate's, had been actively contemplating making Rob a ward of the State, without even raising the need for a home visit. Such a visit, the official wrote in his/her memo, would likely conclude that there 'was no reason for making him a ward'.

A month later such a visit was arranged. The officer who undertook it made a brief and definitive finding:

> At the time of my visit the house was neat and tidy. By native standards the condition of the house was remarkable. Mrs Riley and the three younger children were neatly dressed.

> Mrs Riley said [for the umpteenth time] she would like to have Robert home, and that her husband keeps on asking about having the boy to live with them. In view of the general atmosphere and conditions in this home I recommend Robert's release to the care of his mother.

In August 1966 the communication from the Child Welfare Department to the Native Welfare Department finally confirmed Rob's release from Sister Kate's. There was a final and, as it turned out, prophetic parting comment: 'The child, Robert, will no doubt find it hard to adjust to life outside Sister Kate's home'.

~~~~~~

In the mid-1960s the wider commmunity had little idea why children like Robert Dinah, now Robert Riley, would struggle in their post-institutional life. As in many other institutions set up to serve the policy of assimilation, a gulf separated the official rhetoric maintained by Sister Kate's management and its actual practice. Admittedly, memories of the place range across the emotional spectrum; some children entering it were not 'stolen' from their parents, and without doubt some children benefited from some of the opportunities it offered.

Nonetheless, much damage was done. More recent understanding about the harm done by 'closed' institutions for children highlights their tendency towards regimentation, depersonalisation, capricious management and abuse. This understanding has come from a variety of sources, including the published submissions made to the landmark Human Rights and Equal Opportunity Commission's Inquiry into the Stolen Generations; including two comprehensive reports submitted by the Western Australian Aboriginal Legal Service;[33] the subsequent report of the Commission, *Bringing Them Home*; and most, recently, the Senate inquiry into non-Aboriginal children in institutional care.[34] This latter report documented the shocking lives of children taken from their families in the post-war era by welfare authorities or placed in homes by families unable to provide for them. There are striking similarities in the findings of all reports.

The most fortunate children in Sister Kate's seem to have been relatively better off than many other Aboriginal and non-Aboriginal children in institutional care in post-war Australia. This is not the place to engage in a direct comparative study between Sister Kate's and other child welfare institutions, or between children placed in Aboriginal-specific homes and those for non-Aboriginal children. As previously discussed, Sister Kate herself had been acutely aware of deficiencies in the care of institutionalised children and tried to develop an alternative model. However, she did not succeed in this endeavour with many children — and especially those entering the Home after she retired. Rob experienced the best and the worst of the institution, and this fractured his emotional development. One distinction, however, between institutions for Aboriginal and non-Aboriginal children must be emphasised. Children placed in the former, including Sister Kate's, suffered the deliberate undermining of their racial identity to further the Home's social purpose: assimilation.

Rob came to understand the psychological damage he had suffered. In 1991, he told an audience that institutionalisation made 'us grow up thinking that we were totally alone in the world. We had no family, no belongings, no identity'.[35] These feelings came to be powerful shapers of Rob's emotional makeup. And he was not able at this stage to confront his sexual abuse. That experience lay dormant for years in whatever way children find to banish bad experiences from their thoughts.

There is a sad irony to this. In the years when Rob lived in Sister Kate's, the psychoanalyst Donald Winnicott formulated his theory that a fragile emotional relationship between child and mother or mother substitute could impede the child from establishing a sense of inner security.[36] Few people would associate the adult Rob Riley with a propensity for anxiety; after all, he was the fearless political campaigner. But the extent to which his public existence helped him conceal his vulnerable self is crucial to understanding Rob's life.

Rob would spend his adulthood trying to resolve his feelings about Sister Kate's and the circumstances surrounding his placement there. As a young adult, he felt torn between its positive and negative aspects. 'The idea of assimilation', he explained in an interview in 1984, 'has been fairly successful' in that people like himself who had lived in a home had the benefit of being instilled with the ideals of being successful by acquiring an education and a career. He elaborated: 'So I suppose there have been those fringe benefits that I will always be grateful for, but there will always be things that I vehemently detest. I don't think there can ever be a happy medium between the two'.

Asked, 'What sort of things do you vehemently detest?', he replied that it was growing up in an environment 'without any knowledge of my background'. There was also the deliberate misleading 'about where you come from and not even being aware of your Aboriginality'. Thus, 'you finally confront the big wide world and suddenly are met with the changes from a Home in metropolitan Perth to a place called Pingelly which has got a fairly notorious reputation for its attitudes to Aboriginal people'.[37]

Living in Pingelly would indeed thrust the adolescent Rob Riley into a cauldron of racism, which would change his life profoundly.

Meanwhile, in Sister Kate's, Rob's 'brothers and sisters' were not immediately told that he had gone, let alone where he had gone. It took time for word to filter through that he had left. To most of them, a 'brother' had simply disappeared.

CHAPTER THREE

Life at the Margins: Growing up Aboriginal

Rob reached adolescence in Sister Kate's without having a clear idea of who he was. He felt neither Aboriginal nor white. He had had no family with which to identify, and the bonds with his substitute mother had been broken. His primary identity was simply as one of a group; Rob felt comfortable in the boisterous collective of Sister Kate's, which was all he had known. Reunited at the age of twelve with his family, he had to come to terms with his new home environment: a smaller family unit, an unfamiliar culture, and stressful social circumstances. Rob's transition from apprentice white to claimant of Aboriginal heritage was a painful one. By his early teens, Rob had consciously chosen his Aboriginality, and started to look at his new world with the zeal of a convert.

Following his release to his family, Rob spent a short time at their West Perth residence where he also attended the local primary school. Jackie Oakley — who became a life-long friend, as well as a senior Aboriginal bureaucrat and community advocate — used to pass by his house on the way to school: 'he was a skinny little kid who was the fastest runner we'd ever seen ... he'd want to race all the kids and no-one ever beat him'. Jackie's observation is significant. Rob had a will to win; he wanted to take others on and not be beaten; he wanted to prevail. Inherited from his grandmother, Anna Miller, and honed in the bustle of coping in a large institution, Rob's will to win acted as his emotional buoyancy, his means of surviving the tough challenges he faced.

Nevertheless the transition to home life was troublesome. Competitive as his underlying make-up was, it existed uneasily alongside his equally innate vulnerability. His family situation heightened his feeling of uncertainty about the world. An outsider to his brothers and sisters, he was especially sensitive to being teased by them. His brothers mocked his lighter skin, calling him 'willy white onions'. He missed the children at Sister Kate's; his new family had their own collective identity. Rob felt alienated.[1]

Violet was acutely aware of the upheaval going on in his life. Mindful of his shyness about his unfamiliar surroundings she tried to encourage him, telling him he would be all right; his brothers and sisters were there to talk to; but 'he kept to himself as much as possible'.[2]

In later life, Rob shared with only a few how troubled he had been during this time. Former 'Homie' Sue Gordon recalls that Rob once told her that his transition from institution to family 'was very hard ... that he didn't know how to handle it and he had trouble fitting in'. But, as she confirms, he was not alone: 'there were quite a few kids who had to go through that, who went back to families'.[3] Living with people that he didn't know stripped away the security blanket of the 'family' he had known all his life. The highly regimented system at Sister Kate's 'ran like a little clock'. Children knew each day of the week what they were going to have for dinner, they knew that after school they had jobs to do, and every Sunday night their hair was checked for nits. There was comfort in knowing these patterns. Even though Rob's family tried to give him support, his new life with them and his former life in a closely disciplined institution were like different worlds: 'the transition must have been horrendous'.

The transition was also abrupt. The authorities at both Sister Kate's and the Child Welfare Department mishandled the situation. Firstly, the Daniels's did not allow his mother and step-father to cement the relationship prior to his release, and secondly Child Welfare offered no support to the family despite acknowledging that Robert would face problems in his readjustment.

Rob's situation worsened dramatically when Bill and Violet's marriage collapsed soon after he returned to live with them, and he lost his mother for a second time. Rob has never recorded his reaction to this event. Violet had few prospects of paid employment and was therefore unable to provide for the children; she moved to Port Hedland to stay with relatives and did not see Rob again for several years. Her move underlined the intergenerational impact of Neville's original policy: the family networks that might have provided support had been scattered. Bill, meanwhile, packed the children off to live with his mother on Pingelly Reserve.

In the late 1960s, the town of Pingelly, situated 160 kilometres south-east of Perth, was a segregated town, like others in the state's prosperous agricultural region; there was a gulf separating the town's 960 whites and its 200-strong Aboriginal population, nearly all of whom lived in abject poverty on the town's reserve. Racial antipathy to Aboriginal people among whites, following the dispossession of Aboriginal land generations earlier, had, by the 1960s, hardened into decades-old prejudice and discrimination. In many such insular rural communities in an isolated state, racism had long been institutionalised. Only a few questioned why Aborigines were forced to live apart, not only on reserves but often barred from town sporting, educational and communal facilities. In a few towns, 'whites only' signs were erected on public toilet blocks[4] and some towns earned unfavourable comparisons with the Deep South of America for the belligerent attitude of their white populations to the issue of race. Rob Riley was to live in Pingelly for three of his formative adolescent years.

Located on a 10-hectare site, on a back road about one kilometre out of town, the Pingelly Reserve was established sometime before World War Two to cater for 'the drift of aboriginals, from surrounding farms, into the fringe areas of the town'.[5] By the late 1960s, 'a big mob of Noongars' — up to two hundred people — was living there. On the hard, clay ground Aboriginal people erected 'lean-tos' made of pieces of corrugated iron. The tin houses were swelteringly hot in summer and freezing cold in winter. There were concrete floors and a gap between the wall and the floor so the floor could be washed out. They had three small rooms, each about five square metres. The front door led to the middle room, which acted as dining room and kitchen, and on each side of this was a door; one led to the parents' bedroom, the other to the children's bedroom. Families were large, and boys and girls slept together in the same room, often with visiting aunties and uncles.

Facilities were basic. Toilets and laundry were shared. The sheds were without running water. Acute health problems arose from the effluent, which overflowed from the decrepit sewerage system and ran out onto the Reserve grounds. From October to February every year the local hospital was over-run with patients from the Reserve, most of whom were suffering from chest complaints, gastro and malnutrition, due to their poor living conditions.[6]

Pingelly's only doctor, Frank Fischer, said 'that many of the houses were serious health hazards'. He had found one house where twenty people, including thirteen children, were living crammed together: 'There was no glass in the windows. Water leaked through the roof. It was cold and draughty. The lavatory was 200 yards away. The tap was 20 yards away'.[7]

Such was the pressure for a place on the Reserve that — unbelievable as it seems — some lived in worse conditions on vacant, adjoining land. As part of the media's 'discovery' of the shocking conditions at Pingelly in the late 1960s, a journalist visited Alice Winmar's 'rabbit hutch' home, several hundred metres from the reserve boundary.[8] It was built in less than a day by lopping off branches from the gum trees, and driving them into the ground to form the framework of the small residence. Rusty tin remnants were added to form the walls and roof and wired together: 'Alice and her children (Kevin aged six, Ian, five, Sandra, two, and Christopher, fifteen months) moved in with her widowed mother-in-law the night their old humpy flooded. Their furniture — two old iron bedsteads, a laundry basket and an oil lamp — were drying in the sun when I visited the squalor they call home'.

Aborigines were forced to endure such conditions because the white residents of Pingelly, like many other white Australians in regional areas at the time, did not want to live with Aborigines in their midst. The local Pingelly shire was indifferent to the opportunities for better housing supposedly opening up for Aborigines following the declaration of the policy of assimilation ten years previously. The official state government policy was for 'transitional' houses to be built for Aboriginal people on the edges of country towns as a lead-in to their full integration within the town. However, Harry Lucas, a local minister, maintained that 'there were no transitional houses' in Pingelly in the late 1960s.[9] Pingelly was not alone in dragging its feet in meeting the requirements of the new era. In the nearby town of Gnowangerup, there were six transitional houses for an Aboriginal population of about three hundred.[10]

Official neglect was the order of the day. Alice Winmar knew as much. 'The Native Affairs people', she explained 'come and visit every week. They always say the same: "Is everything all right?" They can see that nothing's right, but it doesn't make any difference'.[11]

———

By the late 1960s, change was starting to filter through from both state and federal governments. First came extended citizenship rights, including the right to drink, and then, in the first half of 1967, a national referendum was held on the need for greater Commonwealth involvement in Aboriginal affairs. It was carried by more than 90 per cent of voters throughout the nation, although the strongest 'No' vote at 19 per cent was recorded in Western Australia.

These developments unsettled the rigid views on race that whites in towns like Pingelly had comfortably shared for generations. In May 1967 their anxieties came to a dramatic head when a Pingelly magistrate, in sentencing a seventeen-year-old Aboriginal youth to six months detention for a misdemeanour, joined with a colleague in issuing a statement calling for the caning of Aboriginal people as the only means to prevent 'a wave of lawlessness caused by young natives in the town'.[12] One of the town's magistrates, E.O. Lange, explained to the press that:

> No matter what all the do-gooders say in Perth, a whipping is the only form of punishment that Aborigines around here fear. A spell in Fremantle gaol does not worry them. They get good food and a bath and that is all they want. Whipping is the only punishment that makes them reflect on their actions. Physical pain is antagonistic to their nature.[13]

It was these comments which sparked the nationwide focus on Pingelly and its race problem. The alleged juvenile crime wave in the town is now difficult to verify. The press reported one incident in which twelve local children broke into a shop to steal sweets and cigarettes; and in the same month eleven children were involved in twenty-nine charges for breaking and entering a shop.[14]

But the police sometimes wrongly targeted Aboriginal youths. For example, on 8 May 1967 residents of Pingelly awoke to the sight of lavatory paper strewn around the main streets of the town.[15] Local white residents believed 'it was done by juvenile natives'. So did the police, who immediately questioned several Aboriginal youths. The next day it was reported that white youths were responsible for the incident; they told the police they were bored.[16] By 1970, the serving Methodist minister, Reverend E.A. Clark, said 'The place is going to blow up one of these days', unless 'something was done about the native problem'.[17]

Whatever the true extent of the delinquency among Aboriginal youth, most of the white townspeople ascribed it to Aboriginal people themselves: to their recent access to liquor, to their refusal to find employment and to 'the greater assertiveness among the natives'.[18]

Only a few thought the causes flowed from conditions on the Reserve and the consequent resentment this had bred over the years. Young people's disaffection with school was a particular problem. Reverend E. A. Clark believed that the reserves 'were a breeding ground of juvenile delinquency'. Moreover, 'Aborigines are still not accepted in our country towns. This is bitterly resented by [them] and this resentment becomes offensive when loosened with alcohol'.[19]

In fact, there was 'lots of drinking of cheap grog' in between the seasonal farm work. Sometimes the men got paid in kind, rather than wages. Ted Wilkes, who became a friend and colleague of Rob's, and had a significant career in Aboriginal politics in Western Australia, recalls that his uncle once received a pig for work he had undertaken. He took it home, slaughtered it and provided a feast for weeks for his family. The people had their own way of dealing with the harshness of the lifestyle: 'You had lots of Aboriginal people living in the one little area so there was a tendency for people to cling onto one another and to share the burden ... there was always a capacity to understand if someone was crying because they couldn't cope any more with the lifestyle; it was on top of them'.

Barely out of an institutionalised life, Rob was thrust into the most poverty-stricken lifestyle imaginable. He once described it as 'a traumatic experience'.[20] He was repelled by the decrepit environment of the Reserve. In 1984, he told Perth's *Daily News* that he had 'spent 2½ years in one of the windy concrete-and-iron buildings they called "the cattle sheds" on Pingelly Aboriginal reserve'.[21]

While living on Pingelly Reserve, Rob had his first confrontation with street-level racism. He was walking down to the shop one day, unknowingly on the 'wrong side of the street' for an Aborigine. Two white boys approached him. They were older than he was and they sauntered up to him and said, threateningly: 'Eh, you're walking on the wrong side of the street for a boong'. Surprised, but not intimidated, Rob shot back: 'Well this street's made for anyone to walk on, and you don't own it'. He paid for his assertiveness: 'they got stuck into me and belted me up and it was just virtually like walking into a brick wall'.[22]

His pride was damaged more than his body. But the deeper wounds were inflicted to his sense of self. 'It was shocking', Rob later recalled, 'to be confronted with those sorts of racist values and ideals that a lot of white kids have'.[23] By the time he related this story in adulthood, he had placed the incident in a broader context: 'In the matter of a few years I had become transformed from a white ward of the state into a bewildered young Aborigine and an object of racist taunts and gratuitous violence'.[24]

Rob's painful adolescent identity crisis was brought to a head by being bashed. As he said, in Sister Kate's 'I knew I wasn't White, but I didn't think I was Black either'.[25] The bashing crystallised his emerging view of himself, a process which he later described as 'the trauma of the awareness of my Aboriginality'.[26] Part of the trauma was the realisation 'that people have ... negative attitudes towards Aboriginals ... the very raw edge of that racism, I've been confronted with it in those terms with those kids belting me up'.[27] The incident was a turning point in his life: 'From then on I was determined to do something'.

As a young teenager, his first response was to hit back. He would 'approach white kids in the street and ask them if they were looking for trouble. If they said "no", I'd tell them I was, and then punch them'.[28] This anti-social response did not continue, but it highlighted an essential part of his character: a fearless, get-on-the-front-foot approach to the world.

Easing him through his family and identity difficulties was his newly-acquired grandmother — Bill's mother. As one of his cousins explained: 'Granny took him in and got really close to him. She had no favourites but she knew Rob needed more love. She gave him that extra because that's what he needed'.[29] Rob acknowledged the role his grandmother had played in his life, by saying in 1984, at the time of his emergence as a national Aboriginal leader, that she was one of the two influences that 'pointed him to the position he now holds' (the other being the racist bashing).[30] Lila Riley was, he said, 'a caring and capable person who had me and all my brothers and sisters at Pingelly'. It was from Lila, too, that Rob started to hear some of the history of oppression of Aboriginal people, and especially the forced removal of children. He would recall sitting down and hearing Granny tell stories about the time when the police used to ride into Aboriginal communities to remove children and the desperate efforts of mothers to hide them.[31] Surely such stories fed Rob's political consciousness, giving him a wider understanding of his own suffering and helping lay the foundation of his later interest in the history of Australia's race relations.

Relationships with his family, apart from his grandmother, continued to be a painful struggle. He was torn between his desire to belong and his not feeling fully part of the family unit. He felt unable to tell them about the racist bashing because, he said, 'I'd only been living with them for less than a year and I was still going through the stage of being accepted in that sense'.[32]

One hot Saturday morning when he was about twelve, Rob returned from his paper-round about mid-day and heard his sister Denise sobbing in the back yard. He asked her what was wrong. When Denise told him she was not allowed to go to the swimming pool with the other children, Rob told her to go inside the house and get her bathers. He said, 'You're going swimming'. Because it was so hot, Rob piggy-backed Denise into town. He stayed to make sure she had a good, long swim before walking back in the cool of the evening.[33]

One of Rob's cousins also remembers Rob's sensitive side: 'once when mucking around he accidentally pushed my younger sister down an embankment. He realised she was hurt and felt sorry for her so he went up to her and apologised and put his arms around her. He never liked to be bad friends with anyone'.[34]

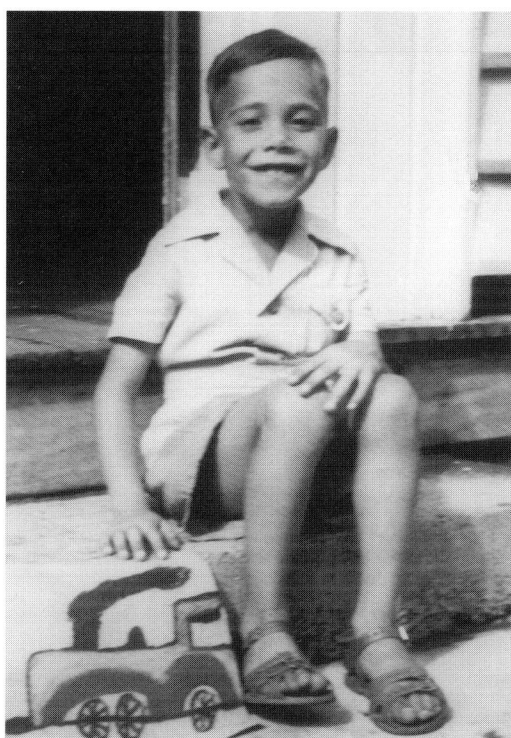

Robert Dinah (later Rob Riley), aged about five, at Sister Kate's Children's Home.

Rob Riley (right) with friend from Sister Kate's.

Rob Riley and his mother Violet, early 1990s.

Dennis Daebritz, Rob Riley, Beth Daebritz, Megan Riley, Jeannie Riley and Emma Riley. The Daebritzes took Rob for weekends and holidays away from Sister Kate's over many years.

Lila Riley, Rob's grandmother on his stepfather's side. Lila took a special interest in Rob while he was living on Pingelly Reserve.

Rob Riley and his stepfather, Bill Riley.

Newly married and leaving for the army. Rob Riley and his wife Jeannie (née Morrison) with friends in 1974.

By the age of twelve, Rob was sensitive and empathetic to individuals, but also angry and disbelieving about the social conditions he had witnessed. He had been forced to make a choice about who he was, and he already had premonitions about his future purpose in life.

Rob's natural personality became evident in other ways during his Pingelly years. Despite the considerable daily adversities, Rob shone at Pingelly High School. He was fortunate in having some family support when he started there. One of his cousins recalls that her sister 'acted more or less as his bodyguard ... She was his guide showing him around the High School'. Even early on he 'didn't like anyone standing over him and he stood up to domineering people', just as he had to the white school students who bashed him when he challenged them.[35]

He was popular at school. In fact, in a pattern he later repeated at Perth Modern School, 'Rob used to have all the girls in the school mesmerised — they all seemed to be after him, maybe because he always joked around and made sure to get in their good books'.[36]

Rob excelled at sport. Still a fast runner, he was nicknamed 'Roo Dog' at Pingelly because of his prowess on the track. As one of his cousins recalls: 'He used to have a unique running style — he used to hunch his shoulders and his head used to come down to give him that extra speed. He won the 880 and 440 yard races at the inter-school sports day in Pingelly — he would have been fourteen. I was so excited I shouted'.[37]

He also loved playing Australian Rules football. Utilising his leg speed, he played ruck-rover or on the wing. Aboriginal boys were barred from the Pingelly football team, so a Noongar team, based around those living on the Reserve, had been formed some years earlier. Later, Rob and one of his cousins were the first two Noongars to break through into the white football team.[38]

In 1968, when Rob was fourteen, a Community Liaison Officer with the Department of Native Welfare discussed with its headmaster some concerns about the poor relationships between the school and its Aboriginal students. It had come to officials' notice that teachers believed that Aborigines should be moved on from the town, both because they were unemployed and because of threats they believed Aboriginal students made against them. The Headmaster supported their stance.

However, the meeting between the headmaster and the Department failed to resolve the school's negative attitudes towards its Aboriginal students. Officers representing the Native Welfare Department maintained that at no stage did they detect that the headmaster felt any sympathy for the difficulties experienced by Aboriginal youth. As the officers tried unsuccessfully to explain, these difficulties were 'an inevitable result of reserve conditions'.[39]

The struggle to thrive in the face of such underlying prejudice must have been a challenge to Aboriginal students who wanted to do well. But Rob also had continuing struggles at home. He remained torn between his life at Sister Kate's and his life outside it: 'It was just a traumatic experience of not being totally accepted by the family and then again not being accepted by white kids ... the experience in the Home had been just a total contrast. It was devastating. I still don't know how I was able to cope with the situation'.[40]

Yet, just as Rob may have begun to adjust to his difficult circumstances, another major change unfolded for him, when he was about fifteen. He left his brothers and sisters in Pingelly, to live with his mother's relatives in East Perth, in what was seen by outsiders as a notorious Aboriginal 'ghetto'. For Rob, this was part of his on-going struggle over his identity: having to live in what he described as 'a metropolitan slum of run-down houses'.[41]

It was not by accident that in Rob's early twenties, when he was working for the Aboriginal Legal Service, he became an eloquent spokesperson for the poor living conditions of metropolitan Aboriginal people and the attendant social problems these conditions spawned.

In a society still hostile to the presence of Aboriginal people in built-up areas, East Perth offered Aborigines a kind of security.[42] To Aboriginal people visiting the city it was a comforting place; somewhere to access 'our mob' and enjoy the familiarity of people who talked and looked the same. There was also a strong sense of shared hardship. Everyone was poor and families had to rely on each other to get through lean periods, also helped by agencies such as the Daughters of Charity, who operated a soup kitchen in the area.

Despite their solidarity, there was no escaping the severe social problems which afflicted the Aboriginal residents of East Perth. As a visitor to the area, Ted Wilkes remembers being struck by the 'very poor lifestyles' of the people: the 'little terrace houses' and the cramped living conditions; the poverty; and the drinking habits of the older Aboriginal people who frequented places like the Tiara Wine Bar.

East Perth in the late 1960s and early 1970s was a creation of the social forces that had shaped Aboriginal–white relations over the past several decades: the policies of dispossession and discrimination; the lack of access to education and training; the forced removal of children; and the lack of access to affordable housing. Marginalised Aboriginal people were forced into a marginalised urban area, once restrictions on their entry into Perth started to relax in the late 1950s.

Once a fashionable district, East Perth was transformed into an industrial enclave by the First World War. The large and stately houses which dotted its streets became run-down as their inhabitants took flight to the outer suburbs.[43] From the 1950s, Aborigines were drawn to the area because of the availability of low-paid factory work, the corresponding downturn in rural employment and the increasing numbers of people leaving the mission system who had lost their family ties. Once a critical mass was achieved, 'chain migration' ensured that others followed to be with family members or just to be able to live secluded lives. By the 1960s, East Perth had become a socially stigmatised area in the eyes of the rest of the community.[44]

The most visible social problem in East Perth was the sub-standard housing. The housing crisis worsened for Aborigines nationwide after the Second World War. With governments reluctant to commit anything but token amounts of money to address Aboriginal housing needs, most Aborigines existed on squalid reserves — such as the one at Pingelly — or in the low-cost districts such as East Perth where private landlords were prepared to rent to Aborigines. However, landlords did little to maintain the standard of their properties, which deteriorated further through overcrowding. It was common for landlords to evict Aboriginal tenants the moment the rent became overdue.[45] Meanwhile, poorly maintained houses contributed to ailing health, especially among children, who were continually afflicted with colds, influenza and throat infections.[46]

The poor health and housing conditions in East Perth had their roots in low incomes and intergenerational trauma and poverty. While most of the district's families were said to earn enough to make them self-sufficient,[47] wages were low and jobs insecure. Even in a family with 'a steady and reliable income, the margin between bare subsistence and serious lack of essential food, clothing and medical requirements is often very small'.[48] Many of the residents came from reserves and missions and lacked extended family networks.

Prostitution and crime were the inevitable outcomes of the low incomes, poor housing and general cultural breakdown which have so often characterised oppressed and disadvantaged minority groups. Teenagers in East Perth were particularly vulnerable. According to one contemporary, many Aboriginal girls became prostitutes before turning fifteen years of age and boys commonly drifted into peer-influenced crime.[49] This slowly brewing social crisis was left unaddressed by government.

The racism that lay at the heart of government indifference is well described by Peter Yu, who was born in the Kimberley but spent his young adulthood in Perth. It was, he recalls, an everyday occurrence. Getting on a bus, getting in a taxi, getting served in a shop, walking along the street: 'You get the looks from the bus driver ... people don't want to sit next to you on the bus ... you get comments, not so subtle comments like coons and boongs'. Peter remembers being chased up St George's Terrace one night in the early 1970s by skinheads and having to take refuge in the Supreme Court Gardens. He recalls that although all Aborigines were targets of racism, Noongars 'used to cop it more than anybody else'.

The police were vigorous in their targeting of Aboriginal people. 'You'd walk out of the pub and you'd get pulled up, the spotlight shining in your face, you get frisked. It was that bad that most Noongar people probably knew cops by their first names ... certainly the ones who were the oppressors in a particular squad.' It was difficult getting served in hotels; Aborigines would regularly be stopped and questioned at the front door and often refused service inside.

Rob attended Perth Modern School while staying with his mother's relatives. Once a selective state high school, and boasting Bob Hawke as a former student, it was by the 1960s a comprehensive high school for the surrounding suburbs and the feeder school for Aboriginal students in East Perth. Rob was a social success at Perth Modern, just as he had been at Pingelly. Jackie Oakley remembers that Rob and a friend would be the centre of attention outside the upstairs classrooms 'like two Prince

Charmings' where 'they would hold court with anyone who wanted to talk to them'. Bright, good-looking, and successful at sport, Rob was confident and outwardly happy. Even at high school his charisma was evident.

However, the experience of prejudice was ever-present. Educational opportunities for Aboriginal students in the school were restricted. The school maintained three streams: professional, commercial and trades. With up to twenty-five Aboriginal students in Rob's year alone, none was allocated to the professional stream.

Capable and well-motivated students like Rob were unlikely to be encouraged to achieve their best, given the systemic discrimination in the education system. A study of Aboriginal education undertaken by a University of Western Australia sociologist in 1968 confirmed the causes of the problem: 'many, if not most, teachers ... tend to play part-Aboriginal problems by "ear", develop stereotyped reasons for retardation, and, with few exceptions, eventually give up on any real endeavour to help these children'.[50] Rob claimed that he was prevented from sitting his final high school exams by the school. He was extremely angry at being denied this opportunity.

Not surprisingly, few Aboriginal students stayed on at school. In Rob's case the pervasive educational discrimination was compounded by on-going family problems. During his high school years he spent short periods with his Uncle Sam in North Dandalup and Bunbury, in the south-west of country Western Australia, and a period with his mother, who had moved back to Perth. However, his mother's live-in partner was violent towards her, and Rob found himself in the middle. On one occasion, when he was trying to protect his mother, his ribs and nose were broken and he received two black eyes.[51] After this incident, he left home and moved into supported hostel accommodation.

Any one of the incidents Rob experienced as a teenager — his abrupt release from institutionalisation, his fragile relationships with his natural family, the repeated changes of household, the racial bashing, the experience of domestic violence and a crisis over his cultural identity — would, one imagines, be serious enough to cause behavioural or emotional problems in many young people. Combined they add up to a deeply troubled upbringing. Rob admitted to having been 'a very angry and confused teenager'.[52] Yet there was no outward manifestation of his troubled state of mind. Rob had a way of distancing himself from the bad experiences that regularly came his way. He may have learned to do this as a child in Sister Kate's, to spare himself the memories of being raped and of being beaten for asking about his parents. Surviving his childhood and adolescence — and indeed surviving later on in politics — required resilience.

―――〰〰〰―――

Rob started work as an apprentice fitter and turner with the Government Railways, but he was never likely to be suited to such work. He found lodgings in Katakutu Hostel, an establishment for male Aboriginal youth, mostly from the country, who had jobs in the city. Aboriginal young men from all around the state lived in several such hostels, forging important intra-state connections. Separate hostels existed for young Aboriginal women. Each had a maximum of fourteen residents who lived with house parents in a structured yet flexible environment.

Katakutu was run by an elderly couple who looked after their residents well. Strong camaraderie was built up among those living there. They socialised together, played sport together, and looked out for each other. Some were ex-mission boys, and occasionally stories would be shared about the lighter moments of surviving in an institution. But no-one disclosed their real emotions about having being separated from their families.

Rob was especially popular at Katakutu. He came across as worldly, self-confident and well-adjusted. He was an avid reader. He could seize on just about any subject and help others increase their understanding of it. He showed a caring attitude to the shy, newly arrived boys from the country. The years at Katakutu were carefree times: summer weekends at the beach; winters spent playing football.

One major incident interrupted the cheerful existence. One of the young men from Katakutu was killed on the street by someone from another hostel. In a fit of jealous rage the attacker plunged a bread knife into his chest; he died on the spot. Rob was among the group of boys to witness the stabbing. It was a devastating incident for all the residents. They were like a big family. For a while the hostel was shrouded in sorrow.

While living at Katakutu, Rob met his future wife. Jeannie Morrison was studying at business college and living in a hostel for young Aboriginal women. They met at a dance at a local Aboriginal centre. Jeannie grew up living a sheltered existence in the country, amid the unquestioning silence surrounding the policy of removing children for assimilation. Her mother, Maisie, had spent time in the mission at Carolup. A strong advocate for justice, she only felt she could share her more positive experiences with her children, and there were some she felt unable to talk about. Jeannie's father was away for extended periods, working for the Main Roads Department. She grew up knowing nothing about the Stolen Generations. The family was poor but close-knit; in the early days of her parent's marriage, the eldest children lived in a tent before moving into the town of Katanning. Here they had close connections to the Katanning Reserve, where most of Maisie's extended family lived. Being granted permission to live in the town meant they were not supposed to go to the reserve. But they did visit occasionally, and Jeannie remembers the makeshift tin sheds, the dirt floors and the people living in harsh conditions.

Jeannie found that Rob, like her mother, did not want to talk about his background. She has explained: 'I don't think he was ready to deal with it then ... he was too young to deal with that kind of trauma from his life'.[53] In any event, the silence in Jeannie's own family meant it was hard for her to understand the few details he did discuss with her. She was young and naïve; 'to put myself in that position [Sister Kate's] would have been really too hard to contemplate'. They married in 1974 in the chapel at Sister Kate's. It was Rob's choice, Jeannie explains.

Rob's second job was as a clerk with Beaufort St [Perth] Law Courts, where he worked his way up from mailing clerk to cashier. His job involved collecting all the money that came over the counter from fines issued by the Court. It was menial work, and Rob didn't like it.[54]

In this work environment he again came face to face with the harsh reality of racial discrimination. One day when he was cashier, $1000 went missing. A fellow worker and close friend of Rob's at this time, Fred Reibling (Speaker of the Western Australian Legislative Assembly at the time of writing), has a vivid recollection of the incident, which gave both of them weeks of stress. The system in place at the Court involved closing the door to the public at 4 p.m., after which two cash registers — one for the cheques and one for the cash — had to be balanced. This was Rob's job. He was required to first take the cheques into the clerk's office and have them signed before placing them in the Court vault. In his brief absence, the register holding the cash was left unattended. When he returned from the vault he noticed that $1000 was missing and alerted his superiors.

Shortly after raising the alarm, all the Court workers were assembled in the front office to wait for the police. Because of the timing of the offence — after the public lockout — the offender had to have been someone who worked in the building. None of the workers would have suspected that either Fred Reibling or Robert Riley would fall under suspicion. As Fred recalls of Rob: 'everyone in the Beaufort St Court trusted him implicitly'.

When the police confronted the waiting staff, Rob and Fred were singled out immediately: 'I can still remember the detectives coming through the door and you could see their minds working — there was the blackfella and that long-haired bum [Fred's description of himself at the time]. Before they had even spoken to us they had made up their mind'.

The set-up turned out to be even more selective: the police only ever suspected Rob. However, this was not apparent for some weeks. After searching each of them on the spot and pulling apart their personal belongings, they were separately required to front up to police headquarters on a daily basis. Every day for the next two weeks Fred was taken over to CIB and questioned repetitively while one of the officers continually hit him on the leg with a ruler for hours on end. 'I lost a stone in weight because I didn't sleep. Every car that went past I thought they're coming to get me'.

Fred Reibling's trauma only ended when his father intervened and told police either to charge him or leave him alone. When this happened, police explained to Fred that they didn't think that he had been involved in the theft; they knew that Riley had stolen the money. According to the police, Fred had only been questioned 'to put Riley off'. Rob's ordeal had not ended.

He was moved to another section of the Courts where he was placed under closer supervision. The regular police questioning continued for some time. When the police could not intimidate Rob into a confession of guilt, he was charged under the *Public Service Act 1902 (WA)* with incompetence. He was held responsible for the money going missing and required to pay back the $1000. However, in another early demonstration of his willingness to challenge authority, he appealed and had his penalty halved. He appealed again and had it cancelled altogether.

The incident has left bitter memories for Fred Reibling: 'I was shattered that these two police had made their mind up before they had asked one question'. As well, 'The system that was in place and overseen by senior people allowed the money to be left as it had been for years'.

Even though he was fully cleared of any wrongdoing, Rob felt that his superiors continued to harbour suspicions of him. He explained this to himself as their racism; he was Aboriginal, therefore he must have been guilty. The incident occurred in the early stages of his relationship with Jeannie and she thinks he was traumatised by the experience: 'I don't think he knew quite how to deal with it'. He was 'devastated' and 'shocked' that he had been accused of stealing. Not talking about his innermost feelings was now an established pattern of behaviour for Rob. Friends recall that his attitude was one of: 'if it hurt too much you don't talk about'. He gave his friends little snippets of information that something had happened, but he made it clear that he did not want them to delve any further. Each traumatic experience was being buried like a layer of sediment in his subconscious. So long as he kept busy and engaged, these layers would remain undisturbed.

The processing of traumatic memories is a controversial area of psychology, and concepts such as repressed and suppressed memory are still debated. Without full recourse to professional assessment, it is risky to associate Rob with this branch of psychology.[55] But some of the patterns in his behaviour are relatively clear. Rob did not forget his past experiences. Rather, he seemed capable of both suppressing the memories from his conscious mind and distancing himself from their intensity when briefly recalling details of particular episodes. This, at least, is consistent with the recall of a range of friends.

However, life often finds a way of penetrating psychological defences. During his period employed at the Beaufort St Courts, he had one unexpected and intensely emotional experience: he was reunited with one of his lost 'brothers' from Sister Kate's. Just up the street from where Rob was working, Steve Goodall had a job at the Postmaster General's Department. After years of separation, they literally ran into each other one day in the street as Rob stepped out of the court building. They both hugged each other and cried. As Steve explains: 'He's my brother and I hadn't seen him for five years ... here's this man that I'd been separated from'. From this point, Rob would never be cut off again from those with whom he had shared his childhood.

'Homies' learnt to stick together for reasons other than their shared experiences. Other Aboriginal people 'always viewed Sister Kate's as a place where fair-skinned Aboriginal people went' and the people who came out of the Home always 'had a tag which they carried with them'. Depending on the background of the Aboriginal person, they were seen by some as 'little smart arses'. These differences melted to some extent, however, in the face of the unrelenting racism all Aborigines experienced in the wider community.

Rob's dissatisfaction with his job at the law courts grew, and led, in 1973, to a decision which many Aborigines from his background had made: he joined the army. Sue Gordon recalls: 'Rob could've been a lawyer, he could have been anything he wanted to but he was getting more angry because he thought the system had let him down, and it's an horrific feeling for people. There's more children from Sister Kate's, I don't say hundreds, but there are more who feel they were let down'. Aboriginals from an institutional background felt comfortable in the army — and the army offered seconds at meal times, which did not happen at Sister Kate's!

~~~~~~

Rob fulfilled the minimum three-year term as a trooper with the Armoured Personnel division. He rose to the rank of Sergeant. Achieving such rapid promotion suggests the army recognised his leadership skills. But it was a difficult time for Jeannie. Being only eighteen and newly married, moving away from family was a challenge for her; the more so because Rob was away a lot of the time on military exercises.

From his time in the army he drew one overriding lesson. In the army, he said, he learnt 'there was a system that everybody, no matter who it was, has to put up with, conform to'. But this 'system' was capable of change, if people were prepared to persist and find the means to work around it.[56] When he wrote this in 1987, Rob Riley was often tagged a radical Aboriginal leader. Yet, here, in a few simple words, was an expression of his faith in the democratic system: that 'radical' outsiders could work within it to deliver justice to Aboriginal people.

Going away to join the army formally ended Rob's turbulent adolescence. Outwardly he emerged self-assured and confident yet he bore hidden scars: the damage done by institutionalisation, sexual abuse, broken family ties and racial harassment. By his own admission he was angry. But he had managed to avoid turning this anger destructively inward by distancing himself from the intensity of the experiences. His peculiar achievement would be the channelling of this negative energy into a positive fight to end the kinds of injustice to which he had been exposed.

CHAPTER FOUR

Apprenticeship: Joining the Aboriginal Legal Service

In a photograph taken of Rob at the time of his departure for the army in June 1974, he is smartly dressed in army blazer and short-cropped hair, arm-in-arm with Jeannie, his attractive new bride, and with family members gathered for the send-off. The young couple had an unmistakable air of excited expectation of: a life together unfolding towards conventional aspirations: army service, mortgage, kids. By the late 1970s, the photographs taken of Rob Riley would be very different: protest marches, banners held aloft, megaphones, a face contorted in anger. How did he undergo such a metamorphosis in commitment to his country: from defending it militarily to challenging the legitimacy of its very foundations?

Following his return to Perth from army service in Queensland in June 1977, Rob enrolled in a bridging course for Aboriginal students run by Curtin University. He and Jeannie slotted back into life in Perth;

they met a group of young people through Rob's course. The course exposed them to the history of race relations in Australia, helping to forge their emerging activism. Surrounding them was an exhilarating national and international climate of activist politics.

Rob had a clearly marked path to follow. In 1955, the civil rights movement was born among African–Americans in the United States, with the audacious aim of overthrowing entrenched legal discrimination. The movement continued to grow throughout the 1960s, in spite of the civil rights legislation introduced by Presidents Kennedy and Johnson. This struggle resonated with Rob Riley throughout his life. He maintained a keen interest in the career of Malcolm X, the charismatic African–American leader who was assassinated in 1965. Rob prized his copy of Malcolm's autobiography. Undoubtedly he would have seen parallels between his own life and that of his hero. Growing up in the 1930s and 1940s, Malcolm X also had to overcome poverty, family dysfunction and an identity crisis to become an outspoken leader in the African–American community.

Rob also became aware of the struggles of Native Americans who, while distant from the civil rights struggle, campaigned to overturn their marginalised position in the United States. Members of the Sioux nation, seeking to assert their rights to re-negotiate the status of their treaty with the national government, took a defiant stand in March 1972 when they occupied a site at Wounded Knee and declared their independence from the United States government. The 72-day protest is credited as being the 'first sustained modern protest by aboriginal peoples against the Western European interpretation of history'.[1]

These developments had their Australian parallels in Charlie Perkins's Freedom Rides in the mid-1960s and the Aboriginal Tent Embassy in Canberra in the early 1970s. However, Western Australia was slow to develop its own Aboriginal protest movement. There had been sporadic but important signs of collective struggle in the 1920s and 1930s, mainly centred around William Harris's Native Union, which 'waited' on the Premier in 1928 with a log of concerns about the lack of Aboriginal rights. Then there was the Aboriginal pastoral strike in the Kimberleys in the 1940s. But Aboriginal political activity had petered out by the 1950s. Perhaps the spark of leadership was harder to sustain in Western Australia, where Aboriginal people had suffered the most repressive policies of any state in Australia. For the generations who grew up under the direct control of the *Aborigines Act 1905 (WA)*, and the associated denial of citizenship rights, the lack of involvement in political organisation was understandable; it was the outcome of several generations of the marginalisation of Aboriginal people.

In particular, the generations of segregation and the breaking up of families created a mentality among Noongars, especially, which resisted inter-cultural cooperation or negotiation with white society.[2] Suspicion of government and its motives were deeply etched into the Noongar psyche. Members of the 1958 State Parliamentary Special Committee on Native Affairs encountered this attitude throughout the state: 'Many [Aboriginal people] tend to set up and maintain a kind of self-imposed barrier from the white community, regarding it with hostility and withdrawing from it'.[3]

The entrenched poverty associated with segregation added to people's alienation. Members of a 1975 Commonwealth parliamentary inquiry into Aboriginal health in the south-west region were shocked to discover an emerging inter-generational dynamic to Aboriginal disadvantage. Referring to Aboriginal parents in country towns, members discovered that: 'Few of them could name accurately their child's school grade. Few parents were in any way able to assist with children's schooling; with few skills themselves they did not expect their children to achieve much more than minimal literate and numeral efficiency'.[4]

In these ways, the development of an Aboriginal voice in Western Australian politics remained stifled well into the 1970s. Compounding their marginalisation was the paternalistic way in which organisations for Aboriginal 'advancement' operated. A number of non-government organisations were affiliated with the Aboriginal Advancement Council. These were dominated by whites who occupied the leadership positions and who saw their task as assisting Aborigines to adjust to white society.[5]

Following the 1967 Citizenship Rights Referendum, increased efforts were made to involve Aborigines in the running of local voluntary organisations. Two new organisations emerged in the late 1960s — the New Era Aboriginal Fellowship and the Aboriginal Rights Council — both reflecting the new commitment to nurture an Aboriginal leadership. The Fellowship served as a forum where some of the emerging Aboriginal activists cut their political teeth.

The beginnings of change in Western Australia came with the election of Gough Whitlam's federal government in 1972. Whitlam funded Aboriginal services directly, including the Aboriginal Medical and Legal Services. In addition, in 1973 the Whitlam government created the National Aboriginal Consultative Committee (NACC). This was the first elected Aboriginal body set up to advise government on Aboriginal affairs.

～～～～～～

In what may have been his earliest political activity, Rob Riley was involved in the 1977 elections for the NACC. He acted as an electoral officer coordinating the roll of Aboriginal voters. The NACC stimulated a new wave of interest among Aboriginal people in the democratic process; many had not previously voted in mainstream politics. Great expectations were held for this new voice in Aboriginal affairs.

From this first, tentative involvement Rob made his way through several political organisations and campaigns. He joined Black Action, a radical Aboriginal rights group, and found a job with the Aboriginal Legal Service, where he enjoyed a rapid rise to the position of Executive Officer, and became a key opponent of Sir Charles Court's conservative Western Australian government. These tumultuous years between the late 1970s and early 1980s were an intense apprenticeship in Aboriginal politics for Rob. By his mid-twenties, he was a seasoned political campaigner.

Black Action was Rob's entree into the world of radical Aboriginal politics. Its name carried overtones of the militant 'Black Power' movement in the United States. Black Action encouraged a new generation of young Aboriginal leaders to become politicised; it was the belated response in Western Australia to the rise of a rights movement overseas and elsewhere in Australia.

Brian Wyatt, a Yamaji from the Geraldton region, was one of the key instigators. He was working as a Field Officer with the Aboriginal Medical Service in his early twenties when Aboriginal injustice opened up to him as a political issue. He had observed the frequency with which Aborigines were put at the back of the queue waiting for services at Perth metropolitan hospitals, and he was forced to question whether such people 'ever received adequate treatment and what this meant for their later health problems'. He also visited the fringe camps in the outer areas of Perth — such as the one at the back of the Midland Abattoir — where the tent and tin dwellings and open fires generated significant underlying illnesses, especially tuberculosis. The Medical Service established a mobile clinic in an effort to help these people cope with their health problems.

Rob met Brian and became involved in Black Action whilst they were both attending the bridging course at Curtin University. Brian was concerned that nothing was happening in Aboriginal politics: 'we had to wake everyone up. Nothing was changing. We were not making any progress'. Rob also became a key figure in Black Action. Even though the group was disdainful of structures and hierarchy, those motivated to get things done on the ground rose to prominence. Rob was one of these figures.

Rob and Brian started honing sharp political lines for the media. They argued that the state government was racist and was treating Aboriginal people as second-class citizens. They drew public attention to the discriminatory practices in the state housing authority, where eviction notices against Aboriginal people were running at high levels. They also railed against the high infant mortality rates and the lack of basic primary health care in Aboriginal communities. Such confrontational statements were guaranteed to draw attention, but there was no grand strategy to their campaign.

Nonetheless, Black Action served a number of important functions. It became an active lobby group 'to get people motivated'. In what Brian describes as 'one of the most exciting times in my life', Black Action organised rallies and protest meetings that brought Aboriginal disadvantage to the attention of the wider community. Linking up with churches, trade unions and university campuses, Black Action was a key part of Western Australia's social justice movement. With Brian as one of the key organisers, and with Rob acting as the key speaker at rallies, Black Action was at the forefront of a number of protest marches through the streets of Perth in the late 1970s.

One rally, in particular, was especially influential in the evolution of the Western Australian Aboriginal rights movement. In December 1978, representatives of the newly formed Kimberley Land Council came down to Perth with a demand for land rights. Immediately, they forged links with members of Black Action. Photographer Michael Gallagher remembers capturing a shot of a proud-looking Brian Wyatt 'marching,

Rob Riley and his brother-in-law Jim Morrison at a land rights rally, late 1970s. Both were members of Black Action and involved in its efforts to politicise the land rights issue.

Brian Wyatt at a Black Action Rally, late 1970s. Together, Wyatt and Rob Riley helped turn the radical organisation into a significant voice for Western Australia's Aboriginal people.

Protest on the steps of Parliament House, Perth, against the Court government's changes to the Electoral Act, which aimed to remove Aborigines from the rolls, c. 1978.

holding a banner with two of these blokes from the Kimberley'. The march symbolised an emerging camaraderie among Aboriginal people: the meeting of two different kinds of movements, the one acknowledging the other.

With its militant, confrontational approach, Black Action was carried along with the left-over tide of optimism emanating from the Whitlam years. Sustaining this optimism was the belief that 'the system' could be challenged to produce change for Aboriginal people. Black Action's tactics of protest and media statements began to unsettle both government and existing Aboriginal organisations. As Brian Wyatt recalls, 'people sort of liked us around the periphery but were a bit careful to keep us at arm's length and not bring us into any sort of mainstream consultation or decision-making'. Such a reaction from government might be expected, but it also came from existing Aboriginal organisations. The next phase of the movement was to shake the foundations of Aboriginal politics: to mount a gradual take-over of existing Aboriginal organisations and to replace the old leadership with younger activists. Rob was the key player in this process.

A showdown between the old and new guards of Aboriginal politics was inevitable. To the younger generation, the old guard were pleasant but tame people. They struggled to articulate messages to government and the wider community highlighting the urgency for better health care and education and the racism experienced by Aboriginal people. The young guard chafed at the prevailing cultural protocol which dictated that the elders did all the talking and all the representations to government. Yet whenever they got near whitefellas, they tended to defer to them. The young guard, on the other hand, were impatient for change. They had been exposed to greater educational opportunities and had had the time to reflect on the subservience of their parents' generation. Rob was especially articulate about the young guard's capacity to push for change. Aboriginal activist Ted Wilkes recalls the impact the young Riley made on his colleagues: 'When Riley started talking, a lot of us said, "that's better, that's what we need, we need to have our younger men, our younger leaders saying the words for us because they know what's going on in the world"'.

Rob found an important figure to help him bridge the worlds of old and new guards. During his grassroots work with the NACC several years earlier, Rob had met George Abdullah, then in his mid to late forties, a charismatic and eloquent advocate for Aboriginal rights. In common with most of his generation, George was not a confrontationist, yet his activism had deep roots, dating back to the famed Coolbaroo Club — the social hub for Perth's Aborigines in the 1940s and 1950s. He had also been a member of the Aboriginal Advancement League, a founder of the Aboriginal Rights Council and a prominent advocate for Aboriginal issues in the media during the early 1970s. As Rob's own activism increased, he sought out George Abdullah, believing that this man, steeped in the first generation of Aboriginal leadership, had something important to offer. George passed on — or confirmed — some important lessons: the need to be credible to get a message across; the need to be on top of a brief; and the desirability of educating people in preference to shouting radical slogans at them. While George's sound advice did not diminish Rob's latent anger, it did offer important insights into how to operate within the political system.

Joining up with Aboriginal colleagues had an added benefit for Rob. At the time he became politically active, he was still insecure about his identity as an Aboriginal person. Gradually, as he developed closer connections with his Aboriginal peer group, colleagues noticed he became a lot more comfortable.

As his political involvements increased, Rob steadily demonstrated the qualities needed to make an effective activist. He was articulate, he could focus on the bigger picture, and he commanded moral authority based on his commitment to justice. His way of dealing with life was to involve himself in just causes. He had other emerging qualities that would also stand him in good stead. He had an innate ability to connect up, to make relationships work, and he continued to be very competitive. In politics, as in sport, he wanted to win.

While flexing his political muscles with Black Action, Rob grabbed his first opportunity to combine activism with employment in an Aboriginal organisation, at the beginning of 1979. His appointment as a field officer with the Aboriginal Legal Service (ALS) happened almost by accident. Cedric Wyatt, the gruff, straight-talking and dedicated CEO of the organisation, was having trouble finding sufficient Aboriginal field officers the day Rob walked into the office to pick up Jeannie, who was working there as a secretary. Cedric noticed 'this young bloke was hanging around. I almost had him physically searched — hands up against the wall — he looked like a criminal to me and it was Rob Riley'. Cedric sat down and talked with Rob and was immediately impressed: he noticed the discipline emanating from his days in the army and his knowledge of government from working in the public sector. Cedric asked Rob, '"What are you doing?", and he told me that he was studying social sciences at uni. I said, "Stop wasting your time".' With the wry humour for which he was renowned, Cedric followed up with: 'Come and do some real work and learn a bit about your relations'. Rob submitted a formal, two-page handwritten application for the position, in which he wrote: 'I am extremely interested in Aboriginal affairs and issues and I feel that working in an organisation such as the Legal Service, I would be able to broaden my knowledge of Aboriginal situations as they truly exist, at the same time doing something constructive in helping Aborigines in such a complicated area as legal matters'.[6] Rob's pitch for the position conveys some insights into his character: he had aspirations to develop himself and he wanted to make a mark.

At the time of Rob's appointment to the ALS in early 1979, the organisation was on the cusp of acquiring influence and reputation. Its inauspicious beginnings were small-scale. Studies conducted in the late 1960s showed the serious disadvantage that Aboriginal people experienced in their contact with the criminal justice system. Aboriginal people were seldom aware of their rights and obligations under the law and most went unrepresented in court.[7] In 1970, the first step towards the establishment of an Aboriginal legal service was made in the inner-city Sydney suburb of Redfern, long a home to poverty-stricken Aboriginal families.

In 1973, a small group of Perth-based legal practitioners set up a voluntary legal service to Aborigines. The scheme was affiliated with the New Era Aboriginal Fellowship, which received a Commonwealth grant to operate the service. At the beginning of 1974 it became a fully fledged legal service, with its own premises.[8] After renting for a while, premises were secured in an old house in Aberdeen Street, Perth in an area which allowed Aboriginal people to have easy access.[9]

Designed at the outset to be managed by Aboriginal people, the Service was constituted so that the Annual General Meeting elected an Executive Committee consisting of seven Aboriginal members. However, the aim to make the service self-managing had one major limitation:

few, if any, Aborigines at the time had the legal training to provide professional assistance to clients. Hence authority within the Aboriginal legal services was shared between the Principal Legal Officer (PLO) and the Executive Officer, whose formal responsibilities were confined to management of the field officers. As the ALS broadened its involvement in Aboriginal political issues, the role of PLO came to assume greater significance, setting up a tension in the management of the organisation which was to reach a peak when Rob returned to the ALS in the early 1990s.

The initial objectives of the ALS were very specific: to educate Aborigines as to their legal rights; to provide legal advice wherever possible; to appear in all courts on behalf of Aborigines charged with offences; and to act for these people in civil cases.[10] On the ground, these objectives translated into basic but important work: attending the court of petty sessions each morning, interviewing people before they attended court and representing them in court.[11]

One early measure was to represent all overnight arrests in the central police court, which caused an outcry because non-Aborigines did not have this advantage at that time.

Soon after Rob arrived, Cedric Wyatt offered his young protégé a significant career opportunity. Having served three years as Executive Officer, Cedric was ready to move on, and had been quietly casting around for a replacement. It suddenly struck him that his young field officer would be ideal: 'I had so much confidence, I was just so impressed with this young bloke and he was pretty calm and obviously very intelligent and I thought I'll groom this boy ... and about six months later he had slotted into the role and developed it'. In Rob's mind there were practical considerations. He and Jeannie were struggling to make ends meet on his study allowance and they had hire purchase and other financial commitments bearing down on them.[12]

Cedric's decision to fast-track Rob to head the field operation side of the organisation was astute, the more so because Rob's leadership potential was not obvious to all those working at the organisation in the early period after his arrival. He was characterised by some as shy and intense.

Heading up a key section of the organisation laid the foundations for Rob's later career. His knowledge of the issues facing Aboriginal people deepened, as did his strategic thinking. He gained experience and confidence as a public speaker and media commentator. Rob's first stint at the ALS also saw him develop his style of grassroots political leadership. He had, Cedric Wyatt observed, 'a great vision' for the Aboriginal Legal Service.[13] He tried to prevent the ALS descending into an unmanageable bureaucracy. He did not lose sight of where he was coming from, who he represented and to whom he was accountable. According to Wyatt, Rob 'tried to make the Service far more accountable to the community'.

Being accountable to the community meant making it a priority to deal with police violence against Aboriginal people. The historically poor relationship between police and Aborigines had become a major focus for the ALS by the time Rob joined the organisation. A culture had developed in the police force of sanctioning the mass imprisonment of Aboriginal people. Cedric Wyatt recalls that the 'zero tolerance' policy of police regularly saw Aborigines committed on 'outrageous' charges involving harmless social behaviour. Public drunkenness was a prime target. Persistent arrest for this victimless crime commonly spiralled into more serious charges when Aborigines' protest was met with the imposition of more serious charges including resisting arrest, aggravated assault on a policeman, and escaping legal custody — the latter charge arising when they managed to run a short distance and get caught again. Nearly all pleaded guilty.

The extent of police discrimination against Aborigines was a serious but underacknowledged matter. It came into full view through an ugly incident only a few years before Rob's arrival at the ALS, in the racially troubled goldfields town of Laverton. It became known as the Skull Creek incident. The local police inspector decided to intercept a small convoy of vehicles carrying approximately forty local Aboriginal men, fifteen women and twenty-one children on the outskirts of the town. In testimony later given to the Royal Commission set up to investigate the events of that day, it was claimed that when news of the convoy reached Laverton, the inspector wanted 'to teach Aborigines a lesson'.[14] Travelling with twenty-two officers, he intercepted the convoy and arrested all the able-bodied men without their being involved in any criminal activity. All were taken to the local police station. Allegations of a mass bashing became the focus of the Royal Commission.[15] Bruises, cuts and swollen faces on more than thirty of the detained Aborigines were said to be savage testimony to police brutality on that day.[16] All had been denied medical assistance.

The Royal Commission later found considerable malpractice on the part of police in their treatment of the Aborigines involved. It rejected police allegations of Aboriginal violence towards police: 'We accept that there was a good deal of shouting by the Aborigines. We are not satisfied they were encouraging attacks on police. On the contrary, it is likely that they were protesting at the behaviour of the police'. Worse, there was evidence of a police cover-up. Initially police worked out a common story alleging that 'when police arrived Aborigines were fighting among themselves'. However, this version was later changed to indicate that 'the first violence seen was of Aborigines fighting police'.[17] The ALS represented the Aborigines during the Commission hearings.

The Skull Creek incident was remarkable because of the number of Aborigines involved and the extent of the brutality perpetrated by police. Yet acts of violence committed by police against Aborigines were an ordinary occurrence. Cedric Wyatt recalls an unaccountable police culture steeped in racism and violence towards Aboriginal people. Complaints against police for violent behaviour were 'never heard of'. Aboriginal people, especially those living in country towns, were frightened to complain. Otherwise 'they were too busy pleading guilty to all the charges laid against them until they started getting representation in court'.

ALS field officers had to collect testimonies from Aborigines charged with offences. It was a stressful job. Frequently having little education themselves, and often having grown up away from their families, field officers worked in the front line of the struggle for justice for Aboriginal people. Inevitably, the field officers also confronted wider issues of Aboriginal disadvantage. They got to know everything in their secondary role as unofficial counsellors to their clients.

Rob was thrust into this demanding and distressing confrontation with the gritty world of Aboriginal poverty. He heard stories from his clients about bashings and assaults inflicted by police which were never aired in court. Rob reached the point where he thought the entire legal system was totally wrong.

This immersion in the lives of disadvantaged Aboriginal people had a profound impact on Rob. It forced him to confront the issues in his own background, the grinding poverty of Aboriginal people he had experienced in Pingelly and East Perth, and the way the courts were used to place Aboriginal children in custody and then in foster homes away from their parents. Jeannie thinks the ALS was the crucible of Rob's political career: an awakening which gave him his first insights into injustice on a broader scale, rather than just a personal one. In fact, the two dimensions became inextricably linked in his approach to politics.

The ALS started making an impact on the discrimination faced by Aboriginal people. Rob was beginning to learn that injustices could be changed if committed people were smart about the strategies they used to confront the system. Using the power granted to them under the *Aboriginal Affairs Planning Authority Act 1972 (WA)*, the ALS coopted volunteer lawyers to represent Aboriginal people in court. In addition, during its early years, the ALS was extremely fortunate in securing the involvement of some of the best young legal talent in Western Australia to work full-time for the ALS in the north of the state. John Toohey, Henry Wallwork and Peter Dowding each gave a year to the Service in return for a small salary and access to a car and house. Each made a substantial contribution to changing the way the courts operated.

The availability of outstanding volunteers greatly assisted in the decision taken by the ALS in the late 1970s to begin to challenge the rulings of local magistrates and Justices of the Peace (JPs). At the time, legally unqualified JPs had the power to impose prison sentences of up to six months. Most were shop owners, garage owners or farmers in country areas and strong members of the Liberal party. The ALS, led by Principal Legal Officer Graham McDonald, decided on a policy of appealing their rulings. The organisation purchased a 'truck-sized' IBM machine that could copy, collate and print a document every minute. An initial decision was taken to lodge an appeal every week, but when this increased to several each week, the ALS effectively buried the system in appeals. More to the point, they won 90 per cent of them. Ian Horrocks, one of the foundation ALS staff members, recalls that the decisions of JPs, in particular, were 'so blatant in error that you didn't even have to read deeply in law to know this was an error'. On one occasion, the ALS emptied the women's prison [Bandyup] of Aboriginal people just on those sorts of appeals.

By 1980, the growing effectiveness of Aboriginal groups was making an impact. The popular press noted the change. An article in the tabloid *Daily News* in March 1980 headed 'The New Black Power' brought the attention of readers to the newly found confidence shown by Aborigines in 'confronting whites with their own methods', namely, the law and media. The desire of Aborigines to protect their land in the face of 'new and heavier pressures' from the resources bonanza in the north-west was also highlighted. However, special mention was given to the role of the Aboriginal Legal Service for its efforts to boost the rights of Aborigines. The newspaper claimed that the Service was 'particularly resented' in the broader community, fuelling 'a strong white backlash against Aboriginal activism'. 'Operating from a converted shop in North Perth, it has saved hundreds of Aborigines from prison and won shorter sentences for hundreds more by defending them in court over the past few years'.[18]

The impressive group of lawyers at the ALS also helped Aborigines tackle mining companies and the state government 'in the bush, across the negotiating table and in the courts'. It was this support which, in particular, incensed white elites: 'When Aborigines begin to use the law against whites instead of defending themselves against the law wielded by whites, some whites are angered by it'. Aborigines, it was alleged, were being 'manipulated, used by cunning white political agitators, Labor supporters, left wingers, even communists'.[19] These fears were also being fanned by the Premier, Sir Charles Court.

~~~~~~~

Sir Charles was renowned in Western Australian politics for his role in opening up the north-west of the state to mineral development during the 1960s. He embodied the 'pro-development' ideology which had been the central strategy of governments in Western Australia since the 1890s. The creed of development cast the politics of the state in an especially conservative mould, in combination with its geographical isolation and its accompanying frontier mentality. Until the 1960s, the aggressive commitment to development had been focussed on the rapid expansion of the state's agricultural industries. Millions of acres had been converted from bush to pasture and wheatfields in the south-west of the state in an orgy of land clearing.[20] Steadily, under the patronage of Sir Charles, the baton of development passed from agriculture to minerals and, especially, the booming iron ore industry in the Pilbara. Sir Charles became 'a globetrotting salesman ... wheeling and dealing in the board-rooms of the world'.[21] To protect his vision of a state friendly to international capital, Sir Charles developed a pugnacious political style built around his authoritarian personality.

In terms of his background, Sir Charles had more in common with Labor politicians of the time than with the corporate interests he was later seen to champion in government. His father was a plumber, he was educated in state schools, and to supplement the family's income he sold newspapers in his spare time. The Second World War was a turning point for him. In a remarkable military career, he progressed from private to lieutenant-colonel between the years 1940 and 1946. Returning to civilian life, he established a successful chartered accountancy firm before turning to politics.[22]

In government, Sir Charles's uncompromisingly forthright views were matched by a commanding physical presence: an imposing frame, square jaw, direct manner and unflinching eye contact. These characteristics perfectly complemented his political style. Even some of his own ministers complained of the government being 'a one-man band', such was his reputation for charging into other Ministers' domains. At the time of his retirement *The West Australian* described his uncompromising political style: 'You were either for Sir Charles or you were against him. There was no room in the middle — the critics became the "knockers" and the knockers were the enemy'.[23]

Like other authoritarian political leaders, he was extremely hostile towards opponents of his vision. The early 1970s witnessed the rise of new challenges to conventional politics — from Aborigines, environmentalists, feminists and unionists. Yet, the manner in which he chose to oppose these social protest movements marked him out as one of the most polarising of Western Australia's political leaders. While Sir Charles commanded respect among a largely conservative public, he was, by the mid-1970s, increasingly despised by progressives and political activists for being oppressive on issues of political rights generally and 'colonial' in his response to Aborigines.

His political dominance was underpinned by one democratic anomaly; the state's electoral system boasted the most lop-sided system of electoral distribution in Australia.[24] In the 1980 election, for example, malapportionment resulted in the two-thirds of the voters within the metropolitan zone being allocated under half the seats in Parliament. This bias in favour of rural areas protected the conservative character of the state's politics, allowing the Liberal and Country parties to dominate both Houses of the state's parliament. From these commanding heights they were able to mount attacks on civil and Indigenous rights.

However, some of his harshest statements were reserved for leaders of the Aboriginal rights movement. He likened the claims to land rights as akin to sovereignty and he belittled activists in the movement — both Black and white — as 'stirrers'.[25]

In one controversial outburst to newly graduated police in March 1980, he lashed out at his political opponents. In what amounted to the issuing of a licence for police to use strong-arm tactics, he warned the graduates that the most 'dangerous enemy' they would face was 'the political or social activist'. He said these people 'were evil'.

The Premier was actively supported in his comments by his Police Commissioner, Mr G.O. Leitch, whose tough reputation was keenly felt by many Aborigines. He informed the newly installed officers that they were entering an era when strikes, protests and demonstrations were on the rise and 'even accepted by some people as a democratic right, with virtually no concept of responsibility, decency and the civil rights of others'.[26] It was a line Commissioner G.O. Leitch repeated in his Annual Reports to Parliament. In fact, in 1978, Leitch revealed his lack of sympathy for the right of citizens to dissent. 'Demonstrations are another area of police concern,' he wrote. 'At many of them the same fanatical and professional demonstrators are to be found. They promote and agitate for breaches of the peace, and then feast on the melee they have created'.[27]

The assault on democratic rights mounted by Sir Charles and his Police Commissioner drew a scathing rebuke from the leader of the opposition, Mr Ron Davies. The comments made by the Premier and the Police Commissioner, Davies said, 'reflected a dangerous lack of knowledge or understanding of the fundamental values in a supposedly democratic society, hostility towards different or unusual opinions and intolerance of criticism'.[28] Yet the official view that dissent was 'evil' set the tone for the battles ahead in which Rob played a role.

Rob's elevation to the position of Executive Officer also marked a new stage in the development of the ALS. When Brian Wyatt assumed the position of President of the Executive, he and Rob developed a strategy to 'fire up' the ALS. They realised that the organisation could limit itself to fighting individual criminal cases, but that this was not really going to achieve anything; the underlying issues needed to be addressed. Policy decisions started to flow from the adoption of this longer-term view. The ALS started to become a formidable organisation. Rob and Brian worked particularly closely, collaborating on whatever issues were pressing. 'We would just sit down, work out a strategy and attack ... I can't recall us having an argument or a brawl over an issue'. Together, Rob and Brian Wyatt, and others, including Marie Bartlett, organised large rallies attracting anywhere from 300 to 1200 people. As Brian Wyatt recalls: 'we had the unions involved, campuses involved, church organisations'. Out of this period of activity people came to see Rob as 'the key Noongar'.

Rob's community profile rose, too, as he started using the mainstream media. One of the earliest surviving interviews he gave to television — most probably from the early 1980s — sees him highlighting the problems of Perth's homeless Aboriginal alcoholics. Asked by the interviewer, 'Is there a kind of racism at work here?', Rob replied: 'Certainly is. And it's a very frustrating job ... the causes of alcoholism are not attended to in any way by government departments apart from, you know, just brushing them off ... and then out of sight out of mind'.[29]

Rob became one of the earliest and most effective publicists of the Aboriginal cause. He had the ability to speak directly and with passion about Aboriginal injustice. In the late 1970s he understood the power of the media to create negative images of Aboriginal people. Although talkback radio had yet to find its modern format, Rob had a habit of ringing up commercial radio stations whenever he heard a caller make a belligerent comment. He became incensed at portrayals of racism in the media. One commercial radio station in the late 1970s featured the impersonation of a drunken Aboriginal, in response to which Rob angrily organised complaints to be lodged with the Broadcasting Authority. The Principal Legal Officer at the time, Phillip Vincent, remembers that Rob 'was always on the front foot. He wouldn't want anything to get past him. He would always want the ALS to have a response to that sort of ugly racism'.

One of the first political issues Rob faced when he joined the ALS was the controversial move by Sir Charles Court to change the Electoral Act 1979 (WA) to make it more difficult for Aborigines to vote. The campaign to overturn the proposed legislation was an early lesson in how hard conservative governments played race relations in Western Australia during the late 1970s and early 1980s.

The Court government's push to marginalise Aboriginal people from the democratic process originated in the fallout from the 1977 state election and the bitter contest for the seat of Kimberley. At the time it was not compulsory for Aborigines to enrol to vote, and for some years the state Labor Party had been mobilising Aborigines to enrol in key seats. The Liberal Party watched this development with increasing concern, fearing the electoral repercussions of the growing number of Labor-leaning Aboriginal voters. Following the poll in the seat of Kimberley, the unsuccessful ALP candidate, widely respected local Aborigine Ernie Bridge, contested the result in the Court of Disputed Returns, alleging foul play by the Liberal Party. Mr Bridge's allegations were later raised in State Parliament. The Liberals were accused of 'stand-over tactics deliberately designed to intimidate illiterate people to deprive them of their right to vote'.[30] The allegations caused a furore. Subsequently, the Court of Disputed Returns declared the Kimberley poll void due to malpractice.

The ALS was actively involved in the efforts to overturn the proposed changes to the Electoral Act. When the Bill was before the House of Assembly, in November 1977, about fifty Aborigines occupied the public gallery and refused to leave. It is highly likely that Rob Riley was among them. Most of these protests were organised by Black Action. Rob kept newspaper clippings and correspondence relating to the protest.

To the assembled politicians below, protestors shouted: 'Kick the Liberals out'; 'Fascists'; 'Racists'; 'Democracy is dead in Australia'; 'You are just inciting Aborigines to violence'. Police reinforcements were called to clear the gallery.[31]

After the ruckus, Liberal member J.C. Tozer reiterated the government's intention of removing illiterate Aboriginal voters from the rolls. They were, he said, 'a completely unsophisticated community' upon whom the fate of governments should not depend.[32]

Eventually, Court's Bill proved too contentious even for the state's ultra-conservative Legislative Council, which narrowly defeated the measure. Nevertheless, Sir Charles pressed on. The following year the government established an inquiry into the Electoral Act, headed by Arthur Kay, a retired judge of the District Court and a known conservative.

Although the Inquiry's terms of reference were broader than issues surrounding Aboriginal voters, these matters were considered at length partly because the Inquiry was being monitored by observers sympathetic to Aborigines who ensured that they could put their views without duress.

Kay ventured some definitive findings about Aboriginal voters. Firstly, 'it was totally unacceptable to Aboriginal people that there should be any limitation on their freedom to enrol compared with any other elector'.[33] Secondly, he argued there was no practical way in which a person's literacy level could be determined at the polling booth and, therefore, 'it is not a matter of tests but how can the Presiding Officer assist the elector to complete his ballot paper'.[34] In other words, the Electoral Act could not be changed to restrict the right of Aborigines to vote.

Not surprisingly, the Court government was unpersuaded by Kay's findings. Undeterred, Sir Charles introduced another Bill to change the Electoral Act in 1979. The key part of this legislation centred on alterations to the method of enrolment. Henceforth, voters would need to have their forms witnessed by a JP, clerk of courts, or electoral or police officer instead of the existing practice of allowing any other voter to witness an enrolment form. As *The West Australian* commented on 7 September, 'the State Government is trying to make it more difficult for Aboriginal and other disadvantaged people to vote'. The newspaper stuck by its previous stance, advocating the need to make it 'as easy as possible for a citizen to enrol and vote'. It believed that the government's legislation was 'a case of overkill'.

Brian Wyatt and Rob Riley organised demonstrations against the changes but to no effect. In addition, both worked through the ALS in an effort to overthrow the amendments. In the organisation's 1979 Annual Report, Rob highlighted that the Executive Committee 'had expressed its concern' about the impact of the legislation and particularly the limited opportunities in country areas for Aboriginal people to obtain the required witnesses to enrol. In most areas these were limited to police and justices of the peace, 'neither of which, for historical reasons have been regarded as sympathetic to Aboriginal people'.

The organisation presented a submission on the government's proposed changes and sought a meeting with the Deputy Premier, Des O'Neil. The Principal Legal Officer of the Aboriginal Legal Service at the time, Graham McDonald, tried to facilitate meetings on behalf of the ALS, but was rebuffed. In his letter to the Deputy Premier, McDonald outlined the frustration the organisation experienced in getting its views across:

> You [the deputy Premier] were unable to meet the members of the [ALS] Committee at their meeting place on Wednesday the 12th but the Committee arranged for several delegates and Mr Huelin [the Consultant Legal Officer] to wait upon you at your office at the appointed time. On the 11th September, Mr Riley, the Executive Field Officer of the Aboriginal Legal Service, rang concerning the delegation and was informed that the appointment was made only for Mr Huelin and myself and that you would not see anyone else.[35]

Aborigines, in other words, were shut out of direct negotiations with government. It could not have gone unnoticed to Rob that direct protest seemed to be the only avenue open to Aborigines to challenge issues directly affecting their interests. For, as Graham McDonald said in his letter to the Deputy Premier, 'It is ... a matter of record that often this Service has either had no opportunity to present its case or presentation of its case has been ignored by Government Ministers'.[36]

Rob decided to place himself in the forefront of opposition to the government by rallying against the infamous 54B amendment to the *Police Act 1892 (WA)*, initiated by the Court government in a crackdown against dissent. In September 1979 Parliament enacted amendments to the Police Act designed to curtail public protest meetings, especially in response to the rising tide of criticism of Court's attempts to quash the land rights aspirations of the Noonkanbah community, described in the following chapter. Under the changes, the organisers of any public meeting were obliged to obtain prior approval from an authorised police officer who was empowered to disallow such meetings if there existed reasonable grounds that it may: occasion serious public disorder or damage to public or private property; create a public nuisance; give rise to an obstruction; or place the safety of any person in jeopardy.[37] For those concerned about fundamental democratic rights, the passage of the 54B legislation was a dark day in Western Australian politics.

To Rob, 54B constituted an injustice. Following its passage, there were discussions late into the night at the ALS about the implications of the legislation, and much musing about the ludicrous extent to which it could be used. What about a public gathering of the Country Women's Association; would they be deemed an illegal assembly? Amid the mirth, and with youthful bravado, opposing the legislation became a challenge for Rob; a case of, 'OK you bastards, we'll do it'.

In early 1980, Rob Riley teamed up with Howard Smith, convenor of the Civil Liberties Action Committee (CLAC), to organise a protest rally against 54B. It was a continuation of a campaign of deliberate civil disobedience against the legislation. Already, 54B had produced a string of cases: 28 summons, 11 arrests, 4 convictions and 35 pending cases.[38]

On 3 May 1980 one of the earliest 'illegal' rallies was held in Forrest place, on the steps of the Post Office in the centre of Perth. The rally was well organised. In addition to ten speakers, about a dozen other CLAC members acted as crowd marshals, deliberately avoiding making speeches so that they would be available to disperse the protestors at the end of the rally.[39] Both Rob and Howard Smith spoke to the assembled crowd of around 500 people.

At about 10.30 a.m., not long after the rally had officially started, twenty police officers descended on the Post Office. The inspector in charge warned that the meeting was an illegal one and anyone speaking would be liable for prosecution. The first man was arrested almost immediately. He had seized a megaphone and begun denouncing Section 54B. He ignored the police warning to stop and was led away to a police van. As the early arrests were made, people in the crowd continued chanting, prompting more to come forward and speak. In all thirty-three people were arrested, including Rob Riley and Howard Smith and one fifteen-year-old boy. Of these, thirty-one were charged with offences under Section 54B.[40] Something of an example was made of both Rob and Smith; they were each fined $50 while the others arrested on the day received only $30 fines.[41] Neither was prepared to let the fines go unchallenged.

Rob's name would likely have caught the eye of the Police Minister, Mr Bill Hassell, who seemed not to comprehend the reasons behind the campaign for civil disobedience. Fuming, he told the press on the day of the arrests that 'the next step to civil disobedience was violent disobedience'. The community, he said, 'could not tolerate people challenging lawful authority'. Mr Hassell warned that 'the community could not survive if people were allowed to break the law'.[42] It was the first of many times that the paths of Rob Riley and Bill Hassell crossed. Tall, sharp-featured and acerbic, Hassell would soon take over from Sir Charles as the state's most strident political opponent of Aboriginal land rights.

In May 1980, the challenge Rob Riley and Howard Smith had mounted over their fines reached the Supreme Court, where the original charges were upheld.[43] Rob's own small brush with the law demonstrated the inadequacy of Australia's legal system in guaranteeing basic rights in the face of a government's determination to undermine them.

Amid the demands of a busy political life, Rob found time for several community involvements. A devoted Australian Rules football follower, he coached an Aboriginal team in an amateur Perth suburban competition. Rob's natural tendency to vocal involvement spilled over into anger when he thought umpires were being racist. Old friend and fellow activist Darryl Kickett maintains that 'you could see the umpires were totally biased against them [the Aboriginal team]'. On one occasion he recalls Rob being ejected from the ground by the umpires for verbal abuse and being forced to yell his instructions and encouragement to players from beyond the fence. On another occasion a brawl started when the Aboriginal women chased the umpires, and Rob's team was suspended.

An altogether different community involvement was his role in helping to establish the Aboriginal Child Care Agency with Jackie Oakley in the late 1970s. It was modelled on a similar service established in Victoria to care for children removed from their families and to ensure they were placed in Aboriginal care. The service aimed to overturn the long-standing assimilationist practice of 'getting kids placed in white environments'. The work of the agency was obviously close to Rob's heart. However, he rarely personalised his involvement. Jackie Oakley reflects on the emerging pattern behind his actions: 'instead of Rob confronting what actually happened to him he'd engage himself in strategies to make sure it didn't happen to someone else'. In other words, as well as feeding his idealistic streak, political activity seems to have been an antidote to the unresolved traumas of his own background.

For Rob, the issue of Aboriginal child care was part of his steadily broadening political involvement. He had begun to collect articles and correspondence on all manner of issues affecting Aboriginal people, building an extensive personal file of information: transcripts from land rights conferences, the controversy over uranium and asbestos mining, information about the operation of the mining industry and developments in Indigenous affairs in other countries. His extensive personal archives show that he was building a formidable personal knowledge base on Aboriginal affairs.

He was especially well briefed on the justice system. The ALS took an active role in the Inquiry into the Rate of Imprisonment — which connected to Rob's already established interest in Aboriginal justice issues.

The inquiry into Western Australia's rising imprisonment rate had been established by cabinet on 9 January 1979. In hindsight, the Inquiry assumes an historically important role. It documents the state's journey to the tragedy of the epidemic of Aboriginal deaths in custody a decade later. Here, the first insights into this unfolding social disaster were laid bare along with the official neglect of its findings.

The Parliamentary Commissioner Mr Oliver Dixon was chosen to head the Inquiry in August of that year, with the Committee commencing its investigations on 7 January 1980. Although the Terms of Reference did not specifically mention the need to address the imprisonment of Aboriginal people, it was inevitable that some focus would be given to this issue, all the more so because the ALS ensured the needs of their client group would not be ignored.

Western Australia's dubious reputation in criminal justice matters prompted the establishment of the Inquiry. The state had, per head of population, 'many more persons in and entering its prisons than any other Australian state' (although it was lower than the rate in the Northern Territory).[44] The ALS's concern was the gross over-representation of

Aborigines in this wave of incarceration; with 3 per cent of the state's population, they constituted 32 per cent of the daily prison muster, a proportion that was much higher than other Australian states.[45]

The ALS compiled an extensive submission to the Inquiry during 1980 following the normal procedure of the issue being discussed by the Executive Committee with the active involvement of Rob as the Executive Officer.

Comprising fourteen pages of text, the submission documented the issues leading to over-representation in the prisons, and drew upon available statistics, research literature and the collective experience of the ALS staff. The first issue tackled in the submission went to the heart of Aboriginal disadvantage: most Aborigines were not criminals as such but victims of socio-economic disadvantage.

While this argument is well understood today, at least in informed circles, it was only beginning to be articulated in the late 1970s. Towards the end of the submission the ALS addressed the social conditions fuelling the high imprisonment rates and the long-term consequences flowing from this in terms of even higher rates of incarceration.

The ALS called upon the government to increase the provision of finance for housing, education and other facilities for Aboriginal people in Western Australia. A decade later, the Royal Commission into Aboriginal Deaths in Custody would do the same.

Of particular concern to the ALS was the overuse by police of arrest rather than summons, and the payment of 'meal money' to police officers in country towns, both of which contributed to the high rates of incarceration. The ALS singled out 'meal money' as a corrupt inducement to country police officers to arrest Aboriginal people as a means of earning additional income, and described the system as a 'meals racket'. Paid as a flat rate per meal per prisoner for the sustenance of prisoners both on remand and sentenced in lock-ups, those police predisposed to do so could arrange for their wives to provide low-cost meals and pocket the difference. It was also common practice for a police sergeant to take one of the prisoners out hunting to shoot a couple of kangaroos, which were cleaned up in the paddock, brought back and hung on the fence along the prison compound, and then fed to the prisoners. This booty was charged to prisoners' meal allowances. As testimony to the power wielded by police in government circles, Rob and the ALS were still battling to end this corrupt practice a decade later.

The ALS submission to the Inquiry outlined the existence of systemic discrimination against Aboriginal people in the legal system. While the ALS was able to show that laws purporting to treat people equally did not do so if the underlying disadvantage was a factor in producing the crime, it went the additional step in challenging the idea of criminality in many of the crimes for which most Aboriginal people were convicted. While these concepts are now widely understood, this was not the case in the late 1970s and early 1980s. The Dixon Inquiry was the first opportunity for them to be publicly aired in Western Australia.

In his position as Executive Officer of the ALS, Rob became more actively involved in trying to deal with police violence towards Aborigines. He embarked on his first experience of working inside the system to effect change. A Special Cabinet Committee had been established to try to improve Aboriginal/police relations and Rob served as the ALS representative. In the 1979 ALS Annual Report he criticised the limitations of this structure to deal with the extent of problems. Rob claimed that police were being 'over-defensive' in their participation, none more so than the Commissioner, who refused to meet members of the Committee to answer their questions. A year later the situation had not improved:

> People are not happy with the situation of police investigating complaints against fellow officers ... There are also too many occurrences of Police carrying weapons and searching houses without showing any courtesy to the tenants of the houses. The Aboriginal/Police Relations Committee is not equipped, or established, to deal with complaints. Whilst this situation exists I feel that the relations between Aborigines and the Police will continue to suffer.

Rob believed the police remained 'a law unto their own' — a position he would have to revisit throughout his career.

For now, there was no time for backward glances. Bigger battles loomed. In the remote Kimberley region, a sacred sites dispute involving the Aboriginal owners of Noonkanbah Station was about to unfold into a major turning point in Rob Riley's life, and in the life of the nation as well.

CHAPTER FIVE

Noonkanbah: The Struggle for Heritage

When Sir Charles Court's government took on the aspirations of the Kimberley Aboriginal community at Noonkanbah, the combustible mix of race and politics ignited. The traditional owners of this remote pastoral station were among the first Indigenous groups in the modern era to directly challenge the European view that Aborigines had no ultimate right to their land. In particular, they claimed the right to control the activities of mining companies threatening sacred sites. Rob made the long trek to join the Noonkanbah Community's last stand: a show of non-violent resistance to the combined determination of the state government and the American mining giant Amax to crush the Community.

The Noonkanbah struggle was a decisive episode in Rob's life, as it was for Aborigines throughout the nation. From the ashes of this defeat emerged the modern land rights movement, with a determined Rob Riley at its forefront. Rob would make repeated references to Noonkanbah for many years after the event, drawing bitter lessons from the strength of forces opposed to Aboriginal rights. Learning these lessons was integral to Rob's transition to activist politics.

Before Noonkanbah, few whites had had any reason to re-think the conquest of Aboriginal lands. Frank Gare, the retiring Director of the Department of Native Affairs in Western Australia, wrote privately in 1978 to his national counterpart, Barry Dexter, about this matter. 'The basic trouble', he told his colleague, 'is that Australia as a whole does not appreciate the enormity of what disinheritance has meant to the Aboriginal people'. Gare, a humane figure, respected for his efforts to build relationships with Aboriginal communities, poured out his despair about the future for Aboriginal people. After a career spanning more than twenty years in the Department, he told Dexter that he was leaving his job with 'little optimism'. In what would be a portent for Rob's career, Gare told his colleague: 'It remains to be seen whether the rising Aboriginal leadership will be able to effectively convince the community at large of this'.[1] The protest which erupted at Noonkanbah was the start of this process. Because the traditional owners only leased their land, what started out as a struggle over sacred sites broadened into a campaign over land rights.

The ALS was one of many groups which assisted the Community in their struggle. Others included Aboriginal organisations around Australia, led by their representative body — the National Aboriginal Conference; also the Kimberley Land Council; the Western Australian Trades and Labour Council and its secretary, Peter Cook; the ALP and especially Peter Dowding MP, a young former ALS lawyer in the Pilbara; and members of various churches, notably the Uniting Church of Australia. Steve Hawke, a liaison officer with the Community, provided crucial support, promoting their cause to the public and galvanising much of the support from community groups.[2]

The support provided by the ALS to the Community was crucial. It took legal instructions from them, and both its Perth and Derby offices were in the forefront of several court battles to stop mining companies from overrunning the Community. In Perth, the Executive of the ALS regularly discussed the matters surrounding the resourcing of the Community's legal campaign. As Executive Officer of the organisation, Rob was involved in these discussions. Phillip Vincent, an ALS lawyer, was running the ALS office in Derby when the dispute erupted, and provided most of the direct legal advice and representation to the Community.

The Noonkanbah dispute brought to a head the contrasting narratives of Blacks and whites in Western Australia. Simmering away in the mind of Sir Charles Court and his government was the need to apply renewed energy to the development of the north-west of the state. While the iron ore industry in the Pilbara continued as a beacon of his vision for Western Australia, the development of the massive irrigation scheme on the Ord River failed to achieve the anticipated boom in agriculture. It was labelled by its many critics as 'an expensive monument to development at any cost'.[3] Nevertheless, Court continued to believe in the region's potential. The main hope during the 1970s lay in the opening up of its mineral wealth.

It appears to be the case that the Court government believed that the emerging political activism of the region's Aboriginal population stood in the way of the new bonanza. The proposed change to the Electoral Act during the 1977 state election campaign could be seen as the government's pre-emptive strike against this perceived threat. Another attack came with changes to the *Mining Act 1979 (WA)*, which made it possible for miners to enter Aboriginal Reserve Land without an entry permit and without negotiations with the Aboriginal Lands Trust. In practice this meant that the Minister for Mines could approve mining projects without guaranteeing any consultation with the communities involved.[4]

Driving these changes were the pro-development views held by the Court government. But the Premier's views on race relations were crucial to the unfolding events at Noonkanbah.

Sir Charles has left an extended record of his views on the Noonkanbah dispute. While none of these suggest he was racist in the common meaning of this term, his views do constitute, in the opinion of this author, a sustained attack on the legitimacy of Aboriginal aspirations for self-determination; and therefore should be examined closely.

Like many conservatives before him, Sir Charles cast his views on race relations within a framework of his 'concern for the welfare of Aborigines'. In an article he wrote for *The West Australian* on 8 August 1980, he showed how he arrived at his position of opposing the Noonkanbah community's spirited opposition to mining. He was among the first conservative politicians in Australia to forcefully argue the case. Summarised, his position read:

'Most of the people at Noonkanbah have no direct spiritual or traditional links with that land'.

Despite the efforts of 'romantics' to argue that Aborigines can only find identity in the land, 'the majority of them seek to establish themselves in the broader community'.

He did not believe that 'radical and unlawful' views expressed by them [the Noonkanbah community] were 'truly' theirs.

The 'doctrine of separate laws was being fed to them [the Noonkanbah community] and expressed for them by outsiders'.

Such outsiders were 'political opportunists and others with no constructive understanding of the situation'.

Claims to sovereignty over leased Crown land were 'absurd'.

Critics dismissed such views as being based on outdated notions of Social Darwinism. One parliamentarian categorised the Premier's statements on Aboriginal people as constituting a conviction as sure as 'as any nineteenth-century white liberal was sure of the superiority of our culture and religion and he thinks the Aborigines should join us in due course — get with the strength and join the superior people'.[5] Whether this assessment is correct is obviously speculative, but it raises the question of how Aboriginal activists like Rob understood the conservative mindset of people like Sir Charles. After all, the stated views of the Premier were substantially based on a set of assumptions about Aborigines.

In his article for *The West Australian*, Sir Charles did not make any attempt to argue the broader economic interest which one might have expected him to make. However limited such an argument, the Premier's opposition to Aboriginal rights over land appears to have rested almost entirely on two propositions, namely, the legal rights of mining companies to operate under laws enacted by his government and the lack of legitimacy of Aboriginal claims to their culture and, hence, to their land. One possible construction is to see such views as constituting a system of power based on race. If this view is correct, then Sir Charles's views on Noonkanbah were designed to express the material interests of whites. Forcing the issue of mining on land claimed by traditional owners could overwhelmingly benefit elite economic interests. Thus, the Premier could assert that mining would not entail any disruption to the community's life and that, in return for mining, they would receive unspecified promises of training and employment in the industry. Noonkanbah became a flashpoint in this political struggle over access to, and the distribution of, resources on Aboriginal lands. Importantly, this was a view of race relations which Rob came to hold. Noonkanbah was the first of his many exposures to this system of racial power, as he saw it.

Two thousand kilometres away, across Western Australia's vast, dry and sparsely populated interior, Aboriginal groups in the Kimberley had a very different idea of their future to that being mapped out for them by Sir Charles Court. The steady increase in mining exploration during the late 1970s was causing Aborigines grave concern about the protection of their sacred sites and, by extension, their control over traditional lands. At a Dance Festival held in May 1978 at Noonkanbah Station, 100 kilometres south-west of Fitzroy Crossing, and attended by several thousand people, the Kimberley Land Council (KLC) was formed to represent Aboriginal interests in the region.

The Community at Noonkanbah Station was one of the first groups to actively resist mining on their land. In so doing, they issued a direct challenge to the modern Western Australian state and the long-held fears about Aboriginal people reclaiming their rights. The Yungngora were only one generation removed from the violence of the police operations which brutally crushed resistance to the opening up of pastoral land to whites in the 1890s.[6] They had been living and working on Noonkanbah Station for several decades when in 1971 they joined the mass walk off from station camps following the introduction of award wages several years earlier. They moved to Fitzroy Crossing, where most members of the community slowly drifted into the familiar welfare–alcohol downward spiral.[7] Fitzroy Crossing 'was not their country; the spirits of the land and the river's waterholes were unfamiliar'.[8] Fortunately, their stay was short-lived. In 1976, the Aboriginal Land Fund Commission purchased the 385,000-hectare Noonkanbah Pastoral Lease for the community, whose primary aim became 'to maintain its own culture, free from European influence'.[9] Having purchased the lease, they were united in a quiet determination that they had achieved peace and all they could possibly want.

Initially, the Community focused on rescuing the fortunes of the property. At the time of purchase, it was a shambles: 'The water bores were in disrepair, not a single windmill was working and the fences had in the main fallen down'. Yet rumours started spreading in Perth that the property was 'a holiday camp' draining taxpayers of $2 million a year.[10] The true picture of the Community was hidden from public view. Through hard work the property's infrastructure had largely been repaired and a program of pasture improvement begun. In 1979, the property sold 448 cattle for $95,000, indicating that the community had transformed the station into a successful enterprise.[11]

In the late 1970s, three parallel developments heralded a new era in race relations in the Kimberley. A return to traditional country by Aboriginal communities foreshadowed a renewed assertiveness on their part in safeguarding their own interests. Simultaneously, a large influx of mining companies, thirsting for the region's hidden riches, threatened Aboriginal interests. And growing awareness of Aboriginal culture among whites changed the political context by producing the first legislative attempts to protect sacred sites in Western Australia. The Noonkanbah Community became the first focal point of the clash between these developments.

The move to protect sacred sites in the state originated in the late 1960s in response to a blatant and widely publicised example of desecration. In the late 1960s, mining licenses were granted in the Western Desert in an area adjacent to an important ceremonial site of the Darlot people. Naturally occuring red and pink stones — known as the Weebo Stones — formed concentric circles and represented the spilled blood of ancestors.[12] In the early 1970s prospectors started to mine the sacred stone, including a local policeman who transported it to Perth for sale. The episode sparked an official investigation which highlighted the absence of any legal protection for sacred sites. When the Aboriginal Heritage Bill came before Parliament in 1972, the reputation of the mining industry was already tarnished. The Liberal member for the Kimberley, Keith Ridge, acknowledged that mining companies had come under a deal of criticism, 'accused of desecrating places of significance'.[13] The new legislation established, among other provisions, an Aboriginal cultural materials committee charged with evaluating sites and advising the minister on their protection. This was supported as a long-overdue measure. Noonkanbah would be the first real test of both the power of the Act and the good intentions of government to uphold it.

The community on Noonkanbah Station became embroiled in the clash of values surrounding sacred sites when thirty mining companies applied for 600 mining tenements of 120 hectares each, representing one-third of the property. In addition, the giant American-based petroleum company Amax gained a permit encompassing the entire property. In June 1978, the Community called in the Aboriginal Legal Service, instructing it to take any legal steps available to stop further exploration on the Station.[14] In May 1979, the Community received a letter from Amax, outlining their intention to drill an exploratory hole near Pea Hill, a volcano-shaped formation rising, like a huge geological sculpture, 25 metres above the flat, treeless plain. It was a sacred site to the people; the sanctity of the area lay in 'the belief that a goanna has lived underground there since the Dreamtime; its scrapings are Pea Hill and its eggs are the round stones on the ground'.[15] From this time on, they were a community on a crusade with every reason to fear and mistrust white fellas. Steve Hawke recalls: 'There were people in the Community who had been through massacres which had never been recorded and who had lived through the days when Aboriginal people were chained by the neck'.

When the Community first galvanised its protest, public interest in, and support for, the rights of Aboriginal people to their culture was a recent phenomenon. For conservatives much was at stake. Acceptance of the rights to sacred sites was but a short step to endorsement of Aborigines' right to the land. Such a right would disrupt whites' economic interests. Thus Noonkanbah became a political line in the sand for right-wing politicians in Western Australia and elsewhere in the country. As one unsourced 'senior Liberal' told the *Daily News*, 'the fight for the north has begun. If we don't hold on, the blacks could take over right through the Territory and Queensland'.[16]

The Aboriginal Legal Service positioned itself for the challenge. In its 1979 Annual Report, the first to be issued during Rob's time as Executive Officer, the Service warned that the government's policy on drilling 'can only lead to confrontation, and possibly physical violence'. Further, it highlighted that there was no satisfactory independent means of resolving the conflict such as access to court proceedings.

In its concluding comments, the Service foreshadowed an increased commitment to land rights issues in the coming years.[17]

Battle lines were being drawn. Opponents of the government were aware of Amax's poor record on Indigenous rights in the United States, where in the late 1970s it faced four separate legal actions initiated by Native American groups.[18] Known, too, was the apparent close working relationship between the government and the company. Together, they promoted drilling on the Community's land in the full knowledge that it was simply a 'wildcat' or, in other words, exploratory drilling with little expectation of success. In fact, when a representative of the Mines Department first went to the Kimberley for consultations with the Community, he was reported to have told them that the prospects for striking oil were poor.[19]

For the ALS the issue became how to use the law to take on the government. Initially the ALS tried to stop Amax by challenging its activities under the Mining Act, but this legislation was found not to extend to the protection of Aboriginal sites. The *Aboriginal Heritage Act 1972 (WA)*, while acknowledging the need to protect Aboriginal sacred sites, gave the Minister the power to override any decisions taken. Thus, in advising Amax that it might be in breach of the Act, the ALS could slow proceedings but not stop them.

The government had time on its side. It allowed a veneer of due process to occur, expecting the Community would back down. The government agreed to allow the Western Australian Museum to undertake a survey of sacred sites on the property. The Museum's report recommended that the entire area surrounding Pea Hill be protected under the Aboriginal Heritage Act. The government agreed but insisted at the same time that Amax be granted a 2-hectare site covering Pea Hill, and directed the Museum Trustees 'to raise no objection to Amax drilling on this site'.[20]

Resistance from the Noonkanbah Community, with the assistance of the ALS, forced Amax to delay plans to drill until the 1980 dry season. A senior traditional man later explained their reaction to the clash of cultures occurring on their land:

> From the beginning we started talking to people about mining according to Aboriginal law — the dreamtime law. If you put a bore down there is always something else in

there. There are things under the ground same significance as things on top. So we had a talk with Anthropologists and the Museum to look at all this land without damaging the sacred areas. They asked if another way was okay and we said 'no, you can't do that'. We look at on the map how far the middle of the area is really from the main place — how long, how wide and how square to join the significant places. The true working is about the stories about the goanna and the eel and we told the Museum Amax were not to go in there — that is a special place. Amax didn't worry whatsoever in the Aboriginal beliefs and put a bore on the main waterhole and hit the middle of the spirit of the main waterhole. The Museum went to write a report. And the Government can change that law and we had to stand very firm in that time and the Government wasn't listening.[21]

Meanwhile, the dispute was galvanising opinion throughout Western Australia's Aboriginal communities. Robert Bropho, spokesman for the Swan Valley fringe-dwellers, travelled outback Western Australia and recorded Aborigines' views on the Noonkanbah dispute. Not surprisingly, he returned with tales of solidarity. Freddy Johnson, a tribal lawman of Looma, summed up the response:

> We tribal lawmen like to see sacred sites left alone. We can't give it to him, gardia [white man]. We can't let him go to white man ... the community of Looma every time support Noonkanbah, the same as all the communities in the north-west of Australia support Noonkanbah in their fight to save sacred sites.[22]

In the meantime, the Community continued its defiant opposition. It was blessed with some naturally gifted leaders, who took their case to metropolitan Australia and helped make it a political cause. The ALS played a decisive role in bringing them down to Perth, which helped to further publicise their cause. In March 1980, 21-year-old Ivan McPhee came to Perth and told the Press that 'We want to be asked, not told, what is going to happen to our land and our people'.[23] A young Dicky Skinner also argued the case to a metropolitan audience, becoming something of an icon because he was 'quite at home talking on radio, being interviewed on TV or facing a press conference on land rights'.[24] Such activities infuriated not only government ministers but their senior bureaucrats in the resource portfolios, who had long ago absorbed the pro-development culture of the state. A senior government officer was quoted as saying: 'Mining in this state has been set back ten years by blackfellas suddenly discovering that everywhere we want to put a hole is a sacred site'.[25]

Yet some mining companies, including foreign-owned ones, disagreed with this view. Just as the political heat was being turned up on the Noonkanbah dispute, a more pragmatic approach, based around cooperation rather than conflict, was beginning to emerge. The *Daily News* explained the new approach:

> They [multi-national mining companies] have special liaison officers, they go out of their way to talk with Aboriginal leaders, they hire Aborigines, pay rental money to explore on tribal ground in some cases and generally try to cooperate with the wishes of elders.

The government, it appears, had no interest in fostering such a cooperative approach. In line with the aims of Amax, it wanted to establish the principle of open access to mining. The company showed its hand in March 1980 when, accompanied by police, its employees entered the property and prepared for drilling. The ALS prepared briefs for a Supreme Court writ to stop the exploration, which produced a one-week reprieve. But later in the month a ruling from the Court restored the company's right to mine. In response, Dicky Skinner called the people of the Kimberley 'to battle stations' and they set up camp near the drilling site. In an all-night display of traditional dancing, Amax workers were psychologically intimidated into leaving the site. This defence of their rights was noted at the time for its historic significance: 'never in the modern era had the country seen such a dramatic assertion of Aboriginal power and resolve'.[26]

On 15 March, the Premier reaffirmed the imminence of drilling. This announcement elicited a sharp public response from Rob Riley in his capacity as Executive Officer of the ALS. He told the *Sunday Times* that the Noonkanbah community was prepared to stand by its commitments not to allow mining: 'If that involves confrontation, so be it'.[27]

As March drew to a close the state government's unyielding stance created wider political tension. The federal opposition had called on the Fraser Liberal government to assume control of the dispute. The federal Minister for Aboriginal Affairs, Western Australian Senator Fred Chaney, expressed sympathy for Aboriginal ties to the land and offered to mediate. On one visit to Noonkanbah he left 'shaking his head', distraught at 'the inability of anybody to resolve the conflict'. Yet, he was not prepared to go as far as recommending the Commonwealth take charge. Prime Minister Malcolm Fraser hardened his own position in support of drilling,[28] and neither was prepared to take on Sir Charles, one of the fiercest defenders of states' rights in the country.

Meanwhile, a range of community groups opposed the government's handling of the dispute. In Perth, Noonkanbah became one of the biggest news stories in many years, as churches, union groups and ordinary members of the public expressed their support for the Community. In State Parliament, the Labor member of the Upper House Peter Dowding took up the Community's cause. Following the government's overruling of the State Museum's opposition to mining on Noonkanbah, he brought on an urgency motion in an attempt to expose the government's duplicity. The Premier, he argued, had been repeating the 'misleading and distasteful' statement that the government was prepared to protect sacred sites. Yet, 'the facts of the matter which the Premier cannot escape are that this land is sacred — and the Government has acted on the basis that it is sacred — and the Museum has been forced to consent to mining on this sacred land'.[29]

Still Sir Charles would not yield. The government was steering the dispute towards a showdown. The amendments it made to the Aboriginal Heritage Act further consolidated its power. These amendments were described later by the state-government appointed Commissioner inquiring into Aboriginal land rights in 1984 as constituting:

> a simple operation in relation to sites. The government of the day can decide in the interests of the broader community what Aboriginal sites should be destroyed or damaged, no matter how sacred or important or special their significance to Aboriginal people may be. Aboriginal people have no right to be heard on the topic, although private property owners may appeal to the Supreme Court if the Minister will not authorise a disturbance.[30]

Sir Charles Court now had all bases covered. Buttressed by tougher legislation over sites, legislative restrictions on public dissent, a compliant police leadership and a resigned federal government, he was able to personally guide the dispute to its inevitable conclusion. On 30 May 1980 he flew to the Community for talks. The Community challenged him to see their culture through their eyes. In a revealing exchange, Dicky Skinner asked the Premier to name a particular tree on the river bank. Sir Charles replied with what he must have thought was the obvious — 'it is a gum tree'. Phil Vincent, who overhead the conversation, remembers Dicky pointing out to Sir Charles a central feature of Yungngora culture: they 'had a different name for each of the trees along the bank of the river', underlining to the Premier 'their intense relationship to the land'.

Few in government understood these deep attachments. Graham McDonald recalls how following a visit to the Community, a minister issued a statement to the effect that 'he'd been up there all day and nobody could show him a sacred site'. Not surprisingly, government talks to resolve the conflict came to nothing. Then, on 11 June, the Premier produced a raft of measures further increasing the likelihood of conflict: enlarging the area of the drill site from 2 to 4 hectares; resuming it from the pastoral lease; and declaring the access road across the property a public road.

During July 1980 tensions between the Community and the government reached a new pitch. On 10 July the ALS, acting on instructions from the Community, launched another round of legal action to prevent the resumption of land on Noonkanbah. It challenged the government's attempts to reclassify the road into the Community as a public road through which the company would then gain access to the proposed drilling site. Lodging objections under the *Public Works Act 1902 (WA)*, the ALS cited the following: that a public road into Noonkanbah would allow access by the public, which would have a detrimental social effect on Aborigines at the station, including the introduction of alcohol, interference with women, desecration of sacred sites, and damage to stock. Arguing that the resumption of land was not necessary for the stated purpose — and hence contrary to the intent of the Act — the ALS objection to the proposed reclassification of the road raised the crux of the Community's concerns: 'The resumption of the land for a public road is not necessary for public purposes, but is merely intended for the purposes of a single company, Amax Iron Ore Corporation'.[31]

Behind the scenes, the government drew up plans to enable Amax to crush the Community's resistance: drilling equipment was supplied by the Mines Department, advice sought from a trucking company, and labour hired with the intention of transporting oil rigging to the Noonkanbah site. The convoy would be given substantial police protection for the long drive north. In the second week of August the convoy of forty-five trucks and four support vehicles rolled out of Perth bound for Noonkanbah in what appeared to some as the closest act to military engagement seen in Australia in a long time.[32] Coinciding with its departure, an editorial in the *The West Australian* described the convoy as 'a sorry testimony to insensitive authority'.[33]

As the convoy prepared to roll north, relations between police and the Community descended into open hostility. In late July, the Community instructed the ALS to lay a five-point complaint with Police Commissioner G.O. Leitch over the behaviour of police on the Station. In a letter to the ALS, the Community alleged the police had been:

> harassing the community and visitors in an unacceptable way. Nearly all the vehicles moving on the station roads were stopped and their occupants questioned. They were asked for their drivers' licences, whether they were carrying firearms and when they were returning ... This has taken place on private roads ... and we regard it as an invasion of privacy and open harassment.[34]

Relations between the ALS and the government continued to sour. On 6 August the Minister for Cultural Affairs, Mr Bill Grayden, called for the disbanding of the ALS in a speech he made to the Legislative Assembly. 'The ALS now appears to be an unashamedly politically oriented organisation', Grayden told members, 'professionally engaged in manipulating Aborigines rather than in providing them with legal help'. Grayden went on to claim that the Premier 'was so concerned about the ALS that he planned to discuss the matter with the Prime Minister, Mr Fraser'.[35]

Days later, Rob Riley and Ian Horrocks spontaneously decided to head to Noonkanbah: 'we just said we've got to get up there, someone has to be there to represent these people'. On the arduous trip, the two

Dicky Skinner raising the Aboriginal flag at Noonkanbah, August 1980. Skinner was a key Aboriginal spokesperson for the rights of his community to protect their sacred sites.

The Blockade, Micky's Pool, Noonkanbah, August 1980. Although defeated on the day, the Noonkanbah dispute sparked the modern land rights movement.

The Blockade, Micky's Pool, Noonkanbah, August 1980. Rob Riley on right with camera.

passed the government/Amax convoy lumbering its way towards the showdown.

As it rolled north, trade unionists and Aboriginal groups organised protests to greet the trucks. On 10 August, police put on 'a massive show of strength' and forced about 150 Aborigines off a main bridge outside Port Hedland.[36] On the same day, the Noonkanbah Community took a further defiant stand. Dicky Skinner raised the Aboriginal flag in a symbolic ceremony proclaiming their right to their pastoral lease. The following day his gesture was captured in a front page photograph in the tabloid *Daily News*: Dicky Skinner, his lithe body dressed only in traditional loincloth, looking pensively down at the ground, his raised right hand holding the Aboriginal flag aloft. It was a stage-managed but nonetheless powerful image. In the face of the overwhelming might of the convoy roaring its way towards the Community, the photograph acted as a reminder to a metropolitan audience of the Community's abiding commitment to their protest. The fact that the working-class *Daily News* splashed it over their front page was indicative of the public attention their protest had gained.

The convoy rolled on. On 11 August Aborigines organised passive roadside demonstrations at Roebourne and Karratha, while trade unionists unsuccessfully tried to maintain picket lines. When the convoy reached Broome the confrontation with protesters and police turned ugly. The convoy was pelted with gravel as it broke through a demonstration of 220 protesters including 120 Aborigines, the lead truck smashing a banner and only narrowly missing the men carrying it.[37] Peter Yu, then a young Aboriginal field worker in the Kimberley, was warned by police that he could be prosecuted under section 54B of the Police Act — the same Act Rob had been prosecuted under — after he spoke to a gathering. Some days later, Peter Yu and Rob Riley would begin to forge a friendship of deep personal and political significance.

~~~~~~~

Rob and Ian had arrived — 'absolutely knackered' — a day earlier than Peter and two days before the convoy arrived. Police were already manning the gate into the Station and the two went immediately to a shed on the Community, introduced themselves and offered their legal services. Today, Ian shudders at the temerity of their action: 'I mean we weren't lawyers. Rob knew how a magistrate's court operated, I at that stage was developing a rather rudimentary knowledge of the legal system ... not lawyers, just a pair of cowboys'.

The following day Peter Yu flew in from Broome with some elders after the smashing of the demonstration there. As if to foretell the drama to come, 'we nearly had a bloody plane crash trying to land at Noonkanbah in a cross wind'. For a while Rob and Ian respectfully listened to 'the old men talking about their land as only old men can'. This got them 'fired up' and 'passionate', not least because they came face to face with the strength of the elders' resolve. The elders told the two of them: 'We will do whatever it is we have to do but they are not going to drill on our country'.

There were some difficult undercurrents swirling in the coming and goings of people. Who had the real authority to speak for the Community? The debate boiled down to 'the real blackfellas' versus the non-traditional ring-ins. Even on the sidelines, Rob would have been aware of these tensions revolving around Aboriginal legitimacy.

Mostly, though, a united front was maintained, and planning got under way for the Community's last stand. Confronting them by now was 'half a police battalion at the front gate' to oversee the entry of the convoy onto the property. Out towards Pea Hill on the designated mining site was a fenced-in compound in which another contingent of police had set up operations.

The isolation of the Community created difficulties for the protestors. There were few links to the outside world. The nearest telephone was at Fitzroy Crossing and it only had two lines out. Newspapers arrived days late. Radio could be accessed but only on short wave. Crackling ABC news broadcasts kept the Community informed of the progress of the convoy.

The first decision to be taken was the most critical: where was the best defensive position to make the last stand? There was no hope of controlling the Station side of the gate, so a dry creek-bed in a dip in the road further on the way into the Station — known as Mickey's Pool — was chosen. It was thought that they could not easily be seen in this location until the convoy was almost upon them. By this stage organisers realised that the government would only likely enter the Station with the light of early morning. At night, and with only moonlight to work by, they assembled twenty vehicles and chained them together in the creek-bed, hoping at least to hinder the progress of the convoy. Roughly sixty people prepared to camp out the night, including five Uniting Church ministers, three of whom had come from the Eastern states.[38] The clergy would add significant public relations value to the protest.

During the early part of the evening the atmosphere in the pitch black, dead quiet, dry creek bed was tense: a sense of heightened reality. Among the elders, the coming showdown generated high levels of fear; to have come this far required courage. The twin sources of their fear were the pastoralists and the police. Michael Gallagher, who captured the protest in a series of photographs, recalls: 'Kimberley people could still point out living pastoralists who had shot their relatives. Those people were still walking around in towns like Halls Creek and Fitzroy Crossing … it had genuinely entered their heads that there was a possibility they might get shot'. The fear of the police was no less intense: they all knew the stories involving police murdering Aboriginal people. Non-violent resistance was the elders' chosen method of protest.

The plans for the last stand were fine-tuned amid unnerving eeriness. The silence was all-encompassing.

A police ute was heard to start its engine up at the Compound. As it crossed the country, its gear changes could be heard. Soon the vehicle's headlights came into view and the protesters watched its progress as it came over the hill and, within clear sight of the creek-bed, suddenly came to a stop. The policeman's voice became audible as, alighting from his vehicle, he spontaneously yelled into the thin, night air, 'Oh fuck'. Activating his two-way radio, his excited voice carried unimpeded to the creek bed as he spluttered into his two-way radio: 'Oh fuck boss … oh shit, there are fucking thousands of them, they're in the creek, they've got trucks and cars and mobs of people here'.

Told by his superiors to calm down and head back to the Compound, the constable's unexpected intrusion into their hideout broke the tension in the creek bed. There was great hilarity at the thought of the young constable 'shitting himself' and knowing that he would 'get toasted in the morning' for having allowed the road to be blocked.

Tensions built again as the protesters snuggled down into their swags. There was talk about the imminent arrival of the convoy. But, no sooner had they settled in than vehicle engines could be heard starting, from the direction of the gate. Eventually a posse of about thirty police arrived, among them both superintendents and Aboriginal police aides. Pointing car headlights into the creek, a senior officer alighted from a car armed with a megaphone. His message was brutally straightforward: 'OK you've made your point, now pack up and go home, be peaceful; we understand that you're not happy but bugger off and not a sound, not a murmur'.[39]

No response was forthcoming from the protesters. As part of their strategy of non-violent resistance, it had previously been decided that no one would speak for 'the mob'. This tactic greatly agitated the senior officer who repeated his line three or four times before, in a tone of increasing desperation, he hollered, 'there must be someone who could speak for this mob, come on there must be someone who can speak'. Still there was no response. But no-one could have expected what happened next. In the still of the desert night, and with the forces of law and order bearing down on them, someone in the creek-bed let fly: 'It ripped the night air, this great echoing fart'. The whole place broke up. Unable to get their answer, and unwilling to move against them in the middle of the night, the police backed off.

However, the retreat was temporary. Several more times that night, as *The West Australian* reported, the police turned up and 'members of the group were warned that they were obstructing a public road and that they could be arrested'.[40] On each occasion no-one replied directly to the police.

The next morning 'all hell broke lose'. At 8.15 a.m., overseen by a big police contingent, a front end loader and a grader started dragging the vehicles aside.[41] The protesters were hopelessly outnumbered. Amid 'ugly scenes', police moved into the group and started arresting the churchmen and elders from the Community. The use of Aboriginal police aides for this frontline task disgusted protesters. Newly appointed to the police service, the aides, whose designated job was liaising between the police and Aboriginal communities, were no doubt caught in an impossible situation. Nonetheless, Rob, Ian and a few others yelled 'shame' as the aides dragged the elders up the hill and into the waiting paddy wagons. In the confusion, Ian and Rob stuck to their formal roles of representing the ALS, and monitoring the treatment of the elders who were arrested. They scurried after those being dragged away and, trying to be in all places at all times, attempted to make sure the elders were read their rights and weren't abused or manhandled.

Once the road through Mickey's Pool had been cleared, hours of stalemate followed as police lined each side of the road to prevent it from being re-occupied. Police carted away all the senior people in the Community to Fitzroy Crossing. Then news was relayed via the short-wave radio that Bob Hawke and the ACTU had black-banned the drilling crew from erecting the rig. Literally, as cheers erupted over this news, the convoy roared past.

In the surrounding chaos, and still standing in the dry creek bed, Rob was introduced to Peter Yu. With little time for formal introductions beyond a quick handshake, they helped to organise a forum of those that were left: 'He [Rob] was obviously preoccupied in getting the legal team and the support to the people who'd been arrested ... I was more reacting to what was happening to the Community'.

The two emerging young leaders camped overnight, too exhausted to talk. But their meeting on the day the trucks came to Noonkanbah would have great significance for each of them and for Aboriginal politics. As Peter explains: 'We grew up in the struggle'. They had both spent their teens in racist Perth (Peter went back to the Kimberley in 1976), enjoyed a similar larrikin humour and, importantly, were bound by their commitment to advance social justice for Aborigines. Peter Yu had already broken new ground in Aboriginal politics by becoming the first Black government welfare officer in the Kimberley and the first Field Officer for the Kimberley Land Council. They had both done their apprenticeships by the time they met.

Following the clearing of the road, the ACTU ban on the erection of the rig lasted a few weeks, until Sir Charles Court organised 'a scab' crew to do the job. The crushing of the Noonkanbah protest is remembered by those close to it as one of the bleakest days in contemporary Australian political history. One of the arrested Uniting Church ministers called the action 'arrogant materialism', while another said 'he had been involved with Aborigines for the past sixteen years and had never seen anything like this before'.[42]

No-one involved was left untouched by the Noonkanbah dispute. The old men at the Community were 'deeply upset by the arrests' and, in the days after the blockade ended, had commenced a series of meetings 'to decide what to do under Aboriginal law about any drilling'.[43] Fortunately, when the cases of those arrested came to court, Phil Vincent successfully had the charges dropped, the magistrate agreeing that it was impossible to determine from available map references the exact location of the road in dispute. Longer term, the crushing of the protest unfolded into a disaster for the Community. Steve Hawke recalls: 'They never got over it. They were never able to get the community fully back on its feet to fulfil the promise the property had. Most of the key leaders from the protest withdrew from political activism'.

For Sir Charles Court and his government, the impacts were no less pronounced. The relentless pursuit of the dispute damaged Sir Charles's reputation. It exposed him nationally, in the eyes of many, as an extremist, a tag which he carried until he retired and was evident in the press commentary at the time of his departure from politics.[44] Fortunately for Sir Charles, much of this reputation faded over time. In the immediate aftermath of the dispute, the Court government continued to exploit the dispute. The Cultural Affairs minister, Mr Grayden, was accused of scaremongering about Aboriginal land rights. In one provocative statement he declared Noonkanbah to be 'no more significant than a huge number of sites elsewhere in Western Australia'. In fact, according to Grayden, 'there were several hundred thousand such sites and many were now cities, towns, dams and farms'.[45] Criticised by the President of the Anthropological Society of Western Australia for 'a massive overstatement', Grayden's comments foreshadowed the tactics conservatives would use to undermine land rights in the decades ahead.[46]

For Aboriginal activists, Noonkanbah was a pivotal experience in their lives. It thrust Rob, and many other young, politically active Aborigines, into a nationally important fight for Aboriginal rights. Although Rob and Brian Wyatt were away from much of the lead-up to the main action at the Community, they were involved in important work in Perth organising support among the broader community, holding rallies and resourcing the legal fight. All of this activity served to raise Rob's profile.

The ALS was now the key Aboriginal political body in Western Australia, with a network of regional offices and powerful people on its committee. Rob was beginning to acquire the standing of a leader at state level.

Noonkanbah completed Rob's transition into activist politics. It sharpened his understanding of the complexities of historical dispossession as central to the Aboriginal story. For those involved, it was clear that dispossession of land was not simply an issue for 'southern'

Aboriginal people. Noonkanbah showed that traditional owners in the north (outside of the Northern Territory following the passage of the 1976 Aboriginal Land Bill) lacked effective control over the land they lived on. Rob absorbed this lesson deeply. For him, land rights could not be divided into a 'north' versus 'south' issue; it was a battle for all Aboriginal people. In forging early links with people associated with the Kimberley Land Council, Rob developed a pan-Aboriginal network initially spanning the state and later the nation.

In addition to Peter Yu, Rob also met John Watson at Noonkanbah. A charismatic traditional leader of the Nyikina people, south-east of Derby, Watson went on to have a distinguished career at the KLC. He and Rob worked closely together in the land rights struggles that lay ahead. In the close bond they forged, Watson deepened Rob's understanding of traditional Aboriginal lifestyles and aspirations.

The post-Noonkanbah period was 'an intense and heightened' era of Aboriginal politics. Noonkanbah highlighted the failure of governments, both federal and state, to deal with Aboriginal aspirations, a situation which lasted until the 1992 High Court Mabo decision upholding native title. As a consequence, the Noonkanbah dispute energised both the ALS and the KLC, fostered the internationalisation of the Aboriginal cause, engaged the ALP at both state and federal levels with the land rights issue and radicalised activists. As Peter Yu explains, Noonkanbah meant they were now in Aboriginal politics for the long haul; 'Whether we liked it or not, we didn't really have much choice'.

But how to move forward? It would have been understandable if Rob had drifted into a more radical version of direct action politics. That this did not occur seems to have been a combination of his personality and the organisational culture of the ALS. He was aware of the responsibility that came with being Executive Officer. The ALS was a legal service; its activities must rest on the law. How could its boundaries be pushed and what would be the response if they did not yield? But he had also seen the failure of governments to enact and uphold laws for the rights of Aboriginal people. How could they be convinced to pursue an Aboriginal rights agenda? At this stage Rob seemed to have no answer to these questions; they would stalk his entire career.

Alongside the political issues, Noonkanbah left conflicting emotional reactions. For Rob and others, the last stages of the protest had had an inspiring quality. The elders's bravery in 'fronting up' on that day to confront the Western Australian police force left a great impression. For Rob, who was only twenty-five, it was an especially big day: a lesson in political courage.

Underneath the highs of the collective struggle was the bitterness of defeat. It brought home the scale of the battles ahead. It left scars on everyone involved and none more so than Rob. With his uncertainties over his Aboriginal identity only just behind him, Noonkanbah brought home to him what it meant to be an Aboriginal; they were not fighting a vague cause, but a struggle over Aboriginal cultural identity. The extensive contacts he made with traditional people helped reinforce what it meant to be Black.

The period from joining Black Action until the defeat of the Noonkanbah campaign brought to an end the first phase of Rob's involvement in Aboriginal politics. It had been an eventful period; a rollercoaster of issues, confrontations and challenges. He had seen race politics played at its most determined. The perceived intransigence of the Court government had forced the adoption of direct action as the principal strategy, but these tactics had proved unequal to Sir Charles Court's determined application of state power. The young guard lost all their battles during the late 1970s and early 1980s. Developing resilience was part of their learning process. As Brian Wyatt reflects, the young guard learnt to keep going 'even though we got done over in the end'.

In the next phase of his career Rob would need to summon all the resilience he could muster: the battle over land rights was set to go national.

CHAPTER SIX

A Bigger Stage: The National Aboriginal Conference

As Rob Riley began casting around for a bigger stage, he sought election to the National Aboriginal Conference (NAC). This was the reformed National Aboriginal Consultative Committee (NACC), the so-called Black Parliament, and the only national Aboriginal voice. His decision was driven by two factors. Firstly, Noonkanbah had left its legacy of anger in Rob as it had in other activists. Secondly, Rob had come to see the limitations of direct action in tackling the conservative political structure of the state and its links to the mining and pastoral industries. But his transition from protest politics to mainstream political lobbying involved a leap of faith: would the NAC be equal to his commitment for change?

Rob was elected in 1981. He would become Deputy Chair in 1983 and National Chair in May 1984. In anybody's language this was an extraordinary achievement. Aboriginal politics in these years was dominated by the land rights issue, and in the period between 1981 and his election as National Chair, Rob played a critical role in helping to shape the Aboriginal response. In the process he made the transition from angry radical to skilled inside operator. He became a Black politician in a white political structure. He mastered the skills of travelling between the two worlds; but these very different worlds were set to clash.

The NAC had a troubled history. Set up by the Whitlam government in 1973 as the National Aboriginal Consultative Committee, to provide Aboriginal people with their first national political voice, it was destined to disappoint. The expectations of Aboriginal leaders and those of the government were fundamentally at odds. How much power and authority should a body representing Aboriginal people have? The government wanted it to provide advice only, while Aborigines wanted to be given the autonomy to manage their own affairs. This struggle for self-determination overshadowed the NACC and its successor, the NAC.

Meeting for the first time on 13 December 1973, the members of the NACC were the focus of great expectations in the Aboriginal community. The NACC excited a new wave of interest among Aboriginal people in the democratic process; many had not previously voted in mainstream politics. In Western Australia, public meetings were held to educate the Aboriginal community about the new organisation. About 70 per cent of the total eligible Aboriginal population had enrolled to vote, and many of these people felt 'that the Committee would give the Aboriginal people a united voice which was urgently needed'.[1] Those harbouring aspirations for the organisation did not appreciate the limited role envisaged for it by the Whitlam government. Indeed, people were misled into thinking that it had more power than it could deliver.

In the government's mind, the Committee was to provide a 'forum for the expression of opinion' on Aboriginal affairs and 'a channel through which the Government might receive representative advice'.[2] Those attending the first meeting saw its role in far broader terms: operating as an executive body with the power to direct funds. Among the first tasks undertaken by the Committee was the drafting of a constitution which proposed a change in name to the National Aboriginal Congress. The proposed constitution also identified fifteen powers and functions including the ability to negotiate with government, the payment of compensation to Aborigines, the power over Aboriginal assets and the ability to control and distribute moneys. This rush to expand its role unsettled the Whitlam cabinet, which refused to accept the new constitution, including the name change.

Unbowed, the NACC continued to refer to itself as the National Aboriginal Congress for the next few years, showcasing the name with pride at its occasional meetings. At its March 1975 meeting in Townsville, Evelyn Scott, General Secretary of the Federal Council for the Advancement of Aboriginals and Torres Strait Islanders, echoed the expectations of the broader Aboriginal community by giving the 'Congress' a rousing message that Aboriginal people were waiting to hear what had been done about housing, education, trade training for young people, reducing the burden of everyday racism and the future of Aboriginal youngsters. Governments still did not appreciate, she told her sympathetic audience, 'the fact that many Aborigines with their culture destroyed, their way of life wrecked, our people being corrupted — is due to the lack of understanding of our real problem'.[3]

As Scott's address testified, Aboriginal people were longing for a strong and effective Indigenous political voice. But this was unrealistic in the form of the NACC. A purely advisory body, and especially one that lacked sufficient resources to engage in consultation or even to maintain an effective secretariat, would struggle to be taken seriously.[4] By 1976, the new Minister for Aboriginal Affairs, Ian Viner, acknowledged to members the 'unhappy history' of the NACC and the 'frustrations you as members suffer in trying to achieve an impossible task'. Viner also admitted he had sensed 'the disillusionment of Aboriginal people throughout Australia as to where the NACC fits into the processes and programs of Government.[5] But Viner rarely consulted the organisation in crucial negotiations he had with Aboriginal communities on issues affecting their interests.[6] He did initiate an inquiry into the NACC which examined its failings and the neglect of government to adequately support it.[7] In response, the Fraser government restructured the organisation, transforming it into the National Aboriginal Conference (NAC).

However, the basic dilemma had not changed. The new body, like its predecessor, lacked any real autonomy. Frustration led NAC members to internationalise their struggle. Almost by accident, they realised they had the power to embarrass government, giving them some hope of additional influence. In April 1976, the NAC declared that 'all Aborigines in Australian jails should be regarded as political prisoners'. In a proclamation presented to the Governor General, Sir John Kerr, 'the NAC said it would take the claims of all Aborigines to the United Nations in an effort to win support for the fight for Aboriginal rights'.[8] On this occasion the threat did not materialise.

The day before the smashing of the last stand at Noonkanbah, a delegation from the NAC left Australia for Geneva to attend sittings of the United Nations Human Rights Commission's Sub-Commission on the Prevention of Discrimination and Protection of Minorities. Australia's first Indigenous delegation to appear before the United Nations consisted of its chairman, Jim Hagan, the two representatives from the Kimberley, Jimmy Bieundurry and Reg Birch, and Phil Vincent from the ALS as its legal counsel. Rob was in transit to Noonkanbah as it left.

Before their departure, delegates had to confront a worried Prime Minister, Malcolm Fraser. He telephoned members and invited them over to Parliament House for morning tea. The meeting with the Prime Minister emboldened the delegation. Fraser begged them not to go, but his anxiety only made the members of the delegation realise that they had hit upon something. Hagan's media adviser, Peter O'Brien, recalls: 'They became so excited and this was the moment in their mind, the making of the National Aboriginal Conference. Suddenly, they were someone that people had to take notice of ... they could make the Prime Minister beg them to come to morning tea!'

At the United Nations hearing, Jim Hagan's speech created an international stir. Commencing with a sketch of the treatment of Aborigines in Australia, Hagan went on to outline the situation at Noonkanbah as an example of how Aborigines' oppression had continued unabated. Stirring words followed: 'The Noonkanbah Community have sought justice, and have been given obstruction. We have sought peace and have been given violence. The Australian government's acquiescence in this continuing breach of human rights must see it condemned in the eyes of the world'.[9]

To his own surprise, Hagan created the first international furore over the treatment of Australia's Indigenous people. The delegation was told that Hagan's address had achieved the biggest media exposure of any delegation to the Sub-Committee on Human Rights. Newspapers from Britain to the Soviet Union covered Hagan's speech, and the Australian government was seriously embarrassed. 'They were very angry and there was a flurry of meetings', O'Brien recalls. After his return from Geneva, Jim Hagan wrote of 'the excited reaction of the world's press, the huge support of our own people and the interest of the many other indigenous minorities around the world'.[10]

Government policy on Noonkanbah at both state and federal levels did not change. Nevertheless, Hagan's delegation to the UN revealed the extent to which the protest at Noonkanbah had emboldened Aborigines, and provided the NAC with a powerful focus. As O'Brien recalls, Noonkanbah was among the first issues dealt with by the NAC that was not scheduled by government; 'they got highly excited about it and became very involved and that made them realise that as a body they did have extraordinary influence if they wanted to exercise it and they didn't have to toe the line and say yes sir, no sir, to the Minister'. Hagan also confirmed the impact of Noonkanbah on the evolving Aboriginal rights movement. It had, he explained, 'presented the Aboriginal people with a cause behind which to unite. There had been similar instances, many of them, but none had stirred the emotional consciousness of the people to such an extent'.[11]

In addition, Hagan's UN delegation highlighted how threatening the internationalisation of the Aboriginal cause could be to the Australian government. Hagan foresaw that the trip would energise the NAC with a new determination: 'to adopt this new international role with vigour'. The world had known little of the historical treatment of Aboriginal people; Australia's isolation had insulated its policies from scrutiny. Now, Aborigines had found a new lever of influence.

Emboldened though the NAC was by its international actions in 1980, it was at the same time sliding into self-destruction. Members felt hurt and disillusioned over governments' failure to heed their advice, even more so when figures including the Prime Minister, Mr Fraser, addressed NAC forums with reassuring words about the importance of the organisation.[12] Underlying personality tensions among the members infused meetings with often incapacitating levels of distrust. There was constant lobbying about who was to occupy the Chair. Jim Hagan was voted out and Roy Nichols from Tasmania became the new Chairman.

In 1980, the NAC was failing to develop effective policy advice and was largely irrelevant to the communities it purported to serve.

Part of its dysfunction was due to the confusion of loyalties some of the members had between their Aboriginal roots and their ties to evangelical Christian churches. More broadly, the NAC was cut off from the newly emerging land councils. The Northern and Central Land Councils had been created as statutory bodies as part of the Fraser government's *Northern Territory Land Rights Act 1976*. Underpinned with secure funding and given the task of to representing Aboriginal people's interests in the land, they changed the dynamics of Aboriginal politics in Australia.

Indeed the powerlessness of the NAC stood in stark contrast to the autonomy and influence exerted by both the Northern and Central Land Councils. Royalties gave the councils 'a chance to make and pay for their own policies, even when these are not what the Commonwealth government wants'.[13] Rob was well briefed on the operation of Territory land councils, having in his possession a copy of Justice Toohey's 1984 Report into the Northern Territory Land Rights Act, which explained the real power they possessed: 'The Act seeks to implement two principles. One is to ensure that the traditional owners understand and consent to any action that may affect the land. The other is to interpose a Land Council between the traditional owners and those who wish to deal in some way with Aboriginal land'.[14]

Within the federal ALP the Northern Territory Land Rights Act functioned as the benchmark for national land rights. Unsurprisingly, the very existence of the Northern Territory Land Rights Act sent shivers down the spine of the Court government, and served to harden its resolve to oppose any intrusion of Commonwealth legislation on land issues. Government ministers invoked the fear of racial tension which, it imagined, would erupt over the introduction of similar legislation.[15] This fear was part of an historical resistance by successive Western Australian governments to outside interference on Aboriginal land issues.

Thus the challenges facing Rob Riley and Peter Yu when they stood for election in 1981 were enormous. Two young and politically inexperienced activists had set their sights on a fight of David and Goliath proportions. They aimed to take on the history of colonial domination, the power of international capital and the institutionalisation of racism. Behind them was a group of young activists including Aubrey Lynch, Margaret Mallard and Frank Chulung. Nonetheless, the obstacles confronting them were daunting.

Especially daunting was the entrenched attitude of racism in the community. Rob would not have been able to ignore the return to public notoriety of his boyhood home of Pingelly. The town had recently been under scrutiny again for 'blatant discrimination'. Splashed across one page of *The Sunday Times* on 6 January 1980 was an article about an incident in which a local hairdresser refused to give a haircut to a part-Aboriginal child. Aboriginal groups protested to the media that this was not an isolated occurrence: the townsfolk were so prejudiced against Aborigines they could not get jobs and faced a barrage of police brutality. The hairdresser was said to be scared by the consequences of her actions and sought police protection.

On-going racial tension in Pingelly was part of a broader pattern of discrimination. A compelling insight into racial attitudes in Western Australia was compiled in 1981 by the Office of the Commissioner for Community Relations in Canberra. An inquiry was launched in the state in response to the volume of complaints made to the Office from individuals and organisations, including the ALS while Rob was still Executive Officer. Its Report was an indictment of the failure of successive governments to deal with the level of community discrimination and institutionalised racism within government agencies and the wider community.[16]

The Report highlighted the extent of institutional racism, which was being driven by some of the state's conservative elite. It included the details of a recent outburst from 'a prominent industrialist and leading citizen' of Western Australia who said during an interview on Queensland television that 'half-caste' Aborigines should be sterilised and confined to a small area of north-west Australia. He also said that most of the racial trouble and demands for Aboriginal land rights came from 'half-castes'. His 'solution' was to make their social security cheques receivable only at Karratha. 'When they had gravitated there I would dope the water up so that they were sterile and would breed themselves out in the future. That would solve the problem', he said.[17]

Among other documents produced before the Office of the Commissioner was a letter from a politician who wrote: 'it was a degrading experience to have to campaign amongst aborigines to the extent I did, and it offended me to know that whilst I was concentrating my efforts on these simple people over the last couple of weeks, I was neglecting a more informed and intelligent section of the community'.[18]

The Commission detailed discrimination against Aborigines in just about every social institution: the magistracy, police, transport, the media, and government departments. Hotels were singled out as a major repository of racist attitudes. In one hotel, three Aboriginal men entered the saloon bar only to be told they could not be served as the bar was 'sacred to whites'. At another hotel, a party of schoolgirls which included Aboriginal children sought to use the toilets during a stop on a bus trip. Hotel staff told the Aboriginal girls that they could not use the hotel's amenities but should go to the 'Aboriginals' hotel' across the road.

Nothing in these reported attitudes would have surprised Rob and other activists who had battled them throughout their careers. Yet the NAC seemed puny in the face of such entrenched racism.

Rob secured a narrow victory and joined the NAC. Elated though he was, not all on his own side cheered his victory. Politically, Rob's rapid rise through Noongar politics put him off-side with sections of the old guard, several of whom were defeated in the 1981 election. Antipathy to Rob and to Peter Yu ran deep among these people, one of whom sneeringly depicted the two as 'hard-core radicals'.[19] Cedric Wyatt remembers handing out 'How To Vote' cards for Rob at a shopping centre during his first election, after which 'some blackfellas wouldn't talk to me again'.

The election highlighted the divisive and unpredictable world of Aboriginal politics which, like its mainstream counterpart, had a reputation for factionalism. Even as a newcomer to this world, Rob could not have escaped the reality that Aboriginal politics was, as *The West Australian* once commented, fraught with 'jealousies and infighting', such that 'movers and shakers can be at the top one day and on the scrap heap the next'.[20] The newspaper failed to point out the obvious similarities with the mainstream political system; but Aboriginal politics was not immune from blood-letting. Throughout his career, Rob would have to fend off sniping and undermining from a few people within Noongar society who were seemingly jealous of his profile or wanted to settle what became the 'old scores' associated with his first victory.

There was also a personal issue arising from his election. Membership of the NAC involved constant travel to both intra-state and national meetings in Canberra and elsewhere. Jeannie could see that his election to the NAC would allow him to become more outspoken on Aboriginal issues, and she was happy that he felt excited about being able to make a difference to the lives of Aboriginal people. However, Rob was acutely conscious of the implications for his family from his constant absence. He was worried that the pressures might break up his family; that he wouldn't be able to be a proper father. By this time, the couple had two daughters: Megan, born in 1979, and Jaymea, born the following year.

Before he was elected Rob talked to Jeannie about how the family would stay together. As Ian Horrocks observed, 'He was patently aware that all the network supports were going to be pulled out from underneath them, that Jeannie would be home on her own ... that he wasn't going to be there enough'. For Rob, family had a deep psychological meaning. Rob was passionate and protective of his family; he could be anywhere, anytime and he would want to know what was happening at home. But in entering the world of Aboriginal politics, Rob created a dilemma he would never resolve. The birth of his children intensified and personalised his interest in politics. Rob didn't want his children exposed to the injustices Aborigines had for so long faced. But, in attempting to provide a better future for Aboriginal people, his family, although proud of the role he was playing, would pay a heavy price.

Despite the personal and political challenges, Rob Riley and Peter Yu began their national careers with optimism. It was an exciting time to be joining the NAC. Irrespective of its internal difficulties, a new climate of ideas had been slowly percolating through Aboriginal affairs: a revisionist history challenging old fictions about Australia's past, an interest in examining new ideas about the legal status of Aboriginal people in Australia, and a growing international outlook among Aboriginal leaders. In Western Australia, the changing political climate was symbolised by the retirement of Sir Charles Court, the old warhorse of conservative politics. On the day of his departure from the political stage, which, some believed, he had so ruthlessly dominated, *The West Australian* noted that he had become a man out of his times; his style of labelling critics as 'enemies' was increasingly out of sympathy with 'the sensitivity of the electorate on matters stirring a social conscience'.[21]

When Rob and Peter came to Canberra for their first meeting, they made a big impression on the NAC. Peter O'Brien recalls: 'I think the whole conference was a bit in awe of these two new exciting, vibrant, energetic young bloods from Western Australia'. Peter Yu and Rob Riley were the two youngest representatives ever elected to the NAC, and their outspokenness and team approach upset some of the older members. They came to the moribund organisation with high expectations of being strong, independent voices.

Rob was driven to succeed in the organisation. He gave every impression of a person comfortable with himself. On one occasion early in his friendship with Peter O'Brien, media adviser to the NAC, he shared the story of his background in Sister Kate's and his rape in the institution. But there was no hint of any emotional trouble: 'I didn't detect any great anger. It was like recounting an overseas trip; this was something that happened and he would seem quite calm in saying the names of those involved, but he'd say, "Oh I don't want you to say that to anyone"'. The subject was rarely raised again.

The exchange is a revealing insight into the layers Rob had placed between past and present. Many of Rob's contemporaries have noted, more in hindsight than at the time, that he was unable to disclose his vulnerable self. This would not have been unusual for someone with his background. Emotional pain from childhood is often difficult to disclose and especially in the context in which Rob was operating. Most of his Aboriginal friends came from backgrounds of hardship and could instinctively understand each other without dwelling on the details. It was also a male-dominated movement, continually focused on the fight ahead. It was not an environment conducive, one suspects, for the sharing of deeper feelings and experiences. It would have been hard for his white friends to understand what it meant to be institutionalised, undergo family reunification and be thrust onto a segregated reserve. The process of distancing and disassociation from his background became routine behaviour, the more so because he had adopted such a purposeful public role.

Rob relished his new role. He liked the perks involved in being at the NAC — the access to government cars and interstate travel and lunches with Prime Minister Malcolm Fraser. In his dealings with Fraser and other Liberal government ministers of the day, Rob developed a dual response; while respecting the office and the chance to influence attitudes, he had an irreverent attitude to power generally. He never changed his manner when in the presence of senior politicians.

Part of Rob's irreverence was a disdain for the often grinding meetings that were part of the NAC process. He liked things to be happening and he disliked getting bogged down in administrative detail. Peter O'Brien remembers how at the prospect of a bout of organisational tedium, Rob would sometimes whisper, '"This is pissing me off, let's go to the pictures". I'd say, "I can't go to the pictures, I've got to go to the meeting", to which he would insist, "Come on, let's go to the pictures", so we'd say, "Oh, we're going to meet the Prime Minister" and off we'd go into Canberra and sit and watch the movies'.

Rob would not shirk, however, when the deliberations became serious. By the late 1970s, the two issues which had come to dominate the work of the NAC were the most vexed matters in Australian race relations: land rights and the call for a treaty. For all the criticisms levelled against it, the NAC did play an on-going role in ensuring these issues remained before government. However, in promoting them, the NAC risked its own credibility. It lacked the resources to consult widely in the Aboriginal community and the necessary political clout to make any real progress through negotiation with government.

By the early 1980s, the idea of a Treaty with Indigenous people was gathering some momentum. It had been first formally raised in 1975 in a motion in the Senate by Neville Bonner, Australia's first Indigenous federal parliamentarian. A second decisive step occurred several years later when a group of interested citizens formed an Aboriginal Treaty Committee chaired by Nugget Coombs, eminent public servant and long-standing supporter of Aboriginal people. On 25 August 1979 the Committee took out a one-page advertisement in *The National Times* newspaper with the opening words: 'We the undersigned Australians of European descent believe that the experience since 1788 has demonstrated the need for the status and rights of Aboriginal Australians and Torres Strait Islanders to be established in a Treaty, Covenant, or Convention freely negotiated with the Commonwealth of Australia by their representatives'.[22]

These words, which went to the heart of Australia's history of colonisation and dispossession, foreshadowed a divisive, decade-long debate about the legal recognition of Aboriginal rights. Rob lived through this debate, firstly in his capacity as a member of the NAC, and later as adviser to Gerry Hand during his tenure as Aboriginal Affairs Minister in the Hawke government.

The Senate Standing Committee which in 1983 extensively examined the issues surrounding a Treaty, highlighted the fundamental division which it raised. 'On the one hand', the Committee wrote, 'is the legal concept that this country was not conquered or ceded but peacefully settled, a concept that has served as the basis for the settled colony principle, whereby the law has regarded Australia at the time of settlement as *terra nullius* or land belonging to no one'.[23] The contrary view, representing Aboriginal opinion, combined traditional knowledge with a new wave of historical research which highlighted the existence of complex systems of social, cultural and religious networks and land tenure within Aboriginal society at the time of settlement. Drawing directly on the work of historian Henry Reynolds, the Committee debunked the idea of peaceful settlement: 'Aboriginal people set out to defend their lands and their society against the superior force of those Europeans dispossessing them of those lands which were the basis of their identity'.

In 1979, two years before Rob arrived at the NAC, the organisation endorsed its support for a Treaty at a meeting in Canberra. In response to the NAC resolution, Prime Minister Malcolm Fraser indicated the government's willingness to examine the concept, a commitment he repeated when addressing the December 1981 Annual Conference of the NAC, the first which Rob attended following his election.[24]

By the early 1980s, Rob Riley had become an eloquent advocate of the revisionist view of history and the moral obligation it placed on the country's leaders. Writing in the NAC newsletter, he took a swipe at the 'old' version of Australian history:

> Historians, however, hold to the belief that this occupation was as peaceful in intent, as it was inevitable. While abhorring the genocidal skills of Australia's first settlers they insist that the intention was never to brutally dispossess the Aboriginal people. This rationalisation however presents modern day white Australia with a dilemma. If the settlement of Australia was not an

aggressive invasion followed by forced occupation, they must accept a moral obligation to recognise the rights of the people that occupied the country beforehand, in retrospect at least. For only under the accepted terms of invasion and occupation would it be inevitable that such rights would be forfeited.[25]

His choice of such bold language is significant. It shows he had grasped the key historical experiences of Aboriginal people and framed them as a political struggle. But he gave no indication in this article that he appreciated just how threatening his newly acquired synthesis could be. The Treaty concept opened up a veritable minefield of constitutional and political issues: what form would a Treaty take, how legally binding would it be, and how could it be sold to a public ill-informed about Aboriginal history and unsympathetic to their rights as a people?

Buoyed by the initial indicators of support from the federal government, the NAC threw itself into the task of producing a draft document outlining its ideas. At a meeting on 12 November 1979, the NAC Executive formed a sub-committee to consult Aboriginal people and adopted the term 'Makarrata' — a Yolnu word from north-east Arnhem Land — in place of 'Treaty'. In a report to the NAC in June 1981 the level of organisational commitment was acknowledged: 'The Makarrata continues to be a major priority of the National Aboriginal Conference and the last year in particular has seen our resources, both physical and financial, heavily committed to bringing preparations for a final draft to a satisfactory conclusion'.[26]

In July 1980, following the sub-committee's first journey around Australia, the NAC issued its *Makarrata Report*. It called for recognition of prior ownership, compensation for losses of land and culture, the return of existing land occupied by 'the tribal people' and freehold title of all land upon which Aboriginal people live. It sought negotiations with the Australian government 'as an equal partner'. In essence, the Makarrata had become an all-embracing land rights treaty.

Yet some Aboriginal groups accused the NAC of watering down its commitment to the concept. For some, there were important differences between a Treaty and a Makarrata. In 1982 *Land Rights News* explained the emerging schism between advocates of the two concepts: 'A Treaty is an agreement between *nations*. A compact is an agreement between *parties* (groups of people)'. The former, the paper argued, would mean that government recognises Aborigines as a Nation; 'and Nations *own* land'. The latter means different things to different people and could be reinterpreted by succeeding governments.[27]

The emerging complexities over the concept only hardened the scepticism of the Fraser government. In March 1981, not long before Rob's election to the NAC, it stymied the organisation's aspirations for a Treaty. While accepting the idea of recognition of prior ownership, the government drew an ideological line against any notion of separate legal status for Aboriginal people, invoking the principle that they were 'part of one Australian nation'. Hence, the government 'cannot legitimately negotiate anything which might be regarded as a "treaty", implying as it does an internationally recognised agreement between two nations'.[28]

Despite the efforts of the government to bury the Treaty proposal, it would not go away. In 1983 the Senate Select Committee on Constitutional and Legal Affairs examined the call for a Treaty, formalising official concerns about its legal impacts. In its submission to the Committee, the NAC acknowledged legal arguments about the use of the word 'treaty' but supported its use in a domestic sense to describe an arrangement between Aborigines and the Commonwealth. The Committee rejected this view, but it did recommend the need for a compact between the Commonwealth and Aboriginal people and it foreshadowed a prominent role for the NAC in achieving this change. In his capacity as Deputy Chair of the NAC, Rob gave evidence to the Committee, outlining for the first time his frustration with the organisation: 'at times we have thought that because of the lack of resources, the lack of information and the lack of being able to research information in relation to the Makarrata, it was an impossible task'. For now, Rob seemed to be saying, the concept was beyond the capacities of the organisation. But he did not dismiss out of hand the prospect of achieving it, telling the Committee that if its preferred model of a legislative compact (using the race and external affairs powers of the Constitution) with Aboriginal people were to be put on the table, the NAC should be the representative body 'to handle the necessary consultation and negotiation with Aboriginal people'.[29]

In his early days with the organisation, Rob watched the intense focus on the land rights/Treaty issue with some underlying concerns. He was becoming intellectually committed to the ideas behind the claims of sovereignty, but as an urban Aboriginal person he wanted a broader agenda developed by the NAC — one that spoke to the specific issues of the dispossessed — and he was frustrated that one never really materialised. He always felt that too much emphasis was put on discussions about land rights and Makarratas that took days, weeks, months, and years and came to nothing. He worried that the land rights issue was never going to come to anything, and that it would not impact on the Aboriginal residents of East Perth.

Yet, the land rights issue continued to move at a snail's pace. With the slow demise of the Makarrata, discussions on land rights inside the NAC became 'very muddy'. According to Peter O'Brien, nobody in the NAC during the early 1980s knew or understood or had a vision for how it was actually going to work.

Towards the end of 1982, Rob was growing disillusioned with the organisation's lack of effectiveness. He was frustrated with the lack of government support. To be effective, he claimed, the NAC needed a team of researchers, legal advisers and support staff, not only in the national secretariat, but in the state branches as well.[30] Six months later he told the press that the organisation had 'been rendered a lame duck through lack of recognition by the state and federal governments'.[31] Meetings continued to be fraught with personality conflicts; they even had to be taped because members did not trust each other to get the minutes right.

Despite his waning optimism Rob continued to grow in stature within the NAC. He was made State Chair at the end of 1981 and he continued to make his presence felt on the national body. He was loud when he wanted to be; he had opinions on everything; he was very good at cutting to the chase and coming up with logical responses. He was always on top of any brief. In fact, he was an avid reader of all government reports dealing with Aboriginal affairs. And he impressed those around him with his open, passionate commitment to Aboriginal justice.

One of Rob's developing strengths was his ability to communicate information to the media. Peter O'Brien observed: 'Rob always had media skills from day one. He could front up to the media and say the most impressive things'.[32] He had the qualities journalists loved:

a concise and incisive message, a willingness to confront opponents, and an ability to convey authority through his statements. He strove to develop his command of language because he thought that this was how fights would be won. He maintained this view until the end of his career. Pat Dodson, who started working with Rob Riley in the early 1980s, acknowledges his friend's mastery with the media: 'Most of us were pretty inexperienced in terms of the media and I think Rob was the best at it in that early period'. Media skills were critical in an area like Aboriginal affairs where the lack of formal power had to be compensated for in some other way.

Through its periodic United Nations work, the NAC had discovered the power to embarrass government. More than any other single member of the NAC, Rob would demonstrate another avenue of influence: the power to make a noise in the press. First as Deputy Chair and then as Chair, Rob brought to the NAC a relish for engaging with the media and the skills to do the job. His naturally competitive personality made him a good match for ministers. He is remembered by Canberra-based journalist Kate Legge as being fast on his feet, politically deft and well liked in the press gallery.

Rob's skills in this area inspired other Aboriginal leaders. John Watson of the Kimberley described his influence:

> I never knew anybody as straight-talking as Mr Riley. He really put it to politicians. He was very strong. He might have been younger than me but I learnt a lot from him about arguing with gardias [whites]. I argued with gardias, but seeing him arguing with politicians he would say things and I'd be thinking, 'He'll go to jail for that'.

Rob had other qualities that quickly won him supporters within the NAC. Among its often squabbling personalities he commanded attention with his incisive oratory and calm authority. Rob's character came to the fore when discussion between NAC members became heated. Peter O'Brien observed:

> When the situation had developed into utter chaos, Rob would come through and say something quite simple and profound ... [the other members] would be at each other's throats, abusing each other and he would just say, 'Righto,

this is the situation' and he would actually calm these people down and get them back on track.

Rob would always be on the front foot, fearlessly taking on opponents, often with little regard for the consequences. He described mine owner Lang Hancock, owner of the *Sunday Independent*, as a 'racist mining magnate', and referred his newspaper to the Australian Press Council over a belligerent anti-land-rights editorial.[33] He was also adept at honing a sharp political line. When, in the 1981 Federal Budget, the funding to Aboriginal affairs was increased to $147 million, Rob sought to take some of the shine off the Fraser government's announced lift in funding. He argued that in comparison to total budget outlays, the $147 million represented just 0.003 per cent of government expenditure; 'it is only then that you realise how little the Federal Government is trying to accommodate the needs of Aboriginal people throughout Australia'.[34] He was becoming a Black politician to be reckoned with, and he enjoyed his growing profile.

His abilities were acknowledged with his election to the position of Deputy Chair in 1983 in only his second year with the NAC. But nothing changed the lack of status of the organisation. To the government, the NAC was little more than a political toy, worthy of only occasional formal recognition. One of these rare moments came on 16 February 1982, when the National Chairman, Roy Nichols, was invited to address the Prime Minister and cabinet. In his address, Nichols warned the government that the pressure for results in Aboriginal affairs was accelerating rapidly, and that Aborigines and Torres Strait Islanders were angry and frustrated over the failure of successive governments to come to terms with their problems.[35]

With Rob Riley's growing public profile came other kinds of attention. At the beginning of January 1983, Rob was visited by state police, who accused him of distributing a pamphlet which urged armed revolution by Aborigines. It included a sketch of an automatic weapon and crude instructions for making a self-igniting napalm bomb. No doubt the authorities had cause to be alarmed, especially if the pamphlet could be traced to a recognised Aboriginal group. Rob informed police the pamphlet was a political plant: an attempt to discredit the land rights campaign. Police claimed he was responsible for its circulation in Western Australia, a charge he vehemently denied. He told them the pamphlet had been mailed to him and other Aboriginal figures in Western Australia. He further explained: 'I had only shown it to Aborigines at consultative committee meetings to illustrate what people are prepared to do to misinform the public'. He decided to go public about the incident, telling the media: 'There is no doubt that some agency in Australia has produced the pamphlet to discredit Aboriginal organisations involved in the land rights struggle'.[36] The claim that some Aboriginal land rights activists were terrorists was bizarre, and Rob's counterclaim of a clandestine attempt to discredit the movement highlighted the undercurrents being stirred in extremist political circles.

At the beginning of 1983, a change in Aboriginal affairs was promised by the election of a rejuvenated ALP under the leadership of the charismatic Bob Hawke, the former ACTU leader. Hawke was armed with a new approach to government: one based around national unity and consensus. It was a style of leadership which might be able to find a resolution to the deep divisions in the community over Aboriginal issues. But it was also clear that Hawke aimed to entrench Labor in power in Canberra by blending caution and popular opinion into the mix of decision-making. Which side of this fault-line Aboriginal aspirations would fall was unclear.

Rob was guardedly optimistic about the federal Labor government's prospects. Attending a conference on legal pluralism in Vancouver in June 1983, he told the audience that the incoming Australian government offered hope that the 'political voice' of the NAC would be heeded: 'Under the former Conservative Government this did not happen and the NAC found itself obliged to pursue its campaign for equity and justice in the international arena in the belief that world indignation would force a change of attitude'.[37]

This was Rob's first overseas trip and, apart from his comments on the political situation, it marked a significant step in his evolution as an activist. Accompanied by Peter Yu and Margaret Mallard, NAC member for the Geraldton region, the delegation used the opportunity as another occasion to promote their cause internationally. Rob gave his reflections on the trip when, on his return, he was invited to speak to the Aboriginal Treaty Support Group of Western Australia. He told the gathering:

> One of the discoveries made by the first international NAC delegation was that basic facts about the Aboriginal situation were largely unknown outside these shores. A succession of governments, with the exception of the Whitlam Government, had approached international forums with the aim of showing how good it was in Australia for the Aborigine. They quoted increased spending, new projects and so on without feeling any obligation to accurately relay the corresponding picture of homelessness, joblessness and general oppression of the Aboriginal people. The NAC saw then that it had a responsibility ... to use every opportunity to expose the realities of our situation. Our trip to Vancouver was to be no exception.[38]

The new Australian government promised to address these long-standing injustices through its commitment to introduce national land rights, to increase funding to Aboriginal affairs, to examine the possibility of a treaty, and to expand the role and funding of the NAC, while also backing an inquiry into the organisation to examine ways to make it more effective. At much the same time, Labor returned to power in Western Australia, led by the youthful and energetic Brian Burke, after nine years in the wilderness. As opposition leader, Burke had given a strong commitment to land rights to a delegation of Central and Western Desert Aborigines in 1982. This new commitment from federal and state Labor governments ushered in a change in status for the NAC, and hence for Rob's role. Gradually, the NAC was drawn closer to the centre of power.

Land rights quickly occupied centre stage in Aboriginal affairs. In their initial embrace of national Aboriginal land rights, both the state and federal ALP had been influenced by the events at Noonkanbah. In the last days of the dispute, the ALP's federal spokesperson on Aboriginal affairs, Stewart West, publicly declared that a federal Labor government would solve the dispute by invoking the so-called 'race power' in the Constitution (based on the power conferred by the 1967 referendum for the federal government to act in the interests of Aboriginal people), and he went on to commit Labor to a national approach on the matter even in the face of acknowledging 'the probability of a divisive white backlash in Western Australia and Queensland on these matters'.[39]

However, consensus about land rights within the ALP proved elusive. The party was divided along factional and geographic lines. The commitment was strongest in Victoria, which was controlled by the party's left wing, and weakest in Western Australia, especially from the time Brian Burke became Labor leader in 1983.

Burke's approach to governing was a complex amalgam of populism, pragmatism and factional hatred. Deploying his background in journalism, he had successfully projected a 'good bloke' image: that of an ordinary man representing a housing commission constituency. His father, Tom Burke, had been a Labor member in federal parliament, and the son carried the scars of his father's battles with the party's left. Burke's allegiances were solidly with Labor's right-wing faction, a base from which he represented a new face of the Labor Party: pragmatic, shrewd and pro-business.[40]

None of these complexities were evident to Aboriginal leaders in the lead up to the 1983 state election. In the aftermath of Noonkanbah, Brian Burke worried that a softening on land rights might cost the party votes in what the Party hierarchy considered would be a close election. Rob Riley had predicted a year earlier that land rights would be a major state election issue,[41] and following the poll he maintained the Aboriginal vote 'was instrumental in the defeat of the Liberal Government'.[42]

The representatives of the Western Australian branch of the NAC — led by Rob Riley and Peter Yu — had tried to develop a working relationship with the ALP preceding the state election. Literally hours before the election campaign commenced, Burke and senior backbencher Peter Dowding came to an NAC meeting in Rob's office to reassure them of the Party's commitment should it win office. Burke said that he would be assuming the responsibility for Aboriginal affairs, such was the importance of the land rights issue. In addition, the government would appoint an inquiry into land rights and then proceed with legislation. Peter Dowding then jumped out of his chair and declared his total commitment: 'If Brian doesn't do it I'll resign'. Rob and Peter were reassured but sceptical.

On the other side of the political divide, the mining industry viewed with alarm the election of the Labor government in Western Australia.

The sector was infused with extremist views about the incoming government and its agenda. Peter Dowding, in his newly appointed role as Minister for Mines in the Burke government, recalls how the industry's lobbyists categorised the government as threatening the future of mining in the state 'because the Marxist-Leninist Labor party is in charge'.

Initially, federal Labor also approached its land rights agenda with enthusiasm. The newly installed federal Minister for Aboriginal Affairs, Clyde Holding, told his first national meeting with the NAC, at which Rob and Peter were present, that the government was rock solid on the issue. 'The principle of land rights', Holding told members, 'is non-negotiable ... we cannot in any way erode or whittle away our commitment to the principle'. He also conveyed a message from the Prime Minister to NAC members, letting them know 'of his firm personal commitment to your cause'. Rob, in his role of Deputy Chair, congratulated Holding for 'his sincere approach'.[43]

So began a frenzied two and a half years in Rob Riley's life: a merry-go-round of meetings, press conferences, and protests to try to secure advances on land rights and justice issues. Adding to the hectic pace was the need to fight simultaneously on both the federal and state political fronts. On the home front, Jeannie was left to bring up the children virtually alone, a 'political widow'.

In their home state, Rob Riley and Peter Yu had to provide oversight to the land rights inquiry which the Burke government established in May 1983 against the advice of Holding.[44] An inquiry posed certain risks for the state government; firstly it would provide a public platform for extremist groups to air their views, and secondly it risked raising expectations in the Aboriginal community that the NAC was now in a constructive engagement with a progressive government. For Burke, the political stakes were higher than simply managing Aboriginal aspirations. The inquiry was a pre-emptive move. Burke had a desire to keep the federal government out. He saw it as electorally unpopular for the federal government to move in on land rights in Western Australia, and a great loss of power to the state in terms of its mining and development.

Paul Seaman was charged with heading the Inquiry and was later joined by Deputy Chair Graham McDonald, Rob's old colleague from the ALS. Seaman's appointment was a bold one for Burke's government to make. He had a distinguished history of conducting litigation on behalf of Aboriginal people, including acting for Ernie Bridge in his challenge to the 1977 election result in the Kimberley, and he had also acted as counsel in the subsequent Electoral Act inquiry. Consequently, he was well regarded in the Aboriginal community and, in equal measure, viewed with suspicion in conservative political circles. He was forced to wait a long time to become a QC.

Nevertheless, at least one senior government minister believed that the Burke government expected Seaman to produce a politically palatable report. Clyde Holding claimed that there was a belief:

> that Seaman would recommend the automatic giving of reserves and areas of land to Aboriginal people and that at the same time he would recommend against any form of Aboriginal control over mining in respect of Aboriginal lands. I did not share his optimism in that. I thought he was trying to read into that situation his own expectations of what would have been, for him, a politically acceptable formula.[45]

If Holding's assessment is accurate, then clearly Burke did not fully grasp the nature of the person he had appointed. Seaman was about to commence a quiet crusade which would have national repercussions for the direction of the land rights debate.

The Inquiry had a rocky start. Within a few weeks, Rob threatened to boycott it unless the government guaranteed greater Aboriginal involvement in planning the Inquiry.[46] In July 1983 substantial money and assistance was allocated to enable Aboriginal communities to make submissions to the Inquiry.

Such was the scale and complexity of the land rights issue that the Seaman Inquiry came to have significance beyond Western Australia. No other process offered the potential for such detailed findings on the issues involved, and especially on the highly contentious matter of the right of veto over mining. Confirming its strategic importance, Clyde Holding later told federal Parliament that 'the Seaman Aboriginal Land Inquiry is of tremendous relevance. Our duty is to get legislation on land rights properly based. We are waiting on the outcome of that inquiry'.[47]

However, the findings were months away. In the meantime federal Labor kept good its promise to establish an inquiry into the NAC, which it did in July 1983. It appointed highly respected public servant and promoter of the treaty committee, H.C. 'Nugget' Coombs, to conduct the inquiry. Holding offered reassuring words to the NAC about the conduct of the Inquiry; it was to address long-standing concerns over the structural weaknesses in the organisation. He left no doubt about his commitment to its future. The Conference, he said, would 'play a very substantial role', alongside the Department for Aboriginal Affairs, in working up the government's approach to land rights, 'and in securing the kinds of political answers that we need'.[48]

The Inquiry proceeded without disrupting the NAC. Rob was closely involved. He and Peter Yu gave evidence to the official hearings and Rob was in regular personal contact with Coombs. However, behind the scenes Coombs was devising a very different view of the NAC than foreshadowed in his original brief. Rob sensed that Coombs had a predetermined agenda.

While land rights and the future of the NAC were dominating the government's agenda in Aboriginal affairs, the running sore of police violence in Western Australia was about to explode onto the national stage. In the remote Pilbara town of Roebourne, described by one journalist in the early 1970s as 'the saddest place in the North' because of its growing 'dispossessed black population',[49] a tragic incident occurred which would shape race relations throughout Australia for the next decade, and sweep up Rob Riley into yet another campaign on police violence.

On the night of 28 September 1983, sixteen-year-old John Pat died in the juvenile cell of the town's police station lock-up from 'closed head injuries'. Pat was typical of many Aboriginal youth in remote Western Australian towns. Born to a teenage mother and a father who drank too much, Pat's family life was marked by poverty, dislocation, early school leaving and unemployment. It was a background destined to get him into trouble.

The Roebourne police closely patrolled the areas of the town frequented by Aborigines, and at night, homes in the area known as the Aboriginal Village were regularly spotlighted by police.[50] This surveillance had long been deeply resented by local Aborigines and had become the catalyst for the downward spiral in race relations. As a consequence of continual and intrusive surveillance, Aborigines were subjected to an endless round of arrests, mainly for offences relating to alcohol and fighting.

In the three years before his death, young John Pat had been trapped in the web of racial antagonisms between police and his own people. He had been arrested several times for liquor offences and for assaulting police officers. He claimed to have been provoked by police on these occasions and, with no permanent ALS representative in the town, had pleaded guilty each time.

Just what occurred on the night of 28 September was to be the subject of claim and counter claim up to and following the Royal Commission into Aboriginal Deaths in Custody, which in 1991 investigated the issues surrounding Pat's death. One thing was not in dispute: a fight took place outside the Victoria Hotel between off-duty police officers who had been drinking in the hotel and several Aboriginal men, one of whom was Pat. One version of events claims that the fight broke out when one of the police officers told an Aboriginal man to 'piss off'.[51] It is surprising that so much else is in dispute given the very public nature of the brawl. Much was at stake: the possible prosecution of members of the local police for manslaughter, and the exposure of the racist culture rampant in sections of the police force.

On the night of John Pat's funeral, a riot broke out when Police Commissioner Leitch ordered the very men who, Aborigines alleged, were responsible for his murder to go on duty with other officers to control drinking in the hotel. Within weeks, Aborigines in Roebourne were loudly proclaiming that the police were guilty of Pat's death. They believed he had 'died as a result of police action during a brawl outside the Victoria Hotel'.[52] From this point, John Pat's death became a symbol of injustice and oppression for Aboriginal people across the nation and a rallying cry for emerging demands for an inquiry into Aboriginal deaths in custody.

For Rob Riley, Pat's death was reason enough to step up the campaign against police violence which he had begun several years earlier at the ALS. Rob was familiar with this ground. Ironically, just days before Pat's death in September 1984, he had dispatched a press statement critical of the police for their 'hypocritical' outrage at the screening of a

NAC WA delegates: Rob Riley, Margaret Mallard and Peter Yu, early 1980s.

Robert Riley in his late twenties, early 1980s.

Rob Riley and Peter Yu in Broome, c. 1983. The two met during the Noonkanbah dispute and went on to become close friends and comrades in the struggle for Aboriginal rights. Both were members of the National Aboriginal Conference in the early to mid-1980s.

Rally protesting the death in custody of John Pat, September 1983. Pat's death became a focal point for the outrage of Aboriginal people over their treatment by police and prison officers.

controversial ABC drama — *Scales of Justice* — depicting police corruption. Speaking with all his ALS experience and in a barely disguised tone of indignation, he said: 'Aboriginal legal agencies have plenty of evidence of police brutality and corruption in relation to Aborigines ... those who champion the squeaky clean image of the police force had never been threatened with firearms, been beaten up in a cell or forced to give "favours" to avoid a prosecution'.[53]

Sharp words: and ones which ensured Rob Riley's name was kept uppermost in the minds of many police officers.

~~~~~~

Throughout much of the second half of 1983 Rob worked tirelessly to bring a broader voice to the NAC by linking it with other Aboriginal organisations and especially with the Federation of Land Councils. This was groundbreaking, if unheralded, work. It was in the development of these linkages that the modern Aboriginal rights movement became fully formed. Part of his thinking on the need to broaden the reach of the NAC was influenced by Sally Weaver, a visiting Canadian anthropologist who undertook an academic study of the failings of the NACC and who acted as unofficial advisor to some of the members of the NAC. She later sent Rob a signed copy of her 1983 paper 'Australian Aboriginal Policy: Aboriginal Pressure Groups or Government Advisory Bodies?' which he kept among his personal papers.

Weaver's study examined the challenges facing Aboriginal people when federal governments attempted to stymie 'the protest mode in Aboriginal politics' by sponsoring national Aboriginal organisations in ways that were designed to contain and manage them.[54] In other words, Aboriginal organisations like the NAC would have to strike out on their own or be rendered irrelevant like the NACC. Certainly, Rob was trying to position the NAC to shake off its past irrelevancy and become a more influential player in Aboriginal politics. Unity was the key to his thinking.

Nothing served to highlight the underlying weakness in Aboriginal politics more than the divisions between the various organisations, especially those existing between the NAC and the land councils. The Federation of Land Councils was formed to provide an organised voice for its constituents. By the early 1980s, considerable bad blood existed between the Federation and the NAC. From the Federation's perspective, the NAC had not given it any support nor any protection against the vilification that went on in the corridors of power.

Rob linked up with another emerging Aboriginal leader, former Catholic priest Pat Dodson, to forge historically important links between the two arms of the Aboriginal rights movement. Ordained in 1974, Dodson had recently transformed his commitment to the Aboriginal cause by becoming Director of the Central Lands Council. Even at this early stage of his career, he combined a striking physical presence with an intellectual and philosophical rigour that increasingly placed him at the centre of the Aboriginal political movement.

The two emerging leaders shared a common aim: to get more power in their relationship with government and a stronger strategic direction to the objectives which should drive the rights movement. Rob took the view 'that all these people in together made the strength of the Aboriginal movement'. Rob's role was crucial in creating this unified force. Secretary General at the NAC, Les Malezer, remembers: 'He was the person that could pull all these people together and hold them together and feel united. He was great at keeping people positive and supporting a common goal'. Rob had to stake some of his credibility within the NAC in forging these relationships, because not everyone in the organisation welcomed the creation of this broader alliance. In fact, on occasions Rob had to go out on a limb within the NAC to get a hearing for the land councils in policy processes. The testiness within the NAC was partly because some members feared a reduction in the organisation's status, but it also reflected a difference in cultures between the two arms of the Aboriginal movement. As Dodson recalls, the 'roughness' of the remote areas was foreign to the experience of the mostly urban-based NAC members: 'We went to battle for people who lived in humpies ... and to stop the pastoralists from locking their gates and shooting Aborigines' dogs'.

However, Rob was learning as much from this process as he was contributing to it. In linking up with people like Pat Dodson and the Federation of Land Councils, he was discovering another dimension of the land rights aspirations of Aboriginal people. At Pat's invitation, Rob attended a number of the Federation's meetings. These were held under 'Federation rules': in the bush, around a camp with a swag, sitting on the ground, eating from a common kitchen. It was the Federation's way of demonstrating that 'if we're talking about land we sit on the land'. Such occasions could only have stirred Rob's passion for the cause. However, to these meetings Rob brought the position of the urban dispossessed and how to deal with their issues. Through such linkages, a united Aboriginal voice was being formed.

Through Pat Dodson, Rob was also introduced to a wider network of Aboriginal political strategists. The Northern and Central Land Councils, in particular, were influential. As the key advocates for the principles of the Northern Territory land rights model, they had spent considerable time perfecting their abilities to deal with the lobbying process in Canberra.

The importance of the emerging alliance between the NAC and the Federation of Land Councils is described by Pat Dodson: 'When Riley came onto the scene we were able to work out a strategy for how best to engage other organisations and how best to orchestrate our lobby on the federal government in a far more concerted and consistent way'. This involved ensuring 'that all bases in the parliament were covered': monitoring the committees dealing with Aboriginal affairs; ministers' offices; factional heads in the ALP; ALP conferences and the federal Liberal opposition. The outcome of this effort was to ensure that 'policy positions were being set in a way that wasn't detrimental to us and to provide arguments to those who were supportive of our views'.

But how unified was this emerging voice in Aboriginal affairs? There were contradictory signs in the early to mid 1980s. On the one hand not all Aboriginal organisations embraced a united political voice with the same enthusiasm as did parts of the NAC and the land councils. Beyond them were a range of Aboriginal community service organisations which had a more closed political culture. And, as mentioned, urban-based Aborigines had a tendency to political infighting largely absent among traditional communities because of the presence of cultural rules emanating from responsibility for land. Still, Rob saw the potential for a pan-Aboriginal voice to deliver good outcomes for communities.

A positive indicator of the cooperation achieved in Aboriginal politics was a formal agreement struck in early October 1983 between the executive of the NAC and the National Federation of Land Councils for a cooperative and joint approach to pursue Aboriginal rights.[55] It was an historic agreement uniting for the first time Aboriginal people in the city and the country in a political framework. The rapport between Rob Riley and Pat Dodson and their combined capacity to realise the political importance of unification was central to the process. In practical terms, the agreement resulted in the establishment of an Aboriginal Land Rights Steering Committee — formally combining representatives from both organisations — to try to bring greater conceptual clarity to an Aboriginal position on land rights. Rob would have had a major input into this, representing the NAC. The report of their deliberations was subsequently published as a discussion paper in February 1984.[56] The 80-page document is a detailed consideration of the moral, legal and political issues involved in land rights as perceived by the Aboriginal leadership. The approach taken was grounded in historical, if not political, realism:

> It may be argued that the Aboriginal people as a *sovereign nation* were deprived of the continent of Australia in 1788, and have continued as a sovereign nation who seek the restoration of their lands ... This starting point leads inevitably to the conclusion that compensation must be paid for the harm done, for the culture lost, and for the deprivation of land, payable to the successors in title to the sovereign nation concerned. This argument proceeds upon the assumption that sovereignty has never been lost, since the contest has never been the subject of any resolution or treaty, yielding up such sovereignty.[57]

As expressed in the paper, sovereignty and the need for compensation became the twin pillars of the emerging unified Aboriginal position on land rights. By the early 1980s, the matter of compensation had gained added intensity for Rob, who by now had researched parts of his family history and felt a personal sense of responsibility for what his relations had suffered. However, the new federal Labor government was increasingly sensitive about these ideas, especially the claim of sovereignty. Minister Holding 'expressly rejected' the Committee's position, categorising it as 'politically unacceptable' because it challenged 'the foundation of and the existence of the Australian government'.[58] Battlelines were already being drawn.

Rob was also a member of the Steering Committee on Land Rights set up by Holding soon after the Hawke government's election in 1983. It comprised senior members of the NAC and representatives from the various land councils. Charles Perkins, Secretary of the Department of

Aboriginal Affairs, attended meetings along with Holding. The stated purpose of the Steering Committee was to 'decide the policy issues in the national land rights legislation'.[59] The Steering Committee was assisted by a panel of lawyers to advise it on options and for drafting the actual Land Rights Bill. To all appearances, it was a powerful body. At the time of its establishment it was envisaged that legislation would be ready for presentation to the Australian parliament by August 1984. However, the final version of such legislation required the approval of the full NAC membership.

Land rights continued to dominate Rob's efforts at the state level as well. In December 1983, the state NAC, of which he was Chair, prepared a submission to the Seaman Inquiry. Rob immersed himself in this task, working long hours and often late into the night to help put the submission together.

By this stage, Rob's position on land rights reflected the views discussed and later published in the NAC discussion paper. They were based around historical claims of sovereignty and the attendant legal/moral issues flowing from occupation and dispossession. The Western Australia branch adopted this as the framework for their submission and applied it in a political context: as the rights had never been ceded, Aborigines had a 'right' to the land of Western Australia from which legislation was needed to cover 'the moral right of Aborigines to reparation and compensation for their dispossession, exploitation and other injustices suffered by them'. More than anything it was intended as a philosophical statement offered to Seaman as a guide to formulating his recommendations.

Largely ignored by the Western Australian press, the submission was seized upon by *The Australian* newspaper which, over several days, ridiculed the contents in a front page article, an editorial and cartoon. 'Aborigines lay claim to all of Western Australia' screamed the front-page headline. The accompanying article stated that the NAC 'has claimed on behalf of the Aboriginal people all of Western Australia and its waters up to the 200-mile international limit'. It did not acknowledge the context in which the statement was made.[60] The paper treated the submission's philosophical statement of principle as an actual land rights claim and, hence, categorised the submission as the most 'all-embracing' made to an Australian government by an Aboriginal organisation. The next day, the paper's editorial accused the submission's authors of stupidity and of inciting a white backlash against land rights. It argued that the sympathy of the broader Australian community 'will evaporate if claims which could only be met in a dream world are made to such bodies as the West Australian Aboriginal Land Inquiry'. Such 'ludicrous' claims, the paper moralised, would not only fuel anti-land-rights campaigners, 'but ordinary people must begin to doubt the integrity of the NAC and its supporters'.[61] To complete its denigration of the NAC submission, *The Australian's* cartoonist, 'Mitchell', depicted a crowd in central Perth falling about in uproarious laughter at hearing the news of the land 'claim' and with a lone Aborigine trying to gain a hearing amid the hilarity with the words, 'seriously though'.[62]

Overlooked in *The Australian's* denigration of the submission was an important point central to the Noongar experience: the intergenerational impacts of colonisation. Rob, like most of those involved in the submission, could draw on first-hand experience of the plight of their families when commenting that:

> The effects of colonisation are now being experienced by Aboriginal people throughout the state. The socio-economic position of Aboriginal people is not the result of maladjustments in the social system, such as those which create inequality in the general population. Rather the position of Aborigines has been created and is sustained today by the continuing processes of colonisation and dispossession.[63]

These were significant comments to place on the public record. Rob and others were warning of a social crisis brewing: its incubator the sense of hopelessness pervading those living on reserves, in fringe camps, or in East Perth. By the early 1980s, the crisis was beginning to manifest itself among jobless school dropouts. Although Rob would develop a more powerful language with which to describe their alienation, he had signalled that he would champion the dispossessed.

The warning about mounting intergenerational disadvantage was ignored. There was little time to worry over this because of the pressing need to respond to the treatment the Western Australia NAC had received over the land rights submission. Outraged that they had been set up by the media, Rob accused them of 'lending strong-arm support to an already well orchestrated anti-land-rights campaign'.[64] The Western

Australia branch issued an immediate complaint to the Australian Press Council which was not resolved until six months later. Ever the toothless tiger, the Council, upon hearing all the evidence, found that the article was 'erroneous, resulting in the public being misinformed'. However, the Council 'did not believe this was done deliberately or mischievously, but it did result from a misrepresentation of a complex and lengthy submission'. The Council merely censured the newspaper.[65]

It would be easy to conclude that Rob and the others working on the submission paid insufficient attention to the way in which they presented their case and the possible misinterpretation it might receive in a highly charged political climate on land rights. After all, the submission acknowledged 'the public's feeling of resentment to them'. In this context, Rob may have allowed his passionate convictions to override his political judgement. Peter O'Brien believes that the submission was symptomatic of the continual dilemma facing NAC members: the need to present positions to their own constituency in a forceful manner while, at the same time, trying to influence the debate within mainstream politics. He believes the NAC often did not get the balance right.

On the other hand, a significant issue arising out of the Western Australia branch's grilling at the hands of the media was the very point raised in their submission, namely the need for an urgent public education campaign. In its preparation of the submission, the Western Australia branch was acutely aware that reference to concepts such as 'dispossession', 'genocide' and 'colonisation' were foreign to most Australians. Consequently: 'There needs to be a concerted effort by the government to mount a real program of public awareness which will adequately and seriously support the Aboriginal point of view on land rights'.[66] As a media-savvy activist, Rob was frustrated about the obstacles the Aboriginal rights movement encountered in obtaining media coverage to present their case. It was ironic, to say the least, that the Western Australia branch became a victim of the very lack of understanding they were calling on government to address.

The NAC submission was only one of several hundred submitted to the Inquiry. Aboriginal organisations, communities and individuals from throughout the state petitioned Paul Seaman in an overwhelming demonstration that land rights and access by miners were grassroots concerns. The NAC may have provided the political context, but out among the disparate Aboriginal communities there was overwhelming support for this political struggle. Rob was familiar with all these submissions, having, at some point, gained a copy of most of them.[67] The submission from the Djugerari community on Cherrabun Station in the South Kimberley gives the flavour of this grassroots movement for land rights. Spokesman Warford Badjiman told Seaman,

> We are Walmadjeri people, we speak Walmadjeri and we are all looking at Walmadjeri country. We are all the same people. If our mob got some land Walmadjeri relatives from other communities and Fitzroy [Crossing] would come and visit and work. People want to get out of town and back to their own country ... We would like freehold land for ever and ever ... We want to picnic and hunt anywhere, even National Parks. We would like to be asked if National Park can be made. We want our language taught in schools as well as English. We think mining mob should see our local organisation (Marra Worra Worra) first and then they would arrange meetings with the right mob. We can show companies where not to go, and we can put this on a map ... We don't want any big holes made in hills, usually they are important. If a mining company is working we don't want them to come too close to where we live. They mustn't stay for ever. We should get a royalty if a mining mob find anything.

Rob does not record his feelings about the submissions but the expression of such direct and assertive views must surely have highlighted the purpose behind the fight for land rights: it was to represent people like Warford Badjiman. With so many submissions from Aboriginal communities calling for land rights, the conservative claim, long propagated by Sir Charles Court, that their aspirations were the work of 'stirrers' was exposed as the scaremongering it had always been.

In remote parts of Western Australia, Paul Seaman was completing the transformation of his understanding of the depth of Aboriginal attachment to the land. His was a journey of self-discovery as well as investigation. His willingness to see the world through Aboriginal eyes stood in stark contrast to the historical denial and racial antipathy of most whites at the time. His close contact with Aboriginal communities brought some emotionally affecting experiences. At One Arm Point, several hundred kilometres north of Broome, he was taken out to an island the community regarded as part of their traditional land. The party left in two boats in the early evening under cover of moonlight and across a sparkling silver sea. When they arrived on the island one of his guides alighted from the boat and immediately glowed with pride 'like a woman with a child'. On the return journey, strong currents threatened danger, which was averted only by the intimate knowledge his guides had of the local conditions. It seemed impossible not to acknowledge that this was Aboriginal country.

Similarly in the Western Desert Paul Seaman was confronted, like few whites ever had been, with traditional cultural ties to land. In an area just below the Gibson Desert, in a locality whites had given the nondescript name of Well 33, Seaman met the Western Desert people. Arriving by light plane in the dark, guided by a line of spinifex torch fires, the travelling party was greeted by a big mob. A night of singing and dancing by firelight followed, after which custom dictated where everyone slept. In the morning, all the people appeared ready for the business of relaying their evidence to the Inquiry. Proceedings were nearly derailed when one of the accompanying local white officials, familiar with Aboriginal protocols, ventured into an area held to be sacred and commenced taking photographs. The Aboriginal people became distressed at the site being mistreated in this manner and invoked the power of a mythical being which would bring destruction upon them. The situation was retrieved only by the official handing over his camera and being escorted from the site.

———

Meanwhile, the federal ALP was finalising the framework of its approach to land rights which Clyde Holding announced in a speech to parliament on 8 December 1983. By this time, New South Wales, under the Wran Labor government, was about to introduce land rights legislation covering that state, and South Australia had undertaken a similar measure in 1981. Queensland, Western Australia, Victoria and Tasmania were without legislation. National land rights legislation, in addition to its application to these states, would ensure consistency and continuity of approach.

These continued to be Holding's aims. But Holding placed them in a broader context. In what was arguably the most expansive and inspiring declaration of political intent in Aboriginal affairs to date, Holding sponsored a motion to Parliament outlining 'a new set of principles' to guide race relations in Australia. The specific five principles on land rights were included as part of this broader agenda. The goal of this agenda, Holding announced, was 'a Government of national reconciliation'. In addition to land rights, the government undertook to work towards 'real justice and equality' for Aboriginal people; to recognise the 'pain and anguish' of children removed from their parents under assimilation policies; to value Aboriginal culture; to address the crises in schooling and health and the national need to come to terms with the past. This commitment to reconciliation, Holding promised, would usher in 'a new phase in black–white relationships in this country'.[68] To complete the impression of the opening up of an exciting new era in Aboriginal affairs, Holding reiterated the central role to be played by the NAC: 'On the great issues of policy, I expect the NAC to advise me and I expect to be guided by that advice'.

The year could not have ended on a more hopeful note. Yet aspects of the land rights issue troubled Rob. He sensed the battle was being lost in the media. Through the public hearings to the Seaman inquiry, the media was giving publicity to the often extremist anti-land-rights views of organisations representing miners and pastoralists and their supporters in the Liberal and Country parties. In November, Rob publicly called upon the Commonwealth and Western Australian governments to back up their land rights initiatives with a public awareness campaign, accusing both governments of failing to counteract the 'spread of confusion and fear about the land rights issue'.[69] The publicity he received generated a letter of support from the Minister. Holding wrote: 'you can be assured ... that the issues you have raised are currently matters being considered by the Government and in which I will be seeking the full involvement of the NAC'.[70]

As Rob clearly understood, the need for a public awareness campaign was growing more urgent. Land rights were beginning to be exploited by talkback radio, a new form of political discourse steadily growing in popularity. Local Perth talkback identity and *Sunday Times* columnist Howard Sattler, one of an emerging breed of commercial radio's right-wing populists, focused on the land rights issue in his column of 20 November 1980. Sattler began with the high-minded, if conservative statement that: 'We owe nothing to Aborigines except equality of opportunity'. However, he then continued by painting a picture that would inevitably have alarmed many a reader: 'first Ayers Rock, tomorrow ... who knows ... maybe they'll declare your street and your house a sacred site'. As was his custom, Rob couldn't allow such a wrong claim to go unchallenged. He rang Sattler's show to challenge his views which, as it transpired, simply became grist for Sattler's next newspaper column, which he focused specifically around the call he had received from Rob, 'one of my most vocal critics'.[71] The encounter was an early lesson on the new media formula: presenters laid down the terms of 'debate' and controlled its course. 'Mr Riley did not want to pursue the argument', Sattler enthused, as if claiming a verbal victory, that equality of opportunity, not land rights, was the most important issue facing Aborigines. Moreover, 'over 85 per cent of callers supported my stand on the issue'. Riley and Sattler would cross swords many times in the coming decade, their exchanges conforming to much the same pattern. Rob would ring in, compelled to defy what he and many others saw as Sattler's brand of inflammatory opinion and populist stereotyping of Aboriginal issues. The format was well-suited to Sattler's particular style, and while critics would often verbally spar with him, they were rarely able to score points. It was testimony to Rob's commitment and competitive spirit that he continually entered the fray knowing he was on a hiding to nothing.

As if talkback radio was not enough of a challenge to rational debate on land rights, the extremist League of Rights added yet another layer. Throughout 1983 and 1984, the League was very active across Australia, but especially in country Western Australia and in outer suburban centres where they gave public addresses on their anti-land-rights stance. National Director Eric Butler and Queensland State Director Geoff McDonald travelled Western Australia with an updated version of Cold War rhetoric: land rights was a communist plot and the Aboriginal rights movement had been infiltrated by Marxists.[72] Strangely, Rob did not draw particular public attention to the League's activities, though he was fully aware of them. In the early 1980s he attended one of their meetings in the country town of Northam, north of Perth. The League had hired the town hall, where about thirty locals were in attendance. A look of shocked surprise overcame the organisers as Rob and a few colleagues walked in and sat down. Rob understood the speakers' messages to be the last gasp of 1930s biological racism. While contemptuous of their beliefs, he saw the League as a sideshow to the main game of fighting the mining industry and its political supporters.

The rise of a politics of fear over land rights was only one issue unsettling Rob at the end of 1983. The second concerned the drifting apart of the federal and state efforts on land rights. Rob raised the issue. There was little public comment at the time on the obvious ambiguity of the two governments producing parallel legislative frameworks. In early December Rob wrote to both Burke and Holding about the NAC's concerns. To Holding he wrote: 'It now seems that neither Government is willing to confide in nor have confidence in the other. The N.A.C. members in W.A. consider that this situation is putting at risk the ambition of both Governments and of the Aboriginal people to have Land Rights granted in this State'. Rob urged Holding to develop a more cooperative approach to achieving uniformity of legislation.[73] In a separate press release he referred to fractures in Hawke's consensus politics regarding land rights.[74]

Rob's letter to Premier Burke was written in a different tone, hinting at perceived personal differences between the two. Rob had been sceptical about Burke's commitment to land rights. After an opening salvo at the emerging drift in state–federal policy on land rights, Rob wrote:

> The excitement at your announcement of the state land Inquiry has faded in the light of the confusion that has emerged as to its direction and final intent. Members of the state Branch, attending meetings of Aboriginal communities around the State, have become aware of growing disenchantment and doubt ... If we are to be criticised as 'one issue zealots', then so be it. We can make no apologies for concentrating on an issue which is at the very heart of Aboriginal hopes and dreams for a better life by way of a more equitable share of the responsibilities and benefits of equal citizenship.[75]

Rob also raised with Premier Burke his worries about 'the barrage of anti-land-rights propaganda in the media' and the need for a public education campaign. Several days later, he received a reassuring letter from the Premier which affirmed his view that complementary state/

federal legislation offered the best protection to Aboriginal people; Burke said he was in continual dialogue about this with the Commonwealth. He also informed Rob that he had set aside money to counteract the 'irrational and ill-informed Land Rights propaganda'.[76]

As events unfolded the next year, Rob's feelings of unease about the underlying political climate proved to be correct.

~~~~~~~~

Meanwhile, in January 1984 Paul Seaman issued a discussion paper which jolted the land rights issue to the forefront of public debate. Although he clearly signalled that existing freehold titles were safe, Seaman advocated, among other things, that Aborigines be granted inalienable freehold title to land and that they should have the power to veto mining on their lands. A power of veto was guaranteed to raise the ire of the mining industry, but Seaman believed it was necessary to be upfront about the issue and to confront the powerful industry lobby groups.[77] In his discussion paper he offered the following rationalisation for a veto:

> It seems to me that Aboriginal land owners who have the power to permit or veto mining development have every opportunity to protect their concerns and to control the social impact which results from development. They have the opportunity to provide by contract for their 'compensation' and for payments in the nature of 'royalties'.[78]

Complementing his clear preference for the right of veto was the need to revamp the Aboriginal Heritage Act which, he wrote, 'offered weak protection ... [and] no realistically enforceable legal protection in its present form'. Hearings had revealed to him 'the most profound anguish' caused by 'the desecration of certain sites'.[79] In these and other statements on key issues, Seaman had served up a political *tour de force* on land rights; but not necessarily a comprehensive one. Rob offered his assessment on the discussion paper in an interview with the media. In his capacity as Western Australia NAC Chair, he said that Seaman had not completely fulfilled the organisation's expectations. While acknowledging some positives in the paper, missing was the exemption of pastoral leases from land claims and the matter of compensation for the dispossessed. The latter was shaping up as a central plank in the framework of the Aboriginal rights movement's view of a just land rights settlement.[80]

Miners, on the other hand, condemned the discussion paper. Duncan Bell, from the Chamber of Mines in Western Australia, who would emerge as one of the key spokesmen in the miners' anti-land-rights cause, drew attention to Seaman's advocacy of the veto as the prime focus of the industry's concern. 'It would', he said, 'have harsh consequences for the economy'.[81] For now, he held in check a fully fledged attack on the land rights cause.

Behind the scenes, the release of the discussion paper mobilised the mining lobby into devising a strategy to persuade the ALP to drop its commitment to introducing state and federal legislation. Their opposition had been brewing for several years. From the time Hugh Morgan took over as president of the Australian Mining Industry Council in 1981, he provided much of the ideological backbone to the campaign by arguing that the industry had to reclaim its legitimacy from its opponents. To do so, miners had to 'rediscover the religious basis' of their activity: 'miners could only counter religious arguments for land rights with religious arguments of their own'.[82]

The miners were on fertile ground in opposing the land rights agenda. For decades the industry had presented itself as essential to Australia, and therefore mining lobbyists found it relatively easy to sell the message that what was in the interests of developers was in the interests of Australians.

The first shot in the miners' campaign was devised by the Chamber of Mines. On 9 March 1984 a full-page advertisement defending the mining industry's economic contribution to the state appeared in the press; the $3 billion in revenue and the $100 million in royalties. The advertisement — run over several weeks and supported by similar radio material — depicted a cheque symbolically written out to 'the people of Western Australia' beneath a banner headline which read, 'Every time our mining industry makes a successful discovery, we all strike it rich'. Only by inference was their opposition to land rights mentioned through invoking 'the principle of Crown ownership'. A separate advertisement, more dramatic in its tone, was run several times from 7 April. It was headlined: 'Beware future prosperity hangs in the balance' and featured the scales of justice weighing 'security' in perfect balance with 'crown ownership'. This 'balance', this 'democratic principle', central to Crown ownership of land, the Chamber asserted in the accompanying 'advertorial', would be undermined by land rights because 'all rights in land should be equal'; minerals below the ground belong to 'all the people'. It was an appeal to fairness with an accompanying threat to the loss of continued prosperity should Crown ownership pass to Aboriginal ownership. Run to coincide with the Seaman Inquiry hearings, it is hard to avoid the judgement that the purpose of the campaign was to condition the public perceptions against the Report's eventual findings, in light of the controversial pro-land-rights perspectives which had emanated from the discussion paper.

As events later unfolded, the first phase of the miners' campaign was a softening-up tactic designed to reinforce the historic ties to the benefits of developmentalism. It was a foretaste of a comprehensive campaign which Rob came to view as linking fear, politics and land rights. Its impact had already been felt. Holding acknowledged as much to the March 1984 NAC meeting, telling members: 'What is happening in Western Australia and the pressure that is being applied by the mining companies are doing a lot of damage in the land rights area'.[83]

Indeed, the damage was more multi-layered then Holding acknowledged. The first phase of the miners' publicity campaign coincided with the efforts of a number of conservative political leaders. The Western Australian Liberal leader at the time was Bill Hassell, whose path Rob had crossed in his days at the ALS. Hassell painted an alarming picture, warning in March 1984 that the granting of such rights would 'do untold damage to this State', which he listed as economic destruction, a racist backlash and a divided society.[84] The following day, Rob tackled Hassell's views head-on, dismissing them as 'wild and unsubstantiated' and accusing the opposition leader of declining to put in a submission to the Seaman Inquiry because, unable to be specific, his anti-land-rights views were 'based simply on racist grounds'.[85] Rob accused Hassell of appearing to 'believe that mere repetition of wild and groundless allegations will make the public accept them as facts'.[86]

The conservative press had also been galvanised by the simmering anti-land-rights campaign and duly came to the industry's defence, reinforcing the concerns Rob had previously raised about the propaganda effect of the media. Foremost among the cheer squad was the influential *Bulletin*, which in a series of articles abandoned any pretence at objectivity to argue that land rights amounted to national economic surrender: without mining and mining-related investment 'the rest of the Australian manufacturing industry is exposed as a sheltered employment agency'.[87]

The pace of events quickened. In April 1984 the Coombs Report was released with its key finding that the NAC had failed to perform. Few could question Coombs's intellectual commitment to working to find effective approaches to the problem of Aboriginal governance.[88] In light of previous findings on the NAC it is not surprising Coombs found a range of failings in the organisation. His favoured model for Aboriginal self-management — a congress based around regional assemblies integrated with the existing department of Aboriginal Affairs (in other words the foundation model for ATSIC) — had some compelling logic. More contentious was his recommendation that the NAC be abolished immediately, with no interim organisation, until negotiations produced a new structure.

In the opening sentence to his report Coombs laid out the case for change: 'There has been almost unanimous agreement among Aborigines with whom I have been able to consult, that the NAC in its present form is ineffective as an instrument of Aboriginal political influence or action'. The organisation was, he said, unlikely to develop into a political instrument with which Aboriginal groups and communities would identify or one which would be capable of providing Ministers with sound advice.[89] Coombs believed the failings of the organisation could be explained by a lack of adequate resources provided by government and inexperience on the part of many members. While he did not single out inadequacies in the leadership of the NAC, he privately thought that it 'seems to lack leaders with political and executive capacity'.[90] Publicly, he wrote: 'In the conduct of its own affairs the NAC's performance has also been disappointing; being marked by its inability to manage staff, by a failure to mobilise expertise, by poor communication with communities and other Aboriginal organisations and by periodic bouts of destructive internal dissension'.[91]

In hindsight, Coombs did not fully analyse the possibilities of the NAC being transformed by effective leadership. Once Rob was elected Chair, he would demonstrate its potential; with strong leadership it turned into an effective political lobby group, if not a fully representative one. Of more pressing concern was the likely fallout from Coombs's report. In the lead-up to crucial decisions being taken on land rights, he had handed the Hawke government the rationale to disband the organisation in the event that it proved politically troublesome. While Coombs may not have been able to foresee exactly how the politics of land rights would unfold, it was a dangerous scenario to call for its abolition in the midst of one of the most critical times for Aboriginal people in living memory.

While Coombs's recommendations awaited a response from the government, the work of NAC members went on regardless. The demands on NAC representatives were equal to, and perhaps greater than, those on parliamentary backbenchers. In Aboriginal politics, achieving credibility meant regular face-to-face contact with communities. In addition, their job was to consult with a range of interest groups and government agencies and attend NAC meetings. The travel was constant; they were never at home. Rob and Peter lived together on the road, always staying in the same hotel, and hardly ever unpacked their suitcases. Peter stayed at Rob's place when coming down from his Kimberley base to Perth. As Peter Yu explains: people 'don't appreciate how exhausting it is, how tedious, how boring, how lonely it can be when you're away from your family and your kids ... we both had young families and the first word they probably learn is aeroplane'.

As the future of the NAC hung in the balance, it remained actively involved in working with the federal government on its land rights agenda. Through the mechanism of Holding's Steering Committee, work was proceeding slowly on the drafting of national legislation. However, the Steering Committee immediately became bogged down in the technicalities of the legal issues involved. Interim Chair of the NAC during the first half of 1984, Lyall Munro senior, issued a circular to NAC members reporting on this process; the panel of lawyers had posed thirty-eight questions requiring policy directions from the Steering Committee, which then requested the lawyers to prepare options on the various issues. This resulted in a discussion paper to guide the Committee's deliberations.[92]

As the Steering Committee slogged through the technical issues of national land rights legislation, the parallel issue of protection of sacred sites re-emerged. As opposition to land rights had started to mobilise both in and outside federal parliament, Holding decided that introducing sacred sites legislation could be a Trojan horse, helping to break down some of the impending resistance to achieving the broader objective of national land rights legislation. The recently unified Aboriginal rights movement, which Rob had worked so hard to achieve, helped draft legislation for Holding, which had its first reading in the House of Representatives in May 1984. As the Minister explained to the House, the Aboriginal and Torres Strait Islander Heritage Bill had two purposes. First, it would preserve and protect areas in Australia and Australian waters which are of particular significance to Aboriginals or Islanders in accordance with their traditions; secondly it would preserve and protect objects, including Aboriginal and Islander human remains, which are of particular significance to these groups. The Bill was designed only as an interim measure until national land rights legislation was implemented, and it would only be used in emergency situations where state governments were not upholding their own heritage laws. In outlining the need for such a measure, the Minister referred to the events at Noonkanbah, but only as the most recent example. As Holding explained: 'Time and again the Federal Government has been powerless to take legal action where State or Territory laws were inadequate, not enforced or nonexistent, despite its clear constitutional responsibility'.[93]

As one of the senior members of the coalition of Aboriginal groups, Rob was part of the framing of the Bill and the political objectives behind it. The Head of Research at the NAC at the time, Les Malezer, recalls, 'the Bill was in our view hasty but we agreed with Holding that let's get it passed through parliament and worry about amending it afterwards'. The introduction of the Bill certainly achieved the immediate objective of flushing out the mining and pastoral industries and Liberal and National parties, both of which immediately declared their opposition to the use of such wide-reaching Commonwealth powers for the protection of Aboriginal land.

Whether the Bill succeeded in breaking down the opposition, or whether it provided a dress rehearsal for the lobby against national land rights, is of more than passing interest. The mining and pastoral industries mounted a strong lobbying campaign against the legislation, claiming it was land rights by 'the back door'.[94] The opposition parties also worked themselves into a lather, as debate in the House raged on throughout May and early June. Leading the charge against the Bill was the opposition spokesman on Aboriginal Affairs, James Porter. He pursued a conventional line of attack: the government had conferred on itself unlimited discretionary powers; it had failed to consult on the Bill; mining and pastoral interests opposed the measure; and it was an attack on the power of the states. Among the most florid assaults on the Bill was delivered by Tasmanian Liberal Max Burr, the plain text of which revealed the depth of conceptual opposition in sections of the Party to the notion that Indigenous people had rights: 'This legislation gives advantages and privileges to one class of people because of the colour of their skin. Other Australians who do not have the same skin colour or are not of the same racial background will be denied those privileges and advantages. That is apartheid. Apartheid is being practiced in this country by this Government'.[95]

Linking support for land rights as somehow akin to the near-universal moral repugnance of the South African apartheid system was symptomatic of the extremist language in which a range of conservative groups — miners, pastoralists, the conservative press and sections of the state and federal Liberal parties — couched their opposition to land rights. The recourse to such language is interesting. A range of conservatives at the time experienced profound difficulties with the meaning of race. Explaining this difficulty goes to the heart of contemporary debates about the nature of modern racism. Theorists of race argue that 'old-fashioned' racism based around perceptions of biological superiority and stereotyping were replaced in the modern era — at least among officials — with symbolic racism: focussing on Blacks as a group and their excessive demands for special and undeserved treatment.[96] This was the context in which Rob fought for Aboriginal rights during the 1980s. He certainly believed the anti-land-rights cause was fundamentally racist. But as the concept of racism itself became more complex, the charge became harder to make stick.

No doubt, the Heritage Bill was a hasty measure. It might well have been improved by a consultative process. But to what end? Of the Liberal/National Party speakers, only Philip Ruddock conceded as a matter of principle the need to protect sacred sites. In fact, in protesting so loudly about the unrestrained power to protect sites being granted to the federal Minister for Aboriginal Affairs, nearly all on the conservative side conveniently overlooked the fact that some state ministers had long been able to use such power against Aboriginal interests. Moreover, the adoption of extremist language to express their opposition was a driving force in polarising debates about Aboriginal Affairs policy.

On the government side, the debate over the heritage legislation raises a specific question about the relationship between the Aboriginal rights movement and the Hawke government. Was it good politics to proceed with the sweeping provisions of the Heritage Bill? Together, had they enhanced or damaged their longer-term cause? The full impact of the passions raised over the heritage legislation would not become clear for several months. For now, the signs were ominous. As *The Australian* summed up the situation: 'the Bill has been noticeably successful in creating yet more antagonism towards the justifiable needs of Australia's original inhabitants'.[97]

But the real antagonism was occurring behind the scenes. The passage of the legislation was straining the relationship between the mining industry and the federal government, but in a way which demonstrated the lengths to which the industry would go to secure the defeat of the legislation. Representatives from the industry peak bodies were tough on the issue. Holding had publicly criticised the mining industry for its 'overreaction and dishonesty'. The industry was infused with the belief, he said, 'that they have a divine right to mine anywhere there is an ore deposit ...[and] that is not acceptable to the average Australian'.[98]

Holding had, in fact, grown alarmed in his dealings with the industry. In a confidential briefing to a joint meeting of the NAC and the Federation of Land Councils, held in October 1984, at which Rob was in attendance, Holding expressed forthright views about the mining lobby. He said that 'putting it mildly, I found them a body that is very difficult to deal with. They will often distort what seem to be the facts of the situation to suit their own preconceived political position'. The situation had become so serious, Holding said, that the Prime Minister had to twice inform the Australian Mining Industry Council that it had misrepresented the government's position on the legislation.[99] Holding instanced the following example: 'I understand that during the discussions in the Caucus in Western Australia notes were circulated to members of the Labor Caucus there which purported to represent the agreement of the Commonwealth with the mining companies. That was basically a circulation of the notes which AMIC had sent to us and which had in fact been repudiated by the Prime Minister'.

Rob was present at the 5 October joint meeting of the NAC and the land councils at which Holding was candid about the government's response. Holding told those present: 'I was also concerned about the kind of footage which was being pumped out over the television stations by the Australian Mining Industry Council. I have told AMIC and the Prime Minister has also told them that not only do we regard that material as inaccurate ... but we also regard it as racist'.

Rob would have been deeply disturbed by such revelations. The miners' lobby groups must have appeared to him as a hydra-headed monster, capable of influencing public opinion while exerting significant political pressure on politicians, including the Prime Minister. This would surely have added to his underlying uncertainty about the ultimate fate of national land rights.

By the close of May 1984, Rob was about to be elected to the position of Chair of the NAC. The political environment in both Canberra and Perth on land rights was contradictory. Publicly, the federal Minister had remained resolute and the Seaman Inquiry remained on track. But behind the scenes Labor governments in Canberra and Perth were growing nervous about fulfilling their commitments. Land rights was proving more complex and contentious than governments had expected. Sovereignty, compensation, a right of veto over mining and the protection of sacred sites had begun to unsettle conservative white opinion. Miners and pastoralists were already at battle stations. The Liberal and National parties were sniffing the opportunities of ramping up their opposition to land rights. At this critical juncture, Rob was one of a handful of prominent Black politicians in the country. For the lonely boy from Sister Kate's and the later, angry young radical of Black Action, it had been a remarkable journey. But as tough as the struggle had been so far, it was about to get still harder.

CHAPTER SEVEN

Betrayal: The Demise of National Land Rights

On 10 October 1984, Rob Riley strode to the podium of the National Press Club in Canberra to address the assembled media. He was the first Chair of the NAC to be offered this opportunity. It was a prestigious occasion, and we can only speculate how Rob felt about the honour. Surely he would have allowed himself a fleeting sense of triumph?

In his speech he launched 'a powerful attack' on Bob Hawke. The Prime Minister had betrayed Aboriginal people. Land rights had been sold out. Aboriginal people had been duped.[1] The speech was a calculated risk because both federal and Western Australian state Labor governments were still trying to stich together a deal on land rights legislation. But the very existence of a deal meant that key principles had been betrayed, and that was enough for Rob to pull off the gloves. As it turned out, Rob's speech crystallised the political drift: the struggle for national land rights was slowly collapsing.

How had the nation let slip from its grasp this historic opportunity? Had the rights movement and its principal activist, Rob Riley, pushed politicians too far too quickly? As he strode to the podium Rob was furious about Labor's cave-in, and in no mood for self-reflection. Although he did not fully acknowledge it in his speech, he saw federal Labor's betrayal of key principles of its policy on national land rights as part of a broader pattern of betrayals of the Aboriginal cause.

In under twelve months from the time of his election as NAC Chair, Rob had seen just about the entire mid-1980s agenda of the Aboriginal rights movement collapse under the weight of political expediency: the integrity of the *Commonwealth Heritage Act (1984)*, the commitment to the public awareness campaign on land rights, and the continuation of the NAC itself. The promises made to Aborigines only a few years earlier were in tatters.

These betrayals were forged in the divisive debates about race which raged throughout 1984. Historian Professor Geoffrey Blainey sparked a 'race debate' in March of that year when he publicly opposed Australia's current levels of Asian migration; and the debate intensified as the year progressed. Claiming to represent popular opinion, Blainey was forced to mount a continuous defence of his view that Asian immigration threatened the social harmony of the nation. He faced a growing number of detractors in the nation's liberal intelligentsia and in the federal government. In essence, much of the controversy ignited by Blainey centred on whether his views revived Australia's old-style, racist image. Were Anglo-Australians still trapped in their history of white Australia? Did the nation still struggle with cultural diversity? His critics raked over his widely acclaimed books on Australian history and found a value-laden view of the past: from the heroic roles he ascribed to European entrepreneurs to the myopic views he was seen to have on Aboriginal culture.[2] To his critics, Blainey depicted Aborigines in the larger story of Australia as triumphant figures, but only in their prescribed role as pre-settlement 'nomads'.[3]

Blainey's views on race were part of a broader resurgence of conservatism in Australia. An intellectual movement known as the New Right combined concerns about Australia's economic competitiveness with a disdain for progressive causes. As the Liberal Party drifted into irrelevance, the New Right captured public attention. Apart from Blainey, key spokespeople in this new movement were widely seen to include Western Mining's Hugh Morgan and former Treasury head John Stone.

Determined to forge an aggressive new direction for the nation, these apostles of resurgent conservatism confirmed their public status by giving the 'big speeches' of 1984: Blainey on immigration, Morgan on land rights and Stone on government regulation. Morgan's speech on land rights, delivered to the Mining Industry Council, was typical of the approach taken by the New Right towards the issue of land rights. Impeccably groomed and haughty, Morgan told the Council that land rights would wipe out the mining industry. But Morgan went further, claiming that the concept represented an anti-Christian spiritualism, would create a white backlash and was founded on nonsensical Aboriginal allegations of genocide by whites.[4]

A few months earlier, at the end of May 1984, the thirty-six NAC members gathered in Perth for their annual conference amid a rapidly changing political climate. Bob Hawke's appeal for consensus was facing an incoming tide of new opinion, some of which complemented the government's economic reform agenda but parts of which threatened to test the strength of Labor's commitments in Aboriginal and multicultural affairs.

Just before the Conference, Rob had been approached to stand for the position of Chair. Among the strong egos and highly factionalised politics of the organisation, Rob was seen as independent, articulate and principled. In the few short years he had been with the organisation he had commanded respect for his aggressive pursuit of political issues together with his willingness to hear others' views and to acknowledge his own mistakes. In addition, Rob's profile benefited from the organisation's preoccupation with the land rights issue, in which he took a major role in developing a united Aboriginal position. Charles Rowley, a widely respected academic in Aboriginal affairs, noted the impact of the land rights debate in changing the NAC.[5] Without referring specifically to Rob, Rowley wrote: 'the radicalisation of the land rights debate in 1984 helped to produce a marked change in the leadership of the NAC'.[6]

In being sought out as Chair, Rob was at a pivotal moment in his life. The NAC was moribund, but it could provide a platform to influence both politicians and the media if it could be driven by decisive leadership.

Rob's candidature, however, was no mere formality. The NAC was an intensely political body and the process of being elected Chair involved securing some of the larger voting blocks as well as the support of the more independent-minded members. Queensland and New South Wales were a voting block, as was Western Australia. The remainder of the states were relatively neutral, and it was among these representatives that Rob picked up additional votes. But Rob had powerful opponents in the NAC. Standing against Lyall Munro senior from New South Wales, he received no support from that state, or from Queensland, which was headed by 'Sugar Ray' Robinson. Yet Rob had specific qualities propelling him to the top. He accommodated all views and made each group feel important. Whereas some people disliked many of the other delegates, no-one actively disliked Rob.

When the outcome of the secret ballot was announced, Rob jotted down a few quick notes on the back of a bank slip before gracefully accepting his Chairmanship. As a close colleague noted, underneath, he was 'bubbling with excitement': 'It was a big coup for a young Noongar man to get the vote. It was a great moment'.

Upon his election, he made his intentions clear. He told the press that the NAC must act more positively than it had in the past. 'We need to make firm decisions to present to the Government and we must not waver on them'.[7] In the past, he further declared, 'Aborigines have tried to put across their point of view politely and rationally but we have been frustrated by the vicious and slanderous campaigns being conducted by mining and pastoral groups and conservative political parties. Now it is time to fight back'. These were emphatic statements, a call to battle. But could he put them into action?

The debate on the Heritage Bill was reaching its climax in federal Parliament. Despite the mining industry's extensive lobbying of the Prime Minister, the Aboriginal Affairs Minister and the Resources Minister, the government had refused to heed its call to withdraw the Bill.[8] Rob's first task was to put some heat on the opposition. He arranged for a telex to be sent to the Minister for Aboriginal Affairs from the NAC which Holding read out in Parliament. It bore the hallmarks of Rob's take-no-prisoners approach. The telex informed the Minister that the NAC intended to ask for James Porter to be transferred out of his shadow portfolio for his failure to consult with Aboriginal people over his opposition to the Bill and for his 'sellout of Aboriginal interests for mining interests'.[9] Rob dispatched a separate telegram to the Leader of the Opposition, Andrew Peacock, urging him to support the Bill and explaining that the legislation represented a harmonious discussion between government and Aboriginal people. How decisive these interventions were is difficult to gauge. According to Les Malezer, they made an impact, especially the letter to Peacock: 'the minute they [the federal opposition] got that letter the legislation was passed through, the Opposition stopped the debate'. Nonetheless, the government was always going to get the legislation through the House and the Senate. In the Upper House the Bill had the backing of the Australian Democrats. Rob realised the significance of the legislation. The granting of power to the federal Minister to protect sacred sites represented a negotiated outcome; as such it was a milestone.

Following Rob's election to Chair and the intervention on the Heritage Bill, the NAC Conference was dominated by the two most emotive issues in Aboriginal affairs: land rights and deaths in custody. On both issues Rob's more assertive style of leadership was evident.

A unanimous call was made at the NAC conference for the establishment of a Royal Commission into the John Pat case, together with funding for the Western Australian Aboriginal Legal Service to conduct its own investigation. In the preceding months the case had continued to arouse anger in the Aboriginal community. An 'ineffectual' police investigation and a subsequent coronial inquest, at which none of the police officers gave evidence on the grounds that they might incriminate themselves, failed to determine the culpability of police.[10] A Supreme Court trial in Karratha followed, which acquitted police of manslaughter charges despite Aboriginal witnesses who alleged police had hit Pat, dragged him to a van and threw him in 'like a dead kangaroo'.[11] Aboriginal groups were incensed at the conduct of the trial maintaining the acquittals represented a further breakdown of the justice system in its dealings with Aboriginal people. Rob was in the forefront of highlighting Aboriginal concerns over the conduct of the trial. Interviewed on ABC national radio days before becoming national NAC Chair, he raised three serious concerns which went to the heart of accusations by Aboriginal people of discrimination in the justice system.[12] Prosecution lawyers, he said, 'may not have prosecuted the case as well as they ought to'. The selection of an all-white jury from the surrounding area was a second concern, because of the high probability that negative community attitudes among some white jury members may have influenced the jury's decision. His last and perhaps most serious charge was the claim that police had intimidated witnesses during the court case, a charge which he supported with the additional claim that witnesses had 'lost jobs because they were prepared to testify against police'. Whether or not he could verify all these accusations, it took significant courage to take on the Western Australian police force in such a public manner and over such a highly charged case, particularly given his direct experience of the strong-arm tactics employed by sections of the force and of the recent police scrutiny over the incendiary pamphlet calling on Aborigines to engage in violence.

By the time of the NAC Conference, Aboriginal anger over the Pat case had reached a new pitch. Following their acquittal, the five police officers involved had been reinstated. However, several were transferred to other country towns with high Aboriginal populations in what was either an insensitive or provocative move by the Police Department. Consequently, the NAC took up the case at its conference, and, in so doing, marked the beginning of the struggle for a royal commission into Aboriginal deaths in custody. The NAC called for an inquiry to investigate the alleged police harassment and victimisation of Aborigines, the intimidation of witnesses at the John Pat trial, police action in the brawl which led to his arrest and subsequent death, the process behind the selection of the all-white jury, and the general state of police–Aboriginal relations.[13]

After his election as Chair of the NAC, Rob continued to press the media over the specifics of Aborigines' concerns about the Pat case. He informed the public that the NAC would be making representations to state and federal governments concerning the establishment of an inquiry.[14] Characteristically, he said that 'police appear to be a law unto themselves. If they decide to persecute a disadvantaged minority then society will turn a blind eye. We are seeing growing evidence of a police vendetta against Aboriginal people and no one, not even the state government, seems concerned'. Referring to the posting of two of the policemen to Geraldton and Merredin, Rob was equally blunt: 'Aborigines took the postings to Aboriginal areas as a "slap in the face". They [the police] are telling us quite plainly that they are the power and that we had better not get in their way'.[15]

Clyde Holding was not prepared to involve the federal government in what he deemed a state matter and the Burke government refused to commit itself, on the basis that it had supported previous inquiries into the matter and it had no right to interfere in the judicial process. The state opposition leader, Bill Hassell, issued another in his long line of unsympathetic statements on Aboriginal issues. 'What they [Aborigines] seem to be saying', he argued, 'is that because the police were not convicted, the justice system had not worked'.[16]

Hassell further raised the ire of Aborigines when he spoke at a Land Rights Forum arranged by the NAC to coincide with the NAC Annual Conference. Speaking before 'a big Aboriginal audience', Hassell made further comments that warned of dire consequences from the introduction of land rights. Federal legislation would, he said, 'cause faction fighting similar to that in Ireland'.[17] In sensationalising such wild and irrational statements, the media fed public fears.

Rob was clearly worried about the impact of Hassell's comments conveyed to the public via the media. In characteristically forthright language he wrote a letter to *The West Australian* in which he charged the Liberal leader with having gone too far in his public comments. 'Mr Hassell has waged a highly successful, highly immoral and highly racist campaign against a people who have been subject to two centuries of intimidation and dispossession'.[18]

Did Rob go too far in his accusations against Hassell? After all, in his letter to the editor Rob raised a key issue about the motivations of conservatives like Hassell who pursued the issue relentlessly: were they concerned for the economic good of the state, or 'simply anti-Aboriginal'?

The day after the Forum on land rights, and coinciding with the end of its Conference, the NAC organised a land rights rally on the steps of Western Australia's Parliament House. Attended by about 3000 people, bonded by 'strong feelings', it is thought to have been the largest demonstration of Indigenous people in the state's history. There was a small forest of placards and Aboriginal flags and chants of 'Land Rights Now'. Rob was the key organiser of the occasion and one of several speakers. His message to federal parliamentarians was blunt: 'Don't short-change us. We've been short-changed for far too long. If that legislation [national Aboriginal land rights legislation] doesn't go the way Aboriginal people want it to ... they are going to find out very loudly and very clearly that the Aboriginal people will not tolerate it'. To the mining and pastoral lobbies, he expressed his utter contempt:

'They see us as second class citizens. After all, why should a few no-hoper blacks be allowed to share in the profits of their own land?'[19]

Several days after Rob's election as Chair of the NAC, Jeannie gave birth to the couple's youngest daughter, Emma. A story and accompanying photograph appeared in *The West Australian* depicting Rob visiting his wife and new-born daughter in hospital accompanied by his two other daughters, Megan aged five and Jaymea aged three. Rob highlighted the plight of people with his background. He said his children 'would have a better childhood than he did'. He further explained that 'he was taken away from his mother', and declared that his children would be brought up 'with the knowledge that they have a family that love and care for them, which is something that I never had when I grew up'.[20] But the comments were brief, the account devoid of intensity.

His election as Chair of the NAC further increased his profile in his home state and nationally. He became the object of media interest, as his invitation to the National Press Club testified. Karen Graydon, a journalist from *The West Australian*, interviewed Rob at this time. She sensed a man of contradictions: 'Rob Riley, the tough-talking Aboriginal land rights activist is, in fact, a surprisingly moderate man'. In becoming a public figure he again faced the scrutiny of his personal life. But what could he would he say about this background when there was little public understanding of the plight of Aboriginal people removed from their families as children? To most white Australians, assimilation remained an uncontested ideal. One senses that Rob knew that his efforts to dispel this ignorance were in vain. He said in the interview that he was bitter at the policy of assimilation, and he mentioned his life in the slums of East Perth and on Pingelly reserve where 'the conditions were even worse'. But readers learnt little. The full horror of Rob's background remained hidden. Then came the inevitable question about his Aboriginality: 'When asked what percentage of Aboriginal blood he has, Mr Riley replied that he was "as Aboriginal as an Aborigine can be"'. This focus on 'blood' showed that the old attitudes towards Aborigines survived. At this stage of his career, Rob was continually being asked to legitimise his Aboriginality.

The interview then turned to Rob's views about the land rights issue. He described the state Liberal/National parties as using a 'deliberate ploy to instil fear in to the community'. Liberal leader Bill Hassell was firmly in his sights. Drawing on research undertaken for the land rights campaign, Rob allowed himself on this occasion to indulge in personality politics — a rare occurrence. By highlighting the personal affairs of Bill Hassell, Rob wanted to underline the hypocrisy he saw in the hearts of those who vociferously opposed land rights but who had been beneficiaries of the takeover of Aboriginal lands:

> Between 1880 and 1900, the Hassell family were given, just given, approximately 700,000 acres of our land. Yet when we ask for the right to have that land back again we're told that it's nothing to do with us. It's just such incredible double standards ... People say to us that we've already got land in the form of reserves, but they don't realise that Aboriginal people don't have control over it. The Government does.[21]

A map of the south-west of Western Australia was drawn up, showing the extent of the Hassell family land grant, which Rob filed for later use.

One of Rob's first official duties as Chair was to lead a delegation of the NAC to address the United Nations Human Rights Commission's Sub-Commission on the Prevention of Discrimination and Protection of Minorities. He was accompanied by Clyde Holding as Minister, whose own address to the gathering confirmed the government's commitment to land rights based on its already stated five principles.

This was Rob's second overseas trip. Internationalism was a developing aspect of Rob's rights agenda, and his speech had a characteristically strong political edge. It was framed around Australia's obligations as a signatory to the International Covenant on Civil and Political Rights. The Noonkanbah struggle was his starting point for arguing that that the convention was not being adequately adhered to in Australia because the mechanism for monitoring it — the Australian Human Rights Commission — was 'wishy washy'. Rob pointed out that when the Western Australian government overturned the Museum's decision to protect the Noonkanbah site, it did so without any challenge from the Commission, which had confirmed its lack of power to call a Minister of the Crown to a compulsory conference. He argued this lack of action set a precedent that Ministers were 'a protected species' and, as such, was contrary to the International Covenant. This, Rob pointed out, explicitly encompassed the actions of persons 'acting in an official capacity'. Warming to his theme, he made a direct attack on the Human Rights Commission, a construction of the Fraser government, and which, in his view, incorporated 'a conservative wishy-washiness into its structure and role'. Its ties to government meant that it could do little more than 'nibble at the edges of injustice, recording acts of discrimination and conciliating when it is all over'.[22] His paper confirmed again why Rob could be such a formidable opponent. Always well prepared, he brought a sharp intellect to the analysis of issues and linked this to his framework of justice.

When he returned to Australia, the extent of his new workload became apparent. As national Chair of the organisation he was responsible for about thirty people in the Canberra office, and although he had stood down from the position of state Chair, he maintained an active involvement in the Western Australian branch. He was always in demand. He had media constantly at the front door. Everyone wanted a piece of him. He was working full on; some days he was inaccessible to his staff. He'd be locked away in his room on the phone or meeting people. On many evenings he attended community meetings trying to allay fears raised by the miners' scare campaign, explaining that ordinary people's backyards were not at risk.

Rob was a natural, charismatic leader. He was good at managing staff, demonstrating a relaxed but team approach. He would help paint the land rights banners for marches and help organise volunteers. He was 'a people person'. Yet, there are conflicting indicators about how well he handled the pressures. He started putting on weight with all the travel, constant airline food, and lack of a balanced lifestyle. In common with many young people at the time, he was a recreational dope smoker, although some thought he used the drug to relieve tension. Sometimes, on his own and behind closed doors, he would smoke a joint before confronting a media throng. Nobody really noticed this at the time, but Rob was beginning to feel the pressure of being an Aboriginal politician in an unrelenting, adversarial political environment.

Early on his chairmanship, Rob made it clear that he was not going to be intimidated by politicians, least of all by the Minister, Clyde Holding. In one of his earliest dealings with Holding as Chair, Rob staked out his approach. Holding had told the NAC that under no circumstances were they to commit funds for the purchase of motor vehicles for use by NAC members. When told of this imposition, members were incensed. They had been pressing for access to vehicles as instrumental to their job of representing Aboriginal people. With Rob as Chair they passed a resolution unanimously ignoring the direction of the Minister. Cedric Wyatt was with Holding when Rob delivered to him the news that his directive was going to be ignored. Holding thought 'that it was quite fundamental that the ultimate authority of the Minister was being overturned by a group of Aboriginal people led by Rob Riley basically saying, "You can go get stuffed"'.[23]

Rob took a similar attitude to one of the darker sides of the job: the constant surveillance from the domestic intelligence organisation, ASIO. His personal secretary at the NAC, Jill Abdullah, remembers walking through one rally and Rob saying, 'See those guys over there — they're ASIO'. It is a measure of officials' perception of the threat posed by Aboriginal activism that the nation's top domestic intelligence agency monitored the activities of Aboriginal leaders. Fellow activist Darryl Kickett says a standing joke existed among the network of activists in the mid-1980s over their status as perceived domestic political threats. When phoning each other they would greet the person at the other end of the line with, 'Oh, hello ASIO'.

How seriously ASIO viewed the Aboriginal rights movement is impossible to gauge. But there was plenty of activity to feed their imagination. In August 1984, the government faced its first test of commitment over the Commonwealth Heritage Act. This went to the heart of Labor's commitment to Aboriginal people in general. The focus of attention was the Harding River Dam in the Pilbara, built to service the towns of Roebourne and Karratha. Commenced in 1981 by the state Liberal government, it was constructed in the face of clear objections from the local Yindjibarndi and Ngarluma people and the then Labor opposition. Peter Dowding led the charge, claiming Aboriginal interests were not adequately considered.[24]

When federal cabinet announced its decision not to invoke the powers of the Commonwealth Heritage Act to stop Harding River Dam, it appealed to common sense: 70 per cent of the work on the dam had been completed. Nothing could bring back the already destroyed sites. But this did not make the decision a correct one, according to near-unanimous Aboriginal opinion. Two of Rob's closest colleagues,

Rob Riley face to face with Roger Shipton, opposition spokesperson on Aboriginal Affairs, at national land rights rally, Canberra, May 1985.

Rob Riley addressing national land rights rally, Canberra, May 1985. The rally was a culmination of moves to create a unified Aboriginal protest movement.

Rob Riley with Prime Minister Bob Hawke, Hazel Hawke and 'Sugar' Ray Robinson, c. 1984. Riley never forgave Hawke for caving in on national Aboriginal land rights, and was an opponent of Robinson's within the National Aboriginal Conference.

Rob Riley taking photos of the handing over of Uluru in October 1985. The Hawke government shocked the Northern Territory government by handing over Uluru (formerly Ayers Rock) to Aboriginal ownership.

Rob Riley and Aboriginal Affairs Minister Clyde Holding c. 1985. Riley and Holding had a testy relationship.

Peter Yu and Brian Wyatt, led the attack over the government's decision. Yu claimed the federal government had betrayed Aboriginal trust and made the heritage legislation worthless. Wyatt drew the link to the yet unfinished Seaman Inquiry, claiming the decision meant that the state government might as well tell the inquiry 'to pack up its bags and go without wasting any more time and taxpayers' money'.[25]

Rob, too, was incensed. He rushed into action a high-risk strategy to close down the NAC in protest. The day after the cabinet decision, he organised a telephone hook-up of the thirteen-member NAC executive 'during which he would suggest that the Conference pack up rather than become a "scapegoat for government"'. Was he serious, or was this a political stunt? For most others acting in his role, it might appear the latter, but Rob was prepared to carry through with his call. Growing weary of continually fighting in vain, he was asked directly by the press whether he was engaged in a stunt, Riley replied: 'No. This is an ultimate position forced on us by the attitude of the Government'.[26]

But Rob's opponents in the organisation were never likely to allow him to become a political martyr by closing it down. When the executive hook-up did take place, a compromise strategy emerged and direct meetings with the Prime Minister were demanded. Explaining his position to the press, Rob threatened direct action: 'If we get no joy in Canberra we will have to embarrass the government by exposing them as a sham'.[27]

The government's refusal to invoke the powers of the Heritage Act to protect sacred sites was not confined to Harding River Dam. By mid-August, two other applications for the protection of sites had also been rejected: Stradbroke Island and the Daintree Rainforest, both in Queensland. These were clear warnings about the future policy battles ahead. Rob told the National Press Club that the government was cowering before 'politically threatening applications'.

In a further retreat from stated commitments, Holding announced no funding would be forthcoming for a public awareness campaign on land rights. In a significant defeat for the Minister, the application for funding was rejected by the cabinet sub-committee on government advertising because 'the committee did not want to expose the government to charges of extravagant spending or government propaganda in an election year'.[28] At much the same time Burke also broke his commitments to a publicity campaign. Rob felt these backdowns acutely. He fully understood the power of the media, and he had gained personal commitments from both governments about the need for such a campaign.

Rob was still fuming about this Labor betrayal a year later. In a 1985 article in *Land Rights News* his language was laced with anger and resentment at the ALP: 'The massive impact of this massive campaign of fear and threats has demonstrated the brutal effect of the hypocrisy of the Labor party'.[29] He was only barely more temperate when he informed a conference in 1986:

> They [the federal government] didn't even try to educate or even provide information to the public about why it is necessary for the Labor party to have specific policies in Aboriginal affairs. The mining industry's campaign was simply an appeal to prejudice. This was an easy campaign to run because it took advantage of the present consciousness of most white people ... We said to them: if you've got money there and are not prepared to use it, why not provide those moneys to Aboriginal organisations that have the capacity to use it and develop the arguments and publish them.[30]

~~~~~~~~~~

In September 1984, amid intense interest from both state and federal governments, Paul Seaman was getting ready to release his report. It would be a decisive moment in the land rights debate. Seaman had been involved in a unique process. Few white officials had had such extensive contact with the hearts and minds of Aboriginal people and their communities. In the previous twelve months, he had met with 2,200 Aborigines and clocked up in excess of 53,000 kilometres in flights to the four corners of the state, journeys on which he 'frequently rolled a swag'.[31] The experience, he acknowledged, had changed him. He had grown closer to Aborigines and their aspirations.

Although he faced no interference from government in the preparation of his report, Seaman felt the pressure in the days before its release. A journalist visiting his city office headquarters the day before he handed it to the Premier found a well-marked 'countdown calendar' and 'bags of shredded drafts'. The journalist learned that Seaman and his staff had been 'up till 3.30 yesterday proofing the report which earlier had been thoroughly checked by a team of lawyers to make sure it said what it meant'.[32]

Seaman knew that his case for land rights would need to be convincingly argued if it was to withstand the expected assaults from powerful lobby groups. He developed his case around an integrated historical, cultural and political framework. Underpinning his approach were two distinguishing features: the pains he had gone to in finding and presenting the Aboriginal voice on land rights and, secondly, the frankness he showed in acknowledging the attitude of historical denialism among key sections of white opinion. He pointed out that: 'A few non-Aboriginal people at hearings seemed to think that it was somehow wrong to refer to the past [as oppression and neglect]. The past was to be forgotten ... There were at times suggestions in the hearings that initiatives in favour of Aborigines ... were the product of some misplaced sense of guilt'.[33]

Seaman's willingness to give voice to the Aboriginal version of history led to some bold findings. On the status of pastoral leases, he acknowledged that 'this land is theirs, it was forcibly taken from them'.[34] He was also critical of the state Aboriginal Heritage Act, noting the reality that 'nobody has ever been successfully prosecuted under its provisions, despite reports of desecration'.[35]

Concern for the Aboriginal voice together with his commitment to legal principles also led Seaman to recommend a veto (within prescribed limits) over mining. This issue, more than any other, rattled government confidence in the Inquiry. It straddled the fault line of responses to land rights. The veto also asserted the legitimacy of Aborigines controlling their own land. Seaman argued the case for a veto by highlighting that 'their society may completely disintegrate unless the process of using their land at our will is not halted'.[36]

Seaman fired a direct shot across the bow of the miners' lobby. He found their arguments self-interested: 'the mining industry wishes the government to exercise its power over its minerals so as to give mining interests paramountcy over Aboriginal interests in land, and for that matter most other interests in land'.[37]

Lastly, Seaman's advocacy of the Aboriginal voice in land rights was fully revealed when he argued for a justice-based approach. Land rights, he argued, were an issue for all Aborigines. Foreshadowing a debate which would be revisited in an intensely painful way by Rob Riley a decade later, Seaman wrote:

> It is clear from the hearings that not only traditionally orientated Aboriginal people but Aboriginal people throughout the state speak of the land as theirs ... The conflict between that Aboriginal view and the legal position will not, in my view, be resolved by a land rights system which accords benefits only to those who establish Aboriginal traditional ownership.[38]

Seaman knew that without a political solution to the plight of the dispossessed, 'Many would be unable to obtain any land under a process which demanded proof of Aboriginal tradition'. But he was constrained by his terms of reference, and the matter was stored over until another day, when Rob would also be forced to return to it.

Seaman identified four main types of land which could be subject to land claims by Aborigines. These included Crown land, reserves, missions and pastoral leases. To implement his proposal for land rights, Seaman recommended a combination of political and legal processes. Aboriginal people would be placed in a position as equal negotiators with minimum interposition of bureaucrats: 'emphasis should be placed upon negotiations between public authorities and Aboriginal regional organisations and their constituents with a view to satisfying Aboriginal claims by administrative grant'.[39] Where such negotiations could not be satisfactorily concluded, Seaman proposed setting up a tribunal to resolve such cases.

Rob had mixed views of Seaman's report. While praising his 'enlightened thinking', he was disappointed about his failure to challenge, 'by way of inference or recommendation', the legal fiction of *terra nullius*, which 'sadly perpetuates this attitude'.[40] Seaman had failed to challenge the fictitious principle on which the nation was founded: that the land was unoccupied at the time of settlement.

Rob's criticism of Seaman was drowned out in the political furore after the report's release. Burke had not expected the moral force of the report. Seaman had not played pragmatic politics with land rights; he had ignored the political static coming from the gathering forces of land rights opponents; and he had set out a clear course of action to deal with the injustices from the past.

Both the federal and Western Australian governments had been awaiting the outcome of the report. Once it was released, they could no longer avoid declaring their respective intentions.

At this point, the federal Labor party's commitment to a process of change on land rights proved to be a mirage. The hard work of Rob and others was undone in a matter of weeks, between the release of the Seaman Inquiry in late September and Hawke's announcement on 16 October that the federal government would not be clarifying its position on national land rights before the December 1984 election. This announcement marked the beginning of the end for land rights based on the government's five principles.

During these weeks Rob was rarely out of the limelight. He tried to maintain constructive involvement with the government process, notably the Steering Committee on Land Rights, and with Minister Holding through the formal processes of the NAC, hoping to influence the course of events. As it became clear that the government was bowing to the pressures around it, Rob used his extensive media involvements to pressure the government to hold the line on land rights. When this prospect too waned, and the battle appeared lost, he used his office to expose the government's duplicity. It was a time of immense personal pressure which, outwardly, he handled with calm authority.

Rob was alive to each of the pressures that came to bear on the Hawke government. He and others in the NAC and land councils were briefed by Holding on several occasions. It was the simultaneous intersection of these powerful pressures that profoundly shocked Rob and prompted his pre-emptive strike against the Hawke government in his Canberra Press Club speech. Paramount among these pressures was the growing impact of the second round of the miners' anti-land-rights campaign, which elevated public fears to new heights. Launched at the beginning of August, it blitzed newspapers and television with advertisements that shocked Bob Hawke, Brian Burke, Clyde Holding and many others in authority as 'unethical, frightening and emotional'.[41] Newspaper advertisements featured a 'Keep Out' sign with the accompanying warning 'This land is part of Western Australia under Aboriginal claim'. Television commercials ramped up this theme by depicting a pair of black hands building a brick wall across a map of Western Australia. Rob was one of the few to say that Australia was in the grip of a high stakes propaganda campaign.

Public opinion was now under pressure from a blatantly partisan commercial intrusion into political debate. In Rob's view, the miners' strategy had two prongs: firstly to use the campaign to create a state of public alarm, and secondly to leverage this shift to intimidate the federal government. The ease with which the strategy worked unnerved many.

Rob told *The Age* newspaper how 'shocked' he was by the miners' campaign, 'and its very evident influence on public opinion'.[42] He was more specific about its impact in an interview with ABC radio in mid-October. The miners' campaign had been successful because it had 'been directed at the psyche of people who fear the sort of unconscious terror about black people and what Aboriginal people might do if they had land rights. I would think at least 75 per cent of people are misinformed'. Of particular concern to Rob was the impact of the campaign in eroding support among more progressive members of the public, who had been shamed into a more liberal position on Aboriginal issues by events at Noonkanbah.

Rob's concerns were shared by expert opinion. Psychologist Andrew Broadribb argued that the mining lobby was 'unleashing deep-seated white fear and jealousy of aboriginal people, especially in their unique relationship with the Australian hinterland'.[43]

Rob planned a counter-attack which was instrumental in stopping the 'black hand' advertisements. Clyde Holding explained his dealings on the matter to those present at the 5 October joint NAC and land council meeting:

> I managed to get them [AMIC] to agree to withdraw their ads on the basis that I persuaded Rob Riley not to release the material which he had ready to go, and which was equally racist. I indicated that it was Rob's intention to release that material and they were rather concerned about their corporate image.[44]

The only clear reference to the existence of these advertisements is an item discussed at the NAC meeting on 13 June 1984, Rob's first as Chair. It involved a briefing on a pilot television advertising program involving half-minute advertisements, twice a night for five nights at a cost of about $10,000. But the content of the advertisements was not discussed.

Rob devised a series of advertisements to appear in *The Canberra Times* during the first week of October. These depicted the history of Blacks and whites around visual images which were designed to prompt community thinking about the current state of race relations, their shortcomings and potential outlook at the time of the Bicentennial year, 1988. To conclude the series Rob reprinted the text of his recent speech to the National Press Club. It was vintage Rob Riley: positive, on the front foot, eye on his opponents. But what could it hope to achieve?

Having primed public opinion, the second prong of the miners' strategy — to leverage a vengeful public to intimidate the government — came into play as a meeting was arranged between them and the Prime Minister sometime around the end of the first week of October. *The Bulletin* reported: 'It is understood that representatives from Australia's largest mining houses, including CRA, WMC and BHP, have been involved in discussions with Hawke ... It is understood, from highly placed industry sources, that Hawke has been presented with the choice of ceding the veto rights or facing the wrath of the mining industry and electors'.[45] Rob had smelt a rat; Holding had been marginalised and Hawke had taken control of Aboriginal Affairs. Clandestine meetings had been arranged outside of any consultation with Aboriginal people. The result, he said, had been a sell-out to the mining industry.

But there was another, parallel, part to the miners' campaign which Rob had witnessed and which formed part of his disillusionment over the 'gutter politics' of land rights: the deal between Hawke and Premier Burke. Rob understood that the miners' campaign had been most effective in Western Australia where it had started and had run for longest. Burke had been placed under significant political pressure for months prior to the release of the Seaman report, and this pressure intensified in the weeks afterwards. While Burke had worked hard to resist the intrusion of national land rights legislation, Seaman's far-reaching recommendations, including support for the right of veto, marked a political line in the sand for Burke. On 28 September, the Premier announced his rejection of Seaman's main recommendations; he would frame his own legislative response to land rights.

Burke had other political concerns on his mind. He believed his electoral prospects were being determined by federal policy on land rights. Therefore, national legislation had to be stopped. Just after the release of the Seaman report, rumours began circulating of a deal already worked out between the two governments. Federal cabinet was said to have discussed the Seaman report several days prior to its release.[46] Cabinet was reportedly sensitive to the imminence of three by-elections in the West. It was also assumed that Hawke took to these discussions the results of ALP polling in the state which foreshadowed an electoral disaster: 68 per cent of voters were opposed to land rights. No-one in the cabinet room would have needed reminding that these potentially ruinous findings were, in large part, a product of the media campaign waged by the miners. Rob was an earlier subscriber to the existence of a deal between Burke and Hawke in the weeks before it became apparent. Even the press judged the Premier's denials unconvincing.[47]

Fears of a deal raised a key issue for Rob about proper democratic process. He maintained Aboriginal groups had engaged with the government in good faith. They had held off putting too much public pressure on government and they had acceded to the warnings from political leaders 'to behave ourselves or risk ending up with nothing'.[48] And to what end? To be marginalised by grubby political deals. Rob was furious that politicians were quite prepared to talk about issues that directly affected Aboriginal people without having any Aboriginal participation in those meetings and without consistent Aboriginal opinion being considered as part of the discussions.[49]

More galling still, the processes in which they were engaged had, according to Rob, become a sham. He was incensed over the failure of the federal government to deliver on its promise of full consultation and he accused the government — in the full glare of the National Press Club with the Minister in attendance — of rendering the Aboriginal Land Rights Steering Committee a virtual rubber stamp for the Minister and his Department. It was being stifled by limited funding, infrequent and hastily called meetings, and inconsistent government communications, despite constant protests.[50]

~~~~~~

Pessimistic as Rob's thinking had become about the politics of land rights, further shocks were in store. The threat of public opinion and its capacity to determine the course of action loomed as a new threat on the political landscape. In the late 1970s and early 1980s, ALP spokespeople on Aboriginal affairs had committed themselves to holding out against any hostile public opinion on land rights. But that was before the ALP came to power, and before the miners' campaign and, importantly, before the full impact of public opinion surveying. Rob Riley was acutely aware of the rise of sophisticated qualitative polling, otherwise known as public opinion polling. By the early 1980s, the ALP's enthusiasm for the application of these techniques was closely associated with the work of Rod Cameron, ALP sympathiser and former whizzkid turned oracle, the founder of ANOP Market Research.[51] What was once 'guesswork, gut feeling, and often blind faith' was being 'turned into a science', with profound ramifications for the handling of sensitive political issues. Already, a 'law' of politics was being formulated in response to the developments: 'Do the research and then on the basis of the findings, maximise the positive responses and minimise the negative ones'.[52] Unfortunately, this 'law' did not explicitly cover the eventuality that responses might be mostly negative on some especially sensitive topics. The land rights issue highlighted this very point.

After declining to fund an awareness campaign on land rights, the Hawke government commissioned Rod Cameron to undertake a survey of community attitudes to the cause. The combustible mix of sampled public opinion and political decision-making would affect Rob Riley for the remainder of his career. On 16 October, while the survey findings were still being completed, key findings were leaked to the press. The results, it was claimed, 'shocked the Government'. These showed that only 18 per cent of Australians supported land rights, while more than 30 per cent strongly opposed them. Significantly, opposition was strongest in Western Australia where the miners' campaign had been the most intense. Foreshadowing a rise in government anxiety about its commitments to land rights, the survey found that many Australians maintained stereotypical images of Aborigines 'as lazy alcoholics or desert-bound "noble savages"'.[53] At some point, Rob was given a briefing on the findings and obtained a full copy of the report. He was thus appraised of its detailed findings. Two would have stood out. The negative attitude of white Australians towards Aborigines was described as 'quite monstrous', while opposition to land rights was based on an unwillingness to transfer power to them. Such views were found to be, in part, a mix of 'general ignorance, misconceptions, fears and doubts, and... lack of understanding of Aboriginal welfare and rights'.[54]

Cameron recommended a multi-million-dollar public awareness campaign to counter negative stereotypes of Aborigines. The urgency which Cameron attached to this campaign complemented Rob's views on the matter. Cameron wrote: 'The Federal government must bite the bullet in 1985 and start to wear down the prejudice in middle Australia ... unless the government is prepared to spend a great deal of money, the chance to influence white attitudes will be greatly diminished. Some form of campaign must go ahead'. These findings had a great impact on Rob. He felt vindicated in his criticism of both Burke and Hawke for backing away from such an education campaign, and he would return to the ANOP findings in the 1990s native title debate.[55] For now, no-one was interested in listening to appeals to reason, and the government was trying to keep the results of the poll secret.[56]

Disturbing though the ANOP's findings were, Rob saw the exercise of commissioning the poll as 'a cynical move to suppress debate until after the December Federal election'. Further, he thought that to place polling at the centre of political decision-making was a travesty of ethical government. He told the National Press Club at the time of his address: 'Our future well-being should not depend on favourable opinion polls. Nor should our rights be jeopardised by the desire of political parties to gain or maintain office'. But that, in part, is what happened. Pat Dodson thinks the ANOP poll was decisive in the government's decision. The point could not have been lost on anyone, least of all Rob Riley: public views on Aboriginal issues could be manipulated for economic self-interest; government would passively collate the changes in sentiment and acquiesce.

Some of Rob's critics in the Labor Party thought that he failed to take account of the realities of the political process. Both state and federal governments were in a quandary; if they could not buy time on the issue they would be swept from power. To this criticism Rob would retort: show some leadership.

Public opinion was not the only dark cloud on the horizon. The federal Liberal party chose to exploit the issue in a transparent push for political advantage. Rob's old nemesis Bill Hassell played a decisive role in breaking the federal Liberal party's brief bi-partisanship on federal land rights intentions. Along with New South Wales Liberal opposition leader Nick Greiner, Hassell addressed state Liberal leaders in July 1984, making an impassioned plea for a change in the Party's position on land rights. Just a few weeks later, federal Liberal leader Andrew Peacock announced that he would repeal any federal legislation passed by Labor. The press was clear in its view of the reasons for the change: 'The Liberals see their stand as a vote winner in country areas and the outlying states'.[57] This, too, had Rob Riley crying foul about Australia's political system. He told the Press Club gathering: 'The Liberal party has quite shamelessly stated that they will repeal any national land rights legislation. This deliberately exploits anti-Aboriginal sentiment within the community for the sole purpose of getting the Liberals back into power'.

Thus, when the day came for Rob Riley to address the National Press Club on 10 October and he accused the Prime Minister of duping Aborigines, he was not acting precipitously. The time had come to tell the truth. But, as he himself said to the assembled media, his message may have come too late. Although it took until the early months of the new year for the full extent of the federal government's departure from official ALP policy to become clear, Rob already knew the chances of achieving land rights legislation favourable to the Aboriginal position had evaporated.

However, the Aboriginal rights movement was not about to throw in the towel. Rob exploited every opportunity available to highlight the Hawke government's retreat: media interviews, articles to the press, and a constant flurry of official correspondence.

The details of Hawke's deal with the Burke government were announced at the end of January. The deal saw Hawke announce that there would be no federal interference in the development of Western Australian land rights legislation.[58] Playing a deft political game, Burke trumpeted the deal in an effort to play to his Western Australian constituency and, in the process, succeeded in lowering the benchmark for national land rights legislation. Importantly, he had kept the mining lobby on side.

Rob was scathing. By now he loathed Burke. He told the press the Premier had struck 'a blatant sweetheart deal', which resulted in a 'complete sellout of Aboriginal and human rights'.[59] The impetus for the deal, he further explained, was a 'political exercise', framed in response to opinion polls.[60] He telexed Hawke to express his 'total frustration that exclusive meetings between the federal government and various states can determine the future and make unacceptable political compromises on behalf of Aboriginal people without the courtesy of proper advice and negotiations'.[61]

Several weeks later the Hawke government finally announced its principles for land rights legislation to be submitted to cabinet. The political shadow-boxing was over. There would be no land rights according to the five principles which were announced in Federal Parliament in 1983 and declared before the United Nations the following year. Under the Hawke proposal there was to be no right of veto over mineral exploration, no guarantee of access to mining royalty equivalents, and no mention of compensation for lost lands.

The package was denounced at a briefing of the NAC National Executive. Rob Riley and Pat Dodson issued a press release explaining that they were not prepared to meet with Holding or the ALP Caucus sub-committee on Aboriginal Affairs to discuss the proposed legislation. Their joint statement said the proposed legislation was a 'sellout'.[62] The two called upon the federal government to reverse its policy direction: to intervene in any proposed Western Australian land rights legislation; to desist from making any changes to the Northern Territory land rights legislation; to abandon their proposed national legislation; and to convene a national summit on land rights.

Rob used his position as NAC Chair to issue a continual round of press releases and official correspondence, as if believing that the words conveying the justice behind the cause would win out in the end. When the Bulletin engaged in another round of land rights bashing with the headline, 'New land rights plan creates Australian apartheid',[63] Rob wrote a stinging rebuke to the editor about press manipulation of the issue:

> The cover title employs a popular catch-cry used by land rights opponents since the early 1970s, that 'land rights is apartheid' and yet you have used the word apartheid only twice in the article without any qualification ... Your article promotes the same fears [as miners and racist organisations] without any substance to support its allegations, and for no obvious purpose other than racism.[64]

Not surprisingly, perhaps, the letter was never published. In Rob's mind there were few examples of unbiased media analysis of the issues underlying land rights. When on 8 March the Melbourne *Age* produced a lengthy editorial arguing that the government's original five principles 'were nothing more and nothing less than justice', Rob sent a congratulatory letter to the Editor, a rare moment when he could express positive thoughts: 'In an era when mediocrity in journalism is the norm and prejudice abundant, intelligent and compassionate pieces of writing such as your editorial are prized and deeply appreciated by Aboriginal people'.[65]

Revealing both his talent for innovative thinking and his increasingly despondent state of mind, he came up with the idea of writing to the Reverend Jesse Jackson, the prominent American civil rights leader. But as he conveyed to Reverend Jackson in his letter, the invitation was very much a last ditch effort: 'If we could be successful in convincing you to visit this country to monitor the current situation and to make constructive criticisms, we feel that we would have moved to show the government the error of its way and convince it to re-examine its intent in the land rights issue'.[66] Unfortunately, Jackson's response, if any, cannot be located.

~~~~~~

Meanwhile, Rob's efforts to mount a united Aboriginal movement on land rights were bearing fruit. He was instrumental in organising a national Aboriginal meeting in Melbourne on 1 and 2 February 1985, which he later described as the first time such a diverse group of Aboriginal organisations met with the specific aim of developing a common strategy.[67] Rob was also an organiser of a week-long meeting held in Canberra in May 1985 on land rights, which had as its centrepiece a land rights rally held outside Parliament House in Canberra on 13 May. This protest was seen by contemporaries as marking the most potent level of unity among Aboriginal groups in recent history.[68] Over 1000 Aborigines (some said as many as 5000) were drawn from around the country and from urban, rural and remote locations.

Tempers flared as the assembled group gathered behind police lines outside the steps of the Parliament. Standing alongside his friend and colleague Pat Dodson, Rob spontaneously instigated a pivotal moment in the protest. He grabbed hold of a megaphone and started shouting 'Come out Andrew, [Peacock]. Show yourself'. He was 'really angry'. At that stage, 'the mob just took off straight across the road', rushing for the steps of Parliament House. The protesters were momentarily content with the ground they had occupied, when Roger Shipton, the opposition spokesman for Aboriginal Affairs, came out and made his way towards the protesters on the steps. His presence almost incited a riot. Rob, who was still clutching the megaphone, yelled straight into Shipton's face: 'Is your name Andrew? Are you Andrew Peacock? We want to speak to Andrew'. Rob convinced the police to escort Shipton from the rally and, according to Pat Dodson, everybody made a dash, like 'a mob of cattle racing ... towards Parliament House and some bloke actually got into the Grand Hall'. Eventually they retreated, but Rob's anger had not only defined the mood of the crowd, it had raised feelings to a fever pitch. A telling photograph in *The Australian* showed Rob Riley with megaphone to his mouth face-to-face with an incredulous-looking Roger Shipton. It conveyed a powerful image: Aboriginal people would not easily be pushed aside.[69] However, the recourse to protest politics had come too late to prevent Labor reneging on its commitments.

Rob had also been caught up in the political quagmire that enveloped Burke's Western Australian land rights legislation. In this debate, a critical choice faced Aboriginal activists and especially those who, like Rob, had been campaigning on the national stage: whether to support a Bill which gave some benefits to Aborigines, or mount a concerted attack on any proposed legislation which fell short of agreed the national principles. The latter strategy was the more compelling because of the fear that any support for Burke might undermine the larger campaign against Hawke, while also sanctioning the Burke government's own retreat from the Seaman Inquiry recommendations. There seemed to be little room to move.

However, the issue was not clear cut. The Western Australian Aboriginal Land Bill, while rejecting key recommendations of the Seaman Report, had one positive: the area of land available to be claimed was extensive. This included the 7.5 per cent of the state vested in Aboriginal reserves and available for freehold title by land rights corporations, and vacant Crown land amounting to 38 per cent of the state. A prominent advocate for Aboriginal causes, Jesuit priest Frank Brennan, acknowledged the dilemma. In a briefing to the Western Australian Branch of the NAC, he argued: 'I have no doubt that the proposed legislation contains much which will benefit the state's Aboriginals giving them access to land previously unavailable to them. Equally, I have no doubt that it falls short of what Mr Seaman proposed and what is implied in the Commonwealth government's five principles'.[70]

By now, Burke was a deft pragmatist who drew quiet enjoyment from the opportunity the land rights debate offered to 'lay into the left'.[71] He began by inviting all major interest groups to be part of the advisory process of drafting the legislation, possibly hoping that the long-standing divisions in Aboriginal politics would open up. Rob and the NAC accepted the invitation at the end of 1984 to be part of the consultative process, even though he and others realised by now that Burke had only a limited measure in mind. From this point Rob's relationship with Burke rapidly deteriorated. No sooner had the NAC agreed to join when Burke took the opportunity to dismiss the NAC because he claimed Rob had leaked details of the proposed Bill to *The Age* newspaper. It was a claim Rob vehemently denied. In a stinging letter to the Premier he wrote: 'Your unwritten allegation was that I had deliberately "leaked" the Draft Bill to the media and in the classic ALP tradition of finding people guilty before proven, you used that as a reason to ban the NAC from further involvement in the drafting process. I believe you have an obligation to substantiate this inference or apologise'.[72] Rob further accused the Premier of pursuing 'a deliberate' strategy to alienate and isolate the NAC and to create divisions among Aboriginal groups.

Whether or not Rob was correct in his analysis of the Premier's motives, the ban had the effect of opening up the anticipated divisions in Aboriginal politics. Bodies including the Aboriginal Lands Trust stayed in Burke's process, causing Rob to complain to Robert Isaacs, Chairman of the Trust, that he was willing 'to cement the "split" in the Aboriginal ranks'.[73]

However, having been forced out, Rob was now free to maintain an uncompromising approach to land rights. As he told the Premier: 'Aboriginal land rights, in our view, are more important than the political expediency of the W.A. Government, and more important than the NAC'.[74] He became one of the Bill's most bitter critics.[75]

Rob resisted attempts by the state ALP to bring him back into the fold. Peter Dowding recalls: 'Rob wasn't the sort of guy you could have a discussion with at that time ... he was just so angry'. He maintains that Rob and other activists criticising the Bill miscalculated in their opposition to the legislation: Rob was 'shooting himself in the foot and his all or nothing approach was a hopeless political stance and once you had significant bodies attacking the legislation from within the

Aboriginal community, we didn't have a leg to stand on in trying to get it through as a reasonable compromise'.

How much additional support the Bill would have received in the Upper House, where it eventually failed by a few votes, is obviously impossible to determine. Dowding acknowledges it was always going to be a tall order to secure its passage through the conservative chamber. In any event, the bottom-line position of Aboriginal activists was the retention of the veto over mining; anything less was tantamount to defeat and therefore unworthy of support.

By the beginning of 1985, activists working at both the national and Western Australian levels stared defeat in the face. Publicly, Rob's reactions articulated the impact of this betrayal for Aboriginal people, but there was also a private dimension. How much responsibility should he shoulder? Could he and other leaders like Pat Dodson have done things differently? Publicly, Rob ascribed the defeats over national and state land rights to forces outside their control. The case for this view is persuasive. But what if more compromise had been applied, and especially over the vexed matter of the veto? Rob must have realised that this was a key sticking point for governments in their dealings with the mining lobby. Why did he not propose cutting a deal and building on its provisions later? The simple answer is: no-one close to the Aboriginal side thought in this manner. As Rob pointed out several times, the need for a veto was upheld by all major inquiries into land rights since the early 1970s. Noonkanbah had solidified the view that gaining land rights without a right of veto would be a hollow victory. Rob was aware from briefings given by Holding that Hawke retained a strong commitment to the need to protect sacred sites. Moreover, Aboriginal rights leaders tried in vain to counter the myth that Aborigines were against mining. As Nugget Coombs argued at the height of the land rights debate, Aborigines 'are not absolutely opposed to mining but will reach agreements which authorise it provided their reasonable interests are protected: their religious, cultural and social life and access to a livelihood which does not require them to become a dependent, landless proletariat with no other options'.[76] The right and the need for Aborigines to have effective control over their land had, by the early 1980s, become the accepted position. Thus the question about the failure to achieve outcomes should not be posed as a failure of the

Aboriginal rights movement to show flexibility but as a backdown by government from this accepted position.

Perhaps the Aboriginal rights movement should have engaged the federal government in a different process to achieve land rights. Aboriginal rights leaders appeared to underestimate the time and complexities involved in articulating land rights as a legal, rather than simply a moral, cause. But, then so did the government, which dragged its feet in providing the details for its five principles. Both sides should have, and could have, realised that the initial deadlines for legislation were unrealistic. The call to a summit on land rights from Rob Riley and Pat Dodson was made late in the debate and failed to fully exploit the connection to Hawke's consensus approach to government. Why was consensus only being applied to some problems and not others?

But there was no certainty that the federal government would agree to such a proposal or that consensus would have been possible, with such implacable opponents as the mining and pastoral industries. In fact the land rights debate highlights the deficiencies in the concept of consensus as a model for governing. Rob placed the onus on the government for failing to plan out the process: 'You'd think that the people who drafted the policy would have planned a strategy to implement it. But they didn't'.[77] Yet the counter-criticism also has some merit: that Aboriginal leaders put too much effort into defining the shape of land rights and too little into how to achieve the outcomes.

It must be remembered there was a pent up feeling in the Aboriginal rights movement for change and the enthusiasm to achieve it was, in large part, generated by the absolute commitments given by Labor at both state and federal levels. This is where Rob felt the sense of betrayal so acutely: the trust broken by Labor. A year after the defeat he was still bitter: 'you can imagine the frustration and anger people feel after having specific promises from the Labor Party, having trusted them and organised Aboriginal people to vote for them. All that trust and hope has been dashed'.[78]

~~~

Rob felt frustration, exhaustion, despair, and the weight of responsibility. In a rare acknowledgement of the emotional strains he told an ABC radio interviewer that 'getting kicked from pillar to post' was 'an incredible feeling'.[79] He told the National Press Club of the weariness of continually confronting the government's unfulfilled promises. The land rights struggle came to assume a wider, symbolic importance as a fight against all the wrongs done to Indigenous people, and it pushed to the sidelines most of the other critical issues facing Aboriginal people. And, for Rob, land rights was fought partly as a battle for compensation for his own dispossessed people. The all-embracing significance of the issue must have heightened both its perceived importance and the impact of its defeat.

His close colleagues recall Rob's exhaustion. Pat Dodson testifies to the enormous pressure he was under. Firstly, he had to hold the line with the National Federation of Land Councils, often with only lukewarm support from some of his NAC colleagues, when his political instincts told him that the bottom-line position was probably going to fall apart. Secondly, he was under pressure to maintain confidentiality. Rob, because of his access to government information and to the Minister, knew much more about events than his colleagues outside the formal structure of the NAC. Yet he always maintained a fully professional approach. He was in a position to reveal some damaging information about government dealings, but never did so. He kept close to his chest personal briefings he had about the ANOP poll and declined to share these even with Pat Dodson.

Deeper in his psyche, though, he felt shattered. Late one night after a long meeting with Holding, Rob emerged 'terribly depressed', feeling that 'there was no way forward' and 'nothing was going to come out of the process'. Pat Dodson had been waiting for him and he tried to get Rob to focus on something else, but there was little he could do; Rob 'felt the pain of it very acutely and I think he felt a certain level of personal failure of not being able to deliver, even though it was clearly not his personal failure'. They drove home together and Rob put on a mournful country and western tape which seemed to Dodson to sum up his mood: 'He thought we had been bloody castrated by Holding and his henchmen'.

Stressful as it was to maintain the struggle, the real issue for Rob was the further stripping away of his hopes for change. The fights with Sir Charles Court were exhausting and debilitating but they could be placed in perspective: he could be dismissed in their view as an extremist. The Labor Party was supposed to embrace change and protect minorities and the disadvantaged. What Rob believed he discovered in his dealings with the federal and state Labor governments was the lack of underlying morality in the political system. Pat Dodson recalls the personal challenge to Rob from the land rights fights: 'I think the vast and crude aspects of the political cutting edge was something that he didn't appreciate as much as we did. He did think there was a fair degree of good in the process that could deliver ... Rob believed that public opinion could help sway the day'. But his hope for an enlightened public had also been dashed by politicians' failures to stand up for Aboriginal rights.

Exhausted and disillusioned though he was by mid-1985, the struggle for land rights greatly enhanced Rob's thinking about politics and power. He emerged from this period as one of the most articulate advocates of human rights ideals within the Aboriginal rights movement. Being closer to the centre of political machinations and the interaction of the players than most others in the movement, Rob had observed the fusion of race, power and politics. He drew some bitter lessons from this involvement.

He abhorred the elitist underpinnings of Australian politics. Hawke may have been preaching consensus, as if this implied a level political playing field, but the reality was that the most powerful economic groups dictated policy to government. Even as Chair of the government's Aboriginal advisory group, he had no direct access to Hawke and had few meetings with him. Miners, on the other had, enjoyed high-level access. This meant, Rob said, 'the interests of Aboriginal people are being eroded because of the influence of these other interests'.[80]

Rob's ideal of justice was badly sullied by his dealings with the political process. He doubted that politicians were motivated by such ideals. To them, land rights was 'a gutter political brawl' rather than the legal and moral obligation it should be.[81] Consequently, politicians operated as populists rather than as statesmen. He told the National Press Club: 'Our future should not depend on favourable opinion polls. Nor should our rights be jeopardised by the desire of political parties to gain or maintain office'. Rob found it hard to believe that neither Hawke nor Burke were willing to seize the political moment: 'we have two of the most popular leaders that have ever been elected and yet they're not prepared to use their popularity to take an issue onto the wider community and convince people that governments have to recognise the obligations it has to Aboriginal people'.

Justice, equality and the responsibilities of government complemented Rob's growing international framework. Rob, as has been previously noted, visited the United Nations in Geneva and was around when the Aboriginal rights movement first internationalised its struggle. He called upon the government to extend its compliance with international human rights treaties so that Aborigines could be given power to place Australia 'under direct international scrutiny'. It is no wonder that the federal government increasingly regarded Rob as a threat.

Such international links were, in Rob's mind, all the more important in light of the conclusions he had reached about Australian politics. Change, as opposed to political tinkering, did not seem possible. In this regard he belongs to a long line of political thinkers on the left of politics critical of the limitations of reformist, left-of-centre parties like the ALP. But there was a darker dimension to his conclusions about the nature of power: Aborigines were forced to exist in a state of domination from which there was little escape. And, by extension, social justice in society at large was a forlorn project. Thus when he lamented that Labor had forgotten 'the people who have traditionally shown their support, be they migrants, Aboriginal people, women, or low income earners' there is a real sense of knowing that this view had emerged from a leader of rare conviction.[82]

By May 1985 when the political landscape appeared at its bleakest, Rob Riley was still Chair of the NAC. Nevertheless, he had one further battle ahead: a move to oust him from the position. This time he would be exposed to one of the harshest lessons of politics: the need to watch your back.

CHAPTER EIGHT

Enemies Within: The End of the National Aboriginal Conference

When a journalist came to interview Rob Riley on 5 July 1985 at the empty Perth headquarters of the NAC, Rob had an air of defeat.[1] By now he was tagged by the press as the 'angry young man of black politics' for his uncompromising attacks on governments. On this July day, though, he had only parting shots to fire. His once bustling office had fallen silent. The telephones had been removed and his staff were out looking for work. Rob was alone, making a final assessment of the Aboriginal rights movement which he had worked so tirelessly to build. The NAC, which had been the focus of this movement under his leadership, had been demolished, torn apart internally by dissension and disagreement, and externally by the federal government.

The contrast in personal styles of Rob and the Minister for Aboriginal Affairs, Clyde Holding, was largely responsible for the drama that ended Rob's leadership. Rob was a conviction politician with an unshakeable political framework. He once explained his approach as 'straight forward'; a willingness to voice opinions 'when I've felt it necessary to do so'; 'not being intimidated by people no matter how senior the position'; and 'forceful/aggressive in defending the N.A.C.'s position'.[2] Holding possessed similar forcefulness and had proved his commitment to ALP policy on Aboriginal affairs over several years, travelling the country with an almost robotic willingness to talk up Labor's commitments in the portfolio. Yet he also belonged to the school of realist politics and accepted the dictates of political survival; the Party's needs came first. Thus, Holding became an equally resolute defender of the federal government's retreat on the heritage legislation, the public awareness campaign and the five principles of national land rights legislation. Opponents recall his desire to control events, his defensiveness when questioned, his intolerance of criticism, and his readiness to denigrate those who challenged him. 'You either did it his way or you were on the outer', is Michael Mansell's recollection. Inevitably, Holding would have to confront the issue of how to deal with the uncompromising, articulate and dogged Chair of his advisory body.

Rob's relationship with Holding started cordially enough. Rob had congratulated his Minister for his sincere approach on the occasion of Holding's first NAC Executive meeting. However, the two men's forceful personalities brought them into head-on clashes over ALP policy changes. Both relished a verbal joust and neither willingly took a backward step. Hostility between the two broke out in an NAC Executive meeting on 16 August 1984, when Holding was forced to defend the government's backdown over the heritage legislation. Rob went public, accusing his Minister 'of developing the Aboriginal Affairs Department at the expense of other Aboriginal bodies and of undermining the NAC and cutting its finances'.[3]

The two appeared together on the ABC's current affairs program *Pressure Point*. Rob challenged the Minister over his handling of the portfolio, complaining that he was bypassing the NAC as the voice of Aboriginal people. Presenter Huw Evans asked Rob whether the problem was between himself and the Minister or between the Department and the NAC members. Rob replied: 'Both. We don't get to see documents until after a decision is made. The government has a policy of self-determination and if the policy is going to have any credence surely things should come to an advisory body'.[4] In his complaint about being overlooked, Rob had put his finger on the precarious position the NAC held within Canberra power structures. In theory the organisation was supposed to act as the Minister's prime advisory body, but in fact Holding took official advice from at least two other sources: the Department of Aboriginal Affairs, headed by the mercurial Charles Perkins, and the Aboriginal Development Corporation, which functioned as a development bank to sponsor projects for economic self-sufficiency in Aboriginal communities.

Of course, Holding had some reasons to be concerned about the NAC. The Coombs analysis had highlighted its inadequacies, and he had had to respond to allegations that substantial monies had been misused by some members prior to Rob becoming Chair. Holding had to call in the Auditor General to examine the agency's accounts.

By the time mismanagement was confirmed, Rob had started to make progress in rectifying the problems,[5] but the combination of this scrutiny, together with the uncertainty surrounding the recommendations of the Coombs Report, had tempers flaring at an NAC Executive meeting. Rob fumed at the Minister. The NAC, he said, had been placed in a 'hopeless' situation, unable to exercise any control or influence. NAC members were, he said, 'sitting down like chooks with our heads on the block waiting for someone to swing the axe'. Rob accused the Minister of threatening the agency with execution: 'You are using the Coombs report as a stick and saying: "you are being naughty" and you are using the Auditor General's report in that way too and flogging us with it and not giving us the opportunity, within the Conference, to deal with things or respond to things the way we think you want us to'.[6] The public impression, on the other hand, was that Holding was undertaking effective negotiations with Aboriginal groups while supposedly neglecting to deal with the concerns of the mining and pastoral groups.[7] Holding was meeting with Aborigines but, his critics allege, he was not engaged in effective negotiation with them, and not using the NAC for such a purpose.

Rob was clearly feeling frustrated, trapped in a *Catch-22* situation: expectations that the NAC perform were being thwarted by the

Minister. Some thought the situation deliberately constructed for this outcome. According to Peter Yu, 'They [Holding and Aboriginal Affairs Department head, Charlie Perkins] appeared to be attempting to sabotage any efforts by the NAC to regain their independence'.[8]

Rob further antagonised Holding in September 1984, when he wrote to him denying the Minister's claim that it was not the place of Indigenous people to involve themselves in international issues of political sensitivity. Quite the contrary, Rob argued: 'Indigenous populations have a community of interest which transcends their national affiliations ... Aboriginal people have an obligation to express solidarity with peoples suffering genocide and exploitation, and to place their own struggle within the world context of human rights'.[9]

Rob's passion for speaking out, his determination to light up the Aboriginal cause in public and private forums, became intolerable for Holding from late 1984, when Rob was among the most vocal critics of the government's deal with Western Australian premier Burke, and the subsequent watering-down of its commitment to land rights. He further unsettled the government by calling on Aborigines to boycott all bicentenary celebrations in three years time unless the land rights legislation was changed.[10]

Was Rob overstepping the boundaries between Minister and adviser? Where should the balance have been struck between the two? Modern practice dictates that a Minister appoints heads of advisory groups with whom he/she can work. But the NAC was no ordinary advisory group: it was a representative organisation. The chair of the NAC was accountable to Aboriginal people. This should have placed the onus on Holding to find ways to work constructively with its head. But with Rob impatient for change and willing to take the issues out from behind closed door discussion into the public arena, something had to give. The problems rapidly surfacing between Rob and Holding spoke to the wider, unresolved tension in the relationship between government and Aboriginal people.

By the time the Hawke government had announced its own preferred land rights model in early 1985, Holding had, according to Rob, decided that he must be ousted from his position as Chair. This account is widely supported by others in the NAC at the time,[11] although not all saw it this way. According to Rob, Holding started undermining his authority among NAC members and invoked the support of Charles Perkins.

The fight was both personal and political. Holding realised that Rob's ability to expose the limitations and betrayals of Labor's changed policy approach to land rights was an obstacle to achieving the legislation. And this mutated into nasty personal politics.

In at least two stinging letters to Holding, Rob accused him, together with Charles Perkins, of waging a war of attrition against his leadership. Acknowledging Holding's anger at the boycott of the Land Rights Steering Committee meeting organised by himself and Pat Dodson, Rob accused Holding of misrepresenting the facts behind their collective stance as NAC and land council members. Rob expressed his 'disappointment and disgust' at the Minister's tactic of 'divide and rule', aimed, Rob said, at ridding himself of opposition to the government's watering-down of land rights. Filled with rage, Rob told Holding: 'To so blatantly and falsely undermine the authority of an elected Chairman of an Aboriginal representative body because that Chairman questions your actions and your motives is gutter politics at its worst'. Rob could already envisage Holding wielding the executioner's axe. Rob challenged Holding to refute his allegation that his insidious campaign of undermining was being undertaken 'in the hope that this will see me removed from office, hopefully to be replaced by a person more amenable to "toeing the line"'. Rob made it known to Holding that his ploy might work: 'It shouldn't be too difficult for you to find the "yes-man" (or "yes-woman") you seek if collectively the Conference and the Land Councils fail to see through your ploy, or if a majority of members are willing to sacrifice Aboriginal unity for selfish ends'.[12] Later, Rob would publicly accuse Holding of engaging in a 'calculated exercise' to undermine his leadership.[13]

As Rob was trying to deal with Holding, tensions within the NAC, never far from the surface, deepened over the response to the government's preferred land rights model. On 21 February 1985, Deputy Chair Lyall Munro senior telexed all thirty-five of his colleagues dissociating himself from the actions Rob Riley and Pat Dodson had taken in refusing to meet with the government over its proposed legislation. Munro was a veteran of the Aboriginal struggle for rights, having been involved in the 1965 Freedom Ride and the Tent Embassy. He felt that Riley and Dodson should have approached the NAC Executive to ratify their action. By joining Dodson in walking away from negotiations with the government Rob was accused of acting unilaterally and ignoring proper consultation.[14] Rob must have been jolted by the criticism. After all, he was accusing the government of doing the very same thing.

But Rob believed that he was now operating on a larger political canvass than that of the NAC, whose capacities he had grown to doubt. This does not excuse Rob's actions; to ignore the body he headed in this way was certain to raise doubts about his leadership. Whether his actions justified the call for his resignation is harder to say. Surely, Munro's call spoke to deeper tensions between the two former rivals for the position of NAC Chair and their differences over styles of leadership. Some of Rob's critics later told him that he was 'the puppet of the more outspoken Aboriginal land councils'.[15]

On 3 April, Holding announced the abolition of the NAC, in clear contravention of undertakings he had given in July 1984 not to 'put the knife' through the organisation while the struggle over land rights was going on.[16] Nonetheless, Rob publicly welcomed the decision and announced his own intentions not to be involved in any future structure, causing disquiet among some of his fellow NAC members. He probably further annoyed Holding by reaffirming his claim that it was being disbanded 'because it had maintained an independent stand in the face of government threats and bullying'.[17] He went further than even these sharp words. The press release he issued contained sentiments of raw emotion missing from the published account. Aborigines had learned lessons from the demise of the NAC, he wrote, the most glaring being that: 'we have no political friends ... we can trust no-one ... too many politicians have betrayed us for us ever to be fooled that way again'.[18]

By the time Rob had played his part in organising the Canberra protest rally in mid May and the week-long lobbying activities involving Aboriginal people from all over the country, Holding could no longer ignore the issue of his leadership. As Peter Yu wrote not long after these events:

> It was becoming increasingly uncomfortable for Holding being criticised from all sections of the community, especially Aboriginal people. Riley and the NAC were becoming a focus for the movement — there's no doubt that for the first time, the NAC was doing what it was supposed to be doing — showing strong leadership.[19]

It was no coincidence, Yu thought, that the moves against Riley's leadership increased after the week of lobbying. From this point, events moved into the shadows. Those critical of Holding claim he turned 'mean and nasty'. He had an ally in Charlie Perkins, who disliked Rob, and who did not agree with the land rights protest; he felt that people were being unrealistic and that they should take more modest views.

With the support of a few fellow NAC members, Rob made several public accusations about Holding's activities. Firstly, he claimed Holding held a private four-hour meeting with twenty NAC delegates on 13 May, four days before Rob was voted out, at which, along with Perkins, he mounted 'a devastating attack' on Rob's leadership. Secondly, Rob alleged Holding 'offered carrots to people who wanted to survive after the NAC was wound up'.[20] In a statement later prepared for legal proceedings, Rob claimed that the attack mounted by Holding and Perkins against himself and Les Malezer (the General Secretary) 'deliberately developed a scenario in which both Malezer and myself were being subject to ridicule. They consistently emphasised that members were obliged to question our actions on behalf of the N.A.C.'[21]

Peter Yu also gave credence to the theory of a deal. Although his claim does not refer to any inducements to particular individuals, it was linked to a political outcome: if Riley was gotten rid of and the NAC under new leadership voted in favour of the government's preferred land rights model, then Holding would consider extending the NAC term further.[22]

Today, the allegations about how Rob lost the chair of the NAC remain serious but cannot be fully substantiated. The allegations of dirty politics were made in the public domain at the time, and Rob's own correspondence adds important details, which mostly flesh out his own side of the account. One NAC member got wind of the allegations of inducements to secure Rob's downfall and strenuously denied the accusation. Whatever the motives of members in taking action to depose Rob, the manner in which it was undertaken was seen by Rob's supporters as being illegitimate, and it later became the subject of court action.

Rob was unaware of the immediate threat to his position until NAC members were summoned by Lyall Munro senior and Sugar Ray Robinson to an NAC meeting held on the afternoon of Friday, 17 May at the Statesman Hotel in Canberra. The numbers invited would be the basis of Rob's claims of a dirty deal. Robinson and Munro claimed the meeting was an Annual General Meeting (AGM), the occasion on which, under the NAC's constitution, the Chair automatically stood down and new nominations were called for. A transcript of the meeting indicates that Rob did not consider the meeting a constitutionally valid AGM but a special general meeting to discuss the closing down of the NAC.[23] He later called it 'hastily convened'.[24] This was an important distinction; a properly constituted AGM could vote on the leadership issue with a bare majority, a special meeting required a two-thirds vote. All but two of those members present agreed the meeting was an AGM. But fellow Western Australian delegate Margaret Mallard insisted that the meeting was not described to her as such. However, eleven members were missing, and it is unclear whether all, or any, of these members were actually informed of the meeting. One of these members, Peter Yu, claims never to have been informed about it. As part of the later court proceedings Yu gave an affidavit testifying to the following: he received no notice of an AGM to be held on the 17th; he received no notice that a proposal would be put that the position of chair was to be vacated; he received no notice that a proposal to adopt the preferred model of the National Land Rights Discussion Paper was to be put to the meeting; and, had he been informed of any of the above, he would have been sure to attend the meeting.[25]

Sugar Ray Robinson was in charge of proceedings. An imposing figure with his tall, well-built physique, rich baritone voice, and commanding personality, Robinson advocated the view that the meeting represented a legitimate AGM. Rob countered, insisting that he 'would not be railroaded into accepting the position of vacating the chair'.

Robinson went on the offensive. Invoking the notorious Premier of Queensland, Joh Bjelke Petersen, and his gerrymandered democracy with its rigged electoral boundaries, Robinson ridiculed Rob's call for a two-thirds vote: 'Now here's the Chairman here saying that he wants two thirds of the vote before he'll vacate the chair. What ridiculous, stupid, bloody rot. That's not a democratic election'. Things were becoming personal. Rob retorted to Robinson's charge that he lacked the spirit for democracy: 'you should know that better than anyone, Sugar, because you come from Queensland'. General Secretary Les Malezer tried several times to hold the position to which Rob was appealing; that this was a special meeting requiring a two-thirds majority to vote out the Chairman. And each time he tried to adjudicate, Robinson would respond: 'No No No Mr Chairman. You're wrong again'. The tension in the room must have been palpable. It was an historic moment for the NAC: to follow Robinson and Munro and ensure some continuing relevance for the NAC and its possible successor, or follow Rob into the uncertain existence of moral protest and ... perhaps irrelevance.

The struggle of wills ended with Les Malezer acceding to a vote on Robinson's motion; the chair was to be declared vacant. Malezer seemingly had little option; somehow the deadlock had to be broken. Rob lost the vote 18–5. Nominations were called for. Lyall Munro stood against Rob and won 15–10.

The real politics behind the meeting may never be known. Outwardly, some members of the NAC may well have been worried by Rob's high-wire leadership style and his readiness to take the NAC to the brink in pursuit of the cause. He might well not have gained sufficient support even if all members had been present. The skills Rob was supposed to have brought to the position had not healed the divisions in the organisation. In fact, his larger vision for it had alienated some support. Moreover, it is not clear why Rob wanted to stay on as Chair for the few months Holding had been prepared to extend to members. If he had lost confidence it in why did he not just leave? Was it because he suspected a deal over land rights? The evidence is not clear to make a judgement, but Rob had his suspicions that all was not as it appeared in terms of the manner of his removal.

He was gracious in defeat, congratulating Munro on his victory. Nevertheless, he had an unplanned, small vindication. As the meeting was about to close, he made an apologetic acknowledgement that it was necessary to sort out whether he or the new Chair should accept the already confirmed invitation to be interviewed on a panel discussion with Clyde Holding on SBS television. Turning to Robinson and Munro, Rob declared: 'Now, due to tragic circumstances you'll have to decide who's going to attend that meeting between the two of you'. Munro responded, without any explanation: 'I'm not prepared to meet

Mr Holding at this stage'. And so there was one final round ... after which it would be all over for Rob.

The NAC itself had an ignoble end, mired in legal battles instigated by Rob over his allegations surrounding his unconstitutional removal as Chair, with counter-action by Munro. Eventually the shell that was left from these bruising encounters was wound up. It was a sad end to an experiment in Aboriginal politics which Rob acknowledged had failed, caught between governments' unwillingness to allow it to function properly and the infighting of its members.

The implications of its demise were significant. It left a vacuum in Aboriginal politics for the next five years until the Hawke government established the Aboriginal and Torres Strait Islander Commission. The National Coalition of Aboriginal Organisations was formed by Aboriginal leaders in 1986 with Rob elected as Chair, in an attempt to fill this vacuum, but it lacked resources for other than occasional meetings. Without a well-resourced and independent voice, Aborigines were shut out of their role as full citizens. Without effective organisations to represent them, they could do little to claim their formal rights as an Indigenous people in addition to the universal ones common to all citizens. Conveniently, this kept land rights and the unpalatable claims to sovereignty and compensation off the political agenda.

Rob had no idea what the future held after he failed to win the vote at the Statesman Hotel. Fortunately, others did. In the room next door to where the NAC was playing out its death throes, Jack Ah Kit and Galarrwuy Yunupingu, both veterans of the land rights struggle and prominent members of the Northern Land Council, were in a meeting. Pat Dodson had sent a message that Riley must be looked after; his talents as a leader could not be lost.

Rob emerged, pushing his glasses back onto his forehead in a sign of resignation, and declared, 'That's it, they've rolled me'. Yunupingu extended his right hand and said, 'Welcome aboard, their loss is our gain, come and work with the Northern Land Council'.

~~~~~~

So, when the journalist visited Rob on 5 July, the 'angry young man of black politics' was about to head north; a 'welcomed self-imposed exile'.[26] Riley warned Aboriginal people that they now had a single choice: to wait for a new cycle in the land rights struggle, which he believed might take ten years, or take matters into their own hands. This, he said, would involve expressing themselves as Native Americans did in 1972 at Wounded Knee, when 200 armed Indians held out for seventy days in a dramatic bid to highlight their plight. The statement was a measure of the collapse in his confidence that Australian democracy would ever be capable of rising to the challenge of addressing the injustices of the past.

Riley attacked all those who he believed had thwarted the cause: Holding for undermining him; Hawke and Burke for their sleazy 'deal'; and ordinary Labor politicians, who had 'just done the dirty on Aboriginal people'.

~~~~~~~

If there was a place to nurse such wounds to mind and soul, it might have been Darwin. It is a city cradled by its stunning physical surrounds. The bay laps the edge of the city. The tropical heat slows and mellows the body. Darwin was a place where Rob should have been able to recover from his exhaustion.

Yet, for Aborigines, Darwin had its tensions. A frontier mentality still pervaded politics and race relations, and the conservative — many would say reactionary — Country/Liberal Party government of the 1980s was forever trying to convince Canberra to whittle back the power given to Aboriginal people under the *Northern Territory Land Rights Act 1976* (Cwlth).

If Darwin was a near ideal location, the Northern Land Council was the perfect place to work. Large, powerful and purposeful, it presented a positive contrast to the powerlessness of 'southern' Aboriginal political organisations. Here, Rob could observe Aboriginal politics at work, invested with legal authority conferred under the Northern Territory land rights legislation. And, to cap off the positives, the NLC was headed by Jack Ah Kit, one of the most respected Aboriginal men in Territory politics, and the perfect mentor for Rob. His large frame was complemented by a generosity of spirit, and he and Rob quickly became close colleagues and friends. Mick Dodson, who worked at the NLC at the time of Rob's arrival, said of Ah Kit that he was 'about the best boss you could ever have'.

For Jeannie and the girls, Darwin was a new adventure. Rob was fortunate in having Jeannie willingly accept the day-to-day challenges of relocation, leaving him to focus on his political role.

In the mid-1980s, the NLC had a staff of about a hundred spread over several regional offices, and a multimillion dollar budget. It was organised along classic public service lines with separate departments. Rob filled the position of Assistant Manager of Field Operations, the largest of the departments, and also advised the organisation on national and international political developments. Rob's role was an all-embracing one to liaise with traditional owners about issues affecting their land, and especially about requests from mining companies. The parallel with Noonkanbah could not have escaped him; here were Aborigines exerting control in a way that the Noonkanbah Community could only have dreamed about.

The job entailed regular bush field trips, which Rob loved, and he participated in quarterly full council meetings. These proved an eye-opener for him, with representatives of all the different peoples from across the northern part of the Territory. He would marvel at how much respect they had for each other, and the process they engaged in to reach solutions. He was impressed with the degree of their control over their own affairs. He wrote to Jill Abdullah, his former personal assistant at the WA Branch of the NAC, with the observation that:

> It's really good when you see these 'big shots' from Melbourne or Sydney front up to these bush meetings. They think that everything revolves around them. They get a bit of a shock when the traditional owners say they'll have to wait or even that they'll have to come back another time because they have more important things to talk about.[27]

Rob eased himself into the relaxed lifestyle of the Territory and his natural disposition resurfaced: people loved him for his happy-go-lucky approach to life, his fondness for telling a joke and his enthusiasm for sports. His latent competitive instincts also came to the fore in social settings. He hated getting beaten in backgammon, and was once sent off in a social game of football cursing that 'the umpire was a cheat and that all the players on the other side were crooks'. But people took his outburst light-heartedly. He enjoyed the frequent bush picnics shared with Jeannie, his children and other families at the NLC. On one occasion, he was ecstatic at the accomplishment of bowling out the three Dodson brothers in a social cricket match. After a few months even Rob noticed the change in himself. But the passion for politics lay just below the surface. He explained to Jill Abdullah: 'Personally I'm feeling allright. I'm really enjoying the break from the up-front heavy politics but at the same time I get a bit itchy when issues break that the NAC would normally be involved in'. This is an allusive description. He was 'all right', but 'itchy'. There is no sense of how much reflection he had undertaken arising from the big defeats of 1984–5. If he had learned anything about himself, his motivations, and what might keep him balanced, he did not let on, even to an old friend.

Eventually, circumstances conspired to terminate his Territory sojourn. The family was homesick for Western Australia, one of the children suffered from a tropical skin condition, and Rob's desire to find his way back into urban-based Aboriginal politics proved overwhelming. In 1987 the family returned to Perth and Rob established himself in a consultancy.

He developed a range of involvements, all of which were directed at providing scope for the Aboriginal voice. The most noteworthy of these was the leadership role he had in organising the 1987 NAIDOC week celebrations. He energised the Aboriginal community by transforming what had been an important but marginalised cultural event into a dynamic political occasion. Rob returned to one of his core themes about change: the need to educate people about Aboriginal issues. He used NAIDOC week as a potent demonstration of how education could be transformed into a political cause for the benefit of Aboriginal people. The centrepiece of the week's celebrations was a colour brochure for distribution in the community with the title, 'White Australia has a Black history'. Rob was very enthusiastic about the slogan because he felt again that the real problem remained Australians' lack of understanding of their own history.

Rob developed a parallel strategy to make this information even more public, by arranging for its publication in the press. This was a novel strategy at the time. In the 1990s, the inquiries into Aboriginal deaths in custody and the Stolen Generations would thrust Aboriginal history out of the confines of academia and onto the front pages of newspapers. Taking out a five-page advertisement in the tabloid *Daily*

News reflected Rob's faith that ordinary people were not all 'rednecks', they were simply ignorant or ill-informed. He wanted to confront this ignorance by educating the broader public about the brutal reality of the colonisation of the continent and its impact on Indigenous people. In this way he ensured that Aboriginal politics was at the forefront of the NAIDOC celebration, with the broader message to the wider community that Aborigines as a people were still around, still hungry for change, and certainly not defeated. After the hurts of the mid-1980s, it was a message many in the Aboriginal community had been desperate to hear, and Rob was able to enlist many eager followers to help with the activities. He struck a deal with the Perth City Council to have the Aboriginal flag flying along the several kilometre journey from one end of the city to the other, although the Council would not allow any of the flags to bear the 'White Australia has a Black history' slogan.

Perhaps, for Rob, the bold assertiveness of the NAIDOC week celebrations carried a dual message. In his mind Aborigines had emerged from the defeats of the mid-1980s, and so had he. Rob was again ready for action. How could he have recovered his spirit so thoroughly? As Peter Yu has reflected, no matter how cynical an activist may feel, 'you always hope that things are going to change'.

Optimistic, rejuvenated, and ready for more tilts at the white Australian psyche, Rob was looking for new opportunities. As it happened, others were searching him out.

CHAPTER NINE

At the Cutting Edge: Political Battles in Canberra

When Gerry Hand was appointed Minister for Aboriginal Affairs in April 1987 by Prime Minister Bob Hawke, replacing Clyde Holding, he needed someone to fill the all-important position of adviser. Sharply etched in his mind was the image of Rob Riley at the May 1985 land rights rally outside Parliament House. Hand recalled this image several times in the years of his parliamentary jousts with Roger Shipton, the opposition spokesperson on Aboriginal Affairs at the time. In the larrikin style for which Hand had become renowned, he had chided Shipton as 'a mug' for 'being the only white man to have been escorted from a black rally in Australian history'.

It occurred to Hand that the person who had orchestrated Shipton's ignoble removal from the rally might have the strength of purpose to hold down the position of adviser. Hand was particular about the person he was seeking. He had grand plans for the portfolio; he wanted to build a replacement for the NAC.

Hand had been involved in Aboriginal politics for many years. He had been Chair of the House of Representatives Standing Committee on Aboriginal Affairs as well as a member of the Caucus Sub-Committee in this area, and he had met Rob several times. Hand was convinced that Rob had the skills needed for the job of adviser: he was a commanding speaker, an effective negotiator and he was well liked. Hand noted there was an edge to Rob: he could get extraordinarily angry but still contain himself. The combination of these qualities appealed to him.

Rob first went to work with Hand as a consultant in April 1987 while he was still operating his own consultancy in Perth. In his letter to the Convenor of the Merit Panel at the Department of Prime Minister and Cabinet, Hand wrote:

> I am now at a very important stage of consultations with the Aboriginal and Islander communities in preparation for establishing a new Commission. It has also become very clear from my recent Australia-wide trip that care will be needed to ensure the operations of the Commission go according to plan after its establishment. Hence I need a respected person with extensive contacts throughout the Aboriginal and Islander communities. This person is Mr Riley.[1]

Rob became Hand's full-time adviser in October 1987.

It is not entirely clear why Rob accepted the offer, especially as a full-time post. Still uppermost in his mind was Labor's betrayal of Aboriginal people. His attitudes and actions throughout the first half of 1987 showed that his views had not shifted. In July of that year the fires of his enmity towards the Labor Party and its Prime Minister were still glowing. He addressed a conference in Perth with the title 'Reconciliation?' in which he attacked Hawke for ignoring the warnings about the miners' media campaign and for 'trading our long-term future for short-term political gain'.[2] How could he have joined forces with the same government while still in this antagonistic frame of mind?

Since his departure from the NAC Rob had maintained his involvement in activist politics. In 1986 he was elected inaugural Chair of the National Coalition of Aboriginal Organisations, established in an attempt to fill the gap left by the NAC. Designed to link up Aboriginal organisations from health, law, land councils, child care agencies, and other community-based agencies to work on common strategies, it was a continuation of his vision to achieve a united movement. Although it lacked funds to fulfil its potential, Rob was hopeful about its future. He informed the above Conference of its activities: 'so far we've had a couple of meetings and these have been encouraging. Aboriginal representatives from various states and organisations have appreciated being able to meet away from the constraints of government funding control and we intend to keep it that way'. His disdain for the federal Labor government was obvious in his caustic remark that 'Aborigines are further out in the political wilderness than they have ever been'.

Another sign of his continuing opposition to the federal government was the public support he had given to the highly controversial plans of Tasmanian Aboriginal activist Michael Mansell to visit Libya with a small delegation in mid-1987. The aim of the visit was twofold: to attract funds for the cause and to discuss with the country's leader, Colonel Gadaffi, the prospect of Libya's imposing trade sanctions on Australia.[3] Mansell, an articulate and charismatic figure who had long been an outspoken campaigner for Aboriginal sovereignty, had also planned to use the trip to promote his concept of an Aboriginal passport which, he hoped, the Libyan authorities would recognise. Like Rob, Mansell had a flair for publicity, and the planning for his trip attracted a rising crescendo of complaints from politicians and editorial writers. Mansell was described as 'playing with fire' by visiting 'the godfather of State-sponsored terrorism' and a murderous dictator. The contradiction between this position and the concern that Mansell's trip might damage Australia's bountiful trade with Libya escaped most commentators.[4]

The Prime Minister, in particular, could scarcely hide his outrage that the trip was going ahead. He does not appear to have reflected that his decision to back away from national land rights would inevitably radicalise sections of the Aboriginal rights movement. Mansell had his opponents among Aboriginal leaders as well, notably Charles Perkins, who described the trip as a serious setback for race relations.[5] In fact Mansell maintains few of the established Aboriginal leaders came out on his side — not that their failure to do so bothered him at the time.

Rob, in his capacity as convenor of the National Coalition, did offer qualified endorsement for the delegation. While expressing 'mixed feelings' about Gadaffi, 'having read all the shock horror stuff', Rob nonetheless offered his support to Mansell, but on the proviso that care was taken not to be seen to be condoning violence as a condition of obtaining money. Rob had a jibe at Charles Perkins for 'being a departmental lackey' in trying to prevent the trip. In the highly charged environment in which Mansell was promoting the delegation, Rob's qualified support put him squarely at odds with the federal government.

Rob's trenchant opposition to the forthcoming Bicentennial celebrations adds to the puzzle of his decision to work for Labor. While he was still at the NAC, Rob promoted the need for Aboriginal protest at this occasion should the federal government not fulfil its promises on land rights. In September 1987, and as Chair of the National Coalition of Aboriginal Organisations, Rob had gone to a meeting in Sydney at which plans to disrupt the Bicentennial were discussed but kept secret. Rob hoped the planned protests would 'prick the conscience of white Australia'.[6] Yet weeks later his consultancy role with Hand was elevated to that of adviser and he formally joined forces with the government which was actively seeking to promote the Bicentenary.

The uncharted waters of Rob's new role adds further to the puzzle of his decision. Up to this point, Rob had been an activist: a public figure with a passion for taking on authority and articulating the cause in the media. Now he was preparing to go behind the political scenes and to work for change in the relative anonymity of the corridors of power. It was an unusual switch in roles. He would no longer be able to speak out in public; Ministers, not advisers, occupy the limelight and engage in the battles with opponents. How would he adjust to this unfamiliar role? Would his principled approach to politics be compromised?

Two factors came into play in his decision to work for Hand. The first was the personality and political profile of Gerry Hand. From Rob's days on the NAC he would have been familiar with Hand's progressive stance on Aboriginal and social issues generally, and he would have had some idea how Hand had tried to carry the fight on land rights through the Party's forums. He clearly liked Hand. Hand was unfazed about Rob's qualified support for Mansell, having himself visited Libya in the late 1970s and been attacked by the same forces that now criticised Mansell. Also, Hand had publicly declared that, as the parliamentary representative of Aboriginal people in federal Parliament, he would not be taking part in any Bicentenary celebrations. Hand was ideologically committed to achieving social justice; for years he had represented the majority of Melbourne's socially deprived housing estates. Serious-minded, he was also irreverent and disdainful of pretensions. A heavy smoker, although a non-drinker, he had a colourful use of the vernacular and he did not back away from a scrap. These qualities no doubt appealed to Rob. Rob's wife Jeannie thinks the personal rapport was crucial to Rob's decision to join his staff: 'he must have just really sweet-talked him ... Gerry's personality is quite infectious'. Nonetheless, Hand maintains that joining his staff was one of the 'gutsiest decisions Rob made', and one which showed his commitment to working for change rather than pursuing his own career ambitions.

The second factor behind Rob's decision was his enthusiasm to rejoin the political fray. He loved the cut and thrust of politics. He was instinctively drawn to its promises and its intensities. Rob enjoyed the struggle, the drama and the machinations of politics. In part, politics was an outlet for his competitive instincts. This may partly explain why he drove himself to stay involved, but it does not explain his motivations. These, as previously observed, lay in a combination of his personal experiences of injustice and his acquired understanding of these in their historical context. Consequently, he couldn't pass up the opportunity to be involved in the realisation of the agenda for change that Hand had in mind. The Minister's approach was summed up in a speech to Parliament in which he stated that 'Australians should not back away from acknowledging, in a symbolically important way, the facts of history and our resolve to address the present effects of past injustice'.[7] But had not Clyde Holding expressed similar sentiments?

Lastly, Rob consulted widely among Aboriginal leaders before accepting the position and was urged by many to sign on.

Hand's reform agenda centred on the creation of a new governance structure — the organisation which became known as the Aboriginal and Torres Strait Islander Commission (ATSIC). He had gained Bob Hawke's backing on this. The Prime Minister's support was crucial; Hand did not want to be politically abandoned, as he saw Holding had been. Nonetheless, any move to create a political voice for Aboriginal people was bound to open up a minefield of problems. As the failed experiments with the NACC and the NAC had shown, Australian governments had never been able to resolve their formal relationship with Aboriginal people. The challenge would be to design an organisation that gave maximum expression to Aborigines' claim for self-determination and one that gave them real access to the executive processes of government. But the extent to which these principles could be embodied within the conventions of the Westminster system, let alone prevailing political opinion, would be the real test.

Rob has left no outline of his thinking on a replacement body for the NAC, but those who knew him at the time recall that his preferred model was along the lines of the Northern Territory Land Councils: an autonomous body/bodies, separate from government. Rob did not want a body staffed by public servants, because that would simply transpose all the old thinking and public service behaviour into the new structure. Based on Rob's experience with Jack Ah Kit at the Northern Land Council, this model made practical as well as cultural sense. Discussions along these lines appear to have occurred between Hand and Rob. However, Rob must have been aware that the final outcome would always come down to a question of how much self-determination the Australian political system was willing to recognise.

In becoming first Gerry Hand's consultant, then his senior adviser, Rob became part of a rapidly emerging circle of influence within Australian politics competing with the traditional influence of departmental structures. Ministerial advisers, working directly to their Ministers, were largely unaccountable to the wider apparatus of democratic government. Rob was in a very privileged position. The role was multidimensional: policy adviser, confidante and problem fixer. Hand says he relied on Rob as one of the key people for his understanding of Black politics. Rob sat in on nearly every meeting Hand had, accompanying him to meetings with other Ministers and Budget meetings to allocate funding priorities in Aboriginal affairs.

When Rob joined Hand's staff as a consultant in April 1987, the first task was to move forward with the ATSIC proposal. Rob made plain to Hand his desire to move beyond the NAC model. But the obstacles in the way of realising any new structure were immense. Proposals for Aboriginal governance divided Blacks as well as whites. On one extreme of Aboriginal opinion were those continuing to advocate forms of sovereignty, while at the grassroots the Aboriginal community held strong views often at variance with the leaders. In addition, there were political 'hard heads' and 'white-anters' in the Labor Party opposed to any move towards self-determination.

Rob was intimately involved in the discussions which led to the original blueprint for ATSIC: *Foundations for the Future*, Gerry Hand's Ministerial Statement made in the House of Representatives on 10 December 1987. It was a bold, and to some, threatening development in Aboriginal Affairs. Picking up the threads of the model 'Nugget' Coombs had laid out in his report on the NAC in 1984, *Foundations for the Future* proposed a model for Aboriginal governance based around the principle of self-determination, within the confines imposed by government accountability. The most innovative part of the proposal was to create twenty-eight regional councils 'to provide the opportunity for Aboriginal and Islander people to have a real say in the running of their affairs and the determination of priorities for action'. In addition, the regional councils would make recommendations about issues on the ground to a central commission, which, in turn, would provide policy advice to the Minister. The proposed Commission would incorporate the Department of Aboriginal Affairs; the Aboriginal Development Commission; the Aboriginal Hostels Ltd; and the Australian Institute of Aboriginal Studies. Adding gravitas to his proposal for reform, Hand announced that the forthcoming legislation to establish ATSIC would contain a Preamble to the Act as a way of acknowledging the 'Australian people's commitment to the recognition and protection of the rights of Aboriginal and Islander people and measures to overcome their disadvantage'. It was envisaged as a dry run for a Treaty: a form of words which might be embodied in a constitutional document. A proposed Preamble was attached to the Statement. As a package, *Foundations* represented the most far-reaching attempt to transform the relationship of power between Black and white in Australia's history.

Foundations for the Future was the outcome of intense discussions involving many people. Rob was only one of these, even though he occupied a crucial position close to the Minister. The completed document contained elements of Rob's views about Aboriginal governance: representation for Aboriginal people; control over budgetary processes; regional involvement to complement a national focus; and an overarching policy role in relation to other government departments in their dealings with Aboriginal people. Yet it also departed in significant ways from his ideal of the land council model. It had umbilical ties to the financial and accountability processes of government, and its proposed three-tiered structure — local, state and national — threatened to make it a bureaucratic monster. Despite these obvious compromises, Rob thought the model outlined in *Foundations for the Future* represented a fresh start in Aboriginal affairs. He and Hand had an understanding, shared by some other key players, that the task to create a new Aboriginal political organisation would be an on-going challenge. In other words, they needed to get in place what was achievable now and develop the structure further at later stages.

Undoubtedly, this strategy carried risks for Rob. In light of his earlier commitments to securing a more autonomous body, was he turning a blind eye to weaknesses that would slowly cripple the effectiveness of ATSIC? In moving to work inside the system, he had come face-to-face with its demands to produce outcomes: some sort of self-determining structure was better than nothing. Or was it? Some evidence suggests that his support for the principle behind ATSIC was tinged with doubt about the bureaucratic structure. While the success of ATSIC would depend on the calibre of the leadership of those involved at the top of the organisation, its unwieldy size and close links to government were unlikely to appeal to many in the existing leadership who were wedded to an activist model of Aboriginal politics. Rob, like others in this mould, was aware of becoming captive to the system of government and of the overwhelming importance of not compromising core principles.

Simultaneously, Rob was intimately involved in the preparation of the wording of the Preamble to accompany the *Foundations for the Future* document. The process involved exhaustive discussions between Hand's office, Aboriginal leaders across the nation including Jack Ah Kit, Peter Yu and Pat Dodson, and a range of departments with involvement in Aboriginal issues. A total of thirty-three meetings were held prior to its release.[8] Given the time differences across Australia, and the difficulty in finding space in people's busy schedules, telephone hook-ups frequently started at midnight Canberra time and went on into the small hours. Various drafts of the Preamble were put up to Hand's office, where Rob oversaw its development. According to Hand, Rob 'talked to me for hours about the importance of the Preamble because it would enshrine in legislation for the first time a recognition of dispossession for Aboriginal people'.[9] Rob was influential in encouraging Hand to hold fast to the recognition of the dispossessed and their rights in the face of opposition from lawyers advising the government on the issue. The outcome of these discussions was included as a proposed form of words in the *Foundations for the Future* Ministerial Statement. This version gave strong recognition to Indigenous people as prior occupiers and original owners of Australia and an emphatic recognition that their dispossession without compensation had rendered them the most disadvantaged group in Australian society.

Foundations for the Future rattled many and varied interest groups. State governments were wary of the potential loss of influence over Aboriginal affairs; developers worried about a reversion to talk of rights; sections of the federal ALP were nervous about local control over Aboriginal affairs; and the Department of Aboriginal Affairs, along with the Aboriginal Development Commission and the Australian Institute for Aboriginal Studies, did not want to be swallowed up into an amorphous bureaucratic structure. As Hand explains, once *Foundations for the Future* was released, the Aboriginal Affairs Department, in particular, 'went feral'. Every brief coming out of the Department had to be carefully checked because it was 'leaking like a sieve' in its efforts to undermine the change. Faxes were being sent directly from the Department of Aboriginal Affairs to the federal opposition. The ATSIC Task Force established by Hand to develop the details of the legislation had to be moved out of the Department because of the hostility directed to it by sections of senior Departmental personnel. The Head of the Department, Charles Perkins, did not support the move to establish ATSIC, preferring the Westminster model of accountability. Some saw this conflict as the product of a power struggle over the control of Aboriginal affairs. Lurking in the background, waiting to pounce, were the conservative parties who were sharpening the edge of their verbal assault on what they regarded as another attempt to treat Aborigines as a minority group with special interests. The political blowtorch was about to be directed at Gerry Hand's office.

~~~~~

As consuming as developing the blueprint for ATSIC had been, another more pressing matter had arisen to divert Rob's and Hand's attention. A spate of Aboriginal deaths in custody in the first half of 1987 had steadily intensified concern about the issue. In the early weeks after Rob took up duties with Gerry Hand, a cluster of deaths occurred in rapid succession. Rob took special interest in the issue because of his previous efforts to advocate for a Royal Commission over the John Pat case and because a disproportionate number of deaths occurred in his home state of Western Australia. From his earlier days at the ALS, Rob was acutely familiar with the circumstances leading to deaths in custody: the high levels of imprisonment, the revolving door of recidivism and the culture of police intimidation and violence.

As agitation from families and the Sydney-based Committee to Defend Black Rights ramped up pressure for a Royal Commission, representatives of bereaved parents went to Rob to discuss the distressing events surrounding the death of their loved ones and calling for something to be done. As the pressure on Rob and Hand increased, the timing of the government's decision to establish a Royal Commission was influenced by one final spontaneous incident. In late July Hand was sitting in Parliament at Question Time when a lull came over proceedings. The momentary silence was filled by an Aboriginal woman screaming at him from the Public Gallery, 'You're a murderer, you're killing our people'. Hand was stunned by this outburst, which made an immediate and deep impact on him. He grasped the essential truth behind the barbed words: the 'system' was killing people and he and the government bore overall responsibility for its management. He shared his distress with Rob and soon after enlisted the support of acting Attorney-General Michael Duffy, who also felt the emotional weight of the woman's comments. Hand and Duffy and their respective staffs, including Rob, prepared an initial two-page letter to the Prime Minister asking for his support to establish a Royal Commission. Later, when the matter came before cabinet, some Ministers expressed outrage at the lack of consultations on the proposal and questioned the absence of detailed costing. However, the proposal was agreed to by cabinet.

While the crucial work on oversighting the Royal Commission and the development of the blueprint for ATSIC continued, Rob formalised his role with Gerry Hand and became his senior adviser. The decision, announced in the press at the end of October, polarised sections of his Noongar circle.[10] He carried the expectations of many: he was both a Western Australian and a Noongar. Somehow, people felt, Rob would get Hand onside. As Dennis Eggington recalls, 'Knowing Rob's strength we thought this would be a time of change and so we were all very excited'. Ken Colbung, Chairman of the state's Aboriginal Advisory Council, and an old sparring partner of Rob's, took a contrary view of his appointment. He couldn't see Aborigines in Western Australia benefiting because 'when these people go to Canberra they forget about the people on the ground and Aboriginal people lose out'.[11] Colbung's own position as Head of the Australian Institute of Aboriginal and Torres Strait Islander Studies, was also located in Canberra, but the irony was, seemingly, lost on him at the time of his outburst.

The decision made, Rob went to live in Canberra full-time, accompanied by Jeannie and their three daughters. By now Jeannie was used to the demands of relocating and finding employment for herself and a school for the children.

Unlike his wife, Rob knew what to expect of life in Canberra. He knew the capital intimately: its grandiosity combined with suburban ordinariness; its extremes of climate; and its culture of obsessive work for those involved with government. Rob initially worked out of a cramped office in the 'old' Parliament House which he shared with six others on Hand's Ministerial staff, including Essendon football great Geoff Pryor, who acted as Chief of Staff. He and Rob shared a passion for talking football. Dawn Casey and Sharon O'Neill joined later. The office was a haven for smokers. So heavy were most of the staff's tobacco habits — including Rob's — that the smoke occasionally drifted down towards other ministerial offices. Strongly bonded, Hand and his staff faced a barrage of opposition to the agenda of shifting the dynamics of race relations in Australia.

As Hand's ministerial office was grappling with the workload of developing the proposal for ATSIC and oversighting the issues surrounding the Royal Commission, Hawke suddenly expanded the agenda by unexpectedly reviving the contentious issue of a Treaty. The defeat of land rights in the 1980s had not diminished the ALP's commitment to a Treaty. Hand had been in conversation with Hawke about the need for a Treaty at the time he was appointed Minister, but it was then decided to use the Preamble to advance the debate more slowly. At the beginning of September 1987, Hand and Hawke were flying to Alice Springs accompanied by Rob when Hand again tried to interest Hawke in a stronger stance on the issue, discussing it in the back of the airplane on the journey across the continent. Hawke was supportive, taking the view that the concept was worth exploring. It was therefore no surprise when, later in the day, interviewed on local radio and asked about a Treaty, Hawke replied that he called it a compact and added that the issue needed to be talked about. The travelling press saw the announcement as a 'shot out of the blue' and transformed it into a major issue.

Hawke's proposal was now officially on the table, but no-one knew the form it would take. The call for a compact delighted Hand, for he had had many representations on the subject from Aboriginal people. But the call revived an old debate for Rob, and one he was not at that stage enthusiastic to re-enter. Rob's views on a Treaty are elusive. In one of his few public statements during his time as Hand's adviser, he acknowledged that 'Australians will eventually have to recognise Aboriginal people in formal economic terms and throw away this welfare mentality and paternalistic attitude'.[12] And, as previously discussed, he had enthusiastically supported the Preamble. Inside Hand's office, he did little to push the urgency of the issue. He and Hand agreed not to present a predetermined position. The idea was that they would let the issue run for twelve months and see what would come of it. Thus, while Rob was among a group of Indigenous leaders who regarded the Treaty as 'a bit of a side issue to the main game', it is clear he was swept up in the dialogue about a Treaty as it gained greater political momentum.

The main issue for Rob continued to be ATSIC. At the beginning of 1988, staff from Hand's office embarked on a major consultation process with Aboriginal communities around Australia. Conducted between 23 January and 10 March, the effort to inform and consult with the Aboriginal community on this proposal was later described as the most extensive ever undertaken by an Aboriginal Affairs Minister about a significant policy change. The effort to consult involved forty-six public meetings attended by approximately six thousand people.[13] Rob went on many of these trips. It was an arduous exercise, partly because Hand insisted that his troupe not appear as 'fat cats' to impoverished Aboriginal communities. Hence, by design, they stayed at the 'grungiest' motels in whichever town they visited. In remote communities they had to 'rough it'. In its organisation, the consultation process took on the appearance of a country and western concert tour: meetings were held in halls, sheds and even creek beds, and at the conclusion of a meeting the Ministerial party hit the road or the airways to attend another.

Most were spirited occasions. Unused to having such political attention lavished on them, Aboriginal communities vented their frustrations on the Minister, ripping into him about how they had felt let down on so many issues for so long. Patience was called for as these broader grievances were heard. However, several clear messages were delivered about the proposed new governance structure: a demand for community elections rather than appointed leaders and for sound financial management. 'Whatever structure is set up,' communities told the Minister, 'don't set us up to fail'.

Rob and Hand shared some memorable trips. One in particular made a deep impact. They were invited as guests of the Pintubi people, whose traditional country was around Lake Mackay on the border between Western Australia and the Northern Territory. In this remote area in 1983, a family had come out of the desert for the first time. By 1988, one of the family members had returned to country and others wanted to visit. Accompanied by these family members, Rob and Hand became the first white people since 1956 to visit this area. Dropped off by a helicopter near Lake Mackay, they spent eight days following the traditional hunting tracks of the Pintubi, bouncing around in the back of a Toyota truck across sand dunes, camping in swags and marvelling at the owners' knowledge of the land and especially their ability to locate waterholes. Hand often recounted this trip with Rob to Pat Dodson as a 'very rewarding experience'.

But the consultation process over ATSIC ran into trouble in the early months of 1988. In being close to government, Rob was risking his credibility in the Aboriginal rights movement. Talk of giving Aborigines more control over their affairs, against the backdrop of the impending Bicentennial with its sharp reminder of the loss of Aboriginal sovereignty, had revived the Aboriginal protest voice after years in the doldrums. The well-known activist Gary Foley poured scorn on the ATSIC model. It was, he said, 'a manipulative trick designed to keep the national voice out of what's going on'.[14] Pat Dodson, who was still working at the Central Land Council, said Aborigines had to have real power and control over their affairs and that attempts at continual assimilation were going to have to stop.[15] Galarrwuy Yunupingu from the Northern Land Council foreshadowed the need for changes to the Westminster system to accommodate constitutional legislation for Aboriginal rights.[16] With Aboriginal expectations soaring, Rob had anchored himself to a reform which would scarcely meet them. Both Gerry Hand and Rob regarded criticism from leaders such as these as a legitimate part of the process of change and not unexpected. But it was an uncomfortable position for Rob to be in. These were people with whom he had shared years of political struggle. Now he was walking a tightrope over ATSIC. He impressed fellow worker Dawn Casey with how he conducted himself during this period.

Rob also found himself in the unusual position of maintaining a public silence on the unfolding debate. In the past he would have been a forceful voice pushing its boundaries, linking up to make governments more accountable for their efforts. Now he was outside the public debate at the very time the consultation process itself came under attack in sections of the Aboriginal community.

Foley predicted Hand's attempt to impose the ATSIC model on the Aboriginal community, rather than resourcing consultation among Aboriginal people themselves, had brought an end to his honeymoon. In Western Australia, Rob came under direct attack for his role in the consultation process. Ken Colbung, one of his long-standing critics in Noongar politics, and Chair of the state government's Aboriginal Advisory Council, issued a stinging attack on Rob. He said the Committee: 'was not impressed by what seemed to be the high-handedness on the part of Mr Hand's senior adviser, Mr Rob Riley'. This charge stemmed from an accusation made against Rob that he had told the Committee 'that the legislation [to establish ATSIC] would proceed regardless of Aboriginal opposition'. Further, Colbung complained that, despite promises, no money had been forthcoming to hold meetings to discuss the *Foundations for the Future* document.[17] The accuracy of Colbung's complaints is not clear. He did participate in a number of meetings with Gerry Hand and took part in some community meetings, including a spirited meeting in Perth where Hand attempted to correct some of his statements. However, it is also possible that Rob did project himself in an aggressive manner to some participants, including Colbung. Rob had staked his credibility on being able to achieve change; his competitive instincts would have likely propelled him into trying to counter the obstacles in the way of the proposed new structure. There is little doubt he wanted a win on getting up a replacement for the NAC.

Defusing Aboriginal disquiet in sections of the Aboriginal leadership about the model for ATSIC became a prime focus of Rob's work. He was made for this task. He was on personal terms with more leaders across the country than probably any other activist, and he loved the telephone. The fact that the ATSIC model ended up with guarded support from the key sections of the Aboriginal community was due in no small measure to Rob's sustained networking.

The consultation phase concluded in March 1988, and the Aboriginal affairs portfolio was rarely out of the media for the next two years. Seizing on the on-going public unease about conferring more rights to Aborigines, the Liberal and National parties created a tornado of objections to try to wreck Hand's agenda. The Minister recalls:

> Some days in Parliament I got every question from the Opposition. They wanted me; they wanted my head; they wanted to stop the Treaty, they wanted to stop ATSIC and they didn't agree with the Royal Commission into Black Deaths in Custody. They put out press releases attacking my staff. They hated Rob with a vengeance; they were obsessed with him because they knew he was a good operator.

~~~~~~

The hours were long and draining, and the lifestyle inimical to normal family life. Rob, Hand and other office staff frequently stayed at work until 2 a.m., and when Parliament was sitting they would be back in their office at 7.30 a.m. When the team stayed late at Parliament House, Hand would order his favourite meal of steak sandwiches for everyone, and it would arrive on parliamentary silverware. Sometimes the team worked the entire weekend. Rob had precious little time for his family. Jeannie said that he lived at the office and came home for a rest. But his family were never far from his mind. He adored his girls and was forever talking about them; he'd come to work in the morning and regale the office with stories of what they were up to. Jeannie just had to accept the situation.

In June 1988 the Liberal opposition sided with the Australian Democrats in the Senate to force a Select Committee into the proposed legislation. Both Rob and Hand regarded the move 'as less than helpful' and an obvious delaying tactic. As the Committee hearings dragged on, frustration permeated all the staff in Hand's office and especially Rob, who had the job of monitoring its progress. Particular concern was expressed about some of the ALP members on the Committee, who, both Hand and Riley believed, were working to undermine any move towards self-determination. Hand elaborates: 'it suited a large section of the government to have the ATSIC proposal drag on until the next election when it was envisaged that I might have moved on and the concept could wither on the vine'.

Rob was becoming the target for opposition attacks on Hand's Aboriginal Affairs agenda. In an effort to denigrate the Minister's handling of his portfolio, opposition spokesman Chris Miles claimed that Hand was more interested in his commitment to promoting 'the radical wing' of the Aboriginal community than in delivering effective welfare measures. 'Why else', Miles scathingly asked, 'would he employ a recognised activist as a consultant on his staff?'[18] Grant Tambling also criticised Rob's role in Hand's office. The personal nature of these attacks did have an impact. Gerry Hand recalls: 'there is no doubt Rob went home some nights hurt by the attacks ... he was subjected to attacks as an individual for working for me'.

The office became a haven for Hand's besieged Ministerial staff, operating as a large, rather dysfunctional family. Especially during 1988, when the staff were under intense pressure, the warmth and affection that built up in their crammed, stuffy office in the old Parliament House sustained them all. Everyone sensed they had a role to play and were part of a team effort. There was little enforcement of hierarchy, even though Hand could be demanding, pedantic and occasionally explosive. A shared fondness for irreverent humour was an outlet for the tensions. Rob was an integral part of this dynamic. He had, Sharon O'Neill recalls,

> a wonderful capacity to defuse a situation when it was really tense. Gerry would be up and down and he had these explosions which nobody was ever seriously on the receiving end of, and he would come into the office and completely go off. Then there'd be silence and Rob would say something like, 'Good one, hero' and everyone would just start to laugh. He just had a wicked, naughty sense of humour.

Dawn Casey fondly remembers Rob's larrikin streak. On one occasion he recast a speech he had been writing for Hand, who had poor sight in one eye. Rob divided the speech into two columns, one in extra large type for the short-sighted eye and the other in normal size. Hand saw the joke and laughed uproariously. On another occasion, close to Christmas, Rob and Dawn Casey were walking down a corridor in the new Parliament House when a prominent Labor female politician strode towards them attired in a bold red dress with a wide, white collar. Instantly Rob quipped: 'Here comes Santa in drag'.

The verbal sparring, bouncing humour off each other, and mocking Hand's occasional black moods helped shield the staff from the hostility of their critics, a number of whom were in the ALP caucus. So isolated was the office that only a few politicians on either side ever visited; it wasn't a good place to be seen.

In mid-1988, the proposal for a Treaty received yet another shot in the arm. Hawke's vague and unexpected call in October the previous year for a 'compact' had not progressed far in Hand's office. But the agitation to revive the commitment continued. At the Barunga Festival, south of Katherine, Hawke issued his famous line — that there would be a Treaty. Rob had had a direct role in helping to organise the Barunga Festival as an expression of Aboriginal culture in the Bicentennial year. The idea for the festival was sketched out at Galarrwuy Yunupingu's home among a small group of people which included Rob, Gerry Hand, Pat Dodson and Mandawuy Yunupingu, each of whom had consulted others. A statement was prepared from the traditional people to hand over to the Prime Minister at the time of his arrival at the festival. Rob became the link between Gerry Hand's office and those preparing what became known as the Barunga Statement.

On 10 June, Rob accompanied Hand, his wife Maree and Bob and Hazel Hawke to Barunga. Amid a 10,000 strong crowd, Hawke and Hand were welcomed by a dance ceremony in which men gathered in a large square and slowly stepped inwards, stomping their feet and gesticulating rhythmically with their hands until the two leaders were completely enveloped. The men dispersed and it was the women's turn to welcome Hazel Hawke and Maree Hand 'to sit down in their midst and be welcomed as important women from another culture'.[19] An

Aboriginal elder, Wenton Rubuntja, summed up the historic nature of the occasion by quipping to Gerry Hand that the gathering of such diverse Aboriginal groups meant it was the first time in 40,000 years that such dances had been performed.

The festival had a huge impact on all those present, including on Rob. The occasion was not only a festival; it was a political statement and this would not have been lost on him. Caught up in the emotion of the occasion, and following direct talks with representatives from the participating communities, Hawke issued his famous statement that there would be a Treaty which would involve a process of negotiation with Aboriginal people. Hawke was then presented with a petition — the 'Barunga Statement' — by the Chairmen of the Northern and Central Land Councils; it was framed by Top End and Centre paintings. It called for Aboriginal self-determination, land rights, compensation for loss of land, protection of sacred sites, return of the remains of ancestors and respect for Aboriginal identity.

Hawke's use of the word 'Treaty' excited both Hand and Riley. It was the first time the Prime Minister had formally used the word and seemed to indicate to them that with this level of commitment achieving a Treaty might not be such an impossible dream. Hawke convinced those present that he, at least, believed a Treaty was politically feasible.

But the announcement of a renewed commitment to the Treaty brought more pressure onto Hand's ministerial staff. Hand explains:

> You've got the Royal Commission underway; you've got a war going on between the Department and the Minister's office; you've got the left-leaning Public Service Union opposed to ATSIC and the Minister. Everybody thought we were mad. John Howard, leader of the Opposition, was frothing at the mouth in Parliament claiming that we were handing over power to Aborigines and that I was splitting the nation by creating a Black parliament. And to top it off we had the Treaty.

Although Rob has left no statement about his reactions to the politicisation of the Treaty debate, it must have confirmed his views about the entrenched attitudes towards race in Australia. From the mid-1980s land rights debate, Rob had formed strong views about the dynamics of racism as an all-embracing system of institutionalised rules, habits and practices. He had maintained his idealistic belief that the public could be educated to understand Aboriginal aspirations, and he continually encouraged Gerry Hand to take every opportunity to get the message out through the media, even cajoling him into appearing on comedian Andrew Denton's *Blah Blah Blah* television program. However, Rob brought to his new role the understanding about the interaction of economic power, community racism and party politics gleaned from his experiences as NAC Chair. The anti-land-rights efforts of the mining lobby showed him that elites ruled to protect their economic interests, aided by the conservative parties. The 1985 ANOP survey revealed to him the embedded nature of racism in the community. The backdown by the ALP on land rights revealed the institutional limitations of reform. The Treaty debate replayed this sordid political scenario on race all over again. This time, however, the mining lobby was less visible, although they stated their case that a compact/treaty 'might spark a more serious rift through the nation than the original land rights debate'.[20] Otherwise, few mining representatives would go on public record, undoubtedly mindful of the attacks from some quarters during their mid-1980s advertising campaign.

It was left to the Liberal party to defend their interests. In his attack on the Treaty, opposition leader John Howard vowed 'to tear up' any Treaty Labor signed. He recycled the fear campaign used against land rights, with a few new twists. A Treaty was, Howard argued, 'a leap into the constitutional unknown'; 'a constitutional nightmare'; 'a form of apartheid'; 'utterly repugnant to the idea of one Australia'. His opposition spokesperson, Chris Miles, injected a note of historical denialism into the dialogue on Aboriginal rights. 'Now is not the time', he argued, 'to look to the past'.[21] In press releases, Howard was even more extreme: a Treaty would inevitably lead to demands for 'a separate black nation'.

None of this would have surprised Rob, but it would have added to his sense of despair that conservatives — in both political parties — did not understand the fundamental nature of racism. White elites — let alone the rest of the population — had little grasp of what it was like to be non-white. There was little evidence of the existence of any 'double consciousness': the ability to think across different cultural perspectives. Howard's ideas on Aborigines did not appear to extend much beyond an unspecified goal of working to overcome disadvantage within the fold of mainstream Australia. A continual theme Rob stressed throughout his career was that whites who commented publicly on Aboriginal people rarely knew or understood their history or aspirations. At times he would sit and brood in the cramped parliamentary office, quietly puffing on one of his many cigarettes for the day. Gerry Hand recalls: 'Rob was frustrated, we were all frustrated. I mean we just couldn't bloody believe the depth of hostility'.

Meanwhile, the Royal Commission into Aboriginal Deaths in Custody hearings ground on around Australia with little interest shown by the general public.[22] And still Aboriginal people were dying. The death in June 1988 of Paul Pryor was widely publicised; it showed that some Aborigines hung themselves out of despair over the justice system.[23] Rob's oversight of this issue in Hand's office continued to be distressing. Rob was the first person in the office to be told of another death, and the first person that Aboriginal people rang to express their frustration and to pass on their criticisms of the government. Rob's early life was similar to that of many of the young men who had died in custody, who had institutional backgrounds and lives of abject poverty. Dawn Casey was struck by the depth of Rob's reaction to each death in custody. On more than one occasion she observed him becoming tearful, contemplating the extent to which many would go to kill themselves.

He was deeply affected by the death of Edward Cameron in Geraldton police station in July 1988, because he knew the young man's father, Leadham, who had also been an NAC member. His son was a talented footballer and a popular figure in the town, but was prone to binge drinking. His life spiralled out of control following an allegation of rape in June 1988 which resulted in his arrest and release on bail. This incident caused Cameron's de facto partner to leave him. On 7 July, Cameron was arrested for being drunk and taken to the Geraldton Police Station. The Royal Commission would later consider his case and find that the Station Orders requiring that prisoners be visited at least hourly were not followed: Cameron was checked once at 3 a.m. and not again until 6.25 a.m. when he was discovered dead.

Cameron's funeral several weeks later brought race relations in Geraldton to boiling point. About three hundred Aborigines went on a rampage, taunting police as killers and murderers. Storming along the main street, the rioters smashed shop and hotel windows and temporarily overwhelmed police.²⁴ State cabinet had scheduled a meeting in the town on the day of the riot, and an incensed Premier, Peter Dowding, publicly blasted 'stirrers' for the riot. A group of permanent protesters, he said, 'travelled Australia ... more intent on making angry statements than being constructive'. He declined to provide names. Dowding took his complaints straight to Hand and Riley. Both were attending an outdoor meeting in North Queensland when the call from the Premier came. According to Hand, Dowding verbally abused both him and Rob. Still convinced of his claim about the role played by outside 'stirrers', he accused both of them of providing funds for Aborigines to attend the protest. The conversation became heated as both Hand and Rob took offence at the Premier's suggestions that they would act in such a manner. Hand remembers the conversation as one of the fiercest he had ever had. Meanwhile, a journalist from *The Daily News* found that the violence was 'simply a sign of the depth of distrust which haunts race relations between Aborigines and police: 'a young man had been hanged in his cell and nothing was going to convince family and friends he had killed himself'.²⁵

Rob's deepening identification with the deaths of so many young Aborigines in gaol intensified during a series of state-based meetings of the families, which was funded by the federal government and which required Rob's attendance. Many of these meetings were explosive, punctuated by passionate outbursts of families' grieving. Some families subsequently came to Rob to discuss how their relatives had died. He held up throughout such ordeals, never indicating to Hand that his own experiences in Sister Kate's were an emotional issue for his work. Dawn Casey agrees. On reflection, she has wondered how Rob could have disclosed his background. Firstly, there was no wider recognition about the lifelong struggles of Aboriginal people who had been institutionalised, and the sexual assault he suffered would have added a layer of shame. Rob kept busy and in the company of other people; he usually did not like being alone. But with his involvement with deaths in custody, some of the cracks began to show.

Rob wanted to broaden the scope of the Royal Commission to examine the underlying causes of deaths in custody, rather than just the immediate circumstances surrounding each individual case. Rob was intimately aware of the need to tackle the pressing social issues driving the high rates of contact Aborigines had with the criminal justice system. The appointment of Elliott Johnson to replace the original Royal Commissioner, Jim Muirhead, provided an opportunity. Muirhead and Johnson were keen to broaden the scope of the inquiry beyond its coronial function, as was Peter Dowding. This confluence of interests led to arguably the most far-reaching inquiry ever undertaken into Aboriginal disadvantage in the country, and one which had a major impact on Rob. It was decided that Western Australia would be examined in depth, in search of the underlying causes of deaths in custody, but only as an example of the broader Aboriginal experience across the nation.

While these discussions were going on, the Select Committee inquiring into the ATSIC Bill handed down its report in March 1989. Highlighting the controversy Hand's office had ignited with their proposed model, Committee members were split along party political lines in their response to the issues of Aboriginal self-determination, although not even the Labor side of the Committee gave unqualified support to the proposal. The majority (Labor) report criticised Rob's and Hand's model for self-determination and the effectiveness of the consultation which had been arranged by them. It called for the retention of a separate Office of Aboriginal Affairs to advise the Minister. Hand maintains that elements within the ALP were 'terrified of handing power over to Aboriginal people' and that ALP concerns about the concept were an obstacle in achieving reform. Indicating the gap which existed between Hand's office and the mainstream of the federal ALP, the majority report noted the 'radical departure' in public administration represented in the ATSIC proposal, which deserved more discussion in the general community. At this point both Hand and Rob realised they were becoming isolated within government circles and that adjustments to the ideal of self-management would be necessary. Despite these misgivings, the authors of the majority report were never likely to abandon the concept altogether because too much political capital had been invested in it by the government.

The minority (Liberal/National Party) report was cast in an altogether more strident tone. In their view, the conflation of the functions of representation, advocacy and program delivery was 'faulty and unsafe' because it would create a separate Aboriginal 'parliament' which would mimic and parallel the Australian parliament. Espousing the inflammatory claim of 'black separatism', the conservatives were appealing to the long-standing fears and uncertainties in the community about the handing over of any powers to Aboriginal people.

The authors of the minority report took a savage swipe at the consultation process undertaken by Hand's office, claiming the Committee had heard 'general allegations of the most serious kind to the effect that the consultation process was corrupted by intimidation, coercion, enticements and stand-over tactics', but failed to provide specifics.[26]

The Select Committee took no account of international developments. The early 1970s marked an upsurge in international interest in the rights of Indigenous people. In the United States in 1970, Republican President Richard Nixon had initiated an era of self-determination for Native American tribes. The reforms were based around the recognition of tribes as being permanent players in the federal system of government and recognising them as sovereign with a capacity to act over matters affecting their interests.[27] From the early 1970s, the United Nations began an exhaustive study of discrimination against Indigenous people which led in 1982 to the formation of a Working Group on Indigenous Peoples. In 1989, at the very time the Senate was considering how to limit the impact of self-determination in Australia, the Working Group initiated a study on the potential utility of treaties and agreements between states and Indigenous peoples.

As these debates acknowledged, it was inevitable that Indigenous people would want to assert their rights and that this required a process of negotiating with them as self-determining people. No such mature debate was able to take place in Australia. Rob observed the ATSIC debate polarised between the outright hostility of the conservative parties and the grudging minimalist position of Labor. His observations became part of what he later regarded as the incapacity of governments to address the rights of Aboriginal people in a fair and equitable manner.

Opposition to the ATSIC proposal came to a head when Hand's amended Bill came before the parliament from May through to June 1989. In what became a marathon debate, especially in the Senate, the opposition attack was unrelenting, broadening out into a fully-fledged assault on Hand's management of the portfolio. The Preamble, which had been packaged as a separate Bill, was a quick casualty, rejected because of concerns that it could be taken to the courts as a prima facie case and could, therefore, be used in future land rights claims. Democrats leader John Coulter, whose party held the balance of power at the time, joined with the Coalition senators in defeating the measure. But Hand maintains that some Labor members were privately relived that the Preamble was defeated. The Coalition parties were fearful that the measure 'could be used to support the development of a common law right to compensation for dispossession, and even to repossession'.[28] Hand and his staff were disconsolate. The degree of antagonism shown to this non-binding statement of plain historical facts conveyed a broader message to them. According to Hand, 'We knew then deep down any hope of a meaningful Treaty was never a possibility'.

The Coalition parties mounted a full-blooded attack on the ATSIC Bill in both the House and the Senate. It was cloaked in concerns that the measure would worsen the already atrocious living conditions for many Aborigines, but a closer inspection of their language reveals a hostility to the very concept of self-determination and their willingness to go to extremes to denigrate it. Chris Miles said the proposal 'sprang from the Government's Bicentennial guilt trip'.[29] Howard repeated his line that it 'strikes at the heart of the unity of the Australian people',[30] while Peter Baume expressed the view that the Minister's goals could be better achieved 'in other less radical, less threatening and less destructive ways'. He likened ATSIC to putting Veterans' Affairs in the hands of veterans, a proposal which would be 'laughed out of court'.[31]

Without doubt, the most florid attacks on the ATSIC Bill came from Senator Tambling. He had drawn attention to himself through his long-standing aggressive questioning of Aboriginal Affairs. On several occasions Rob had sat through Tambling's attempts to tear down Hand's administration of the portfolio. In one debate on the Bill, Tambling described Hand's advisers as a radical political elite, and suggested Hand was developing a 'totalitarian state in the heart of democracy'. Then came the accusation of national disloyalty: 'the Minister has turned one section of the community against another'.[32]

In the highly charged atmosphere enveloping Hand's office, Rob engaged in a spontaneous act of recklessness. One night on his way home from work, he stopped at a phone box and rang Grant Tambling's parliamentary office. Pretending to be an anonymous caller, Rob asked to speak to Tambling saying he had some damaging information about

Gerry Hand to pass on. When Tambling came to the phone, Rob yelled, 'Get fucked!' and hung up. It was hardly the act of a professional adviser. But it is revealing of his provocative, risk-taking nature. The fall-out could have been considerable.

When the Bill finally passed the Senate, it had been subjected to extensive amendment which, Rob and Hand believed, fundamentally weakened the concept. What emerged has been described as an organisation 'close to a crisis of legitimacy', because while its representatives were accountable to the Aboriginal community, it functioned virtually as a government department.[33] Its budgets were subject to Ministerial approval and discretionary action.

Rob was devastated that the Preamble, on which so many had pinned their hopes for a future dialogue about the rights of Aborigines, had gone, and he blamed the Senate for turning the ATSIC Bill from a measure aimed at a form of self-determination into a limited form of self-management. Some of Rob's close colleagues were scathing about the emasculation of the original proposal. John Ah Kit wrote that the legislation had been 'diluted to such an extent that it no longer empowered Aboriginal people to directly manage their own affairs'.[34] Many of the prominent leaders critical of the forced changes were now openly wary of seeking election to ATSIC. This fulfilled one of the concerns Rob had at the outset: that the Commission would only ever be as effective as the leadership that sought election to it. In effect, the legislation which established ATSIC offered Aborigines greater power to set priorities but only with the trade-off of increased Commonwealth government scrutiny. For those in Gerry Hand's office, the passage of the ATSIC legislation was a hard-fought battle. It restored an institutional voice to Aboriginal affairs and gave a measure of self-determination. Yet it is hard not to find in the legislation, at least in part, reasons for the slow decline and eventual demise of ATSIC.

No doubt the bureaucratic structure was unwieldy, and the Canberra-based Commission was perceived as remote from the regions. Crucially, the absence of key leaders from the ATSIC structure weakened its effectiveness over time. Whether more autonomy for the regions would have saved ATSIC from its eventual demise is, obviously, speculation. With so little political goodwill for the concept of self-determination, and with the polarisation of the debate on the measure put up for discussion, there was little chance that the best model would emerge.

Rob became disillusioned with ATSIC, telling a conference in 1995 that the ideal of self-determination had been stymied by paternalism.[35]

***

What had Rob been able to achieve as an activist working inside government? He had been a key player in two critical developments: the creation of ATSIC, which, even in its minimalist form, provided a platform for Aboriginal people to re-assert their political voice; and the broadening of the Royal Commission into Aboriginal Deaths in Custody into a landmark social justice inquiry, which guaranteed that Aboriginal issues would continue to occupy the national agenda. Yet, both these achievements were qualified. ATSIC would struggle to gain credibility, and the political commitment to follow through on any of the Royal Commission's recommendations was, at best, uncertain. Not all of those close to Rob believe his time as an 'insider' could justify all the effort he had expended. In effect, he had gone to work with Hand to effect change — from the inside this time — and again turned up with partial victories. Hand agrees that the very concerns Rob had about joining forces with the ALP were vindicated by the obstacles placed in their way by the Party, let alone the virulent opposition mounted by the conservative parties. Dawn Casey concurs that his time working in federal politics were likely a disillusioning experience for him. While he appreciated Hand's commitment to achieving change, his aspirations for what might have been accomplished were dashed.

***

Rob's tenure as Gerry Hand's adviser came to an end as a result of the extension of the Royal Commission into examining the underlying causes of deaths in custody. When his friend and colleague Pat Dodson was installed as the Royal Commissioner for this task, he recruited Rob for the position of Head of the Western Australian Issues Unit attached to his part of the Commission. An Issues Unit was established in each state with the responsibility of identifying what Aborigines saw as the issues and solutions to deaths in custody. To undertake this task each Head was required to plan and organise a process of consultation with Aboriginal communities. Thus, Rob was involved in the largest single exercise ever undertaken to seek the views of Aboriginal communities about their predicament.

Rob, Jeannie and the children came back to live in Perth. He worked out of the same city building as the legal side of the Royal Commission, although they operated separately. Pat Dodson based himself in Broome, according to the regional approach to his work. Rob's work, therefore, was to feed directly into the investigation into the underlying causes of deaths in custody, a function heightened by the Western Australian focus of the Commission's role. In Dodson's mind, Rob was an ideal choice for the task because of the knowledge he had gained at the ALS, his understanding of police issues, and his sense of justice. Simultaneously, Dodson recruited Peter Yu to work with him in Broome, thus bringing the two close friends to work together for the first time in several years.

The task confronting the Commission was immense. It was a multilayered quest to identify the factors behind Aboriginal disadvantage and discrimination which propelled such disproportionate numbers into the justice system. It became a journey into the experience of Aboriginal dispossession and disempowerment. It needed to explore why so many Indigenous communities were dysfunctional: racked by substance abuse, family violence and poverty. Why did women go back to their partners who had bashed them? Why did many men feel more comfortable in prison than in the outside world or with their families? Early on, Commissioner Dodson would throw these questions to Rob, encouraging him to find out what people were saying and to come up with some answers. The process was bound to unleash a torrent of grievances and grieving and was destined to be a hard slog both physically and emotionally. Following years of reflection after Rob's death, both Pat Dodson and Peter Yu believe the experience of this intense consultation was the start of Rob's slide into mental illness.

Rob's formal role as Head of the Issues Unit was to arrive in advance of the Royal Commission in regional centres and liaise with the community, briefing them on the issues on which Dodson wanted to question them, organise them to appear to give evidence, and assist in the preparation of any submissions. Rob's personality and his profile greatly assisted him in undertaking this process. His skills as a communicator paved the way for Aboriginal participation in the proceedings. He explained the work of the Commission in language which people could relate to, and he took the message to Aboriginal people in town camps, community halls and out in the bush. Once the formal hearings commenced, Rob and Peter had a role through Pat Dodson in overseeing the presentation of evidence. In sitting after sitting, in centres large and small, across the length and breadth of the state, Aboriginal people trooped in with stories of police violence, disempowerment, discrimination and disadvantage. Key themes emerged. The impact of institutionalisation was one important issue; Dodson later wrote in his Report: 'Each individual who died was exposed to some degree of mission/welfare interface ... which resulted in family disruption. The disturbance of family group support is a constant theme of the lives of those who have died in custody'.[36] From hearing such evidence, Rob confronted his own background: the background he had distanced himself from, hidden behind the layers of his commitment to politics. But, as was his manner, he was not able to openly share with others what he was going through.

Another theme raised in the evidence Rob sat through was the extent of police targeting of Aboriginal people. Evidence given on this matter was like a tapestry running from one end of the state to the other. The case of a traditional lawman from Broome was repeated many times in evidence. In the lead-up to his death he was arrested on 17 June 1987 and sentenced to six days for being drunk; re-arrested 24 June for the same offence and released on 27 June only to be re-arrested the same day. The man was found dead at 6.30 p.m. that evening.[37] Other evidence raised even more stark allegations about police intimidation of Aborigines: declining to give Aboriginal juveniles in custody medicine when complaining of being ill; threatening Aboriginal people with revolvers; and swearing and making fun of them. During the hearings, instances of police raiding Aborigines' homes caused some people to feel uncertain about discussing the issue because of their fear of being singled out by police and harassed.

Rob had been dealing with police discrimination and violence towards Aborigines for over fifteen years, and he recognised the stories being told to him in the hearings. The institutionalised nature of racism in the police force emerged as a systemic problem in the Commission's hearings. How could it ever be changed? His despair over this issue was only heightened when he and the others working for the Commission re-enacted the circumstances surrounding John Pat's death in what was an emotional and eerie experience, given the intensity with which Pat's death had been felt by Aboriginal people for so many years.

A third theme resonating with Rob in the Commission's hearings was the pervasiveness of community racism. Pat Dodson later commented in his Report that Aboriginal people were regarded as 'criminal, violent and destructive of private property and, as a consequence, as a threat to the social fabric of non-Aboriginal society'.[38] In the face of hearing such evidence, Rob could not have but felt despondent. What had changed since the ANOP survey revealed the depth of racism six years earlier? And did not its persistence highlight again his claim about the culpability of politicians for not having the courage to embark on a program of educating the community?

The challenge of the formal hearings was not the only distressing part of Rob's work on the Royal Commission. Part of the role of those involved in the investigation was to visit all of the state's prisons and lockups. This, too, was a confronting experience, leaving each of them regularly in a state of shock. Part of the distress was actually seeing the concentration of Black faces in each institution they visited. There was a sense of the wasted human potential: bright young men going nowhere. Under different circumstances some may have become leaders in their communities. Some thought of themselves as akin to political prisoners, such was the oppressive surveillance of police. Individuals complained that they were often picked up the moment they were released from gaol by a policeman standing there with a warrant to put them straight back inside again.

The physical conditions of regional prisons added to the feeling of despondency. Most were 'woeful', 'primitive' places consisting of mesh wire, iron beds, tin roofs, and an absence of cold water and exercise yards. In short: hot, dreary dungeons. Rob was particularly hit by such conditions because he so closely identified with the men's institutional backgrounds.

Rob and the others regularly confronted the racist attitudes of prison officers. So unabashed were many of them in their attitudes that they did not bother to hide their prejudices when talking to the visiting Aboriginal Royal Commissioner and his co-workers. Rob had always found it difficult to act with restraint in the face of racism. His childhood experience of being bashed had shaped a combustible anger at the hearing of any prejudice. But the formal process of the Royal Commission required him to hold his tongue. On one occasion after they had all heard a barrage of the worst redneck views imaginable, Rob emerged and finally allowed his anger to boil to the surface. He turned to Dodson and said: 'Don't ever ask me to do that again, sit in that environment'.

This confrontation with injustice — in all its forms — was beginning to unsettle Rob, and all the others involved. He had some intense conversations with Pat Dodson. Rob told Dodson he could understand how some of these young men reached a stage where they wanted to kill themselves as a political statement, a statement against the system, 'against the violence and the abuse that life as an Aboriginal person brings you in this country'. In Rob's mind such an action 'would be an honourable thing to do'. Dodson, perhaps because of his background training in Catholic teaching on the sanctity of life, or a secular version of it, could not understand or condone taking one's own life in this way.

The hearings and visits to prisons involved a punishing round of travel, mostly arduous road trips involving fourteen-hour days and often seven-day weeks. Rob and Yu, in particular, lived this way for almost a year and a half. It was reminiscent of their days at the NAC: living in each other's pockets, pushing themselves to the limit. But there were lighter moments. At night those travelling together would sit around and have a few beers. Rob would feed off people like Darryl Kickett, who was also a noted jokester and story-teller, and there would be lots of laughter. Occasionally they would bet on the horses on a weekend visit to a remote country pub.

The camaraderie got them through some tight spots. Remote area driving has its dangers. On one trip Rob was travelling to the remote Aboriginal settlement of Ngurawaana near the Fortescue River to visit an alcohol rehabilitation project. He was in a Ford sedan with Dennis Eggington and Steve Mickler, while Darryl Kickett and Pat Morrison had the luxury of a four-wheel-drive. The track out to the community was in worse shape than they had imagined, and several hours of jolting and bouncing across the outback desert had dented the underside of the car and blown out one tyre. On the way back from the community to Karratha it started to rain, and then to pelt down. Soon the party was in a full-blown tropical downpour. Lightning bolts blasted the landscape. Water levels at each creek they crossed were rising rapidly. They reached one gully which had become completely washed out. It was touch-and-go whether to risk the crossing or face the uncertainties of turning back. Rob made the decision to press on. The four-wheel-drive vehicle made the crossing first to gauge the difficulty. Water surged around its wheels and bumper bars as it ploughed across to the other side. Steve Mickler

Rob Riley and Jack Ah Kit, Uluru, late 1980s. The two became close friends during Rob's time at the Northern Land Council, of which Ah Kit was Director.

Friends and colleagues Dean Collard and Ted Wilkes with Rob Riley, at the Bicentennial, 1988. Rob took an active part in defining an Aboriginal position in opposition to the occasion.

Male dancers, Barunga Festival, 1988. The Festival, which was attended by representatives from communities across northern Australia, drew a commitment from Prime Minister Bob Hawke to work towards a Treaty.

Aboriginal Affairs Minister Gerry Hand and Bob Hawke, Barunga Festival, 1988.

Women dancers, Barunga Festival, 1988.

watched on anxiously from the back seat, with increasing doubts that the family sedan would replicate the feat of its more muscular rival. Dennis Eggington's expression said the same. Rob, however, calmly said to Dennis, 'She'll be right, just keep your foot planted on the accelerator, no matter what, keep the car straight and don't drop the revs'. In they plunged. The car got about halfway across and the water was up to the door handles, slowing it to a crawl. The vehicle began to drift sideways in the current. Steve was expecting to hear the sound of the engine stalling and a yell to abandon ship. Instead, he heard Rob urging Dennis: 'Keep the revs up, keep it going, keep it going'. It worked: the car, struggling all the way, made it across and all broke out into whoops of relief.

The story reveals some of Rob's key personality traits. On display was his ability to act decisively; to size up a situation; to make a decision; and to stick with the course of action. In a word: leadership. There was a flip side to this quality of Rob's: a willingness to push a situation to its limits. He was a risk-taker.

They continued their journey in the rain-drenched car with water lapping at their ankles. Rob had an instant solution to the problem: he drove the car up an embankment, and while it was tilted sideways he opened the doors. Out rushed the water.

At the conclusion of their consultation work for the Royal Commission, Riley, Dodson and Yu were exhausted physically and mentally. They were torn between being depressed and angry at confronting such huge social problems and the sense of powerlessness that pervaded most Aboriginal communities.

There was precious little time away from the demands of the task. Occasionally Rob, Jeannie and the girls would go camping at Busselton, where Rob would enjoy fishing and briefly recharge his batteries. But otherwise the issues were all-consuming. Each of them felt a sense of responsibility to the Aboriginal community to produce something tangible at the end of the process.

Rob submitted a report to Pat Dodson about the issues he encountered; and this helped inform the writing of the Underlying Volume of the Royal Commission. He resigned before the completion of the writing of Pat's Report to take up, arguably, his biggest challenge: to return to the Aboriginal Legal Service in Perth as its Executive Officer and to transform the organisation into a vehicle for fighting for the recommendations of the Royal Commission.

CHAPTER TEN

War on All Fronts: Return to the Aboriginal Legal Service

When Rob returned to Western Australia to head up the Aboriginal Legal Service in June 1990, the racial faultline dividing the state had opened dangerously wide. According to a state government inquiry,[1] the early to mid-1990s were dominated by an 'us' versus 'them' attitude towards Aboriginal people. This was marked by an upward trend in negative stereotyping and resentment over the perceived status of Aboriginal people as a privileged group in receipt of supposedly generous government handouts. Going back to the ALS was a risky choice for Rob. The racial undertow would mean he would inevitably be dragged back into crude political fights over race. But he was committed to making his career in Aboriginal activism, and job opportunities were few and far between. Even so, the job held strong appeal; he had a vision for the future of the ALS.

Between 1990 and 1992 — the period encompassed by Carmen Lawrence's Labor government — Rob was a key participant in four crucial public policy debates: the introduction of harsher penalties for juvenile offenders; the implementation of the recommendations of the Royal Commission into Aboriginal Deaths in Custody; the request from Hamersley Iron to develop its giant iron ore project at Marandoo in the Pilbara; and the on-going police violence towards Aborigines. The ALS had become moribund and dispirited and needed extensive restructuring. Rob pursued a strategy of waging war on all fronts as he propelled himself — and the rejuvenated ALS — into the role of defender of Aboriginal rights. His profile soared; the demands on his time and energies became unrelenting. Eventually something had to give.

The state government had inherited decades of neglect in Aboriginal affairs, and its own approach was reactive rather than strategic. Even when controversy was raging the government lacked a clear policy framework with which to resolve disputes. Consequently, Rob's was a chaotic existence. Contentious issues continually streamed across his desk, forcing him to campaign simultaneously on several fronts. The debate over juvenile crime ran throughout the period, while the other three issues flared at different points. Juggling these competing demands, Rob became the highest-profile Aboriginal leader in the state and the one most in demand by the media.

When Rob applied for the position of Executive Officer, he wrote: 'My work with the Royal Commission presents a rare opportunity to identify and address some of the complex issues which confront Aboriginal people on a daily basis. My view is that the A.L.S. would be both a practical and natural progression at the completion of the Royal Commission'.[2] He surely realised the difficulty of securing change on the scale envisaged by the Royal Commission.

He relished a return to activist politics. Rob had a vision — shared by other key players at the ALS — that the organisation could be transformed into a political vehicle to fight for Aboriginal rights. This was a bold move. Major changes were needed to to make the organisation effective. Not everyone was persuaded that this was the appropriate strategic direction. How would it affect its core business? Where would the funding come from to enhance its role? What tangible outcomes could such a move expect to reap? While there were doubts in some minds about the strategy, the balance sheet appeared to have more positives than negatives. The findings of the Royal Commission's Underlying Issues report — well known to Rob even though the Report would not be released until June the following year — demanded the active involvement of Aboriginal people in the mainstream political system. And the same dilemma about the ALS confronted Rob as it had done ten years earlier. Was there any point in its operating as a giant sausage machine for criminal justice cases, when the issues underlying Aborigines' involvement in the criminal justice system went unaddressed? Rob thought not; he saw the potential for the ALS to be at the vanguard of the Aboriginal community in challenging discrimination and disadvantage. But he may not have anticipated just how vicious some of the political fights would be, or that, in making his role at the ALS into an overtly political one, he would become a bigger target, not just for governments but for some of his critics within the ALS and in his own Noongar community. In short, Rob was in for the fight of his life.

From his time working with Gerry Hand, Rob had learnt much about the processes of politics: advancing policy proposals, dealing with bureaucracy and arranging press conferences. Moreover, he was used to maintaining a punishing work schedule. His time with the Royal Commission had further developed his public speaking skills. Working with Pat Dodson had matured him; he had become more skilled at negotiation and developing strategic ideas. Dodson had been part of the process of transforming him from the angry young man of radical activist politics into a skilled political operator. Lastly, more than a decade in the Aboriginal rights movement had given Rob the opportunity to develop a formidable national political network; he knew all the major players and how to co-ordinate with them. Thus, at the time he re-joined the ALS, Rob was outwardly very confident.

But at a deeper, emotional level, there were problems. Rob was already exhausted. The Royal Commission had taken its toll. He had had virtually no break between leaving it and commencing at the ALS. His physical health had deteriorated, the most obvious manifestation being his significant gain in weight. Less obvious was his continuing use of recreational drugs. Personal issues which he had had to confront during his time at the Royal Commission were starting to bubble to the surface, tugging at his psyche. The exposure he gained through the

Royal Commission to the impacts of childhood institutionalisation brought to the surface nagging questions about the circumstances leading to his placement in Sister Kate's. His anxiety to find out more was continually thwarted; the subject was just too painful to raise with his mother, whom he loved and respected. And his marriage was under strain from all the years he had spent away from his family. Thus, Rob's return to the ALS coincided with the beginning of his dual life: the public face of a campaigner for justice, and a private life of increasing pain and fragmentation. Somehow he managed to keep the two from colliding for several years.

The backdrop to all of Rob's work with the ALS over the next five years was the racial tension fraying the social fabric of Western Australia. Rob persistently claimed that Western Australia was 'the most racist State in Australia'.[3] While he was never asked to substantiate such a claim, he had well-formed views about the nature of the racism he confronted. These were outlined in evidence he gave in 1989 to the Human Rights and Equal Opportunity Commission's inquiry into racist violence in Australia. He made a number of telling points. Firstly, and remembering that at the time he gave the evidence he was still working for the Royal Commission, he conceptualised racism as constituting 'a very structured, a very entrenched, a very institutionalised and a very psychological violence'. Secondly, because there had not been any proper recognition of Aboriginal people they had no equal status in the eyes of government; merely 'beggars' to people in authority. Thirdly, as Aboriginal people lacked economic clout they could not exert any political influence. Lastly, the police represented an oppressive force for Aboriginal people.[4]

How could the ALS be reshaped to meet such formidable challenges? First and foremost, Rob realised that it had to be professionalised. Its structure and constitution were dated. It needed to be transformed into a state-wide representative body, and not just an urban-dominated one.

Behind the scenes, undue influence was exercised was wielded by a few power-brokers in the Noongar community. Principal among them was Robert Bropho, an enigmatic, uncompromising and, to some, bullying Aboriginal leader. For several years prior to Rob's return to the ALS, Bropho had steadily developed his profile and influence.

Bropho was the key spokesperson protesting the decision by the state Labor government to allow re-development of the disused Swan Brewery on the picturesque Swan River foreshore immediately underneath the imposing cliff face of King's Park, and just a short distance from Perth's central business district. At the point where cliff face and brewery intersect is a freshwater spring, widely acknowledged to be part of an Aboriginal camping ground and dreaming track.[5] In the late 1980s, Premier Peter Dowding had plans drawn up to convert the building into a tourist centre, boutique brewery, restaurant and museum housing a collection of Aboriginal art. Bropho challenged these plans citing the damage development would incur on the sacred site. Using funds and legal expertise provided by the ALS he successfully pressured the government into stalling development. In the process, Bropho became a prominent activist and, not unlike Rob in his earlier career, succeeded in transforming the heritage issue into a wider community cause.

Thus, by the time Rob recommenced as the head of the ALS in June 1990, Bropho had an impressive power base within Aboriginal politics and, specifically, within the ALS itself. Rob disliked Bropho. Their political styles were different. Bropho was a grassroots activist with an unyielding, in-your-face and, some thought, egotistical style. Rob was a political player trying to negotiate systemic changes. The dispute over the Swan Brewery drove a wedge through his new approach to politics. While supportive of the heritage issues at the centre of the dispute, Rob was frustrated with the tactic of protracted, all-out confrontation, which, he felt was damaging the perception of Aborigines in the community. But there were also personal issues at stake. Bropho was clearly a rival, and a formidable one. In addition, Rob had little influence over the course of the dispute, even though the ALS was funding the various court actions to delay work on the site.

In moving to change the focus and direction of the ALS, Rob invited opposition from within Noongar politics. Throughout 1991 and 1992, a series of meetings were held about the future direction of the organisation involving the change to a state-wide executive structure and the continuation of funding for selected projects. These amounted to 'horrific' battles between the forces of change and those of the status quo: scrappy brawls in which principles and personality issues became deeply entangled. No doubt Rob's opponents thought he was marginalising them, taking away their community-based organisation to fight his own grandiose political battles. Rob saw the influence of the Noongar old guard as an obstacle to his larger vision. Several were dissatisfied because the ALS had turned down applications for funding particular projects. But, from Rob's perspective, old scores were again being fought out and he believed the organisation would get nowhere unless the influence of his few Noongar opponents was reduced. The dispute got very nasty, involving, at one point, a short-lived takeover of the ALS office by Rob's opponents. Staff had arrived for work one morning and could not get into their workplace.

Rob persisted with the changes. Bropho had his supporters in the white community too, and not all of these people agreed with Rob's tactics of sidelining sections of the Noongar community. But by 1992 Rob had engineered the changes he wanted. A state-wide committee structure had been established with an accompanying state-wide process of election to the ALS Executive. In October 1992, elections to the Executive brought about a substantial change in membership which, once operating, Rob thought 'demonstrated a far more responsible and objective team approach'.[6] Rob had worked hard to get some of his key supporters elected, including Ted Wilkes and Dennis Eggington, both of whom were close friends and active campaigners in Aboriginal politics. Wilkes, who was Executive Officer of the Aboriginal Medical Service, became the Chair of the Executive. The changes were significant in terms of the capacity of the ALS to fight on a broader front. Rob's highly political approach to heading the ALS was backed by Wilkes and most of the Executive.

Rob's old mentor at the ALS, Cedric Wyatt, observes that establishing the ALS on a state-wide representative basis was essential to its professionalisation but a Herculean task to achieve: 'I had no intention of doing it because of the difficulty'. In the process Rob had shored up his position on the Executive with sufficient members sharing his ideas about change. Clearly he had learnt a crucial lesson from his dumping from the NAC: the politics of organisations was as important a focus as the wider political struggles. But his position was never fully secure; his opponents had long and bitter memories of the struggle. Bluntly, there were a few people on the ALS Executive waiting for the chance to undermine Rob.

Alongside structural changes, Rob set about to increase the profile of the organisation. In his first Annual Report, he emphasised his view that the media portrayal of Aboriginal people would be a crucial battleground under his leadership: 'The media does itself a serious disservice by insisting on portraying Aboriginal people in a biased and sensational manner'.[7] Rob introduced press conferences at the ALS. Initially these started as regular media 'door stops' but Rob set aside a room within the organisation for press conferences, which were announced via press releases. A media throng usually turned up on such occasions. Part of the success of this operation was Rob's style in dealing with the media. Journalists liked Rob because he was accessible and he understood their demands for a twenty-second grab. But his integrity also won many over; even those who disagreed with him on particular issues respected that he was desperately trying to deal with serious issues. Crucially, though, in making himself a media figure for the Aboriginal cause, Rob created tensions within the ALS about the focus he placed on this part of his job to the detriment of the wider management of the organisation.

In addition to his media work, Rob extended the profile of the ALS by engaging in a tireless round of community speaking engagements. He rarely said no to any organisation asking him to speak. The commitments he made to schools, community groups, universities and conferences started to pile up in his diary. There would be double and even triple bookings, causing headaches for his secretarial staff, and Rob would race from one to another. His disorganised style sometimes frustrated other senior ALS figures.

The final component of Rob's quest to professionalise the ALS was the plan that he and other senior staff laid out to expand the service. In his first Annual Report, Rob wrote: 'There is a growing capacity for more resources and the need for a greater capacity for the Aboriginal Legal Service to be able to respond to the reasonable and practical needs of Aboriginal people throughout the State'.[8] In this quest, Rob and other ALS senior staff were fortunate. Following the release of the final report of the Royal Commission into Aboriginal Deaths in Custody in 1991,[9] the federal government made $150 million available nationwide to address the key issues. Plans for a new strategic vision for the organisation emerged from ideas put together by discussions among Rob, senior staff and the Executive. Rob was fortunate in that some talented people joined the organisation. The ALS made successful bids for a share of the RCIADC money. Thus, within two years of his return, the ALS nearly doubled its budget of just over $2 million and went from an organisation employing seventy-one people in fourteen offices around the state to a hundred people in eighteen offices. In addition, the organisation created three new units: Public Interest (headed by Tony Shelly), Community (several people headed this unit but Peter O'Brien was a key force), and Land and Heritage (headed by Greg Benn). Together, these units were involved in a wide range of projects. In a short space the ALS had gone from an organisation overwhelmingly focussed on criminal matters to a broadly-based human rights organisation fighting across the range of interests of concern to Aboriginal people.

To complement his vision of a revitalised ALS, Rob had a clear understanding of the political challenges confronting the organisation. He set these out squarely in the public arena in his first Annual Report. They were: youth issues (Aboriginal juvenile crime); Aboriginal/police and community relations; land, mining and heritage issues; and the Royal Commission into Aboriginal Deaths in Custody. Indeed, these matters consumed Rob for the next five years in a frantic round of public advocacy, lobbying and direct protest.

Herein lay a flaw in his plan for the ALS, both personally and professionally. Rob oversaw the creation of a large and impressive political machine for the advancement of Aboriginal rights. But could he control it? And could he control the agenda that he had set for it? Two problems quickly emerged. The first centred on the conflicting demands of the political and criminal dimensions of the ALS. Technically, Rob was supposed to look after the management of the field officers and the non-legal staff. With a vast clientele, this was a demanding job in its own right. If these staff members were not trained and managed, 'the wheels fell off'. Several of the ALS staff attest that Rob had little interest in this role; his heart was in the political side, and especially the role he created as public advocate for Aboriginal issues. The periodic reports from the field officers in each of the eighteen regional offices piled up on his desk unread. In turn, this placed additional pressure on other senior staff and created something of a dysfunctional underside to the work of the organisation.

Rob saw his role as engaging in the big political fights, taking on the vested interests and cutting through the political resistance to change. He excelled in this role. He had the Executive's backing in this role. But it brought underlying tensions to the organisation. He was torn between having an organisation to run and carrying the burdens of Aboriginal advocacy.

In addition to delegating the daily administration of the criminal justice side of the ALS to others, Rob did not regularly engage in the daily grind of managing the organisation's policy positions and strategy. While keeping informed of developments, these tasks frequently fell to his Principal Legal Officer, Catherine Crawford, and to other senior staff.

The sheer size and diversity of roles within the ALS created personal problems for Rob. The organisation he helped build threatened to consume him. His work load was relentless. He would sometimes arrive in the mornings looking shell-shocked. He ran from one commitment to another all day long, rarely getting home before 8 p.m., when often there would be telephone calls about one problem or another. Sometimes the field officers or legal staff rang him to complain about the problems they were having gaining access to a client. Rob would drop whatever he was doing and go down to East Perth Lockup and sort the problem out.

Even at social gatherings he would often be backed into a corner and spend the evening rummaging over political or community issues. His personal assistant, Jenny Bedford, remembers: 'If we went for lunch in town, people in the street would stop him and do the same sort of thing ... he was Rob Riley and everyone knew him'. Family time was fleeting. He grabbed moments with Jeannie and the children, but his role was not conducive to cultivating the personal dimensions of life. At times he did not cope with the pressure. Occasionally he would 'go missing in action', head to the golf course and have some time out. He relied heavily on two old and close colleagues — Peter O'Brien and Ian Horrocks — to help him manage the organisation and ease the tensions between himself and some of his senior colleagues. Both had been with him off and on since his early days in Aboriginal politics. Both understood how he functioned and could often second-guess his views. In different ways they managed the swirling demands around him.

Despite undercurrents of dissatisfaction with his style of management, most of the ALS's large workforce admired Rob's high-profile championing of the Aboriginal cause. In the flurry of issues coinciding with his return to the ALS in June 1990, the one requiring his most immediate response was the disproportionate involvement of young Aborigines in serious crime. Over the next two years, the issue would define Rob's public profile and his vision for the ALS as a human rights organisation for Aboriginal interests. His efforts to steer the state away from recourse to harsher penalties involved him in some of his most creative roles as an activist: public advocate, lobbyist and protester. Because of the weight Rob attached to his campaign over juvenile crime, some context as to its origins in the modern era is necessary.

Between 1990 and 1992, a spate of high-speed car chases involving police and Aboriginal teenagers, some of primary school age, resulted in the deaths of ten innocent road users. In one horrific crash a young pregnant mother and her young son were killed, leaving only the father, Peter Blurton, alive. The random nature of the road accidents, the recklessness of the young drivers, and their brazen behaviour shocked the community. However, the intensity of the reaction — culminating in a massive demonstration of community protest for harsher penalties for young car thieves — suggested deeper forces at work. In part, Western Australia's own version of a 'race war' was fought over how to deal with young, alienated Aboriginal criminals.

How Western Australia drifted into this race war over juvenile crime was a subject with which Rob was intimately familiar. He knew the damaging intergenerational impact of reserve living; the damage done by the removal of children from their families; the failure of the education system to provide opportunities for successive generations of youth; the high rates of imprisonment which deprived adolescent boys of male role models; the unemployment which bred an outsider mentality; and the lack of cultural connection brought about by generations of assimilation and which fostered a crisis over identity in many young urban Aborigines. In short, Rob understood the cumulative effects of alienation in fuelling the angry aggression of some Aboriginal young people. In a speech he gave to a criminal justice conference in 1991 he cleverly constructed an imaginary, but typical, offender to highlight the complexity of the forces driving them to crime, a device which he used to provocatively raise the claim that such young people were the 'REAL victims'.[10]

The alienation of significant numbers of urban Aboriginal teenagers had been a slow burning fuse since at least the late 1960s, when the first generation of Aboriginal children allowed into state schools failed to thrive. In the early 1970s, educationalists started to observe that many Aboriginal youth had an acute sense of their own low socio-economic status and the limited opportunities open to them. Generations of reserve living had bred hostility towards wider society.[11] In 1980, a report compiled for the State School Teachers Union highlighted a crisis among Aboriginal youth. It pointed to the lack of adult male role models for Aboriginal boys arising from high rates of unemployment, imprisonment and unstable marriages. The Report concluded that these young people 'are presented with a view of society that does little to motivate them to seek the same goals and values as white children'.[12]

In 1987, a new and dangerous form of social behaviour emerged — the high-speed car chase. *The Daily News* reported that young Aboriginal boys driving stolen cars were deliberately taunting police into high-speed chases.[13] In the previous two weeks police had chased more than a dozen cars. All were driven by young Aboriginal boys, and on six occasions they deliberately rammed pursuing police. Moreover, the boys were intentionally letting themselves be seen by police, to taunt them into a chase. Immediately police noticed a stolen car, the young driver accelerated away: 'They throw things like shoes and beer cans they have found in the car'.[14]

A study conducted by the Department of Community Services not long after Rob took up his position at the ALS documented the social context of the problem.[15] Nearly half of the offences were committed by ninety-three young people, 67 per cent of whom were Aboriginal. Most of these young people came from impoverished and socially marginalised backgrounds: single-parent families; truancy; regular patterns of drug use; and child abuse and recidivism.

The figures reflected a continuation of the social crisis which had engulfed many Aboriginal families living in the metropolitan area of Perth. The seriousness of this crisis was also documented in 1990 by the Department for Community Services in an internal study comprising 250 interviews with Aboriginal people living in metropolitan Perth. The Department was under pressure to address the problem of Aboriginal juvenile offending, and the study was an attempt to grapple with its social context. It painted a bleak picture: 'the human issues presented portray a people isolated, rejected, ignored, and desolate, with their children facing uncertain but not pleasant futures'.

Five broad themes emerged:
- the removal of Aboriginal parents' authority and control over their children;
- the complexity of the legal structure stemming from a different culture which has little understanding of or sympathy towards those of an entirely different culture;
- the effective removal of Aboriginal children from the mainstream educational system;
- the effective removal of Aboriginal children from the mainstream employment system; and
- the negative relationship between Aboriginal people and their children, and the police.

Those interviewed spoke of an epidemic of Aboriginal young people 'getting into trouble'. Two-thirds of interviewees noted that their own children or children of relatives had been in trouble with the police: breaking and entering, stealing, shoplifting, substance abuse, truanting and disorderly conduct. Police intimidation of interviewees' children or relatives was a common experience: bashings, harassment and verbal abuse. The survey's findings were never publicly released. As the Royal Commission's Report into Deaths in Custody had yet to be completed there were few voices able to depict the realities facing Aboriginal juveniles and their families. Rob tried to fill this void.

For Rob, the furore that broke out over young Aborigines involved in high-speed car chases was not just core business for the ALS; it was deeply personal. In 1991 he offered some insights into his passionate interest in the problem. Addressing a criminal justice conference he talked about his own outbreak of anti-social behaviour following his first confrontation with racism in Pingelly. He said that it would have been easy for him to continue to seek revenge 'against a community that had treated me with such contempt'. He then posed a rhetorical question: 'Why didn't I continue with this anti-social attitude and behaviour?' He had, he said, spent 'many hours', reflecting on what stopped him becoming a juvenile delinquent. He knew that his own life could easily have become trapped in a downward spiral of alienation and the desire for revenge; fate saved him from becoming one of the kids who were now being targeted for harshly unsympathetic, 'get-tough' approaches on crime.

Rob's passionate involvement in the juvenile crime debate raised themes integral to his broader political activism: the need to address the interplay of race, racism and power. Rob understood that the alienation fuelling the outbreak of high-speed car chases was the product of historical forces: the intergenerational impact of poverty and hopelessness that he had witnessed on Pingelly Reserve and had first raised in public in the NAC submission to the Seaman inquiry. While Rob never sought to minimise the seriousness of crime among sections of the Aboriginal juvenile population, he believed that institutional racism and media propaganda were integral to understanding how the criminal activities of the age group became depicted as a community social problem whose only solution was further punitive approaches. And, of course, fresh from his ordeal with the Royal Commission, Rob was acutely aware that a 'lock them up and throw away the key' mentality would inevitably produce more deaths in custody.

In the months before his return to the ALS, Rob had watched the media commentary on Aboriginal juvenile crime grow into a frenzy. *The West Australian* ran a headline at the end of February 1990—'Aboriginal gangs terrorise suburbs' — which stirred Rob into immediate action.[16]

On his morning radio show Howard Sattler had conducted an interview with the victim of an attack. By this time Rob and Sattler were dogged political combatants. Sattler had become the highest rating morning presenter in Perth and part of the select, but powerful group of national talkback presenters capturing the attention of politicians. Critics alleged this select group were cynical populists for their ability to exploit public prejudices.[17]

Howard Sattler was reaching his peak when Rob verbally tangled with him on the issue of juvenile crime. Rob made several concise points: that race was driving the media's interest in high-speed chases; that the problem must be seen in its social context of disadvantage; and that the community must cooperate in finding solutions. These were rational, reasonable points. But the talkback format always held pitfalls for activists like Rob. Sattler interjected with what appeared to be a well-rehearsed line guaranteed to trap Rob:

Sattler: But Rob, I've made this point for some time, and you'll probably disagree with it, I think its time we stopped treating Aboriginal people as a separate race. We're all Australians under this sun.

Rob Riley: Well, I class myself as an Australian, but my priority is that I identify as being an Aboriginal, and no one's going to convince me that I should deny my Aboriginality because there's this one push of one Australia. ...

Sattler: But doesn't being an Australian come first?

Rob Riley: I believe, in my mind, I want to identify as being an Aboriginal first ...

Sattler: Before you're an Australian?

Rob Riley: Yeah.

Sattler: Well, that's where I think you've got it all wrong, Rob ...

And so the exchange drifted from Rob's preferred ground to Sattler's even more contentious line about nationalism versus Aboriginal identity. As much as Rob tried, he could never claim to have triumphed in the talkback format.

In April 1990, and still in his capacity as Head of the Aboriginal Issues Unit with the Royal Commission, Rob wrote to the Australian Press Council with a formal complaint against *The West Australian* for the article headed 'Aboriginal Gangs Terrorise Suburbs'. The offending article was, he wrote, 'a gross breach of journalistic ethics fuelling ignorant and prejudiced attitudes toward Aboriginal people'. While Rob was at pains to point out that the reality of Aboriginal juvenile delinquency was serious, he charged that the story was 'a beat up'. He argued that it was based on unsubstantiated information, especially the claim of a 'terror' gang involving thirty Aboriginal youths. This information had come from undisclosed sources. He reported that a television crew had privately told him that the incident involved between half a dozen and a dozen young Aborigines who were shoplifting. He acknowledged the isolated physical assault but claimed this did not constitute terrorising of the suburbs, and, furthermore, none of the material justified a front-page article. Rob's final complaint was the lack of attempt to verify the alleged incident by talking to Aboriginal people.

In his letter of complaint to the Press Council, Rob expanded on his concern about the pattern of biased reporting on Aboriginal people. He had surveyed the contents of the offending edition and reported that:

> Two smaller articles on page two 'officers sent to assess problem' and 'woman, 19, scarred by gang attack' were linked to the page one lead. A very cynical and racially derogatory cartoon by Alston capitalising on both that edition's lead story and previous sensationalised articles about federal funding to the Aboriginal Legal Service to defend a sacred site was run on page ten. A misinformed feature on petrol sniffing (e.g. 'they sniff to get away from their heritage') on page 11 was the subject of criticism from various quarters.[18]

Rob refused to let up on the issue of press bias. Just days before he took up his position at the ALS, Rob gave evidence about the role of the media to the Royal Commission into Aboriginal Deaths in Custody. He took along his own small survey. He had culled all the stories in the press about Aboriginal people in the previous week and was able to report that of the eighteen separate articles, 'there was not one positive story in that whole week', which, he elaborated, was 'a fairly typical situation'. Rob told the Royal Commission of his concern over the power of the press to influence public opinion and to render a sense of powerlessness in the Aboriginal community because of their inability to redress the negative reporting of their communities.

In his evidence, Rob returned to an old theme: the need for a public awareness campaign, one which was commensurate in scope with the anti-smoking, anti-drug and keep Australia beautiful campaigns. The campaign, he said, should inform the general public 'of why Aboriginal people are in the socio-economic position they are and some of the fairly difficult social circumstances that Aboriginal people have to face on a daily basis'.[19]

At the ALS, Rob increased the tempo of his efforts to curb the impact of the media in its sensationalisation of Aboriginal juvenile crime. A string of negative headlines appeared: 'Fear and speed in the streets'; '60 Minutes of Terror' and 'Aborigines in half high-speed chases'; all of which were run on either the front page or inside front page of *The West Australian* and *The Daily News*. More bad publicity followed. In July 1990, and in contravention of the *Children's Court Act 1988 (WA)*, the police orchestrated the release of the name and photograph of a teenage Aboriginal escapee from a detention centre. The 'mug shot' and accompanying story became front-page news. Rob fumed over the disclosure. He shot off a press release in which he accused police and some media outlets of whipping up an atmosphere of hysteria over Aboriginal young offenders which was creating 'a climate of fear and racial hatred' towards Aboriginal young people. He elaborated. 'The front page story and "mug shot" in *The Daily News* of a 16-year-old Aboriginal boy who escaped from Longmore Detention Centre on Monday were totally out of proportion with the seriousness of the offences for which the youth had been convicted'.[20]

Warming angrily to his theme of a 'police–media witch-hunt', Rob argued the incident was a serious violation of the United Nations Declaration on the Rights of the Child. He called upon the state government to halt the 'racist persecution of Aboriginal youth'.[21] Such was the climate of hysteria about this one boy's escape that Rob gave eight media interviews on the one day.

Rob also had an angry exchange with Howard Sattler about the matter of releasing the names of juveniles who had escaped from custody. Sattler adopted the police argument that such releases were in the public interest, while Rob claimed the police deliberately broke the child protection law with the aim of having it permanently weakened.[22] In the eyes of his critics, Sattler had generated moral panic over juvenile crime. By this stage, Rob had adopted a pugnacious stand against Sattler. Whenever he was in his ALS office in the mornings, he would tune in to the 'Sattler File'. He continued to engage with Sattler, against the better judgement of some of his colleagues, who warned Rob, 'You can't win with this bastard'. But, as one of these colleagues recalls, Rob felt he had started to develop a measure of the man from listening to him. As Ian Horrocks recalls: 'Rob felt there was no other way than to crash or bash. It had to be confronted. Sattler had the town inflamed'.

There are no records available to show how many times Rob appeared on Sattler's program. On a few occasions Rob rang the program without identifying himself. But his strategy of confronting the media and trying to put across a different message earned him the respect of many in the white community. People would stop him in the street, shake his hand and just say, 'G'day Rob, I've been seeing what you're doing in the media for your people and just want to say well done and keep it up'.

Rob was able to acknowledge the seriousness of the issue but to place it in its historical and socio-economic context. In this way he usually appeared reasoned and reasonable. In one extended profile for *The West Australian* he laid out his views about the social context of Aboriginal juvenile crime in this style: 'He did not condone criminal activity. His point was that there were burning issues behind juvenile crime'. Some of these young people commit crime, he suggested, 'to get back at society for what it has done to their people'.[23] Feedback he was getting from Aboriginal juveniles in detention centres highlighted their sense of alienation, their crises over identity, and the intimidation they faced from police. Taking a shot at Sattler and his listeners, he elaborated:

> It was easy for the community, media and politicians to take a simplistic view of the issue — calling for harsher penalties. But while a black-bashing attitude might provide some short-term relief, the shadows of the issue would remain. The social issues aren't being addressed as to why there is such a big problem.

Rob's calmly stated but confronting views earned him a rare endorsement from the press. In its editorial on the same day as the feature article, *The West Australian* found much to praise, endorsing his explanation of alienation and of the need for consideration of profound social and cultural factors. The paper supported his call to end the negative stereotyping of young Aborigines: 'The solution will not be found if sections of the white community continue to adopt a negative and hostile attitude towards Aborigines because of the wrong-doings of a few confused and angry young people'. It was a measure of the impact Rob had had in changing the debate that such endorsement was offered.

~~~~~~~~~

In May 1991, with the debate over harsher penalties still simmering away, came the long-awaited release of the Report of the Royal Commission into Aboriginal Deaths in Custody. Rob saw the release of the Royal

Commission's $30 million, eleven-volume report, containing 339 recommendations to government, as a landmark in Aboriginal affairs. In fact, the Royal Commission had acted in the manner of a truth and reconciliation commission. It had garnered the voices of Aboriginal people, heard their stories of injustice and victimisation and reported back to government with a vision for a new relationship between Aborigines and non-Aborigines. Rob expressed his admiration for Pat Dodson's 'charisma, objectivity and patience' in focussing national attention 'on the powerlessness and dispossession of the Aborigine'.[24] He saw the recommendations covering education, housing and employment as a blueprint for the future. It fact, Rob had staked his role at the ALS on his ability to ensure that governments implemented the Report. All his prior experiences working in Aboriginal affairs were embodied in the findings of the Report and especially the link that the Underlying Issues volume made between contemporary socio-economic disadvantage and historical dispossession. And he had been an integral part of it. Rob's fate and that of the Royal Commission would be interwoven.

On one issue, though, he was vehemently at odds with the findings of the Royal Commission. Commissioner Johnson found that none of the deaths in custody were the product of deliberate violence or brutality by police or prison officers, but rather of their lack of appreciation of a duty of care. This was a crucial issue for Rob. Police brutality had formed most of the testimony he had gathered from Aboriginal people during his work with the Commission. How had Johnson come to such a finding? The Commission's hearings into the John Pat case had been conducted over three months in Roebourne during the first half of 1990, just after the Underlying Issues team had undertaken their own reconstruction of the young man's death.

Not everyone associated with Commissioner Elliot Johnson's hearing felt that the process worked to produce the fairest possible outcome for Aborigines. Some people were concerned about the adversarial nature of the hearings, the unfavourable treatment of certain evidence from Aboriginal witnesses, and the persistence of irregularities in the police case. Rob was likely aware of this dissenting opinion. It would have complemented his long-standing view of police culpability in the John Pat case and his view that the justice system had repeatedly failed the Aboriginal community. He continued to believe that the strongest actions should be taken against offending police and prison officers. He would have understood the warning of contemporary French philosopher Emmanuel Levinas: 'A world where forgiveness is almighty becomes inhuman'.[25] Rob had lived too long with police violence for a blanket act of forgiveness. In his angry reaction to the Royal Commission's lack of finding on police culpability in some of the deaths — and particularly that of John Pat — Rob was already staking out his opposition to any kind of reconciliation that did not include retributive justice.

Rob's position was complicated by the divisions within the state government on the matter. The Police Minister, Graham Edwards, made an early declaration that disciplinary action against officers was unlikely because of the lapse of time.[26] Meanwhile the Premier, Dr Lawrence, announced the formation of a taskforce to investigate whether police should be prosecuted or disciplined. This decision was quickly reversed following strong opposition from the Police Union, which took out a full newspaper advertisement with a blunt warning: the Union would use all its resources to resist attacks on its members 'to satisfy minority groups seeking revenge, not justice'.[27]

Rob made several calls for prosecutions and disciplinary action to be taken against police or prison officers involved in the deaths of Aborigines in custody. He argued that 'those responsible had to be brought to account no matter how long ago people died'.[28] He went on:

> It's nonsense for anyone to be claiming that charges cannot be brought after seven years. Police are charging people with incest twenty years after the event. The Royal Commission was about investigating the circumstances leading up to the deaths and the fact is that so far all the reports show criminal negligence. This is inexcusable and we are demanding that the system changes and we will be pressuring the Government until it does. The ALS will be demanding it does.

This time, he had powerful backing for his views. Under a new editor, *The West Australian* castigated the Royal Commission Report and the state government for failing to initiate disciplinary charges. It was unacceptable, the paper argued, for officialdom to 'merely close the books on tragic events in which the behaviour of police and prison officers was shown to be appalling'.[29]

Rob organised a 'Rally for Justice' through Perth's central business district to protest the government's decision not to proceed with investigating disciplinary action. In press releases advertising the rally, Rob used characteristically forthright language to press his main charge against the government: 'Either the WA Police Union is dictating Government decisions or the Government is in basic agreement with the view that violent, racist and negligent officers should remain welcome in Government employ'.[30]

Rob expected up to a thousand people to join the Rally, but less than three hundred did. The failure of the Rally to excite greater support is difficult to explain. It was held at short notice and received little advance publicity. Also, not all Aboriginal leaders agreed with the stance Rob adopted. A counter-view held that punitive action against police would damage changes thought to be under way within police culture. Later, Rob would adopt a more proactive stance in working with police to effect change.

The government's implementation of the Royal Commission recommendations began to occupy Rob's attention. This would be a mammoth task. Most of the recommendations were the responsibility of state governments. Leadership, resources and coordination would be called for. A year after its release, Rob was growing pessimistic about the prospects for change. In the 1991–92 Annual Report he wrote: 'The ALS has not fulfilled its potential of challenging the government on its failure to implement the recommendations of the Royal Commission into Aboriginal Deaths in Custody. To date the government has paid only lip service to the Commissioner's final report and recommendations. It has ignored the Underlying Issues Report prepared by Commissioner Dodson'. Had he set the bar too high? What could the ALS do except continue to exert moral pressure? Nevertheless, he did not let the issue disappear.

~~~~~~

In the meantime, Rob's energies between June and August 1991 were also occupied by a row over heritage issues instigated by Hamersley Iron (part of the Rio Tinto mining giant) and its claims that the ALS was thwarting its efforts to develop the massive Marandoo project in the Pilbara, close to the Karajini National Park and the township of Tom Price. In a re-run of similar conflicts, the mining activity was seen by the traditional owners as posing a threat to their rich and world-class store of sacred rock art.

This issue again brought to the fore the central dynamic in Aboriginal affairs so familiar to Rob. Aboriginal interests were always given second place to powerful, vested interests which campaigned to demonise and belittle the claims Aborigines made for equal consideration. The Aboriginal voice was overwhelmed by contrived arguments which positioned Aboriginal interests as contrary to the national interest. Moreover, bodies that sought to represent the Aboriginal position were criticised for pursuing their own political agenda contrary to the 'real' interests of people on the ground. In these cases, governments inevitably side with the powerful interests.

To some extent this is a reconstruction of Rob's position; he left no detailed account of his overall views on the case, but it emerges through his many statements on the Marandoo dispute and is consistent with his previous experiences of Noonkanbah and the struggle over national land rights. The bottom line was that Marandoo put Rob and the ALS legal staff through the wringer of this contested, winner-take-all approach to resolving disputes over land.

The Marandoo project's problems went public in early June 1991, when Hamersley's public affairs spokesman claimed that the Company had not been able to secure approval from the traditional owners of the Tom Price region for the commencement of site work as required under the *Aboriginal Heritage Act 1972 (WA)*. The spokesperson complained that the ALS was not able to progress negotiations.[31] This publicity was quickly followed by information supplied to the press by the Chamber of Mines and Energy about a systemic problem of backlogs in the mining industry arising from Aboriginal groups exercising their rights under the Aboriginal Heritage Act.[32] In this way, the mining industry defined the 'problem': Aborigines exercising their rights; and the solution: change the Act.

The extent of industry's lobbying behind the scenes is impossible to gauge, but it was only a matter of weeks before the Premier, Dr Carmen Lawrence, warned Aboriginal groups of her intention to step in and break the impasse through legislation. Certainly the Premier had a sluggish economy with which to contend. But the Marandoo project was never a straightforward pro- or anti-development issue. From the Aboriginal perspective, it was about process and timing.

Rob went on the offensive the moment the Premier made her announcement. He told the press:

> Dr Lawrence's attitude was reminiscent of the anti-Aboriginal sentiment whipped up by the WA Chamber of Mines a decade ago. It was nonsense to suggest that the ALS and the traditional owners were involved in some kind of conspiracy to thwart commercial developments. When you have an equation like profit and jobs versus Aboriginal culture and heritage it is predictable that the powerful and vested interest groups like the Government and the mining industry will eventually impose their will.

Few people had the experience to make such prescient comments. He knew the script. The next stage of the campaign was to denigrate the ALS itself. This was kicked off by the Mayor of Kalgoorlie–Boulder when he called for the organisation to be disbanded as being detrimental to the mining industry.[33] Sensing the political opportunity to bag the government, opposition leader Richard Court upped the ante, criticising the Premier for failing to resolve the dispute. At the end of July 1991 Hamersley Iron took out two newspaper advertisements criticising the ALS for its role in obstructing the project.[34] The Premier also criticised the ALS, pointing to part of a letter it had written to Hamersley telling the Company that flying over sacred sites could incur damage, a position on which the Minister for Aboriginal Affairs initially supported the ALS, only to back down the following day.[35]

In early September 1991, the Chamber of Mines ramped up the pressure on the government. It took out a further full-page newspaper advertisement in the form of an open letter to the Premier imploring the government to intervene in the dispute and mounting a thinly veiled attack on the ALS: 'Some people, claiming to act in the interests of Aboriginal groups, are using heritage legislation to assert de facto control over high profile economic development projects for their own political agendas'.[36] The open letter was no different in sentiment to Sir Charles Court's oft-stated slur that it was only outside 'stirrers' who whipped up anti-development feeling among unsuspecting Aboriginal people in remote communities. The Chamber said it was committed to the protection of sites of 'genuine' significance and wanted a clear framework for resolving these issues. But, in this context, 'genuine' was loaded terminology: a tactic to ensure that development proceeded quickly.

Additional pressure was placed on members of State Parliament. The Association of Mining and Exploration Companies sent an open letter to all members written in explicitly ideological terms:

> During the past decade, the Aboriginal community has made constant demands on Australian society for the allocation of land, protection of Aboriginal Heritage, special Government funding packages ... and for assistance with life style developments. These initiatives have often resulted in services or developments which have set parts of the Aboriginal community aside from the mainstream of society. Aboriginals as a result are now seen by many as a privileged group, as this special assistance is not available to other ethnic groups.

The Association further complained that government funds given to the ALS had been used to 'frustrate the legitimate aspirations of the rest of the West Australian community'.[37]

Rob continually stressed that the ALS took instructions from the traditional owners through their body, the Karajini Corporation, in a client/lawyer relationship and was bound to use every provision of the weak Aboriginal Heritage Act to defend their interests. Why, he asked, should Aboriginal people in 'a civilised world' not be accorded the same access as anyone else to contract law and civil rights?[38]

Inside the ALS, there were two aspects of the way the dispute was being conducted which were very different from the version peddled by the Company, the Association of Mining and Exploration Companies Inc. and the state government. Rob did not fully disclose the organisation's concerns, possibly either because it might further inflame the dispute or because it was too complex a picture to be conveyed to the community via the media.

Firstly, the traditional owners wanted a lot more consultation than the standard practice of being asked their opinion and being told what would happen. They wanted proper negotiations to ensure that development would proceed in a culturally appropriate manner, and that the community would be compensated through economic benefits and employment. The ALS's second concern related to the nature of

Hamersley's negotiations: the apparent lack of substance about the actual benefits to the community and, more particularly, the absence of a culturally sensitive approach to the negotiation process.

Mining companies like Hamersley invariably wanted to be given a map containing references to all the sacred sites. But traditional owners often felt uncomfortable handing over this kind of information to anyone who was not a traditional law man. The ALS continually tried to explain to the Company that the matter could not be dealt with in this manner. The traditional owners' preferred method was to be provided with the work site information by the Company, which it would then use to survey the proposed areas. Then, in a process of interactive communication, they would isolate areas of significance and come up with alternative sites where development could proceed. In this way, traditional owners did not have to divulge any cultural information and everyone walked away contented.

Some mining companies had adopted this approach. At the height of the Marandoo dispute, Geoff Stewart, Chief Executive of North Flinders Mines, wrote an article for an industry newspaper arguing that some segments of the mining industry had 'little understanding of the interests of Aboriginal people and too few people appear willing to make an effort to find out what the aboriginal interests in the land really are'.[39] Stewart did not single anyone out, but it was the view of the ALS that Hamersley was opposed to the method of supplying the community in advance with all the information about site works.

By the end of August 1991, the government appeared to change tack. It agreed to conduct an anthropological survey, thereby breaking the impasse. Rob welcomed the decision as a vindication of the traditional owners' position. In his view, it was Hamersley Iron that had failed to meet its responsibilities.[40] For now the matter rested.

Rob immediately switched his attention to the populist debate over harsher penalties for juvenile crime. While *The West Australian* had changed course on this issue, which it credited in part to Rob's persistent calls for greater understanding of the causes of offending behaviour, Sattler continued to beat the drum for tougher approaches. In the months leading up to 20 August 1991, he extensively promoted the need for harsher penalties on his radio program and advocated the calling of a 'Rally for Justice' of which he became convener. Sattler was described as having 'vigorously fanned the juvenile justice debate on his radio station'.[41] On the appointed day, in excess of 20,000 people attended the rally outside Parliament House, having been primed by Sattler to sign a petition which circulated among the crowd by girls in tee-shirts bearing the name of the radio station he worked for. Critics called the event a rally for ratings, suggesting that Sattler was inflaming community prejudice and fears about the juvenile justice system, which was supposedly not being hard enough on young repeat offenders, the majority of whom were Aboriginal.[42]

The sheer size of the crowd was intimidating enough for politicians, but its mood was positively unnerving. Like some modern version of a white knight, Sattler was introduced to the crowd as a hero. Further feeding the fears of the crowd was a man prominently bearing a noose with a placard which called for the hanging of the Children's Court President. The rally's petition called for the state government to introduce, among a range of measures, mandatory minimum sentences for repeat offenders.

Premier Dr Carmen Lawrence's immediate response to these demands was equivocal. On the day of the Rally she told the press: 'It [the Rally] is definitely a message that the Government hears and has been listening to for some time'.[43] But what did this mean? A psychologist by background, intellectual, urbane and sophisticated, Dr Lawrence would almost certainly have seen the merits of Rob's call for a broader approach. However, her government was under constant pressure in the polls. It had suffered on-going adverse publicity from the WA Inc financial scandals, which originated in the Burke government.

Rob continued his advocacy of a more humane understanding of the problem. In November 1991 he gave evidence to the Western Australian House of Assembly Select Committee on Youth Affairs.[44] He forthrightly acknowledged the social reality facing impoverished Aboriginal families. He told the Committee members that theft was a way of life for many Aboriginal young people; 'nobody gives it a second thought'. He also emphasised the effects of drugs and alcohol: 'kids are often freaking out from the effects of drinking ... and then shooting up speed. As a result they are stealing cars and being involved in high-speed chases'.[45] Rob strongly argued against the imposition of harsher criminal penalties: 'The more we criminalise kids, the more crime they commit.

There are better ways of dealing with that problem than putting kids in custody, because from an Aboriginal perspective, often those kids graduate from being put into juvenile institutions to being sent to adult institutions'.[46]

Much of the evidence given to the Committee supported Rob's thrust to address the social crisis in the lives of many young Aborigines and their families. But most witnesses worked in government-funded agencies and were not able to put their views on the public record. Thus, Rob was among the most consistently strong opponents of the emerging calls to toughen the penalties for juvenile offenders.

Sympathetic as Rob was to the plight of alienated young offenders, he boiled over with frustration and anger in dealing with the parents. Many came to the ALS to complain to Rob about the way their sons had been arrested. Rob took them into his office 'and laid into them'. Everyone in the building could hear him shouting: 'Don't come in here and tell me what they did wrong, have a fucking look at yourself'. One case, in particular, had him seething. Talking to parents of two boys — aged eleven and eight — he expressed his utter disbelief to the parents that they could allow their young children to roam around over a six-month period in which they stole several cars. For Rob the couple epitomised the failure of parents to provide adequate care. As these examples show, Rob was equally concerned about the need for Aborigines to show individual responsibility as he was for wider society to show understanding about the impacts of intergenerational disadvantage. He had begun to express interest in ideas emanating from New Zealand and based upon traditional Maori practices which brought together offenders, their family and victims into a consultative process based on offenders' taking responsibility for their actions.

But, for now, Western Australia failed to embrace such far-reaching changes. While the government was formulating its punitive response to juvenile crime, the related issue of police violence towards Aborigines erupted nationally in early September 1991. On her way home from acting in an amateur play about police racism and violence, quietly-spoken community worker and dance teacher Rhonda Collard unexpectedly encountered a convergence between art and real life. Her car was surrounded by armed police officers, who were following a tip-off that a 'glinting object' had been spotted in her vehicle. Forced to lie face down and spread-eagled on the road, Collard and her companion had a pump-action shot gun primed and levelled at them. Collard thought she was going to be shot. The glinting object was nothing more than a drink bottle. When she threatened to report the incident, an officer said to her: 'You people have no voice. Who'll listen to you people?'[47]

But Collard did have a voice, as did her Aboriginal husband, a serving officer in the Western Australian police force. They took their story to the press and it was splashed across the front page. For Rob and the entire ALS team, this was the case they had been waiting for: two highly respected members of the community victimised by the police by virtue of their race, and willing to come forward.

The Collard incident came amid growing concerns at the ALS about the rise in the number of incidents involving Aboriginal complaints against police. In his first Annual Report, Rob released ALS statistics which showed that complaints had increased by 75 per cent since 1988. He expressed particular concern about allegations concerning 'the callous and terrifying methods' used by the Tactical Response Group (TRG) and the 79 Division, which, he said, 'should not be seen as secret police who are answerable to nobody'.[48]

At about the time that Rob wrote these comments, Western Australia's Equal Opportunity Commission released a report into police practices based substantially on cases provided to them by the ALS.[49] The report confirmed what Rob and others had been claiming for more than a decade: that violence towards Aborigines was widespread in the police force. It found 'alarming problems' between police and Aboriginal people, and a culture of ignorance in the force about the meaning of discrimination and the existence of structural discrimination against certain groups. The Report also conceptualised the background factors behind the poor relationships between police and Aborigines: the 'institutional' view among Aborigines of police as an oppressive force, and the opposing institutional view among police that Aborigines had 'something against police' and therefore needed to be dealt with harshly. Interviewed on ABC radio following the release of the Report, Rob put his finger on the difficulty of addressing the problem. He asked: how can the community 'protect the interests of people that feel intimidated about identifying who the perpetrators are?'[50]

Now, less than two years later, came the Collard case, which offered a rare opportunity to erect a solid platform for debate about the seriousness of the issue. Rob pursued a three-pronged strategy:

giving extended media interviews to publicise the wider problem of police violence towards Aborigines; highlighting other cases that had come forward to the ALS; and engaging with the police to address the problem. He outlined his strategy in an extended interview with *The Bulletin*.[51] The only way change can occur, he said, was to 'press home the point' through formal complaints: 'If you walk away from an allegation without seeing it through to the bitter end, you are not doing anyone — including the police — any favours'. Yet Rob also stated that the ALS would not 'jump on the bandwagon of kicking the cops'. In fact, he used the Collard incident to seek a meeting with Police Commissioner Brian Bull to express his concerns about the activities of the heavily armed sections of the Western Australian police force.[52] Rob's approach on this occasion mirrored the new strategy he had hoped would be successful in his role at the ALS: place maximum pressure on government through the media and engage with them to solve problems. On the matter of police violence he could claim some success for the strategy. Rob was a key player in assisting a change of culture in the police force away from institutionalised violence towards Aborigines. He developed a close and constructive working relationship with Deputy Commissioner Les Ayton, and in the process built the first institutionally effective bridges between the police and Aboriginal people in Western Australia.

Following the Collard incident and its immediate fallout, Rob's attention was drawn back to juvenile crime. The government unexpectedly announced its policy stance early in 1992. On 6 January, in his capacity as Acting Premier while Dr Lawrence was overseas, Ian Taylor announced draft legislation to target 'repeat offenders' and 'hard core juvenile offenders' with the aim of removing them altogether from society. On 29 January 1992, and back from overseas, the Premier announced the details of the legislation together with a special sitting of Parliament to be held on 5 February to consider the proposed legislation.

When the legislation came before Parliament, it did so in the form of two Bills: the Crime (Serious and Repeat Offenders) Sentencing Bill and the Criminal Law Amendment Bill, the joint aim of which was to provide for a minimum sentence of eighteen months for violent juvenile repeat offenders; a twenty-year sentence for any offender, adult or juvenile, convicted of driving a stolen vehicle dangerously and causing death; fourteen years for driving a stolen vehicle dangerously and causing grievous bodily harm; and eight years for stealing a vehicle and driving it recklessly or dangerously. A proposal to give the government power to detain recidivists at the government's pleasure was dropped before the draft legislation was finalised.[53]

The government's plans incited a fury of opposition from groups around Australia, including ATSIC, the federal Human Rights Commissioner, the federal Attorney General, the Crime Research Centre at the University of Western Australia, churches and youth legal services, among others. From this point, Rob became one of many voices in this chorus of opposition, although as a prominent local media personality his views were given wide exposure. He attended a national criminal justice conference in February 1992, where he made an impassioned critique of the moral bankruptcy inherent in the state government's embrace of the legislation. There was an unmistakable sense of despair driving his comments. Drawing on his experience at the ALS he challenged the audience to consider the historical context of the legislation. Every day of the week, he said, he witnessed the consequences wreaked on Aboriginal people by past racial policies: 'I witness a sense of hopelessness, I see frustration at a sense of powerlessness, of being unable to change the everyday conditions that compound the misery of so many people's lives'. He moved to his central criticism of the legislation, the crux of which resonated with his own life:

> Once again, despite the years of public breast-beating about the shameful mistakes of the past, young Aboriginal people who need help, understanding and compassion, are to be forcibly removed from their families and communities ... [and] locked away in a system that will turn them into hardened recidivist criminals.[54]

Rob went on the offensive soon after the details of the proposed legislation were made public. He used regular media interviews to disseminate his strong opposition to the measure. The full extent of his feelings about the proposed legislation were conveyed in a letter to the Premier on 5 February 1992. Throughout his tenure as the head of the ALS, Rob was active in writing to persons in authority. His surviving letters show a readiness to use a combination of reason and emotion to convey his thoughts, as if the privacy of personal communication carried more weight than repeated public appeals. The 5 February letter was in this vein.

Rob's letter began by stating his credentials to the Premier, and moved to establish the basis of his concern: how the legislation would impact on Aboriginal people. Almost as a rhetorical device he raised the spectre of the breach of the UN Conventions of the International Covenant of Civil and Political Rights and the International Convention on the Rights of the Child, only to dismiss their relevance as being 'based on clinical, legalistic emphasis' which, while valid, ignored 'the human element'. The human element for Rob was the six hundred young people who, because of prior convictions, were likely to come under the definition of serious and repeat offender, 70–80 per cent of whom would be Aboriginal. Moving closer to his theme of human impact, and wearing his own experiences on his sleeve, he wrote:

> I tell you that Aboriginal people fear the impact of this legislation because we already know what the result will be. We, as a race of people, have been subjected to some of the most harsh and inhumane attempts at social engineering which have ever been imposed, by a supposedly democratic country on its indigenous population ... Our people have lived through and survived genocide and dispossession.

Lifting the emotional tempo of his words even further, Rob invited the Premier to consider her own legislation within this historical context:

> Yet, here we are, after all that we have been through, watching you and your Government enacting these same hideous policies on our children and exacting the same hideous penalties. The tragedy is that we are powerless to stop you. You are making a terrible and irrevocable mistake which is going to destroy the lives of so many young people, whose only crime is to be a victim of society and previous government policy.

If any assemblage of words was calculated to cause the Premier to change her mind on the legislation it was surely these. But Rob did not feel content with the case that he had so far made. He challenged the

Premier to consider the political context of the proposed legislation as a product of unprincipled political forces:

> This legislation is not fair and balanced. It is produced in haste as a result of a concerted campaign waged over a considerable period of time (at least three years) by the likes of Howard Sattler and Radio 6PR, who have been responsible for the media beat up and public hysteria. You and your Government have fallen victim to the powers of influence and the populist media.

It was a devastating critique: emotive, intelligent, principled. But its tone was desperate, a reflection of both Rob's feelings about the actions of the government and frustrations about the limitations of 'outsider' activism. Rob had helped build an organisation to fight the system, but no Aboriginal voice was strong enough when governments were bent on siding with populist opinion. Intellectually Rob knew these limitations, but emotionally he believed that rational argument should win out.

Rob was prominent in a final protest against the legislation on the day of the special sitting of Parliament on 5 February. About three hundred people gathered to express their opposition, among them the survivor of a horrific crash a few months earlier. Peter Blurton was photographed with Rob on the steps of Parliament House, the two men united in a call for more rehabilitative and preventative measures for juveniles.[55]

After the protest broke up on the steps, many people, including Rob, went up to the public gallery of the House of Assembly, with the aim of expressing their opposition to the last. Although recollections differ on the nature of Rob's actions, one close friend recalls that he threw a roll of toilet paper down into the Chamber and that he yelled comments at Dr Lawrence about the racist nature of the legislation. Community activist and future WA Greens Senator, Christabel Chamarette, only recalls Rob mouthing abuse at the Premier but says that he did manage to make direct, penetrating eye contact with her. The moment that the protest made itself heard, security guards made a beeline for the public gallery. Rob organised people to block the corridor, momentarily preventing the guards from getting in. While others drifted outside, Rob stayed to the last. But it was to no avail.

There were a number of key aspects of the debate over Aboriginal juvenile crime that caused deep distress for Rob, of a highly personal

Travelling party attached to the Royal Commission into Aboriginal Deaths in Custody investigation into underlying causes, c. 1990. Left to right: Patricia Morrison, Rob Riley, Steve Mickler, Darryl Kickett and Dennis Eggington. The photographer was Pat Dodson.

Meeting the Dalai Lama in Perth, 1992. His Holiness was attending the Mind Science symposium, while also taking time to meet members of the local community.

Rob Riley speaking on the radio, early 1990s. Rob developed a reputation as an articulate and forceful media advocate.

Rob Riley addressing a rally to protest Western Australia's controversial juvenile justice legislation, February 1992.

Rob Riley with Aboriginal Affairs Minister Robert Tickner, Aboriginal Legal Service offices, mid-1990s.

kind. The community prejudice which drove the debate was reminiscent to Rob of the prejudice which undermined national land rights in the mid-1980s. It is significant that Rob re-visited ANOP's 1985 call for an education campaign in evidence he gave to the 1991 Royal Commission into Racist Violence. As was the case in the 1980s, the debate on juvenile crime was propelled by vested interests, and again the police and the media conveyed images and information detrimental to Aborigines for apparently self-serving reasons. Then there was the cave-in by the state Labor government to populist opinion, in Rob's mind yet another of the Party's betrayals. And underlying these political elements was his close identification with the alienated youths themselves. He saw in them many of the circumstances of his own life. They were victims of the history of injustice dealt out to Aboriginal people, cast adrift from their Aboriginal identities, and destined for institutionalisation.

Western Australia in 1992 must have appeared to him a cruel and unforgiving place. He had been prepared to acknowledge the problem of serious offending. He wanted an enlightened approach to deal with its causes. And he was prepared to work with government to achieve it. Yet, populism prevailed. He was devastated. The actions of the Lawrence government, one of his close friends explained, 'broke his heart'.

His relations with the government were further strained by the announcement of its proposal to resolve the Marandoo dispute. On 5 February 1992, Dr Lawrence announced that it would legislate to block 'unwarranted legal claims' threatening the proposal. The government simply excised the area required by Hamersley from the requirements of the Aboriginal Heritage Act. While it required the Company to protect sacred sites, this was held to be inadequate by the traditional owners. A decade later, the Company's Director, Peter Eggleston, confessed to the misguided nature of the approached taken by it and the government. The legislation had, he explained to a world sustainability conference, 'marked a low point in Aboriginal relations for the Company ... [the case] left a legacy of deep distrust and bitterness'.[56]

Rob publicly criticised the amendments and privately wrote to the Premier complaining that the government had dealt with Aboriginal people in a discriminatory manner 'by virtue of greater consultations with the mining industry' and producing amendments 'designed to facilitate the access of the mining industry to Aboriginal land, in particular areas of cultural significance'.[57]

For the traditional owners of the region, the experience was a distressing one. Greg Benn, head of the Land and Heritage Unit at the ALS during the dispute, explains: 'They felt totally disempowered, totally disillusioned and eventually came to the point where they weren't willing or able to take the matter any further'. As Rob had said, Aborigines were merely 'beggars' to people in authority.

This view only hardened when Eric Charleton, an opposition member of the Legislative Council, initiated a stoush with the ALS, which ran throughout the second half of 1992 but which reached a critical stage in September of that year. Earlier in the year, Charleton had passed a motion requiring the ALS to hand over all its financial statements for the previous three years. His motion, he said, arose from 'a great deal of concern among Aborigines themselves about the way in which the ALS operates'.[58] At its heart the dispute was about the legitimacy of the ALS in the eyes of two disparate groups brought together in alliance: Rob's critics in the Noongar community and the state's conservative politicians, who viewed his effectiveness with growing alarm. At stake was a key principle: to whom was the ALS — and community organisations like it — responsible: to the funding body (in this case the Commonwealth government) or the jurisdiction in which the service was delivered (that is, the state of Western Australia)?

As an Executive, the ALS regarded itself accountable only to the Commonwealth and refused to comply with the Upper House motion that it hand over financial documents. Behind the constitutional argy-bargy Rob alleged dirty politics. He laid out his charge in several statements to the press. Charleton had, he said, a hidden agenda: to close down the organisation,[59] while Rob's Aboriginal opponents wished to see him removed as head of the ALS. Bropho instigated at least one public meeting of Aboriginal people which attacked Rob and at which he claimed Aborigines had lost faith in the ALS.[60]

The simmering row came to a head in September 1992, when Rob announced that the ALS was taking its challenge against the authority of the State Parliament to the High Court. This application was later rejected by the Court, leaving the matter to be decided by the State Supreme Court, which, in November 1992, found that the legal argument put forward by the ALS was without merit. However, the ALS Executive remained defiant: no documents would be handed over to what was seen as a witch-hunt. This decision left Rob and the Principal Legal Officer, Catherine Crawford, in real fear of going to prison. Charleton, for reasons known only to him, chose not to enforce the Legislative Council's motion.

It is tempting to leave this incident without further comment; just a sideshow to the main game. But it resonates at several important levels. Firstly, it shows how Rob's leadership divided Noongar politics — he was strongly backed by his Executive and especially successive Chairs, Sandy Davies and Ted Wilkes, yet bitterly opposed by a small, core group of Noongars. He was unable to reconcile these different groups and showed no inclination to do so. Clearly his opponents were at odds with his style of leadership irrespective of any latent personal issues. Secondly, the row over accountability underlined just how hard conservatives played politics over Aboriginal issues in Western Australia.

~~~~~~

In this hurlyburly existence, there were rare moments of relaxation. Most centred around time with his three daughters. It was with them that he was able to put politics to one side. When he was home he always had something fun organised. To them, 'he was just a big kid at heart', making fun out of every situation he could, even in the most ordinary situations: 'when he dropped us off at school in the ALS [red 007] car he'd do laps of the roundabout, with music blaring loudly'. He had a connection with children that went beyond his own: 'He loved kids, any kids; it's like he'd nearly adopt them'. The fondest times were with his children camping down at Busselton, in the south-west of Western Australia. There was no telephone, television or radio at their favoured campsite, which they shared with friends and relatives. He left politics behind: 'we could spend time with him without a phone on his ear or cameras around'.

Much as he tried to be a good a father, Rob's political career intruded into the lives of his children: 'It was hard. He was always away. It was good when he was around but hard when he left'. Having such a high-profile and controversial father brought unwarranted attention to them: 'In primary school it wasn't so bad because the school was small and they tried to protect us. But once we hit high school we started to get negative comments'.

Periodically Rob would also take time out with old friends. On one occasion Peter Yu sensed that his friend was not travelling well and invited him up to Broome for a long weekend. They went camping out on Manari Beach, about an hour out of Broome: a stunning place with pristine white sands, clear water, and extensive coral reef. Rob spent time on his own, wandering out on the reef at low tide looking at coral, crabs and shells. In that oasis of calm he relaxed. But it was temporary. On the way back into Broome, as soon as they were within telecommunications range, Rob was 'back on his mobile and smiling again. He was back in touch with the world'.

There were lighter moments as well, when Rob's naturally larrikin humour re-emerged. At a media awards night in the early 1990s, Rob ambled past an already seated Howard Sattler and quipped to his on-air nemesis, 'Well, Howard, I guess there'll be no awards for you tonight'.

His upbeat disposition did not last long. By the close of 1992 Rob's emotional life was in turmoil. Rob's marriage to Jeannie broke down. On the surface, at least, it is not hard to understand why Rob and Jeannie went their separate ways. The pressure of politics meant he was rarely home; they had little time to share life as a couple. To some, Rob also seemed to experience difficulty in the intimacy of relationships, the small daily interactions that sustain them. This, too, may have been a consequence of his time in Sister Kate's.

Rob began a relationship with his executive assistant, Maxine Chi, an Aboriginal woman from Broome, but he took the failure of his marriage very hard. He was so distraught at the thought of breaking up his family that he told one friend 'he was thinking of driving head-long into traffic'. Jeannie could not avoid noticing 'the emotional trauma surfacing' and felt powerless to intervene. The separation brought closer to the surface his suppressed emotions about his life in Sister Kate's.

At around this time he wrote a long, revealing letter to Maxine.[61] The emotions poured out as thoughts about the past and present collided. 'The experience I am now dealing with', he said, 'reminds me of my experiences as a child searching for himself in Sister Kate's'. He detailed to her his struggles in the institution and his joy at being reunited with his family as a twelve-year-old. He was beginning to understand how this experience had shaped him, and he was able to explain to Maxine the underlying struggle of his life: 'All my life I wanted to belong to someone. All my life I have wanted someone to belong to me'. But his marriage break-up meant the sudden loss of contact with his children. He wrote: 'The hardest thing I am dealing with now is getting used to my kids not being around, hearing them laughing/fighting or making a noise. I miss most of all their cuddles and hugs ... it brings tears to my eyes just writing this. I can't stop thinking about them'.

Rob began to understand how his childhood had shaped his political career. In his letter to Maxine, he raised the 'internal pressure' created by the split between his personal, personal/professional and professional needs. He wrote of these as three 'different states of mind', separate but inextricably linked: 'They greatly influence who we are and what we do and where we are going'. He had developed the insight that 'If these three things are not in the right measure they cause so much damage and can be so self-destructive. Everyone needs to come to grips with their own reality and the influences which drive them'.

But for Rob, coming to grips with his own reality was extremely painful. His urges to find out what had really happened to him plagued his thoughts. His anger over his institutionalisation — rekindled by his work on the Royal Commission into Aboriginal Deaths in Custody — now burned more intensely inside him. He was suffering mood swings and feelings of anxiety. In November 1992 he booked himself in to see a psychiatrist and took twenty days' sick leave following a diagnosis of 'severe depression and anxiety'.

Rob was directed to a private psychiatric clinic and entered an intensive treatment program based around cognitive behavioural therapy — the idea that patients can learn to redirect their emotional lives and better manage their moods. He was asked to nominate his goal for the program to which he revealingly replied: 'To attend as often as possible and use the experience to assist in the resolution of outstanding conflicts/problems in my life'.[62] Clearly Rob was struggling to fully take on board the nature and implications of his illness.

He wrote: 'I must be completely competent, make no mistakes and achieve all the time if I'm to be considered worthwhile'. He could see the costs incurred by his approach to life: he became used up; he shut out others including his family; he had no time for himself and his health suffered. He wanted to change his life; to lose weight; to make more time for himself and his children. But he had not realised that to meet these goals he faced a dilemma: how could he rebalance his life and at the same time stay at the forefront of Aboriginal politics, where the endless political confrontations over racial politics were burning him out? Compounding Rob's dilemma were other shortcomings in his makeup also likely to have been shaped by institutionalisation. As one of his close colleagues reflects, Rob not only did not provide space for himself, he 'didn't have the ability to nurture himself, he had never been taught to look after himself physically or mentally'. Tragically, he could not face this dilemma. The big political issues just kept rolling around.

There was much to be proud of in what had been achieved in the preceding two years. Rob had helped inject spark and purpose into the ALS. He had a committed staff working on a wide range of justice issues. There was so much energy flying around the place in some weeks, it could feel like 'working in a war zone'. Arguably, the ALS had grown into one of the largest, most diverse and politically strongest community-based Aboriginal services in the country. And, despite ongoing tensions over his management style, Rob carried the politics of the organisation. Most agreed he starred in this role. He could take fights up to the government. But how many of these fights could he win? And at what cost to him as an individual?

CHAPTER ELEVEN

Mounting Despair: The Final Campaigns

Still committed, but increasingly troubled, Rob Riley was a key participant in three crucial policy issues in the mid-1990s: the native title legislation; the on-going struggles with the implementation of the recommendations of the Royal Commission into Aboriginal Deaths in Custody; and the campaign to establish an official inquiry into the Stolen Generations. These three issues went to the heart of Rob's views about the need for a just settlement regarding Australia's racial past.

While his role of public advocate and political lobbyist kept him in the public eye, his emotional life continued its downward spiral. Each of these bitterly fought campaigns left him with yet more layers of disillusionment compounding the depression he was experiencing over the unresolved issues from his childhood.

The symptoms of depression and anxiety are both commonplace and life-threatening; at best they are generalised symptoms, highly idiosyncratic to the individual experience. They can combine periods of relative good health with bouts of incapacity. Much can be hidden from view: private despair can be masked by public lucidity. For Rob, these were the years in which the betrayals piled up, the disappointments mounted, and medical interventions proved ineffective.

In January 1993, the High Court handed down its historic decision on the Mabo native title case. The decision, the outcome of a case instigated by Queenslander Eddie Mabo, confirmed that he and his fellow Murray Islanders in the Torres Strait retained common law rights to land. But how would this translate to the rest of Australia's Indigenous population? There was a minefield of legal and political issues. Robert Tickner in his book *Taking A Stand* has provided an insider's examination of the struggles of the Keating government to formulate its response. The following account is necessarily selective, but it parallels that of Tickner while adding insights from the perspective of a key Aboriginal participant. Rob's journey through the debate on native title is important in highlighting the painful choices that faced Aboriginal leaders.

As Tickner makes clear, one of the crucial issues facing federal government after the High Court decision was the insecurity of land grants in the mining and pastoral industries arising from the *Racial Discrimination Act 1975*, which stipulated that people could not be discriminated against on the basis of race. In effect, the Act protected Aboriginal interests in property, as they had to be treated the same as any other property interests. Governments could always compulsorily acquire native title as they could any other land title, but the Australian constitution ensured that just terms would apply. This raised the problem that many titles to land granted by government after 1975 might be invalid because they failed to take account of Aborigines' common law right to land (as the High Court found in the Mabo case). The mining industry was particularly concerned about thousands of exploration and mining tenements which were now seen as legally uncertain. Early statements from industry representatives called for the suspension of the Racial Discrimination Act so that titles could be validated and native title extinguished on the affected lands as the preferred federal government response to the High Court decision. But there was an even more fundamental conundrum arising out of the decision: should the federal government's response be broadly based and political to encompass all Aboriginal aspirations to justice, or narrowly defined and legalistic, capturing only the impact of the Mabo decision? And what pressure would Aboriginal groups bring to bear on resolving this conundrum?

For months after the June 1992 High Court decision, neither the government nor Aboriginal groups seemed to know what path to take. The Prime Minister established a task force to devise options for a response. Apart from greeting the legal demise of the doctrine of *terra nullius*, no-one on the Aboriginal side of politics had much of an idea about the way forward. For Rob the decision was another huge issue with which he had to deal: yet another campaign of negotiation and contested politics.

In early 1993, Rob was overcome with exhaustion. He described this feeling as like 'drowning, like I'm falling into this big hole and I don't know how to get out'. As part of the on-going treatment for depression and anxiety which he commenced at the end of 1992, Rob attended counselling sessions associated with a program of behavioural cognitive therapy. At one of these sessions in January 1993 he was asked the question he had spent his adult life holding at bay: was there anything about his childhood he wanted to discuss? The floodgates opened. The incident of his rape as a nine-year-old came unexpectedly to the surface. Rob 'went to pieces', fled the session and locked himself in his office, instructing his staff to find his partner Maxine. She was in Broome on holidays with her children. When they found her she went down to the ALS office in Broome and got on the phone. She spent two or three hours consoling him, shocked at these revelations of abuse, which she was hearing for the first time. The confusion of words and emotions tumbling through the telephone appears to have been typical of post-traumatic shock; the memory of his childhood trauma was suddenly the cause of acute distress.[1] Rob told her: 'I was having a session and this thing that I thought I'd buried so deep that it would never affect me again came up when this woman said to me, "Is there anything in your childhood", and it just surfaced'. He related to Maxine what he had blurted out to the counsellor: 'They raped me, they hurt me, they really hurt me'. He related these words in a loud, sobbing voice. He explained that he had dealt with the trauma by suppressing it. Now, just as he was about to enter some of the most important negotiations of his career, he was drawn ever more deeply into himself, trying to deal with his past.

Indeed, mid-January 1993 marks the beginning of his public involvement in the native title debate. Along with senior ALS staff, including Principal Legal Officer Catherine Crawford and President Ted Wilkes, Rob was involved in developing a Western Australian Aboriginal position. The ALS engaged in a round of state-wide meetings to inform the Aboriginal community about the Mabo decision and to consult about the position the organisation should adopt in negotiations with the federal government. On 14 January Rob announced ALS plans to expand its involvement in land rights issues. It would use $2 million allocated by the federal government arising from the Royal Commission into Aboriginal Deaths in Custody, for the employment of two additional lawyers and a researcher.[2]

Rob's early statements on the issue were based on the lessons he had drawn from the 1980s. From these, he felt he understood the underlying forces of Australian politics too well not to warn about the threats ahead. He expected native title to be another bitter fight. On 14 January he told the press: 'After Mabo, much of Western Australia is effectively no man's land, which leaves it open to manipulation for politically expedient ends. We should be wary of conservative forces wanting a backlash against Aborigines over land rights'.[3]

His comments were prophetic. It soon emerged that the recently elected Western Australian Liberal/National Party state government, led by Richard Court, had grasped the political implications of the High Court decision. Rob knew Western Australian politics intimately and suspected the worst. Richard Court was the son of Sir Charles Court. The youthful-looking and affable Premier seemed to lack his father's domineering streak. But he shared his father's conservative parochialism. Richard was raised in a family, in a political party and in a state political culture where being anti-Canberra and opposed to Aboriginal land rights had long been passports to political success. His pedigree made it likely that he would to try to undermine the Mabo High Court decision.

Predictably, Premier Richard Court made an early declaration of his concern about the Mabo decision, well before the federal government had finalised its own response. The Premier captured front-page headlines when he announced that the state government was considering legislation to remove mining and other business interests from the impact of the High Court's Mabo decision. This, he elaborated, was necessary to end the uncertainty for companies looking to invest in Western Australia.

But this was just an opening pitch before making a full assault on Mabo at the end of March. At this time the Premier flatly rejected the High Court's decision, stating that 'he did not accept that a special title should exist for different groups'.[4]

The Court government's muscular political stance was in direct contravention of earlier advice from the state government's own Solicitor-General, who had told the previous Labor government to accept the existence of native title and to come to grips with its implications.[5] Thus, even without knowing which way the federal government was going to go on the issue, Rob knew that the ALS was on a collision course with the Court government over native title in Western Australia. Rob had been correct in his initial thinking; the debate would have a distressingly similar ring to the campaign he had fought and lost in the 1980s. It is not surprising, therefore, that in his first response to Court's rejection of native title he referred to some of the old battles. Court's denial of the existence of native title, Rob told the press, was the case of 'like father, like son', the same destructive 'mine-or-bust mentality' which could 'see a return to the Noonkanbah days'. He criticised the Premier for failing to consult with any Aboriginal leaders since the High Court decision came down, and warned, 'Aborigines are prepared to negotiate but if Mr Court wanted a fight they would not back down'.[6] It was politics as confrontation: the very mode which had already worn Rob to the bone, physically and emotionally.

While the political moves were being played out in the media, the ALS had taken some crucial first steps. The Principal Legal Officer, Catherine Crawford, asked law professor Richard Bartlett, of the University of Western Australia, to conduct a series of seminars to help the organisation determine its response. Bartlett, who had twenty years' experience working on native title issues in the Canadian prairies, brought an intellectual commitment to the desirability of regional agreements as opposed to legislating explicitly for the existence of native title. Rob was very much influenced by the Canadian approach, of which he and other Aboriginal leaders had some prior knowledge. Bartlett warned that legislation both defined and restricted native title rights. Far better to avoid legislation and rely instead on common law (which the Mabo High Court decision had clarified), devising regional agreements which would allow all parties to define their interests, work on what was important to them and reach agreements without unnecessary division.

Rob was attracted to this model because it could be used to develop different kinds of agreements, which could include the dispossessed, the people whose interests he had always tried to include in every debate over land rights in which he had participated.

~~~~~~~~

Within days of Paul Keating's election victory in March 1993, a delegation of Aboriginal leaders — David Ross, Noel Pearson, Peter Yu, Tracker Tilmouth and Rob — went to Canberra to discuss the federal position on Mabo. They met with senior Keating staffer Simon Balderstone, who advised them of Keating's great support for Aboriginal people, pointing to Keating's election eve speech to his staff in which he had spoken of the opportunity offered by Mabo to make peace with Aboriginal people. When Balderstone left the room, Tracker Tilmouth quipped to his colleagues, 'The last time I trusted a whitefella, I ended up in a mission'. His comment broke the solemnity of the occasion, while reminding the Aboriginal delegation of the historical context of their discussions with government.

Soon afterwards, David Ross, Director of the Central Land Council, convened a meeting of about forty Aboriginal leaders and legal and academic experts at the Red Centre Resort in Alice Springs. The historic meeting, which has come to be known as the Red Centre Meeting, was held over a few days at the beginning of April. Rob was invited, with others from the Kimberley, Northern, Central and Cape York Land Councils, as well as advisers including Ron Castan, the Melbourne Queens Counsel who had led the legal argument for the High Court Mabo case. Much was at stake. Failure to produce a consensus would weaken the ability of Aboriginal people to negotiate an outcome.

Amid the intense discussions, sharp differences of opinion emerged about the implications of the Mabo decision for Aboriginal peoples' aspirations for land rights. In the heat of these discussions, the emerging Aboriginal leader Noel Pearson became a prominent figure, along with Ron Castan, in defining what became the dominant Aboriginal position: the need for overarching Commonwealth legislation to defend the newly established right to native title outlined in the Mabo decision. Those associated with this position believed that this right was under real threat from miners lobbying the federal government to change the Racial Discrimination Act and from the resource-rich state governments who, also under pressure from the mining lobby, might seek to legislate away native title within their states. This position inevitably meant that land rights would become a minimalist model around compliance with the requirements of the High Court decision that native title existed in only very prescribed ways, that is among those who could prove continuous cultural connection with the land and where Aboriginal title had not been extinguished by exclusive possession of land title granted to others. It marked a decisive shift away from the previous Aboriginal position on land rights, which had sought to negotiate with the federal government a political settlement based around the principle of Aboriginal sovereignty over land, including compensation for those who had been displaced and dispossessed.

At the meeting, Rob led the counter-argument. It was clear that most of those present rejected the call for a return to the 1980s-style 'grand settlement', even though the spread of understanding about the Canadian comprehensive regional agreement model had cast it in an updated format. Rob and others supporting the counter-view succeeded in gaining in-principle agreement that negotiations with the federal government must include separate negotiations regarding the interests of those Aboriginal people who would not directly benefit from a minimalist model framed by the High Court's decision. The Red Centre meeting foreshadowed a rift in Aboriginal opinion over native title, between a pragmatic approach which sought to take into account the realities of the political climate, and an idealistic one centred around the fight for the principle that all Aborigines should derive some benefit. As the months progressed, this rift developed into a serious split. More than any other Aboriginal leader, Rob became caught between the two sides, pulled politically, intellectually and emotionally to the point of exhaustion.

On 7 April, probably motivated by the Red Centre discussions, Rob wrote to Paul Keating, acknowledging his 'willingness as Prime Minister to take the debate forward ... [bringing] Australia to the verge of the most profound change in the relationship between the descendents of the legitimate owners of this land and non-Australians'. But he wanted to pass on his experience to Mr Keating and warn him of the dangers ahead:

> The debate demands your leadership and direction if it is to be seriously considered by state and federal governments and not hijacked by private and public vested interests. Aboriginal people are acutely aware of the impact the Mining Industry was able to bring to bear on the Australian population, ultimately leading to the then Prime Minister reversing his commitment to Aboriginal Australians on the issue of National Land Rights legislation in 1985.[7]

Was Rob trying to stoke the political rivalry which had existed between Keating and his predecessor, Bob Hawke? Rob appeared to be trying to nudge Keating into standing by his previous comments heralding the historic opportunity presented by Mabo which he had outlined in his famous Redfern speech in 1992.

In his letter to Keating Rob also informed the Prime Minister of the ALS's efforts to develop its position and revealed the influence of the Canadian model: 'Australia can learn a great deal from Canada in this area. After the Supreme Court of Canada's watershed decision in *Calder 1973*, the Canadian federal government announced a comprehensive claims policy which has borne fruit for indigenous Canadians and has not halted development'. Rob also made a strong pitch for the dispossessed: 'Ultimately your Government's response to Mabo cannot ignore the interests of dispossessed people. We believe that the issue of justice and equity for Aboriginal people should not be jeopardised simply because those with vested interests do not like it'. In a final, revealing, comment to the Prime Minister, Rob showed the depth of the psychological impact which the mid-1980s debate had had on him: 'I have attached for your information extracts of a 1985 report produced by ANOP which made very strong recommendations to the Federal Government, but were never implemented'. The extracts covered ANOP's rationale for a desperately needed public awareness campaign on Black rights generally and land rights in particular.

Rob wanted to use native title to develop a system of land rights for traditional Aboriginal people while ensuring that the dispossessed were not forgotten. In fact he was adamant that the Mabo decision should not 'split Aborigines into one group which got status through Mabo and another which did not'.[8] This had long been Rob's stance. During the 1980s he worked hard to develop this position into a coherent political package. He consistently held to the view developed at this time that the dispossessed would need to be compensated. In the early 1990s, he thought such a package would require money.[9]

Several weeks after his letter to the Prime Minister and the Red Centre meeting, an Aboriginal delegation — again including Rob — was invited to address the federal cabinet on 27 April. This time there were twenty-one persons in the delegation.[10]

The significance of the occasion was lost on no-one. The day before the session with cabinet the Aboriginal delegation met to finalise their package and approach. They resolved that because the High Court had validated their rights as Aborigines they would go to the meeting as if it was one between equals. Geoff Adlide, who was a note taker at the meeting, explains: 'They were not going to turn up pleading with the government to give them this or that and they wanted this position confirmed with the Prime Minister's Office right down to how many note takers they might take into the Cabinet room'.

The night before the meeting Rob sat up into the small hours preparing his speech. In the morning his mood was buoyant.

The delegation arrived in time for the 2.10 p.m. cabinet meeting. It was not a meeting of the full cabinet; Keating was joined by eight other Ministers together with two officials. With the media allowed in for the first ten minutes, the first task involved the presentation of a painting by Wenten Rubuntja to mark the historic occasion. With the media shunted out of the room, Keating then opened proceedings with an impressive speech which began with his characteristic ability to invoke a sense of occasion. 'I think this is an historic meeting', he began, 'because we have the opportunity to consider a basis for reconciliation in this country'. Setting the tone of cooperative discussion which followed, Keating described the High Court Mabo decision as offering a 'basis of equality which has not formally applied or obtained in the past'. Further reassuring words followed: the government would not be stampeded into a hasty response by the mining and pastoral industries. And, speaking directly to Rob's interests, the Prime Minister confirmed that the government would seek to do other things 'for those who've lost the right to native title through dispossession or other acts of injustice over time'.[11]

The Aboriginal delegates were reassured by the Prime Minister's words. They also knew them to be an honest reflection of his position.

The previous day, notes from the meeting the Prime Minister had had with miners and pastoralists had been leaked to them. Not only did the words match, but the Prime Minister had been much tougher on the industry groups. It appeared that Keating was going to seize the moment.

The Aboriginal delegation had decided that they were going to open with a series of speakers from different parts of Australia. Galarrwuy Yunupingu straightaway started speaking in his native Gumatj, which caused a momentary 'double-take' expression on the Prime Minister's face as he realised he was not being spoken to in English. Yunupingu then translated what he had said. Other traditional people followed suit, creating a powerful impression of culture. John Watson from the Kimberley Land Council highlighted the importance of the issues at stake for traditional people: 'In my country we have different meeting places, waterholes, rivers. We have significant beliefs from our old people. Old people are crying, dying ... We're a sad people trying to preserve our culture'.

Rob's speech was a powerfully worded and direct appeal to the Prime Minister for leadership. 'You alone', he said, 'can set the agenda in a way nobody else can'. Drawing on his heartfelt experiences, he proceeded to outline why his leadership, as Prime Minister, was essential:

> All of us in this room know what we're up against. There are ultra conservative state governments and commercial developers who believe they have a God given right to perpetuate the notion of 'might is right'. They believe in the scaremongering tactic of telling the Australian nation that the Indigenous peoples of this country are unilaterally opposed to any commercial development be it mining, tourism or pastoralism. That is not true, we know that and so should you and your colleagues. We are dealing with an Australian public who are constantly being told that the Indigenous peoples of this country are hell bent on taking away from them that which they have acquired. The simplicity of this argument is reinforced by general ignorance and prejudice that can so easily be stirred by frightening and misleading media campaigns. We have lived through an experience in 1984/85 when the full impact of

a media campaign generated by the mining industry forced the then Prime Minister with the help of the W.A. Premier Brian Burke, to dump ALP party policy and renege on their commitments to Aboriginal Australia. The exercise of political expediency and maintaining political power should not be the basis on which judgements are made.

Following this plea to correct the mistakes of the past, Rob issued a warning to the Prime Minister. 'Don't exclude us from the process. Don't attempt to do this without our involvement. Please don't dismiss us. If you do, you can forget about reconciliation. We will wind people up. We will hit the streets. We will go to international forums'.

Rob ended by offering the Prime Minister the essential Riley philosophy: 'You don't stop fighting for justice simply because those around you don't like it. We will not stop fighting'.

It took courage to address the Prime Minister so pointedly. Rob showed that he had the capacity to ignore the aura of office; to approach the highest authority from a position of principle. Robert Tickner, the Minister for Aboriginal Affairs, described Rob's contribution as 'politically incisive'.[12]

The delegation then presented to Keating its 'Peace Plan' (named after his election eve speech to staff), consisting of eight principles. Among these, the Commonwealth would commit itself to affirming and protecting Aboriginal rights; establishing a tribunal to determine Aboriginal titles not just on the basis of common law but also on a needs basis; setting up a national land fund to enable Aborigines who could not assert native title to have access to purchasing land; ensuring absolute protection of sacred sites; providing compensation for land disturbance and use of minerals; and entering into a process of negotiation on longer-term issues. In return, Aborigines would agree to the validation of mineral titles which might otherwise be invalidated due to the *Racial Discrimination Act 1975*. Crucially, though, the Peace Plan left open the definition of native title. It said: 'This legislation would not identify where legislation might exist and whatever the rights might involve, but would simply provide a national umbrella for the title'. This held out hope that a flexible 'test' for native title might be established, and would have provided some comfort to Rob.[13]

Following the meeting, some in the Aboriginal delegation became aware that Rob had secretly taped the entire meeting by strapping a small dictaphone to the side of his body. He was brazen about his ploy, explaining to his colleagues that there was no need to worry whether the note takers from each side had captured the entire conversation because he had taped it. As he said this he casually tossed the tape to a colleague. It was a classic high stakes action from Rob. But some of his colleagues believed he had committed a grave error of judgment. His actions had transgressed the hallowed nature of the cabinet room where, by tradition, discussion was supposed to be conducted freely; it had contradicted the 'negotiation as equals' approach to the meeting; and it threatened to derail the process had the government found out about the breaking of trust a secret taping had entailed. But, as Geoff Adlide explains, no-one suspected Rob of other than good motivations: 'Over his political life he had been stuffed over by politicians; they had gone back on their word and so he thought, "I'm going to get this [the cabinet discussion] and keep it"'.

Despite this sour note, the meeting ended on a high for the Aboriginal delegation. The government was listening to them, and a dialogue had opened up about a way forward to negotiate better outcomes for Aboriginal people.

~~~~~

Back in Western Australia, Rob kept the ALS Executive informed of his involvements on native title. At Executive meetings during 1993, he offered a detailed summary of progress to date and the implications as he saw them. He acknowledged that 'only some' Aboriginal people would benefit 'from the strict legal definition of the Mabo decision', but he held high hopes for the total package of the Peace Plan:

> We believe the Mabo decision is not just about the recognition of common law 'native title', which acknowledge the rights that Aboriginal and Torres Strait Islander people have to land (where the requirements of proof can be fulfilled). But it is also a decision on Indigenous Rights and Human Rights. Other important issues involved are social justice, political recognition and the process of Reconciliation.[14]

These comments illustrate Rob's conflicting intellectual and emotional responses to native title. Firstly, he believed it was vital for Aboriginal people to 'hold the line' on the package presented to government, even though he was not a committed supporter of the legislative approach. Secondly, he still had high expectations of what could be achieved, because the Peace Plan had the potential to transform the Mabo decision into an instrument for Aboriginal human rights. Lastly, and as he outlined to the Prime Minister, he harboured deep fears that conservative forces would, ultimately, quash the expectations of Aboriginal people.

The conservative counter-attack was in fact getting under way. Claims about the impact of Mabo on trade and investment were just an opening salvo. Various prominent public figures delivered some extraordinary outbursts denigrating Aboriginal culture and these were duly repeated uncritically in the press. Rob could hardly have missed National Party leader Tim Fischer's Social Darwinist assessment offered in June 1993 that 'at no stage in Aboriginal civilisation did they develop substantial buildings, roadways or even a wheeled cart', which, he argued, provided justification for dispossession: 'Those in the guilt industry have to consider that developing cultures and peoples will always overtake relatively stationary cultures'.[15] At much the same time, historian Geoffrey Blainey weighed into the debate. He argued that the 'extravagant Aboriginal use of land before European colonisation in 1788, if applied to the rest of the world, would support just one per cent of the current population'.[16] Rob challenged Blainey's motivations: 'Professor Blainey's speech was the type of emotive misinformation that generated fear. That's the mindset we have to try to change in this country. It has the effect of developing a backlash against Aboriginal people'.[17]

In May 1993, and still smouldering with hostility, the Western Australian Court government unleashed its own response. Rob's fears appeared justified, as there is little doubt that comments by senior members of the Court government caused fear amongst the community and mobilised public opinion against native title. In early May, Rob's old foe Bill Hassell, now State President of the Liberal Party, called the High Court decision 'illegitimate' and 'racist' and warned that it would stir social division and incite a backlash. Rob was convinced that the statements represented a deliberate attempt to create a hostile reaction and he could not let that go unchallenged.[18] In fact, Rob pursued Hassell at every opportunity. In trying 'to stir up sentiment against Aboriginal people', Hassell was, according to Rob, 'displaying his bigotry'.[19] Rob retrieved the information collated in the mid-1980s about the Hassell family land grant in the south-west of Western Australia in the nineteenth century. Hassell had claimed that suburban areas of Perth were under threat from native title. During an interview on local ABC television, Rob pulled out his map. According to Alan Carpenter, the journalist who interviewed the two men, Rob's tactic 'was a powerful counterpoint to the argument that Aboriginal people were going to appropriate land that did not belong to them ... Rob threw open the other side of the story'.

Premier Richard Court also continually repeated the alarmist claim that native title threatened suburban homes.[20] In contrast to the Premier's comments, deputy Liberal leader Colin Barnett momentarily acknowledged that Mabo would likely have limited application. He quickly withdrew his comment.[21]

Rob threatened to take action against Premier Court to prevent 'the divisive and racist comments' on Mabo from polarising the community.[22] He was rarely out of the press from May through to December 1993, warning about the tactics of conservatives in trying to engineer a public backlash against Mabo as part of their political strategy to overturn the decision. He told ABC radio listeners that claims that Aboriginal people were anti-development were 'a beat up' perpetuated 'by the resource industry to generate fear'. Aboriginal people want development 'on our terms and conditions not somebody else's because invariably if it's somebody else's, the Indigenous landowners get screwed'.[23]

On 26 May 1993, Rob leaked details of the state government's draft legislation granting a much lesser form of title to Aboriginal people, and with minimal compensation to them, to *The Australian* newspaper.[24] He said that the government was 'trying to legislate away the rights of Aboriginal people', and he called on the federal government to immediately legislate to override the proposed state law. Peter Yu later accused the Court government of acting in collusion with the mining industry when he released the Chamber of Mines' draft paper on Mabo which, he pointed out, contained virtually identical principles to the government's own draft paper.[25]

The struggle with the Court government steadily impacted on Rob's state of mind. There were tensions in the ALS from his continual absences; he became less and less visible in the organisation as his visibility soared in public. His prominence on such a controversial issue in a state with a strong underbelly of racist opinion generated a personal backlash. He received hate mail telling him that all Aboriginal people should be shot and, more disturbingly, he received death threats over the telephone in the middle of the night. He acknowledged that the strength of anti-Aboriginal feeling in the community was 'hurtful'.[26]

Rob called a press conference in mid-July 1993 to lash out at the state government's stance. His frustrations boiled over. He went straight to the moral credibility of the Premier by charging him with playing the race card: 'The State Government had resorted to the most simplistic politics of fear to engender a racial backlash against Indigenous people'. But instead of continuing on a political line of attack, he suddenly, and uncharacteristically, turned personal. He dragged the Premier's adopted daughter into the debate by saying: 'it was very convenient for Mr Court to claim he had an Aboriginal child so he could substantiate his claims that he was not racist. But at every turn since the High Court decision recognising native title in June last year, Mr Court had acted in a racist manner'.[27] It was a reckless and hurtful statement, a lapse of judgement which he recognised almost immediately. The following day Rob rectified his personal attack on the Premier by offering an apology for bringing his daughter into the debate. But it was a qualified apology only, for he warned the Premier that his attacks on native title were causing an upsurge of racist opinion in the community.

―――

The emotional strain on Rob over native title was exacerbated through his dealings with individual Aboriginal communities. For some time after the High Court decision was handed down, expectations rose across Aboriginal Australia that their history of dispossession might be addressed. Slowly, as information filtered out about the likely federal government response, optimism turned to disillusionment. Many Aboriginal people rang Rob to express their disappointment that Mabo would bring them nothing. The calls came from around the state: from those moved off their land at the whim of government policy, even in recent decades, and from those who, while they could claim a link to the land, no longer retained a connection to their traditional law. These calls must have caused Rob intense distress, as he knew that he might become a party to what he saw as the moves by the government to extinguish these people's rights. He suspected also that the government would provide nothing to those Aboriginal people, particularly from southern Australia, whose common law rights had been extinguished by the sheer magnitude of European occupation, or, as the High Court called it, 'the tide of history'. It must have felt to Rob that he was selling out his own people. From his perspective, all hope now rested with the efforts he and others could make to nail down the government's commitment to a flexible test of native title and, importantly, to the achievement of measures which would accord justice to the dispossessed and displaced.

While opposing the state government's efforts to destroy Mabo, Rob was having a parallel fight with the federal government. With the legislative response still being developed, Keating made a controversial decision not to oppose legislation introduced by the Northern Territory government to secure protection for the $250 million McArthur River lead–zinc–silver mine. This was roundly criticised by Aboriginal leaders, who were not consulted over the decision. It is hard to overestimate the impact of this decision on Rob's underlying response to native title; it marked the dividing line between his optimism and his growing despair.

He was in the forefront of Paul Keating's critics over the decision. In itself, this was an unpalatable task. For Rob, Keating was the first political leader who had shown any connection to the struggles of Aboriginal people. Keating's December 1992 Redfern speech had deeply affected him, with its historic acknowledgement of white responsibility for the ills that plague Aboriginal society. The speech had even connected to the emotionally charged issue of the Stolen Generations when Keating said: 'We took the children from their mothers'. One of the messages Rob took to the 27 April cabinet meeting had been to remind Keating that Aboriginal people wanted to believe the Prime Minister's sentiments in his Redfern speech.

But following the McArthur River decision, Rob decided that Keating was just another double-dealing politician. He accused the Prime Minister of a sell-out to Japanese share interests. It is worth closely examining his public statements on the issue. They become more despairing as the week progressed. At the end of May Rob told the press:

'After all the pleasant noises the Federal Government has been making to us over the past couple of weeks, the first opportunity they have got to demonstrate their commitment they've shafted us hard and fast'.[28] In an interview on ABC radio on 1 June, his frustrations were becoming clearly evident. 'Quite frankly,' he said, 'after all the involvements I've had at a national level, I'm quite prepared to sit at home and take it easy instead of having to worry about politicians who tap you on the shoulder and say, "Don't worry about it, trust us and we'll look after it"'. On 3 June — the anniversary of the Mabo decision — he enunciated his clearest view about his disillusionment with Keating. He told the press that after making speeches about the need for reconciliation with Aborigines, Mr Keating had sold them out:

> Prior to that time it [the Redfern speech] was the culmination, not only of the political struggle for Aboriginal people, but the ability to bring the Australian people together. But when this deal was done on McArthur River, not only did Paul Keating kick Aboriginal people in the guts, but he lost the opportunity of being recorded in history as the Prime Minister able to address the social justice issues concerning Aboriginal people. It will take a power of persuasion for him to be able to convince people like myself and other Aboriginal people that we should give him another chance.[29]

These comments contain crucial insights into Rob's state of mind. Throughout the native title debate he had been battling depression. Now, it seems, his depression was taking the form described by psychologists as depressive realism.[30] Although the existence of this condition is debated within the profession, it closely resembles Rob's darkening outlook. Depressive realists are supposed to see the world as it more truly exists. It is based on the idea of the uniqueness of melancholia. Some at least of these sufferers are said to possess acute insights into reality, and especially the ability to more realistically predict negative events. This ability derives from the absence of the defensive mechanisms which for the rest of humanity naturally buttress more positive individual moods. Rob's continual exposure to the injustices facing Aboriginal people and the grinding reluctance of the political system to resolve them helped create a depressive realist perspective that nothing would change. And, by the time of the McArthur River decision, Rob must have felt that he knew intimately what would happen to native title in the bear pit of Australian politics: conservatives would posture until they fanned a fear campaign; elite interest groups would peddle influence until they weakened the resistance of politicians; and the Labor Party would vacillate until it sniffed which way the political breeze would blow. He had seen it all before. Native title was becoming one more nightmare.

By the June 1993 anniversary of the Mabo decision, Rob was openly struggling to maintain his optimism. The federal government had released a discussion paper comprising a framework of thirty-three principles which, according to most Aboriginal opinion, left ambiguous the integrity of the Racial Discrimination Act. The paper was savagely condemned by Aboriginal leaders including Mick Dodson and Noel Pearson, the latter claiming that the document treated Mabo as a land management issue rather than one focused on Aboriginal cultural and spiritual ties to the land.[31] For his part, Rob told the press he had doubts that the Prime Minister would come good on delivering 'a better deal for Aborigines'. His worst fears were materialising. International businessmen were winning the struggle over the mind of the federal government: 'They have got more money and greater political influence'.[32] The photograph taken to accompany the story captured his mood. Rob was pictured with his chin resting on his forearms, his forehead creased and a melancholic expression on his face. He had a look of resignation.

Matters came to a head when the federal government's draft legislation was announced towards the beginning of September 1993. The week before its release, Rob said that although he believed Keating had Aboriginal interests at heart, 'he lost control of the Mabo debate when he allowed bigoted comments from Western Australian Premier Richard Court and Liberal President Bill Hassell and mining leaders to gain popularity in the public sphere'.[33]

From this point on, Rob's loosely stitched-together position on native title was stretched to breaking point. He greeted the release of the draft legislation as 'the most serious mass extinguishment of the rights of Aboriginal people since white settlement', expressing his long-held fear of a narrow, legalistic application of the Mabo decision. Yet he would soon join key Aboriginal leaders in urging the two Western Australian Green senators — who held the balance of power in the Senate — to pass the legislation. How did he come to hold two such outwardly contradictory positions? Rob's experiences in the final, desperate stages of the debate over the native title legislation are part of the broader story of wrenching divisions within the Aboriginal leadership over the issue.

The Keating government's draft legislation was not greeted with any enthusiasm by Aboriginal leaders. Like the earlier discussion paper, it left ambiguous the contentious issue of a roll-back of the Racial Discrimination Act. It further stipulated that native title would be extinguished on all pastoral leases, and it imposed a strict definition of native title as handed down in the High Court decision, in contravention of the spirit of the Peace Plan.

Aboriginal people from all over Australia gathered at Eva Valley in the Northern Territory to denounce the Bill. Sporting a Malcolm X T-shirt, key Aboriginal negotiator Mick Dodson held a press conference to lash out at Keating. Aboriginal leaders urged more talks to resolve the impasse.

At much the same time the Western Australian Green senators firmed up their opposition to Keating's planned legislation, expressing concern over mass extinguishment. Accompanied by her key adviser on native title, Cathcart Weatherby, Senator Christabel Chamarette undertook several trips to remote Aboriginal communities to learn more about the grassroots Aboriginal response to the issue. What they found disturbed them. At Bidyadanga Community, 120 kilometres south of Broome, they encountered five different tribal groups, all brought in from the Desert but not all of whom, they believed, would have their native title rights upheld under the proposed legislation. Yet all groups thought that they would get their land, 'the land out there that they had been hauled off'. As Chamarette recalls, the tour also revealed that some Aboriginal communities 'were very concerned that all native title was going to do was drive a wedge through their fairly peaceful communities ... it would force them to have a dispute with white people that they'd been able to live alongside relatively amicably for a long period of time'.

In an effort to influence the development of the legislation, Chamarette started talks with Aborigines representing the interests of the people of southern Australia. But in mid-October, a delegation associated with northern Australian Aboriginal interests, including Noel Pearson, Lois O'Donoghue, David Ross, Mick Dodson and Rob Riley, met the Green senators, with Rob playing an uncharacteristically back-seat role. According to Chamarette, spokespersons for the delegation said that they had just been to a meeting of Aboriginal leaders at which it was decided to recommence negotiations with Keating. Divisions long simmering below the surface over native title were increasingly coming out into the open. How far should Aboriginal leaders go in their willingness to compromise over the legislation?

Behind the decision to re-engage was the worry that the federal government might capitulate to the mining and pastoral industries and the resource-rich states, all of whom were demanding that the government's legislation focus on validation of leases and the extinguishment of native title. Chamarette believed that Keating was rattling the sabre at Aboriginal leaders, and that this had produced the desired effect of bringing them to the negotiation table.

The delegation said they hoped to mobilise support of the Greens — together with the Democrats — to maximise the opportunity to pass acceptable legislation. Chamarette offered the delegation cold comfort. She said that the entire legislation was anathema to the Western Australian Greens: 'It's the opposite of what the government should have done which was to put a hold on further extinguishment and then negotiate with people over what was native title'.

Rob was quiet, standing at the back of the delegation with his face barely in view to Chamarette. On behalf of the delegation, David Ross, Director of the Central Land Council, explained that they understood the position of the Greens, and agreed with much of it, 'but we have to do something, we have to negotiate because we will get nothing if we don't'. Why was Rob so unobtrusive at the meeting? It almost certainly reflected his growing disquiet over the terms of the Keating government's legislation and the pressure he felt under for the legislation to be passed.

Divisions within the Aboriginal leadership came to a head on 20 October, when an agreement was reached between the Aboriginal negotiation team and the Keating government. This decision formalised the split brewing within the Aboriginal leadership over Mabo. The so-called A Team, who were prepared to negotiate directly with Keating, comprised mainly representatives associated with northern Australia: that is, traditional Aboriginal people. This group maintained a pragmatic line that it was better to try to win 75 per cent of something than 100 per cent of nothing. The so-called B Team, representatives of Aborigines from southern Australia, wanted to hold out for a more far-reaching settlement over native title. Under the agreement the A Team reached with Keating, the integrity of the Racial Discrimination Act was to be maintained, which meant implicit acceptance of Indigenous common-law rights. The principles to guide the framing of legislation were:

- recognition of native title rights and some basic principles of its existence;
- provision for the validation of past acts of land occupancy which may be invalid because of the existence of native title;
- provision for a future regime in which native title rights are protected and conditions imposed on acts affecting native title land and waters; establishment of a process by which native title can be established and compensation determined; and
- establishment of a National Aboriginal and Torres Strait Islander Fund.[34]

Crucially, the Bill was to remain silent on the issue of pastoral leases, and also included a special right to negotiate which, in theory, opened up the process more widely for Aboriginal claims. In return, the federal government committed itself to developing a social justice package and land fund for those Aborigines who did not fall within the provisions of the proposed legislation.

Lois O'Donoghue said the negotiations surrounding the historic decision had 'given Aborigines a new, powerful and united political voice in Australia'.[35] However, the claim of unity had a hollow ring in light of Rob's assertion, repeated on the day the deal was announced, that it 'amounted to the most serious mass extinguishment of the rights of Aboriginal people since white settlement'.[36] The bitterness of Rob's language hid personal as well as political hurts. Land rights had now been transformed from a political campaign into identity politics: who could prove their Aboriginal bona fides? Although he was not explicit about this point, it is clear that this was abhorrent to Rob, who had only discovered his own Aboriginality in adolescence.

There was little relief for Rob from the intensity of the political battles over the native title legislation. The government of his own state of Western Australia was on the frontline of opposition to the letter and spirit of the High Court decision, spearheading the first legislative assault on the new-found common-law rights of Aboriginal people. In a matter of weeks Court had rushed his legislation into parliament and guillotined it through both Houses. The legislation had been framed in a tricky manner. It stated that all native title in Western Australia had been extinguished and was to be replaced by a lesser title of 'traditional usage', which did at least have a slight connection to the Racial Discrimination Act. Nevertheless, many saw Court's actions as high-stakes political gamesmanship. Even the conservative newspaper *The West Australian* described the legislation as a 'morally questionable strategy', which, despite the Premier's confidence in its ability to withstand constitutional scrutiny, stated 'there is no guarantee it will survive the inevitable challenge in the High Court'.[37] Rob had seen these kinds of political dealings in his state before. The umbilical cord that tied political leaders to the resource industry at the expense of Aboriginal people was well known to Rob. The problem had always been that it was so hard to defeat. Politicians could play to the gallery of public opinion around this time-honoured strategy and expect plaudits every time. According to Chamarette, Rob had told her he was deeply worried about the potential fallout from the state legislation. He saw it as a threat of similar magnitude to Brian Burke's efforts to thwart the land rights campaign in the 1980s: history repeating itself. He was 'really worried about the ugliness of that racist lobby in Western Australia'. Rob understood that the system would, at best, produce a pallid compromise.

Rob took a barrage of 'grabs' to the Western Australian media. He was fearless in his comments. The preparation of action in the High Court preoccupied the ALS legal staff and drained significant resources from the organisation's core issues. Rob explained to the public why the legislation was morally and legally wrong. He told the press: 'Extinguishment of native title and subsequent compensation has to be on 'just terms' [according to the Australian constitution] and it is an area that the Premier does not make any comment on'.[38] In fact, Rob claimed that Richard Court 'has certainly outdone his father in terms of being provocative and uncompromising'.[39] Whatever its constitutional flaws, however, the political strategy started to pay dividends as Court's popularity lifted on the back of his anti-Canberra, anti-Aboriginal stance. The legal undoing of this strategy had to wait until March 1995, when the Western Australian government's case was rejected by all seven High Court judges, who argued that the legislation contravened both the Racial Discrimination Act and the constitutional right of the Commonwealth through the 'race power' to overrule the states. 'COURT'S $4M MABO FOLLY' greeted readers of *The West Australian* the day after the decision was handed down.[40] By then, Court's hardball political tactics over native title had sapped the energies of key ALS staff, including Rob's, and had helped shift the debate on native title further to the right.

On a wider front, the bitter fight between the ALS and the Court government over native title put the relationship between the two on a 'war footing' which impeded dialogue on other pressing issues facing Aboriginal people. Rob had to defend an accusation made by the Premier in State Parliament that he and Peter Yu wanted a separate Aboriginal state in Australia. Rob's retort went straight to the point. He and Yu were simply advocating self-determination in line with the recommendations of the Royal Commission into Aboriginal Deaths in Custody.[41] In 1994 Aboriginal Affairs Minister Kevin Minson started another public campaign to have the ALS disband because, he said, it had become a 'monstrosity' and a 'political animal'.[42]

In the meantime, political attention shifted to the Western Australian Greens, and how they would seek to exercise the balance of power in the Senate. Chamarette and Margetts had a series of meetings with the government outlining their position on the legislation which included the following: no 'roll back on the *Racial Discrimination Act 1975*; only Federal Tribunals to hear native title claims; native title should be allowed to coexist with other titles except where there is an inconsistency; the right of consent over developments such as mining; and the social justice package to be outlined in the Prime Minister's second reading speech'. In essence, the Greens did not want extinguishment; they 'wanted co-existence to be able to be argued at a later stage'.

From this point on, the Western Australian Greens negotiated for the most part with groups representing the interests of the totally dispossessed and displaced and those associated with the remaining sovereignty movement from the 1980s: the B Team. Rob accused the Greens of dealing with 'fringe Aboriginal elements that did not understand the High Court nor the Government's legislation'.[43] Nevertheless, Rob would have had considerable sympathy with key parts of their opposition to the draft legislation. His comment probably says more about the pressure he felt he was under in holding to his own views. Rob was occupying an increasingly uncomfortable position with a foot in both camps. Chamarette saw little of him and assumed he had chosen to go with the Bill and the A Team. But he was also informally aligned with the B Team, whose members included Geoff Clarke and Michael Mansell.

For much of October and November, Rob was not especially prominent on the Aboriginal side. He did make several decisive interventions in the desperate last days of negotiating the passage of the legislation. He was at a meeting with the Prime Minister, Peter Yu and Noel Pearson which laid out a strategy to try to gain Western Australian support for the legislation. There was an urgency to the discussion. Rob seemed to have become convinced of the need to formally back the passage of the legislation to stave off the potential threat posed by Richard Court's legislation to extinguish native title. Pearson recalls Rob's contribution as impressive.[44]

All attention turned to the Western Australian Greens as pressure on Christabel Chamarette and Dee Margetts continued to mount. Delegations of Aborigines were sent from all over the country to Parliament House in Canberra urging them to pass the legislation. Rob was part of this phase of the campaign. On one particular occasion Rob rang Chamarette and 'pleaded' with her to pass the legislation, to which she replied, 'I've just been on the phone talking to people pleading for me not to pass it'. Rob then asked why she was opposed to the Bill passing, to which Chamarette pointedly replied: 'Because of dispossession'. She sensed that Rob fully understood the sad irony in the situation: 'I had the feeling that Rob wanted me to pass the Bill and he wanted to put pressure on me but he actually understood why I couldn't do it and he never gave me a hard time, not like Noel Pearson and others who really gave us a fairly hard time'. But there was no doubting the pressure Rob was under. According to Chamarette: 'I could sense that he was uncomfortable with what was happening. He just looked miserable the whole time'.

Behind the scenes political nerves were fraying. The federal Liberal leadership was under some pressure from moderate sections of the Party to change its opposition to the very principle of native title. Keating, who according to Chamarette wanted to pass a Bill favourable to Aboriginal people, was under pressure from Caucus not to concede beyond the present framework contained in the Bill. The Greens continued to hold out for amendments. In early October they had had a secret meeting with the Prime Minister, urging him not to give up negotiating with them and highlighting to him the potentially hollow victory which they believed lay at the heart of the proposed Native Title Bill.

As the Greens entered direct negotiations with Labor Senate leader Gareth Evans, tensions reached a new height. Midway through one marathon negotiation, the Greens threatened to call a late-night press conference to announce their intention to vote against the Bill. Evans's legendary temper ignited: 'Gareth just exploded and hurled us out, sort of pushed us out the door so he didn't have this raging argument in front of thirty or forty other people and screamed at us and said, "We'll get serious" sort of thing, and so eventually he calmed down and said, "So if we negotiate some amendments, you'll agree not to hold the press conference"'. Negotiations between the government and the Greens went on over the next five days. The sticking point continued to be how much land the legislation would make available to Aboriginal communities.

As uncertainty continued over the decision of the Western Australian Greens, Aboriginal leaders remained divided. Through his association with members of the A Team, Rob viewed with concern their long negotiations with the government, believing these placed the very existence of native title in danger. The A Team maintained its stance that a minimalist legal interpretation was the only realistic alternative which would deliver any advancement to Aboriginal people.

The Greens did obtain important amendments to the legislation. These included a threshold amendment which allowed Aboriginal communities a right to negotiate through registration of claims with the proposed Native Title Tribunal (as opposed to the government's preferred option of Aborigines having to establish a prima facie case of continuous ownership); and the extinguishment of native title on pastoral leases was removed from the Bill. But the overall Bill remained far short of what they had hoped for. Rob gave every indication that he was sympathetic to their view that the onus was on the government to prove where native title had been extinguished rather than the reverse. But in the end, the Greens had exhausted their own political capital in trying to amend the Bill. Voting the Bill down would have meant losing the amendments they had obtained.

On 21 December, as the Bill was entering its last phase of passage through the Senate, Chamarette rang Rob to let him know of the Greens' decision to let it pass. She told him she felt that the Bill was the lesser of two evils. Outwardly Rob's words were reassuring: 'I'm glad you agreed ... you've done the right thing', he told her. But Chamarette heard no conviction in his voice.

Rob's doubts and disappointments over the Native Title Bill mirrored the wider divisions in the Aboriginal rights movement. There are tantalising insights into Rob's thinking on this question. He seemed to have come to the realisation late in the Bill's journey that his dream of a just settlement for Aboriginal people would not be fulfilled. Six months after the Bill had passed the Senate, Rob told a native title conference in Perth that, 'rather than a dream, [native title] has become a nightmare'.[45] He described himself as 'frustrated, disillusioned and [not] optimistic about the future'. He gave at least a fleeting insight into the basis for his pessimism: 'Really, what the Native Title Act is about is recognising and protecting the existing interests of non-Aboriginal Australia'.[46] But whether he ever shared the Greens' view that 'the A Team had dudded the B Team in negotiations over Native Title' is not clear. Even if he believed that was the case, Rob was probably too loyal to express any criticism of colleagues. To the end, his split position over the native title legislation remained contradictory: it represented mass extinguishment, but nonetheless had to be passed.

～～～～

Rob's involvement with native title issues extended beyond the legislation itself. He was a key participant in parallel discussions with the Keating government about the land fund and social justice package. He attended a meeting of Aboriginal leaders in Canberra in late October 1993 about both issues, which anticipated a quick resolution. However by the end of 1994, the land fund had been referred to a Senate committee and no details had been finalised for the package. Rob had held out high hopes for both elements of the original compromise established at the Red Centre meeting. He informed the December ALS Executive meeting of his view that the core feature of the Fund should be to provide 'land to the *most* [Rob's italics] dispossessed and to those who do not have land'. He said that the social justice package was vital 'if Indigenous people are to be able to revitalise into strong, healthy and independent communities'.[47] The Land Fund was eventually established by legislation that provided $1 billion for dispossessed Aboriginal people to acquire land, but commitment to the social justice package dropped off the Keating government's agenda and was not pursued by the incoming Howard government. In other words, the Red Centre principles and later the Peace Plan with federal cabinet, upon which Rob offered his support to a consensus Aboriginal position, were never fully delivered.

The pain and division caused by native title did not abate. Once the legislation was in place, the task of representing Aboriginal claimants began in earnest. This new phase brought Rob into direct conflict with Peter Yu, who had become Director of the Kimberley Land Council (KLC). How two closely aligned organisations, headed by two old friends, could come into conflict said much about the impact of the Mabo legislation on Aboriginal politics. When it came to deciding which land rights claims in Western Australia should be brought before the newly established Tribunal, and the manner in which they should proceed, issues of organisational culture and authority opened painful divisions between the ALS and the KLC.

For its part, the ALS saw itself as being governed by its charter to try to use the native title laws to advance the position of Aboriginal people. It believed it had the state-wide structure and expertise to be the lead agency in trying to take advantage of the new federal legislation. It settled on accepting instructions from the Miriuwung Gajerrong community, whose land claim straddled a large area of the eastern/western Kimberley and Northern Territory, as the first such claim brought forward in Western Australia.

Conversely, the KLC regarded itself as embodying a different style of decision-making. Under Peter Yu's leadership, it stressed that Aboriginal land claims in the region should proceed only from a fully consultative process run by Aboriginal people, from which informed consent could be given. The KLC maintained that the ALS was remote from the people on the ground in the Kimberley and that a culture of using white lawyers disempowered Aboriginal people. The way forward, it argued, was to try to negotiate with the state government before becoming involved in a legalistic approach.

Yu tried to persuade Rob to have the ALS withdraw from acting for Miriuwung Gajerrong and on any future claims in the Kimberley. Peter Yu and the KLC Executive believed that the ALS involvement in the Kimberley would entrench existing community division, thus undermining efforts by the KLC to develop a coherent Aboriginal political position in the region. Conversely, lawyers with the Land and Heritage Unit at the ALS asserted that they had a duty to take instructions from groups whom they believed had legal merit in a native title claim and to pursue those claims from a legal perspective. This duelling over legitimacy took its toll on Peter's and Rob's friendship, already under strain from the divisions over native title. They rang each other less frequently and no longer exchanged confidences as they had always done since Noonkanbah.

For Rob, the fact that the land rights struggle had come to this — a rift with one of his closest friends — was devastating. As one of his colleagues at the ALS acknowledges, the dispute 'became quite personal between Rob and Peter Yu and I know it caused Rob a lot of grief and heartache ... it took its toll on Rob'. A pivotal point in the tension between the two organisations occurred at a meeting in Derby in April 1993. Yu, who felt thwarted in seeking details of the ALS plans to represent native title claimants, turned to Rob and asked for cooperation. Rob had to say that he did not have authority under the ALS constitution to run legal issues; that responsibility belonged to the Principal Legal Officer.

Rob had long chafed over this distinction and sought at various times to have it changed. He felt he did not really control the organisation he nominally headed. He perceived himself to be isolated from the main game inside the organisation. He and the Principal Legal Officer at the time, Catherine Crawford, came into conflict over the matter. Rob tried to convince Crawford to shift positions so that relations with the KLC might be easier, but she, while wanting to avoid all-out warfare with the KLC, was not prepared to accept Yu's view that the ALS had no place in the Kimberley.

As the dispute over the Miriuwung Gajerrong festered, Rob increasingly wished he could find a way to resolve the dispute between the two organisations. One day he rang Peter Yu, and at some point in the conversation said, 'The day you and I start arguing like this, I'd rather be dead'. In hindsight, such a statement carries a terrible emotional weight; but at the time Rob likely did not mean it literally. Rather it was a symptom of the broader stress that he had been under for years during the native title debate.

~~~~~~

Rob's on-going stress had resulted in an alarming rise in his drug use. A long-term recreational user of marijuana he had, at some point around 1992, began using amphetamines, a habit which was known to some of his friends and a handful of his colleagues. In addition, he was taking prescribed anti-depressant medication, and periodically he increased the dosage when he felt under stress. The combination of drugs became a barrier to overcoming his illness. Ever the risk-taker, Rob was also indiscreet about his drug-taking. Not surprisingly, this brought Rob into conflict with his Chairman, Ted Wilkes, who became aware of the extent of his illicit drug use. Wilkes questioned him about the problem, advised him to quit using illicit drugs and warned him of the protocols that would come into play should he continue with the behaviour. But Rob was in denial.

Somehow, he managed to keep functioning at a professional level in the public realm, if not as the head of the ALS, where his frequent absences continued to create tensions. Between 1993 and 1994, and while the on-going political battles with the state and federal governments over native title continued, Rob was involved in the efforts to ensure the state government implemented the recommendations arising from the Royal Commission into Aboriginal Deaths in Custody. The recommendations embodied every fibre of his understanding of Aboriginal disadvantage which had been gathered from his youthful observations of the decrepit conditions on Pingelly Reserve, the unrelenting discrimination he encountered in his early days at the ALS and, more recently, the grinding work he completed for the Royal Commission itself. Rob knew how extensively the operation of government needed to change for Aboriginal people to begin to achieve equality in society. Here, too, his expectations were dashed. Neither the Lawrence nor the Court governments treated the recommendations with the urgency required by the Aboriginal and wider communities.

Rob was involved in two separate processes monitoring the implementation of the Royal Commission recommendations. The first involved the ALS in the preparation of a detailed report, which he and the Principal Legal Officer, Catherine Crawford oversighted.

The second process involved his membership of the Aboriginal Justice Council, set up with funding from the Royal Commission to provide advice to the state government on criminal justice matters. The Council also compiled a detailed report. Both reports were scathing about the lack of political and bureaucratic leadership in addressing the underlying criminal and social justice issues which had informed the Royal Commission recommendations. Both reports reveal that the lack of progress was not just a case of governments having tried and failed to resolve a complex problem, but one of the lack of effort made to take seriously the report of the Royal Commission. The ALS found that in the two years since the release of the Royal Commission's report, only 57 of the 195 recommendations which it was able to assess had been adequately implemented.[48] In its report, the Aboriginal Justice Council wrote that: 'The findings of the report are of such magnitude as to confirm that the current system has, at best, only effected a superficial treatment of a multi faceted problem'.[49]

Although Rob was not involved in the day-to-day preparation of these reports, he attended meetings associated with their preparation and, at all stages, was well aware of the emerging findings. While everyone involved experienced a deep sense of frustration and disappointment that governments and their agencies were so unresponsive to implementing the recommendations, for Rob, with his long-standing and emotional ties to the issues, the frustration must have been near overwhelming. Whereas in the past he had been witness to community racism towards Aboriginal people and what he saw as the moral failings of party political leaders, his involvement in oversighting the Royal Commission recommendations brought him face to face with the failure of the system of government to produce change for Aboriginal people. Given Rob's steady slide into depressive realism it is important to understand the extent of resistance he and others encountered.

There was a vicious circle of resistance to change. Agencies opposed being held accountable for their performance on Aboriginal issues, and Ministers failed to make them co-operate. Ministers simply ticked off their endorsement for certain recommendations in a perfunctory manner without supplying any supportive detail or, in many cases, policy documents. Thus, it became impossible to tell whether what government was saying publicly was flowing through to the agencies. Robyn Ayres, a lawyer who had worked on the Royal Commission, was employed by the

ALS to prepare its 1994 report. She recalls the frustration of trying to determine how far the government and its agencies were implementing the Royal Commission recommendations. Ministers, she says, were either not prepared to exert authority over their departments or failed to appreciate the level of resistance in them to change their practices and cultures. She had to meet with Ministers simply in order to get basic information. Rob would attend and always made an impression. He was personable and showed a willingness to negotiate an outcome.

But in agencies like the Police and the Justice Department, indifference and resistance to change were just too strong. The meal allowance for country police officers was a case in point. The allowance was paid to police for providing meals to prisoners, but without accountability for either the money spent or the quality of food provided. It had long been regarded in Aboriginal circles as a racket. The Royal Commission found the system unacceptable and recommended its abolition. To those involved it was a simple thing to change, and the corrupt practices it had generated for years compelled urgent action. The ALS had obtained statistics under a freedom of information application, showing that in some cases country police officers were making up to $70,000 a year in the early 1990s welching money out of the system and lining their own pockets.

For several years after the release of the Royal Commission recommendations, the police took the view that the system of meal allowances would not be abolished until an acceptable alternative could be introduced on a state-wide basis. However, it was not until 1994 that an Interdepartmental Committee was established to examine alternatives. Rob was hopeful of a successful outcome. He told the December 1994 ALS Executive Committee that, after sixteen years, the ALS was now in a position to make 'ground-breaking change'. But the Committee became bogged down in the face of the Police Department's inflexibility. An ALS briefing paper noted: 'The Police Department has stated from the outset that it wants a statewide scheme which does not allow for regional variations. It has adopted this position because its research into meal allowance systems operating in other states has shown that allowing for regional variations creates problems for the Police Department'.[50] The ALS regarded their attitude as simple intransigence to 'making any amendment to a scheme which has and still benefits employees to a large extent in country towns to the detriment of Aboriginal people'.[51] The

Interdepartmental Committee continued to meet until September 1995 until changes were finally agreed. This straightforward recommendation for change took more than four years to achieve. And this was only one small area.

On other recommendations, little or no progress for change had been made by the mid-1990s. The system of police investigating complaints against their own officers remained largely unreformed, as did the system of allowing justices of the peace — people with no legal training — to have the powers of imprisonment.

The Royal Commission's recommendations in relation to the incarceration of Aboriginal juveniles was another concern close to Rob's heart. Both the ALS and the Aboriginal Justice Council reports were critical of the lack of progress by the Lawrence and Court governments. The Aboriginal Justice Council wrote: 'The overall picture in relation to Aboriginal juvenile issues remains, for the most part, bleak in many areas of the state. While we may draw some comfort from the success of individual initiatives, the general picture does not encourage optimism in the short to medium term'.[52]

Rob has left two accounts of his response to the failure of governments to fully act on the Royal Commission recommendations. In 1992 he was defiant in fighting for the recommendations of the Royal Commission, vowing: 'I won't ever give up on this cause. When you come from the trenches you know you must fight for these changes'.[53] By 1995 his words echoed his despair that nothing would change for Aboriginal people in Australia. Governments, he told a 1995 psychologists conference, had once again abrogated their responsibilities on the Royal Commission recommendations:

> The pathetic excuses of government (State and Federal) are either 'it's not our responsibility', 'we don't have the dollars', and 'there are no capable Aboriginal people to take charge'. History necessitated an implementation committee to monitor and report on the enactment of the 339 deaths in custody recommendations that were made and it has been found ... that the response has been tepid and unconvincing. The main issue all along has been reluctance by white Australia to transfer power, skills and resources to Aboriginal people to run their own affairs —

in partnership and cooperation with the wider Australian society and its institutions.[54]

The failure of successive Western Australian governments to systematically implement the recommendations increased the pressure on Rob as head of the ALS. He faced the brunt of the Aboriginal community's expectation that the ALS should have been able to make it happen.

───

Rob's final campaign was to press the claims of the Stolen Generations. The ALS was one of several organisations to call for a national inquiry. In 1990 the Secretariat of National Aboriginal and Islander Child Care began the campaign, with the New South Wales organisation Link-Up also active.[55] Rob commenced lobbying in 1994, the year that the 'Going Home' conference was held in Darwin, bringing together Aboriginal people mainly from the Northern Territory who had been removed from their families.

From then on the issue plagued his mind and dominated his private thoughts. Rob's first public statements on the issue are revealing. He said a national inquiry should be used to develop counselling services and give recognition to 'the grief, pain and hurt that assimilation had caused hundreds of thousands of Aboriginal people'. But he warned that calls for an inquiry would be ignored: 'They will wash their hands of it because it might open the floodgates [for compensation] and the government is worried about the truth of the policies coming out'.[56]

In November 1994, Rob Riley and Maxine Chi attended the 'Healing Our Spirit' conference in Sydney. Rob was to present a paper on the history of racial policy, but unannounced he disclosed his experience of sexual abuse in Sister Kate's. It was the first time he had publicly done so. He did it against his partner's advice; she had been urging him to first discuss the issue with his immediate family. While his revelation did not reach the media, word travelled that he had opened up about his abuse. In the following weeks he received nearly a hundred calls from people wanting to share with him their own experiences of sexual abuse.

Over the next six months Rob used every available opportunity to press home to the state and federal governments and to the public the importance of the Stolen Generations issue. In October 1994, a 'Stolen Generations Project' was set up in the ALS Public Interest Unit, employing the services of Tony Buti with the title of Human Rights Lawyer and with the assistance of Catherine Crawford, the Principal Legal Officer. Unique in both its purpose and scale, it aimed to record the stories of Aboriginal people who had been removed as children and to assemble these into a publication. In part, it was seen as another way to keep the pressure up for a national inquiry. However, the involvement of the ALS in this project Rob brought face to face with his childhood demons.

Initially, the project members thought that they might be able to secure 60–70 interviews. But as the call spread through the Aboriginal media network, hundreds came forward with their stories. Simultaneously, six Northern Territory Aborigines launched an action against the federal government, and against the 1918 Aboriginals Ordinance which provided the legal basis in the Territory for the Commonwealth to remove children. Once again, Rob used the opportunity to call for a national inquiry.[57] Rob also wrote to the federal government during the process of collecting the stories for the ALS project. In December 1994, he told his Executive that his call for a national enquiry had arisen as a result of the findings emerging from the project. His outline to the Executive of some of these findings is revealing. He told the members that all the stories of the 130 people interviewed to date 'highlight and confirm the trauma still associated with successive government policies towards Indigenous people. Without exception all the persons contacted felt that a part of them had been removed forever. There is an extreme sense of bewilderment and alienation resulting from their removal, and a sense of being unable to cope'.[58] The project was dragging Rob still deeper into the murky waters of his childhood.

Rob made himself available to be interviewed by Tony Buti for the project. It was an unnerving experience for Buti to interview his boss, and Rob was in control for most of the interview: 'the way he told it was quite beautiful really'. He made the story flow, but there were a couple of poignant moments: the account of his rape and the memories associated with his institutionalisation. He broke down in tears 'when he talked about being punished for asking about his mum'.

Rob's was only one of seven hundred stories which were eventually collected by the ALS. All spoke of the multiple horrors of removal and institutionalisation and its debilitating long-term impact.

Rob used other opportunities to keep the pressure up for the establishment of a national inquiry. When in December 1994, Joy Williams, an Aboriginal woman from New South Wales, won the legal right to sue the federal government for the physical and psychological damage arising from her own removal, Rob was quick to seize upon the significance of the case. The Williams case, he said, 'set a precedent and could spur Western Australian Aborigines to sue the state government for its former policy of separation'. He further claimed that 'this is going to be the most significant issue that the Australian public will have to deal with in 1995'.[59]

While the issue of the Stolen Generations was beginning to occupy increasing amounts of Rob's energy, he was also forced to re-engage in the crime debate. Throughout 1994, the Court government moved to make crime a centrepiece of its political agenda. The focus again was on juvenile offenders. The government's proposal was snatched from the 'get tough' policy basket, which had gained ascendancy worldwide by the mid-1990s. The Court government proposed to establish military-style 'boot camps' for male juvenile offenders as an alternative to prison. Rob was drawn into yet another politically driven skirmish. It lasted on and off for twelve months. For Rob, it was yet another example of governments playing politics with Aboriginal people. As 60 per cent of juveniles incarcerated were Aborigines, they were going to become the prime target of the policy. As he repeatedly pointed out in the press, the government chose to ignore all advice that such 'boot camps' are not effective, transgressed international obligations to children and would make young people caught in their net into tougher and smarter criminals. The underlying motives of the government, he said, were simply political: Aboriginal people were to be a tool to allow the government to be seen to be doing something on the issue.[60]

Throughout this time, Rob was losing faith in medical intervention in his psychiatric problems. By mid-1995, he had spent three years in periodic psychiatric out-patient care and several brief visits as an in-patient, but it seemed to make no difference. His medication also brought no relief from his painful emotional struggles, and on at least one occasion he discharged himself from hospital. Addressing the 1995 Australian psychologists' conference — the first Indigenous person to do so — he provocatively asked the assembled professionals, what would they know about Aboriginal people? He seemed to be challenging the profession to acknowledge that the pain he and other Aborigines had experienced over the years was beyond the life experience and intervention methods practiced in mainstream medicine. How could he tell a white, middle-class psychologist what it was like to have a racial identity crisis, to experience profound social marginalisation, to undergo racial taunts, to want to change society and to be unable to do it, to feel an incessant need to engage with the political system and the continual despair at its belligerence and betrayals?

A number of friends tried to intervene in his life. Some warned him of the perils to his health arising from the stresses he had been under and urged he rest and seek further treatment. He continued to rely heavily on his partner, Maxine.

In April 1995 Rob took the long drive to Derby. He had a range of reasons for going. He wanted to catch up with family who had moved up to live in the town, and he wanted to reconnect with the Kimberley, one of his favourite regions in Australia. He went seeking a change of pace, and a chance to reflect. Packed in his luggage was his Native Welfare file, the contents of which had begun to gnaw at him like a cancer. Along the way he intended to catch up with Derby-based Aboriginal friend Carol Martin. She had been speaking to John Watson of the Kimberley about bringing Rob to the region for some healing and time out. Rob had visited Watson's community at Jarlmadangah, 140 kilometres south-east of Derby, on several occasions in the previous three years, and relished the opportunity to sit and talk with his colleague, who regarded him as one of the family. Watson, himself a long-time leader and land rights activist and mentor to Rob, was keen to bring him out to the community. Rob thought Martin's place would provide the ideal location for a week's rest. Located several kilometres out of town on a five-acre block, it was as far from the stresses of metropolitan political life as it is possible to imagine. Arriving late one afternoon, his introduction to life on the semi-rural block jolted him out of his recent troubles. Confronting him were Martin and a female friend clad in sarongs and steel-capped boots. Martin was mowing the knee-high grass while her friend was bearing a shot gun on her hip ready, it transpired, to shoot any of the snakes in flight from Martin's aggressive lunges at the thick undergrowth with the mower. Alighting from his car, Rob poured immediate scorn on the two horticultural gladiators. Rather than attempting to massacre the snakes, he proffered an uncharacteristic suggestion: take it slowly, give the snakes time to flee before invading their territory. It proved a circuit breaker. He and Martin spent the next two days in continuous laughter about the manner of his arrival. He started to relax.

But choices had to be made. People from Watson's community duly came to Martin's retreat wanting to take him to a healing place on their land. Watson and Martin believed that some traditional healing would help lift Rob's state of mind. But he would not go with them. He explained that to do so would betray his own Noongar culture. So he stayed with Martin. During the next week he ate, painted and drank red wine.

Meanwhile, confronting again the contents of his Native Welfare file loomed as threateningly as a Kimberley downpour. He had not dealt with its distressing implications, he told Martin. He wanted space and quiet to fully consider it. He was plagued by the thought that his carers in Sister Kate's had lied to him. Martin, who had had experience in counselling other Aboriginal people to confront their past in the form of the cold-blooded language of official files, convinced Rob not to re-engage with the contents of the file at this time; to put its contents in a separate place and not let them hurt him. He took her advice. But he was struggling to shake off his immersion in the revisitation of his childhood trauma. He told Martin about the hundreds of Stolen Generations survivors who had rung him either at home or at the office to unload their own burdens. He detailed to Martin the tragedy of individual case histories. Martin tried to shift his focus from the collective struggles of these people onto himself. Let their sadness go, she tried to counsel him: deal with your own cycle of recovery. It was a message he barely heeded. He spent much of the week learning to paint and generally relaxing, but he ran out of time. He needed to get on his way to Broome.

His return to Perth was followed by some positive news. In May 1995 the federal government had announced its support for an inquiry into the Stolen Generations. Rob had played a key role in lobbying for it, helping to shape it by calling for the appointment of an Aboriginal Commissioner to sit on hearings with Sir Ronald Wilson (this position was filled by Rob's friend and colleague, Mick Dodson) and for the issue of compensation to be included in the inquiry's terms of reference.

With the Human Rights inquiry gearing up to commence its arduous task, Rob turned to the launch of the ALS project on the Stolen Generations, *Telling Our Story*. Sister Kate's was chosen as an appropriate location for the launch, which he hoped would add to the potential for publicity for the project. But it brought Rob back to the very site of his unresolved childhood anguish for a very public and political occasion. Several hundred people were invited and seated under a marquee. A mix of church, community and political leaders joined Aboriginal people and representatives from Aboriginal organisations. Rob used his speech to push the cause. He spoke from the heart about his reunion with his family. As he described what had happened to him, Rob had one hand clenched, his audience expecting to see it finally raised in a Black Power salute. Instead, he opened it to reveal the copper coins given to him long ago by his step-father. His voice cracking with emotion, Rob told the story of how his step-father handed over to him all the money he had had on him, which Rob had kept as a symbol of his sense of belonging.

Then he moved on to even more emotionally dangerous territory: his sexual abuse in the institution. The intensity was extraordinary. Rob's close friend and colleague at the ALS, Peter O'Brien, has vivid memories of the occasion. They had previously discussed what he was going to say, but Rob did not want O'Brien to write anything. 'Everyone knew that it was going to be highly emotional and then for Rob to get up and start talking about his own experience, and to mention the rape ... You could hear a pin drop'. O'Brien had no idea that Rob was going to come out with the 'bombshell' of his abuse. No-one did. The electric atmosphere of the revelations added to people's sense of shock. It was as if the audience were collectively drawn right into the horrors of institutional assimilation. The revelations stunned his children. His daughter, Megan later wrote: 'it was really a shock to see him that emotional and just heartbroken, like he was broken down into little pieces'.[61]

Was Rob using his experience and his high profile as a deliberate political tactic, a means to generate additional impact for the publication? It is clear that he failed to prepare himself for his disclosure. Those close to him believe that his speech at the Sister Kate's launching of *Telling Our Story*, in which he spoke in such a deeply personal way, was the beginning of Rob's descent into an emotional darkness from which no-one could rescue him. Something snapped on that day. Thereafter, he was described by one of his close friends as 'shellshocked, almost emotionally paralysed'.[62] On the evening of his launch speech, Rob went on a drinking binge. For weeks after he was at a loss to know how to deal with his situation. His secretary, Jenny Bedford, recalls driving in the car one time with Rob 'absolutely sobbing'.

On 12 July 1995 — the day after the launch of *Telling Our Story* — he made a fateful decision which effectively ended his public career. After work on that day he went to the Claisebrook Tavern, where he drank for several hours, and from there he proceeded to a function associated with NAIDOC Week, where he continued drinking. According to one colleague, Rob may have consumed as much as one and a half bottles of bourbon. In his inebriated state, he was goaded into becoming involved in a drag race by one or more of the four other people in the car. He was driving his red ALS 007 Commodore, known to just about every policeman in the state.

Nonetheless, he set out along a major Perth metropolitan highway, at speeds which police later alleged reached 200 kilometres per hour, although no official measurement of his speed was ever taken. He claimed he was not watching the speedometer but admitted to driving over the speed limit. Inevitably, given the prominence of his vehicle, the police were on his tail. He was followed to his house where he attempted to avoid arrest. When placed in the police van he began kicking the vehicle. He was taken to the central police lock-up, held overnight and charged with reckless and dangerous driving, refusing a breath test and damage to a police vehicle.

News of the incident hit the television bulletins that evening. The whole thing was videoed like a movie, with shots of police lights and police cars chasing him. It has never been conclusively proved how the video left police hands. The likelihood is that someone leaked it to the media. Rob was mortified at the thought of his drunken behaviour being broadcast and even more so at the sensational manner in which the stations covered the event. He later instigated legal action against Perth's four commercial stations for misrepresenting the facts surrounding his arrest and for releasing an illegally obtained internal video of the arrest.[63] Police Commissioner Bob Falconer publicly stated that the release of the video represented a 'serious breach of discipline' and 'may even be a criminal offence'.[64]

While obviously distraught at his own behaviour and its unsavoury coverage, Rob had his own view of the politics behind the police actions. He knew that some in the police force saw him as an adversary: someone who could grab the headlines and use them so effectively to highlight their treatment of Aboriginal people. He had been untouchable; but now the police had him.

The morning of his arrest and detention, Rob rang Ian Horrocks, the Human Resources Manager at the ALS, and asked him to come and bail him out. Worried about the adverse publicity his release might stir, Horrocks rang the Commissioner of Police, who offered to make special arrangements for Rob to avoid any confrontation with the press. Arriving at the lock-up, Horrocks was not able to convince Rob to take a 'back door' exit. Instead, he insisted on facing the media, which had been informed of his arrest and imminent release. Looking dishevelled, he opened the door of the main entrance to the central Perth lock-up and was greeted with a media throng. He made a statement apologising to the community, accepting responsibility for his actions and conveying directly to young Aboriginal people the stupidity of his actions.

The same day as his release, Rob wrote a confidential explanation of events to Ted Wilkes, the Chair of the ALS. Ted, by now an old friend of Rob's, was placed in an invidious position. What action should he take? While Rob informed him of his intention to apologise to staff, the incident had compromised the integrity of the organisation. Later on, Rob felt compelled to resign his position with the organisation in order to give the Executive time to consider its options. At much the same time he rang Deputy Commissioner Les Ayton, and insisted on arranging a meeting with the arresting police officers so that he could apologise to them. The meeting took place in Ayton's office.

News of his brush with the law was seized upon by some long-standing opponents in Noongar politics. Ken Colbung said in an interview that 'Mr Riley had rorted the ALS, fantasised that he was James Bond, was a bad example to other Aborigines and should be sacked'.[65] However, Rob had strong support in both the Aboriginal and wider communities. In the lead up to the August Executive meeting where Rob's fate was to be determined, the organisation received nearly sixty unsolicited letters from the public requesting leniency for Rob.

They form an extraordinary insight into the impact Rob had made on the community's imagination. Letters came from people from all walks of life: government officials, Labor politicians, church leaders, lawyers, journalists and ordinary members of the public. Some were written in the form of testimonials and addressed formally to Ted Wilkes as President. Others were sent directly to Rob as heartfelt personal messages of sympathy and encouragement. Rob had touched a chord in many people by the courage he showed in talking about his own experiences.

A lawyer wrote:

> In the years that have gone by where Rob has been your Chief Executive Officer, I have to say that I have admired the tenacity with which he has fought the cause of the Aboriginal people, many times against great odds. I have not always agreed with his view but I very much felt that the Service needed a man such as he to forcefully put the views required where ordinarily support for your people falls very far short of what it should be from other sources.

A member of the public sent a handwritten note:

> Without really thinking about it, I have for years admired your television appearances ... Under great provocation, facing blatant prejudice from political leaders who should know better, you have been forthright but courteous, showing admirable balance and restraint.

A police officer wrote:

> Over the years I have watched and listened with interest on matters pertaining to the police and aboriginals and whilst we would agree to disagree on some issues I have admired your desire to bring the aboriginal point into focus.

Without doubt, the most encouraging letter came from Rob's three daughters, Megan, Jaymea and Emma. They wrote: 'Came in to give you some support. Although we are upset with what has happened we want you to know we are on your side'.

Rob was deeply affected by this outpouring of emotion. He began to view his contribution to the struggle for Aboriginal rights as involving significant personal sacrifices which, previously, he had simply taken for granted.

When the matter came up for discussion at the August meeting, Rob's resignation was rejected and he was temporarily reinstated. However, he had clearly lost ground. He attended the meeting, at which a number of resolutions were passed, including one to the effect that he remain Executive Officer only until a Deputy could be appointed and a 'handover' period arranged. It was envisaged that Rob would then leave the organisation for a three-year period of study leave, after which he would return as its head. The agreement seems to have been brokered with Rob's tacit approval, but how committed he was to it is not clear.

However, the whole incident had had a deep impact on him. He felt shame that his public credibility had been tarnished and he wondered whether he could any longer sustain a public profile on justice issues. At about this time he started to talk about suicide to at least one of his close friends, while depending on several key relationships for support.

In August 1995 Rob had to attend his court hearing on the driving charges. Another media 'circus' confronted him as he drove up to the courtroom. In answering the charges, Rob received back-up from an unlikely quarter. Deputy Police Commissioner Les Ayton, with whom Rob had developed a close collegial relationship in the cause of developing better relations between police and Aboriginal people, appeared as a character witness. For such a senior officer to appear for Rob Riley took courage. Ayton explained to the press that he appeared because 'I like and respect the man. I admire his courage ... I also admire the way he has worked strongly in the Aboriginal community and strongly with the police to improve the lot of Aborigines and police'.[66] Ayton's actions were regarded by rank and file police officers as treacherous. They were reported as being 'ropeable', compelling Ayton to issue an email within the police force explaining himself.[67] The magistrate eventually decided to fine Rob $1800 and suspend him from driving for nine months.

Also in August, Rob was forced to confront a family issue. One of his brothers was forced into homelessness, and his case generated national publicity. Like many Aboriginal males from families suffering intergenerational discrimination and poverty, Rob's two brothers had struggled at different times in their lives. Rob had previously intervened

On holidays (left to right): Lydia Collard, Rob Riley, Emma, Megan and Jaymea. Rob enjoyed periodic holidays at Busselton in Western Australia's south-west.

Rob and his daughter Megan.

Emma, Megan and Jaymea, on holiday in Pemberton, WA.

Ted Wilkes opening Rob Riley Walk, Curtin University. The Walk was opened following Rob's death in 1996 to recognise his work in Aboriginal Affairs.

Gough Whitlam and Violet Riley on the occasion of Rob's posthumous Human Rights Award by the Human Rights and Equal Opportunity Commission, Sydney 1996.

Rob Riley's grandchildren at his grave in Pingelly. Left to right: Izayoh Riley, Jaxon Mallard and Caitlyn Mallard.

in the life of his younger brother, whose criminal activities were the cause of family unrest. Rob was distraught at the thought that this brother might end up alienated from the family and he was instrumental in bringing him back into the fold. On the occasion that his other brother was made homeless through eviction by the state housing authority, Homeswest, Rob was brought into very personal contact with an issue which the ALS had long championed: the alleged discrimination shown by the authority to its Aboriginal tenants. In an article published in *The Canberra Times*, journalist Jan Mayman wrote:

> At 39 Tim Riley is just another statistic in the endless tragedy of Aboriginal Australia. Once he was a gun shearer, today, he is an epileptic, unemployed, with a frail spouse and five children, one handicapped. They all became homeless last week when they were evicted from their Homeswest house for rental arrears, even though their rental of $320 was paid in full before the court hearing that devastated the family. ... 'I don't think anyone wants us anywhere', Tim said, watching his children carry their few possessions out of the house they called home for only a few months. Also watching were some neighbours who blitzed Homeswest with complaints about alleged anti-social behaviours from the day the Riley family moved into their Perth suburban street. 'I knew it would be no good: it's a street of white people, buying their own homes. They complained all the time about us, to me and to Homeswest. A neighbour even said my kids disturbed him in his swimming pool with the noise they made playing basketball. Another neighbour told me he would never be able to sell his home with us next door.' [68]

Rob would have been acutely aware that the actions of Homeswest were contrary to the findings of the Royal Commission into Aboriginal Deaths in Custody, which highlighted the role homelessness played in creating family breakdowns and which was a contributing cause to cell deaths. But he was unable to prevent the pattern recurring in his own family.

Rob had always been involved at the grassroots of Aboriginal socio-economic disadvantage. It was his willingness to answer calls in individual cases that led to his ultimate undoing.

On the evening of 17 September 1995, Rob received a call from an Aboriginal woman whose fifteen-year-old daughter had been raped. After acknowledging the severity of the incident, he said that he would contact other ALS officers to assist her. He later rang her back to inform her that he could not find anyone. She became distressed and challenged him on the service that the ALS was supposed to offer. Still under suspension from driving, and without funds to pay for a taxi fare, he made the fateful decision to drive himself over to the woman's place to provide support. On his way home he was pulled over by police and charged with driving under suspension. He was subsequently fined $350 and given an additional nine months suspension from driving.[69]

Events now began to spiral out of control. Following the charging, he rang ALS President Ted Wilkes to explain events and offered to participate in an Executive meeting at which he would put the mitigating circumstances behind the second car offence. However, simultaneously, his depression worsened. He was using speed with 'party friends' and spinning out of control. No-one knew how to deal with him and his illness.

Rob admitted himself to Royal Perth Hospital on 18 September as an in-patient. It was the third time he had been hospitalised for his depression. The psychiatrist who saw him at that time later wrote in stark terms about his 'terrifying sense of internal fragmentation': he was 'exhausted, overwhelmed, sad, helpless, hopeless and despairing about his future'.[70]

Two days later, he read of his sacking by the ALS in the newspaper. He claimed not to have received formal notification from the President until later that afternoon. The manner in which Rob's departure was handled by the ALS has caused divisions of opinion within the organisation and within the wider Aboriginal community that have not healed to this day. The Executive was divided in their support for him as, indeed, it always had been. While his long-time detractors would have seized upon the situation, they were all under pressure to be seen to be acting appropriately.

To this day, some of Rob's close friends believe the Executive acted in a hasty and uncaring manner. They claim he was 'shafted' by the organisation to which he had dedicated such a large part of his life, and that this magnified his emotional difficulties. Others can more readily see the invidious position in which the Executive was placed: here was their widely acclaimed leader in a second unlawful incident. Surely the interests of the organisation are larger than the individual? For those close to Rob such as Ted Wilkes, Rob's state of mind and his pattern of drug use must also have been alarming, even though Wilkes did not know the full extent of Rob's illness. Wilkes maintains that after the second car incident Rob's role as Executive Officer and the ALS itself had both been placed in an untenable position. However, he says that it was never the intention of the organisation to formally dismiss Rob, but rather to 'parachute him out and cushion him somewhere else until his health improved and he could return to the ALS, although not necessarily in his former position'. The press, Wilkes maintains, misrepresented the way in which the departure was being handled.

Whatever the intentions behind the moves to deal sensitively with his transition from his current duties, the effect was the same: Rob was no longer the high-profile leader of the ALS. Peter O'Brien understands the dilemma the Executive found itself in: 'In the end the ALS had to decide to get rid of him. That was a very painful process for them. Nobody wanted to do that to Rob Riley. Ted [Wilkes] didn't want to do that to Rob Riley'.

What could or should the ALS Executive have done differently? Should they have let Rob attend the meeting to account for himself? But he was hospitalised and obviously in no fit state to appear. At some later date they could have taken Rob more into their confidence, talked some more about taking time out, the support they could offer. Perhaps they knew that they would be in for an ugly scrap: Rob would fight to hang onto his position. And there was the tarnished face of the ALS to consider. The choices must have been sickening.

Rob did not think he was sufficiently ill to have to step down. As one of his close colleagues explained, he felt betrayed: 'He never got it. He wasn't capable of getting it. He was too sick'. With the benefit of hindsight, those involved at the ALS would have done some things differently. But whether this might have prevented Rob's suicide is unlikely; his emotional struggles just went too deep.

After two weeks Maxine went to visit him in hospital and was shocked by his appearance. He looked pallid, sapped, drugged into an artificial state of passivity and clearly unable to cope. She had to steel herself to see him in this state. He told her he had tried to pray while he was in bed and had even taken himself over to Saint Mary's Cathedral and tried to pray there. He was not a believer and no divine intervention was forthcoming.

Inexplicably, Rob was released from hospital a week after Maxine's visit. He was shifted to an out-patient clinic and was again referred to a counselling regime. This time, he did not hold back on the complex web of issues that had entwined his life in despair. He spoke of his painful family background, the unremitting stress of Aboriginal politics, and the losses of key relationships in his personal life. He made particular mention to the psychiatrist of the absence of grieving over his losses because of the demands of politics. The psychiatrist concluded her report by diagnosing Rob as having a 'depressive illness' brought about by his own striving personality and the stresses of his occupation. It was expected that recovery would take a further six months of treatment. But in a little over six months Rob was dead.

As this book has tried to show, Rob's battle with depression had several layers. The first was the unresolved trauma about his rape, the beatings he received in Sister Kate's for asking about his parents, and his immersion in the unknown world of Aboriginal disadvantage. One theory of trauma holds that it 'shatters the self'.[71] This mirrors the observations of those close to him after he disclosed his childhood distress at the launch of *Telling Our Story*. It also mirrors the description — 'internal fragmentation' — used in his 1995 psychiatric report. Importantly, Rob used the word trauma in his suicide note.

A second layer of Rob's depression was his inability to come to terms with his sense of loss. All his life Rob had needed to feel that he belonged. He appeared to be in a state of mourning over things that he had valued in his life but had lost. He intimated this in his account of his state of mind to the psychiatrist following his release from hospital in 1995. His sense of mourning is also likely to have extended to the loss of his political career, in which he had invested so much of himself. Rob used the words 'sad' and 'helpless' during this visit.

According to a Freudian perspective, inability to resolve mourning leads to melancholia which, in an accompanying state of depression, is characterised by a tendency to suicide.[72] The last layer of Rob's depression involved, as has been previously noted, his 'depressive realism' about the state of Australian politics. This, too, is clearly reflected in his suicide note.

What kind of intervention can be effective in a case like Rob's, with such deep, multi-layered strands? The very notion of 'illness' suggests that he had little control over the choices facing him. These are troubling, complex and ultimately, unresolvable questions. But in the last few months of Rob's life there are hints that he had thought deeply about ending his life.

When Rob was released from hospital his framework of support had all but collapsed. His public role in the Aboriginal rights movement, from which he drew his identity as an Aboriginal person, had ended. The movement had spent itself in the struggle over native title and had gone further into retreat with the election of the Howard government, which early on distanced itself from the 'rights' agenda. Rob's departure from the ALS meant he no longer had a political role within the rights movement. Even his mobile telephone had gone. He was disconnected from his world. His private life had been overtaken by issues from his past and by his disillusion with Australian party politics.

Recovery for Rob would have to involve rebuilding all these facets of his life in some new form: finding another professional role within Aboriginal affairs; repairing personal relationships; dealing with the traumas from his past; and either finding new sources of hope about the capacity of Australian politics to deal with racism or at least reconciling himself to its limitations. Rob attempted to chart a path through these thickets, but it is reasonably clear that, especially in the last two months of his life, he felt unable to construct a new identity for himself. Thus, at some level beyond the symptoms of his illness — his anxiety and despair — was a bleak understanding about where he stood in the world.

Yet Rob's last few months highlight the enigma of mental illness. Outwardly, he was functioning. He was no longer spinning out of control. He had enrolled in a course of university study. Much of his anger was directed at trying to obtain compensation from television stations over the 'illegal' release of the video and from the ALS over work-related stress. He took several drives into the south-west of the state, trying to find a deeper connection to his Aboriginality. He also attended two conferences in the early months of 1996: one in Adelaide on constitutional reform and the other in Perth on Aboriginal media. He was a convenor at this latter conference and gave a characteristically hard-hitting serve to the media, even though his tone conveyed weariness: 'The media exercise sensationalism, or they're only interested in selling newspapers or making big bucks for ... those who deliberately provoke a negative image of Aboriginal people'.[73] These seemed to be the actions of a man trying, at least, to climb back onto his feet.

But the appearances belied the truth. Rob had no stable place to live. He would show up on the doorstep of his friends, stay for a few days, often locked away in a bedroom provided for him, and emerge only partly refreshed. To several of these friends he talked about suicide. He had been thinking about this intermittently since his involvement in the Royal Commission into Aboriginal Deaths in Custody. He seems to have become weighed down by the decision to end his life for at least two months before he died. Some thought they noticed a calmer demeanour in the month before: a demeanour which, in hindsight, indicated to them that Rob had made his decision and was at some peace with it. Others witnessed his on-going troubled side. Rob paid a visit to his old mentor, Cedric Wyatt, then Chief Executive Officer of the State Aboriginal Planning Advisory Authority. He just fronted up to the office one day and Cedric could tell he was not in a good condition; he thought he was high on some substance. He offered to take him home, but Rob insisted that he just wanted to sit. He sat silently in an armchair for an hour and then left.

He seems to have been at some point of transition in this decision-making process when he was invited to stay with a couple — Cheryl Taylor and Stuart Crowe — who became aware of his lack of stable accommodation. When he arrived, he had only a swag and a few possessions in the boot of his car. He was still enrolled in Heritage Studies at university, trying, at least, to carve out the next career move. He imagined becoming a consultant negotiating agreements over access to heritage sites: a broker between Aboriginal groups and mining companies, national parks and tourism ventures. But he was not passionate about the idea. Even the study failed to engage him. Going to a lecture and writing from notes and preparing a paper could not compare to his work at the ALS. In his mind he knew that the move into some form of consulting was not going to be the fix for his professional life. In other words, Rob could not imagine a life outside of activism. Nothing else seemed to him as purposeful.

However, he struggled to reconcile this identity with the fundamental nature of Australian politics and its unyielding attitude on Aboriginal affairs. The on-going failure of the Court government to meaningfully respond to the Royal Commission continued to gnaw at him. But this was simply one focus of his disillusion — his depressive realism — about Australian politics. He came to a point where he seemed to believe that for all the effort, all the work he had expended in the cause of change, nothing had changed or was likely to change. This feeling was compounded by the election of the Howard Liberal government.

Like many people involved in Aboriginal politics, Rob appeared to be cynical about the direction in which the government was headed. He sensed that the political right was going to muscle in hard on Aboriginal politics; that there were tough times ahead. On the Sunday two weeks before he died he read the front-page article in the *Sunday Times*, headed 'Tip Kids'.[74] It was about fifteen Aboriginal kids living in squalor on a former outer metropolitan rubbish dump. The article reported that five hundred Aboriginal children were homeless in Perth.[75]

His private life showed no greater cause for optimism. He continued to take anti-depressants but appears to have discontinued the professional counselling. He sensed nothing was working. The psychiatric profession had failed to find a path that would lead to him being able to heal. Its regime of drug therapy had not produced results, and it does not appear that any of his public or private psychiatrists had assessed him as being at risk of suicide, even though on any measure he had multiple risk factors. Trapped in his illness he still could not escape the demons from his past.

The Human Rights and Equal Opportunity Commission's Inquiry into the Stolen Generations was soon to visit Perth. Rob knew he would be one of its key witnesses. He would have to face giving evidence before his old friend and colleague, Commissioner Mick Dodson. He did not have the strength to face a new round; to keep re-opening the wounds from his childhood and to have these publicised for political effect. He was in a bind; he could not stand back from the inquiry because of his political commitment to it nor could he face up to giving evidence before it. Equally distressing for him was the alienation he felt from key relationships in his life. For someone who thrived on a sense of social connectedness, his growing isolation must have disturbed him. He had cut himself off from many of his former friends, although a few were in touch with him to the very end.

All these issues played on his mind like loose, live wires. But there was a thread connecting them all. Rob's mental illness did not exist separately from his life experiences. And the key to understanding these life experiences is racism.

In short, Rob was a victim of Australian racism in all its interwoven and barely acknowledged historical and contemporary political manifestations. Racism had deprived him of a family and shaped his childhood exposure to assimilation. Racism had forged his anger as he confronted the world of discrimination as a teenager and young adult. And racism lay at the heart of the political battles he fought in the Aboriginal rights movement for land rights, self-determination and an end to grinding disadvantage. He died in the cause of trying to help the country confront and overcome this racism. But, as he said in his suicide note, he believed the nation had turned its back on this quest.

Legacy

At the 1997 National Reconciliation Convention in Melbourne, a small candle burned in the corner to symbolise the suffering of the Stolen Generations. At the end of the Convention, Pat Dodson, in his capacity as Chair of the Reconciliation Council, made a special acknowledgement of the candle's symbolism by paying a tribute to his friend Rob Riley. Shedding his stoic and intellectual persona, Dodson moved to the microphone, his eyes filling with tears. Choking back emotion he told the audience:

> There is one whom I would like to acknowledge and thank who is not here with us today. One who was always prepared to walk together with us no matter what the burden and hurt that entailed. He had the vision when others were still searching in the darkness. He had the courage to walk without trepidation when others had difficulty finding the strength to confront the barriers that were raised before us. Our brother Rob left us physically twelve months ago, but where the candle of the stolen generations has burned in the corner of the stage over these days, his spirit has filled this auditorium. And we thank him for that.[1]

It was a fitting acknowledgment, but how many in the audience would have had any idea about the struggles Rob and the other leaders in the rights movement had had to endure in the previous twenty years? For many the personal costs have been extremely high. To be involved in Aboriginal politics in Australia is to lose many more battles than will be won. A combination of underlying community racism, elite economic interests and a preference for historical denialism deprived the Aboriginal rights movement of all but a few compromised victories. Rob was at the epicentre of this historically significant struggle for most of his adult life. He was involved in most of the major political developments of the time, including land rights, self-determination, reform of the justice system and recognition of the plight of the Stolen Generations.

The twenty-year campaign that Rob and other leaders waged against police violence, intimidation and discrimination in Western Australia helped usher in a change of direction. In recent years, police have developed the concept of community policing, and this has helped foster closer and more productive relationships with many Aboriginal communities. Aboriginal people are still incarcerated at a much higher rate than whites in Western Australia and elsewhere, but few would disagree that the old days of oppressive policing of Aboriginal communities have substantially disappeared.

In the mining industry, similar cultural changes have taken place. Again, Rob was part of a national and international movement to make mining companies more accountable and responsive to the Indigenous communities among which they operated. This change is evident in the efforts of Rio Tinto, for example, to build constructive relationships with Aboriginal people, in Australia and around the world. The company used to have one of the worst records of working in Indigenous communities, but it has reassessed its relationship with Aboriginal communities in Australia, and in 1996 it apologised to Aboriginal people for the company's actions at Weipa, Argyle and the Pilbara.[2] Australian governments have recognised that 'there is a cultural change taking place in relations between industry and Indigenous communities' and has programs in place to further support this change.

This is all a far cry from the days when Sir Charles Court bludgeoned the Noonkanbah community's aspirations. It is a marked improvement, too, on the efforts of the governments led by Richard Court and

Dr Carmen Lawrence to defend the economic benefits of mining at the expense of Aboriginal people.

Rob's views on native title have been given currency in recent times. Those who fought as he had done for a Canadian-style, regional agreement approach to the Mabo High Court decision saw this come to fruition in the recent Ord River agreement involving the Miriuwung Gajerrong people. Pat Dodson led the negotiations, which produced a landmark agreement regarded as being beyond the capacity of the courts to deliver. The deal struck with the traditional owners covered future land use, compensation, economic development and land management. It also dealt with health and educational outcomes and established an $11 million fund co-managed by the state and the traditional owners to supplement mainstream services.[3] In negotiating the agreement, Dodson said that it was 'as much about dealing with past injustice as it is about providing for future land use in the region'. Rob would have agreed wholeheartedly with his friend.

These are significant achievements. However, none of the events in which Rob was a participant produced a clinching victory in Australian race relations, or any sign that Australia as a nation was committed to coming to terms with its past. Achievements like the Royal Commission into Aboriginal Deaths in Custody, the creation of ATSIC, the Human Rights Inquiry into the Stolen Generations and native title were all compromised, diluted or in some way sullied in the political process. There were other, indisputable defeats. Political realists would say that few campaigners get all they want out of the political system. But few groups fought so hard and over such a long period of time to come up with so little for their efforts, as Aboriginal activists in the modern era. Rob understood the unyielding nature of race politics in Australia.

Thus, in the absence of grand victories, how do we evaluate his work?

Rob stood for a set of ideals and a vision for the nation which remain vitally relevant. The value he placed on justice, on the search for fairness, is as universal as it is timeless. All societies are enriched by people who choose the life of moral protesters; they enlarge our vision, disrupt comfortable certainties and shed light on issues that mainstream politics is content to ignore.[4] Rob did not flinch from his belief that Aborigines had a moral and historical claim to justice. He had a vision which encompassed all Aboriginal people in the nation. It was his capacity, commitment and courage in search of these ideals that places him as one of Australia's enduring human rights campaigners.

In December 1996, Rob was posthumously awarded the Human Rights Medal issued by the Human Rights and Equal Opportunity Commission 'for his life-long commitment to advancing Indigenous issues in Australia'.

Rob had an acute understanding of the weaknesses of Australian democracy in dealing with race. He saw the failure of the state to enact and uphold laws to protect Aboriginal interests. He witnessed this failure from the earliest struggles at Noonkanbah through to the debates over the Mabo legislation. He believed that Aboriginal politics was dominated by an ideology of racism, the aim of which was to deny Aborigines any self-determination and any share of the nation's resources. He also identified the tools of this racial politics as fear and historical denialism.

Rob conceptualised the link in Aboriginal affairs between vested economic interests, conservative ideologues and an uncritical media as constituting the politics of fear. Rob understood that fear was being used by one group to rule another, and that it was embedded in the structure of power. He called the tactic propaganda, and drew attention to its emotive, irrational foundations. Few others at the time had such a comprehensive insight. He often drew attention to the miners' campaign that brought down national land rights in the mid-1980s; it showed how the tactic could be used to thwart the political process. He saw parallels at work in the native title debate during the early 1990s.

Rob was well versed in the second tool of racial politics — historical denialism. He witnessed first-hand the transformation of history into an ideological tool. He was in the front row of Australian politics when John Howard and other conservatives used historical denialism as a means to attack the treaty and ATSIC during the late 1980s. He would not have been surprised at the lengths to which Howard has now taken his campaign. The official imprimatur which the Prime Minister gave to historical denialism reached a peak in an interview he gave to *The Weekend Australian Magazine* in 2004, where he paraphrased the conservative argument linking a lack of individual responsibility to past events with a call to close the book on racial history. The Prime Minister said: 'Now I totally agree that they [Aborigines] have been appallingly treated in the past. But I didn't do that. I won't feel guilty about it. But because we feel guilty we have these nonsenses such as treaties. And it is nonsense. I say let's forget about the past, start again, and just concentrate on making things better for the Aborigines'.[5]

Rob's outraged reaction could easily be imagined. Forget history? History made Aborigines what they are today, he would have argued. In saying this he would also have felt a deep connection to his own family's experience: the way racial policy made prisoners of his maternal grandmother, Anna Dinah (née Miller), his mother and his uncle. Then there was 'Granny' Riley, and her family and wider community, condemned to racial segregation in the cattle sheds of Pingelly Reserve because whites could not countenance racial integration. And there was his own experience: the lonely little boy of Sister Kate's; and the traumatised teenager moving from one impoverished Aboriginal community to another. Rob's call for the understanding of history to shape a reconciled future for the nation remains in stark contrast to the Prime Minister's own skewed, blinkered vision.

But, as Rob stated many times, not much separated Australian political parties on Aboriginal affairs. He saw the Liberal/National parties as vehicles for anti-Aboriginal policies which he saw as racist, in that they sought to perpetuate a position of privilege and power to whites by denying Aboriginal rights; and they employed propaganda and historical denialism as tools in this quest. Labor, on the other hand, was intellectually receptive to the moral and historical claims of Aboriginal people, but continually betrayed them by bowing to populism and vested interests.

Rob has also left us a set of ideas about what it means to be a reconciled nation. He rejected the term 'reconciliation' as early as the mid-1980s because, he said, it implied that 'two parties in the wrong were coming together'.[6] Rather, Rob believed that white Australia faced a challenge in coming to terms with its past. This involved dealing justly with the claims of Aboriginal people to their rights as Indigenous peoples, including self-determination. Coming to terms with the past, he believed, also involved governments and the community working to address the intergenerational problems caused by colonisation.

For Rob, reconciling the nation also meant facing the underlying racism in Australian society. His life and career reminds us how pervasive and institutionalised racism has been in contemporary Australian society. He witnessed the flashpoints of racism in the form of police violence and deaths in custody, but he confronted, too, its ordinary manifestations. Nonetheless, he was clearly shocked at the findings of the ANOP poll in the mid-1980s, the first comprehensive attempt to quantify Australians' attitudes to Aborigines. And Rob himself lived in the constant shadow of racism: ASIO files, death threats and hate mail.

Rob refused to let such personal manifestations of racism embitter him towards white Australia. He maintained that racism could be overcome through public education. He waged a long campaign for governments to fund such a campaign. He realised that without such a campaign, Aboriginal aspirations would be thwarted by governments who either manipulated public prejudice or caved in to it.

Rob's legacy can also be seen as a set of approaches to Aboriginal activism. As one of the most experienced activists of the modern era, Rob had intimate knowledge of the unique demands that the political campaigns placed on individuals. Seeking justice for Aboriginal people was, he once said, 'a constant struggle you can't walk away from'.[7] But commitment itself was not enough. He understood that little would be achieved without a united voice among Aboriginal people. Consequently, he rejected as artificial divisions between Aboriginal people. Colonisation, Rob understood, had impacted on all Aborigines.

Rob's career as an activist/leader can be divided into three phases. The first encompasses the period of his entry into political activity in the late 1970s, through to his chairmanship of the NAC. During this time, Rob was at the forefront of moves to create a unified Aboriginal voice with the capacity to make Aboriginal aspirations known to government and the wider community. Great strides were made in this period linking up disparate Aboriginal organisations across the country into a pan-Aboriginal movement; the mobilisation of this unity for acts of civil disobedience; the creation of a national Aboriginal political organisation to articulate the Indigenous voice; the development of a leadership able to communicate with the broader Australian public and engage in negotiations with government; and a commitment to using international forums as a means of exerting moral pressure on government. It was the very success of this model that governments found so threatening. It came close to delivering national Aboriginal land rights on terms articulated by Aboriginal people.

Secondly, Rob involved himself in the 'insider' politics often claimed to be the more effective path for those engaged in social movements. Rob was one of the earliest Aboriginal leaders to take up a senior political role in government. Rob's career shows that the model has potential when there is alignment between the activist 'insider' and the minister/bureaucracy. There have been few, if any, Ministers for Aboriginal Affairs as committed to achieving fundamental change for Aboriginal people as was Gerry Hand. Yet the conflicting opinions about how much change was achieved during these years on the key issues of sovereignty and self-determination caution against misplaced optimism for 'insider' politics. Even so, advances were made in the face of trenchant opposition.

The third and last phase of Rob's career centred on developing an institutionally-based human rights approach to achieving change for Aboriginal people. He helped transform the ALS along these lines. Its key elements were: the creation of a high profile institutional leadership; the extensive use of the media for the purposes of public education and for exerting moral pressure on government; the establishment of specialist units to pursue a broad agenda; and a capacity to engage with government in negotiating outcomes. This model succeeded in making the ALS a powerful political vehicle for advocacy and public education on a range of key issues. Even though it failed to deliver victories against governments motivated by populist agendas, it was highly effective in setting an agenda for political engagement.

In recent times, there has been a hiatus in discussion about the way forward for Aboriginal people in Australia. Michael Mansell has lamented the decline in the Aboriginal protest voice, commenting that: 'Now the streets are silent. The rage seems to have subsided'. But, as he acknowledged, there is 'still plenty to protest about'.[8]

The struggle for Aboriginal rights is unlikely to remain in the wings for ever. The experience of Indigenous politics around the globe shows that states eventually have to reckon with the historical claims of colonised peoples. Memories persist, aspirations are revived. Australia's Aboriginal population has suffered more than its counterparts in New Zealand, Canada and the United States. On all the major social indices, Australia's Aborigines fare worse than their counterparts in these countries and, arguably, they also possess weaker forms of self-governance.[9] The unfinished business of Australia's racial past is unlikely to disappear.

Yet it is also true that Rob may, over time, be seen to have belonged to a unique generation of activists, prepared to devote their lives and their careers to work for change, often outside of government organisations and frequently in antagonistic battles with government. It is unclear whether such a generation will ever be replicated.

Rob's life reminds us that the struggle against injustice is on-going. The obstacles placed in the way by ignorance, self-interested economic elites, cynical media presenters, and populist politicians is, as he was fond of saying, no reason to give up. At the same time his life should cause us to reflect on the Australian political system, which dealt so ruthlessly with his quest for justice.

Notes

Introduction

1. Mayman, 1996.
2. ABC, 'Telling His Story', *Four Corners*, 15 July 1996.
3. WAAMA Radio, 24 June 1996.
4. See Beresford and Omaji, 1996.
5. *West Australian*, 7 October 1995.
6. Macintyre, 2004, p. 35.
7. Riley, 1984a.
8. Riley, 1994, p. 167.
9. Homberger and Charmley (eds.), 1988.
10. Woolf, 1939.

1 Prisoners of Racism

1. Maushart, 1993.
2. PD LA Vol. 28, 1905, pp. 307–16.
3. Jacobs, 1990, Haebich, 1992, Beresford and Omaji, 1998.
4. Jacobs, 1990, p. 27.
5. Beresford and Omaji, 1998.
6. Jacobs, 1990, p. 102.
7. Violet Riley, 'Memories of the Past', n.d.
8. Cited in Beresford and Omaji, 1998, pp. 42–3.
9. Beresford and Omaji, 1998.
10. *West Australian*, 1 March 1939.
11. *West Australian*, 5 May 1934, cited in Maushart, 1993, p. 228.
12. Moseley, 1935, p. 12.
13. Royal Commission on Aborigines, 1974, p. 14.

14. Initial Conference of Commonwealth and State Aboriginal Authorities, 1937, p. 11
15. Ibid.
16. Violet Riley, n.d.
17. Cited in Maushart, 1993, pp. 189–90.
18. Haebich, 1982.
19. Maushart, 1993, p. 183.
20. *West Australian*, 21 March 1940.
21. Legislative Assembly, 1955, Vol. 3, p. 43.
22. Violet Riley, n.d.
23. Commissioner for Native Affairs, 1952, p. 13.
24. Commissioner for Native Affairs, 1951, pp. 19–20.
25. Commissioner for Native Affairs, 1947, Vol. 2, p. 9.
26. See Jessie Street's account cited in Beresford and Omaji, 1998, pp. 162–3.
27. Commissioner for Native Affairs, 1953, p. 5.
28. Ibid.
29. Commissioner for Native Affairs, 1959, p. 28.
30. Commissioner for Native Affairs, 1953, p. 14.
31. Violet Riley, n.d.

2   Bound for Assimilation

1. Morgan (ed.), 2002.
2. Sister Kate's Children's Home, MN 957, 3179A/366.
3. Whittington, 1999, p. 6.
4. Cited in ALS, 1996b, p. 27.
5. Whittington, 1999, p. 7.
6. See, for example Ken Colbung's and Graham Farmer's stories, in Leaming, 1986.
7. Morgan (ed.), 2002.
8. Leaming, 1986.
9. Sue Gordon, interview.
10. ABC, 'Telling His Story', *Four Corners*, 15 July 1996.
11. Cited in Morgan (ed.), 2002, p. 12.
12. Joan Winch cited on WAAMAA Radio, 'Tribute to Rob Riley', 24 June 1996.
13. Interview Peter O'Brien.
14. Interview Joan Winch; see also Leaming, 1986, p. 82.
15. ABC, 'Telling His Story'.
16. Ibid.
17. Beresford and Omaji, 1998.
18. Leaming, 1986, p. 83.
19. Riley, 1987, p. 69.
20. Ibid.

21. State Library of Western Australia, 1984.
22. ABC, 'Telling His Story'.
23. Sister Kate's Children's Home, MN 957, 319A/366.
24. Riley, 1987, p. 69.
25. Riley, 1987, p. 67.
26. ALS, 1995, p. 109.
27. Makin, 1970, p. 99.
28. Cited in Makin, 1970, p. 107.
29. ALS, 1995, p. 110.
30. Child Welfare Department File, 'Dinah, Robert Samuel'.
31. Morgan (ed.), 2002, p. 77.
32. Child Welfare Department File, 'Dinah, Robert Samuel'.
33. ALS, 1995, 1996.
34. Senate Community Affairs Reference Committee, 2004.
35. Riley, 1991, p. 39.
36. Winnicott, 1957, 1964.
37. State Library of Western Australia, 1984.

3 Life at the Margins

1. See Rob's account, 'Malcolm', ALS, 1995, p. 115.
2. ABC, 1996.
3. Ibid.
4. Beresford and Omaji, 1998.
5. Lange, 1981, p. 185.
6. *West Australian*, 28 July 1970.
7. *West Australian*, 17 July 1970.
8. *Weekend News*, 13 May 1967.
9. *West Australian*, 28 July 1970.
10. *West Australian*, 9 May 1967.
11. *West Australian*, 13 May 1967.
12. *West Australian*, 19 August 1967.
13. Ibid.
14. *West Australian*, 23 May 1967.
15. *West Australian*, 9 May 1967.
16. *West Australian*, 9 May 1967.
17. *West Australian*, 17 July 1970.
18. *West Australian*, 8 May 1967.
19. Ibid.
20. Riley, 1987, p. 67.
21. *Daily News*, 8 June.
22. Riley, 1987.
23. Riley, 1987, p. 67.
24. Riley, 1991, p 39.

25. Leaming, 1986, p. 89.
26. Riley, 1991, p. 39.
27. Leaming, 1986, p. 89.
28. Ibid.
29. Rob Riley Memorial Service, 1996.
30. *Daily News*, 8 June 1984.
31. Leaming, 1986, p. 97.
32. Riley, 1987, p. 67.
33. Rob Riley Memorial Service, 1996.
34. Ibid.
35. Ibid.
36. Ibid.
37. Ibid.
38. Ibid.
39. Department of Native Welfare ACC 1667 193/67.
40. Riley, 1987, p. 67.
41. Riley, 1987, p. 66.
42. Kidd, 1967, p. 70.
43. Makin, 1970.
44. Kidd, 1967, p. 26.
45. Kidd, 1967.
46. Ibid, p. 27.
47. Ibid, p. 2.
48. Makin, 1970, p. 123.
49. Makin, 1970, p. 218.
50. McKeich, 1969, p. 23.
51. ALS, 1995, p. 115.
52. Ibid.
53. ABC, 'Telling His Story', *Four Corners*, 15 July 1996.
54. Riley, 1987, p. 71.
55. McNally, 2003.
56. Riley, 1987, p. 71

4 Apprenticeship

1. Deloria, 1985, p. 80.
2. Howard, 1981.
3. Report of the Special Committee on Native Affairs (1958), p. 20.
4. House of Representatives, 1976, p. 85.
5. Howard, 1981.
6. Rob Riley personal papers.
7. See House of Representatives Standing Committee on Aboriginal Affairs, 1980.
8. Royal Commission into Aboriginal Affairs, 1974.

9. ALS WA (1984), unpublished.
10. Ibid.
11. Royal Commission, 1974, p. 371.
12. Riley, 1987, p. 71.
13. Cited on WAAMAA Radio, 'Tribute to Rob Riley', 24 June 1996.
14. *West Australian*, 19 August 1975.
15. Laverton Royal Commission, 1975–76.
16. *West Australian*, 19 August 1975.
17. Laverton Royal Commission, 1975–76, pp. vi–vii.
18. Williams, 1980.
19. Ibid.
20. Beresford et al., 2001.
21. *West Australian*, 19 December 1981.
22. Reid and Oliver, 1982.
23. *West Australian*, 19 December 1981.
24. Black and Peachment, 1982.
25. *Daily News*, 28 March 1980.
26. *West Australian*, 29 March 1980.
27. Annual Report of the Commissioner of Police, 1978, p. 7.
28. Ibid.
29. Cited in ABC, 'Telling His Story', *Four Corners*, 15 July 1996.
30. *West Australian*, 10 November 1977.
31. *Daily News*, 9 November 1977.
32. Ibid.
33. Kay, 1978, p. 44.
34. Ibid., p. 47.
35. State Archives, Aboriginal Legal Service of Western Australia, Mn 2024, Acc 5622A.
36. Ibid.
37. *West Australian*, 5 June 1981.
38. PD, Vol. 224, 1979, p. 1899.
39. *West Australian*, 3 May 1980.
40. Ibid.
41. *West Australian*, 5 June 1981.
42. *West Australian*, 3 May 1980.
43. Ibid.
44. Committee of Inquiry into the Rate of Imprisonment, 1981, p. 255.
45. Ibid., pp. 13–14, 38.

5 Noonkanbah

1. Hutchinson, 2004.
2. The account of the Noonkanbah dispute is necessarily selective in terms of events and the involvement of the main players. My concern has been to account for the involvement of the ALS and its staff. While this account is based on some new research, a full examination of the dispute is available in Hawke and Gallagher, 1989; Vincent, 1983; and Kolig, 1987.
3. *Sunday Times*, 17 August 1980.
4. Bos, 1990.
5. PD, Vol. 28, 1980, p. 247.
6. Hawke and Gallagher, 1989; Pedersen, 1995.
7. *West Australian*, 25 August 1980.
8. *West Australian*, 25 August 1980, p. 76.
9. Vincent, 1983, p. 327.
10. *West Australian*, 25 August 1980.
11. Vincent, 1983, p. 327.
12. PD, Vol. 172, 1972, p. 2970.
13. Ibid.
14. Hawke and Gallagher, p. 21.
15. Hawke and Doyle, 1980, p. 9.
16. *Daily News*, 28 March 1980.
17. ALS, 1979.
18. Hawke and Gallagher, 1989, p. 106.
19. PD, Vol. 28, 1980, p. 397.
20. Hawke and Doyle, 1980.
21. Seaman, 1984b, pp. 140–41.
22. *West Australian*, 20 August 1980.
23. *Daily News*, 28 March 1980.
24. Ibid.
25. Ibid.
26. Hawke and Gallagher, 1989, p. 222.
27. *Sunday Times*, 16 March 1980, p. 3.
28. *West Australian*, 2 July, 1980, p. 5.
29. PD, Vol. 28, 1980, p. 391.
30. Seaman, 1984b, p. 144.
31. *West Australian*, 10 July 1980, p. 9.
32. Ritter, 2002.
33. *West Australian*, 9 August 1980.
34. *West Australian*, 29 May 1980, p. 11.
35. *West Australian*, 7 August 1980, p. 5.
36. *West Australian*, 11 August 1980.
37. *West Australian*, 12 August 1980.
38. *West Australian*, 13 August 1980, p. 9.

39. This account was given in an interview with Ian Horrocks.
40. *West Australian*, 13 August 1980.
41. Ibid.
42. *West Australian*, 13 August 1980.
43. *West Australian*, 15 August, p. 9.
44. *West Australian*, 19 December 1981.
45. Ibid.
46. *West Australian*, 14 August 1980.

6 A Bigger Stage

1. Senate Select Committee on Aboriginal and Torres Strait Islander People, 1976, p. 262.
2. Senate Select Committee, 1976, p. 262.
3. NAC Minutes, Full Congress Meeting, Townsville, March 1975, p. 4.
4. Harris, 1979.
5. Senate Select Committee, 1976, pp. 269–70.
6. Harris, 1979, p. 57.
7. Department of Aboriginal Affairs, 1976.
8. 'Aborigines will Appeal to UN' (1976), p. 16.
9. Cited in Vincent, 1983, p. 337.
10. Hagan, 1981, p. 38.
11. Hagan, 1981.
12. *Aboriginal News*, Vol. 3, No. 4, May 1978.
13. Harris, 1979, p. 58.
14. Toohey, 1984, p. 56.
15. *West Australian*, 6 August 1980.
16. Office of the Commissioner for Community Relations, 1981.
17. Ibid., p. 26.
18. Ibid, p. 10.
19. *West Australian*, 24 October 1984.
20. *West Australian*, 24 September 1988.
21. *West Australian*, 19 December 1981.
22. Cited in Harris, 1979, p. 13.
23. Senate Standing Committee, 1983, p. 7.
24. *NAC Newsletter*, Vol. 1 No. 5, 1981, p. 11.
25. *NAC Newsletter*, September 1983, p. 13.
26. *NAC Newsletter*, Vol. 3 No. 1, June 1981, p. 6.
27. *Land Rights News*, Jan./Feb. 1982.
28. Senate Standing Committee, 1983, p. 17.
29. Ibid, pp. 135, 160.
30. *West Australian*, 18 November 1982.
31. *West Australian*, 6 January 1983.
32. Interview Peter O'Brien.

33. *NAC Newsletter*, May 1982, p. 24.
34. *NAC Newsletter*, Vol. 1, No. 5, 1981, p. 14.
35. *NAC Newsletter*, September 1983.
36. *West Australian*, 4 January 1983.
37. Riley, 1983b, p. 1010.
38. Riley, 1983a.
39. *West Australian*, 11 August 1980.
40. Libby, 1989.
41. *West Australian*, 21 December 1982.
42. *West Australian*, 23 February 1983.
43. Minutes, meeting with Minister, Canberra, 17 March 1983, p. 24, Rob Riley personal papers.
44. Minutes, joint meeting NAC/FLC, 5 October 1984, p. 5. Rob Riley personal papers.
45. Minutes of Steering Committee Meeting, 5 October 1984, Rob Riley personal papers.
46. *West Australian*, 18 June 1983.
47. PD, House of Representatives, 1984, p. 2697.
48. Minutes, meeting with Minister, 7 March 1983, Canberra, p. 54. Rob Riley personal papers.
49. Cited ABC radio, 27 May 1984.
50. Purdy, 1992, p. 2.
51. McGlade and Purdy, 2001.
52. *West Australian*, 14 October 1983.
53. *Weekend News*, 24 September 1984.
54. Weaver, 1983.
55. Undated letter from Roy Nichols to Clyde Holding, Rob Riley personal papers.
56. NAC, 1984a.
57. NAC, 1984a, p. 15.
58. Ibid.
59. Undated NAC circular, issued by Chairman Lyall Munro, Rob Riley personal papers.
60. *Australian*, 29 December 1983.
61. *Australian*, 30 December 1983.
62. Ibid.
63. NAC WA, 1984.
64. *West Australian*, 2 January 1984.
65. Australian Press Council, 1984.
66. *Australian*, 29 December 1983.
67. Rob Riley personal papers.
68. PD House of Representatives, 1983, p. 3485.
69. NAC Media Release, 28 November 1983, Rob Riley personal papers.
70. Letter dated 7 December 1983, Rob Riley personal papers.

71. *Sunday Times*, 27 November 1980.
72. *Sunday Times*, 12 August 1984.
73. Letter dated 12 December 1983, Rob Riley personal papers.
74. Press release dated 2 December 1983, Rob Riley personal papers.
75. Letter dated 7 December 1983, Rob Riley personal papers.
76. Letter dated 12 December 1983, Rob Riley personal papers.
77. Interview Paul Seaman.
78. Seaman, 1984a, p. 59.
79. Seaman, 1984a, pp. 48, 49.
80. *West Australian*, 25 January 1984.
81. Ibid.
82. Cited in Libby, 1984, pp. 59–60.
83. NAC meeting, 13 June 1984, Rob Riley personal papers.
84. *West Australian*, 13 March 1984.
85. *West Australian*, 14 March 1984.
86. Letter dated 25 January 1985, Rob Riley personal papers.
87. *Bulletin*, 31 January 1984; see also 28 February 1984.
88. See Rowse, 2000.
89. Coombs, p. 11.
90. Cited in Rowse, 2000, p. 190.
91. Coombs, p. 82.
92. Undated NAC circular, issued by Chairman Lyall Munro. Rob Riley personal papers.
93. PD, House of Representatives, 1984, p. 2129.
94. *Sydney Morning Herald*, 29 May 1984
95. PD, House of Representatives, 1984, p. 2677.
96. Sears et al., 2004.
97. *Australian*, 29 May 1984.
98. *Sydney Morning Herald*, 29 May 1984.
99. Minutes of 5 October 1984 meeting, NAC/FLC. Rob Riley personal papers.

7 Betrayal

1. *Daily News*, 11 October 1984.
2. See Markus and Ricklefs, 1985.
3. Stannage, 1985.
4. *Bulletin*, 2 October 1984.
5. Rowley, 1986, p. 44.
6. Ibid.
7. *West Australian*, 5 June 1984.
8. *Age*, 29 May 1984.
9. PD, House of Representaives, 1984, p. 2682.
10. Purdy, 1992.

11. Graham, 1989, p. 140.
12. ABC, 24 May 1984.
13. *West Australian*, 9 June 1984.
14. Ibid.
15. *Daily News*, 9 June 1984.
16. *West Australian*, 9 June 1984.
17. *Daily News*, 6 June 1984.
18. *West Australian*, 3 April 1985.
19. *West Australian*, 7 June 1984.
20. *West Australian*, 11 June 1984, p. 53.
21. *West Australian*, 9 June 1984.
22. Riley, 1984b.
23. Cited on WAAMAA Radio, 'Tribute to Rob Riley', 24 June 1996.
24. *West Australian*, 7, 8, 10 August 1984.
25. *West Australian*, 7 August 1984.
26. *West Australian*, 8 August 1984.
27. *West Australian*, 9 August 1984.
28. *Bulletin*, 11 September 1984, p. 38.
29. *Land Rights News*, September 1985.
30. *Direct Action*, 9 April 1986.
31. *West Australian*, 18 September 1984.
32. Ibid.
33. Seaman, 1984b, p. 15.
34. Ibid., p. 69.
35. Ibid., p. 144.
36. Ibid., p. 162.
37. Ibid., p. 166.
38. Ibid., p. 23.
39. Ibid., p. 10.
40. Riley, 1984a.
41. *Age*, 19 August 1984.
42. Ibid.
43. Ibid.
44. Minutes of Meeting, Joint NAC and Land Councils with the Minister for Aboriginal Affairs, 5 October 1984, Rob Riley personal papers.
45. *Bulletin*, October 1984, p. 39.
46. *Age*, 26 September 1984.
47. *West Australian*, 28 September, p. 1.
48. ABC, National Press Club speech, 9 October 1984.
49. Ibid.
50. Ibid.
51. Gawenda, 1984.
52. Gawenda, 1984.
53. *West Australian*, 14 October 1984.

54. ANOP, 1985, p. 27.
55. Rob Riley personal papers.
56. *National Times*, 18–24 April 1986.
57. *Sydney Morning Herald*, 30 July 1984.
58. *Sydney Morning Herald*, 20 June 1984.
59. *Australian*, 25 January 1985.
60. *Sydney Morning Herald*, 20 June 1984.
61. Telex, 30 January 1985, Rob Riley personal papers.
62. NAC media release, 13 February 1985, Rob Riley personal papers.
63. *Bulletin*, 12 March 1985.
64. Telex, 12 March 1985, Rob Riley personal papers.
65. Letter, 15 March 1985, Rob Riley personal papers.
66. Letter, 25 March 1985, Rob Riley personal papers.
67. Document prepared for court hearing on NAC, Rob Riley personal papers.
68. *Canberra Times*, 21 May 1985.
69. *Australian*, 14 May 1985.
70. Brennan, 1985.
71. *Bulletin*, 12 March 1985.
72. Letter, 5 December 1984, Rob Riley personal papers.
73. Letter, 6 December 1984, Rob Riley personal papers.
74. Letter, 5 December 1984, Rob Riley personal papers.
75. *West Australian*, 15 March 1985.
76. *Age*, 4 October 1984.
77. *Direct Action*, 9 April 1986.
78. Ibid.
79. ABC, 30 July 1984.
80. ABC, 21 February 1985.
81. ABC, National Press Club, 9 October 1985.
82. *Direct Action*, 9 April 1986.

8 Enemies Within

1. *Western Mail*, 6 July 1985.
2. Document prepared for legal case over NAC, Rob Riley personal papers.
3. *West Australian*, 17 August 1984.
4. ABC *Pressure Point*, 18 August 1984.
5. Yu, 1985.
6. Minutes, NAC Executive Meeting, 25 July 1984, Rob Riley personal papers.
7. *Bulletin*, 11 September 1984.
8. Yu, 1985.
9. Letter, 24 September 1984, Rob Riley personal papers.
10. *West Australian*, 2 March 1985.

11. Interviews with Michael Mansell, Heather Skullthorpe, Les Malezer, Peter Yu.
12. Letter, 26 February 1985.
13. *West Australian*, 18 May 1985.
14. Telex dated 21 February 1985, Rob Riley personal papers.
15. *West Australian*, 18 May 1985.
16. Minutes, NAC Executive Meeting, 25 July 1984, Rob Riley personal papers.
17. *West Australian*, 4 April 1985.
18. Rob Riley personal papers.
19. Yu, 1985.
20. *Western Mail*, 6 July 1985.
21. Rob Riley personal papers.
22. Yu, 1985.
23. Transcript NAC Meeting, 17 May 1984, Rob Riley personal papers.
24. *West Australian*, 18 May 1985.
25. Ibid.
26. *Western Mail*, 6 July 1985.
27. Letter dated 4 November 1985; used with the permission of Jill Abdullah.

9 At the Cutting Edge

1. Rob Riley personal papers.
2. Riley, 1986.
3. *Australian*, 7 April 1987.
4. Ibid.
5. *West Australian*, 21 January 1987.
6. *West Australian*, 25 September.
7. PD, House of Representatives, Vol. 166, 1989, p. 1366.
8. Senate Select Committee, 1989.
9. WAAMAA Radio, 'Tribute to Rob Riley', 24 June 1996.
10. *West Australian*, 31 October 1987.
11. Ibid.
12. *West Australian*, 7 October 1987.
13. Senate Select Committee, 1989.
14. *Weekend Australian*, 6–7 February 1988.
15. Ibid.
16. Ibid.
17. *West Australian*, 14 April 1988.
18. PD, House of Representative, Vol. 162, p. 73.
19. *Land Rights News*, July 1988.
20. *Australian*, 3 September 1987.
21. *West Australian*, 14 June 1988.
22. *Age*, 18 February 1989.

23. *Australian*, 29 June 1988.
24. For an account of the riot see *Daily News*, 26, 27 July 1988.
25. *Daily News*, 27 July 1988.
26. Senate Select Committee, Dissenting Report, 1989, p. 5.
27. Wilson, 1998.
28. PD, House of Representatives, Vol. 166, 1989, p. 2718.
29. PD, House of Representatives, Vol. 166, p. 1339.
30. Ibid., p. 1332.
31. PD, Senate, 1989, Vol. 135, p. 243.
32. Ibid., p. 335.
33. Ivanitz and McPhail, 2003.
34. Cited in Brennan, 1985, p. 5.
35. Riley, 1995.
36. Dodson, 1991, Vol. 1, p. 57.
37. Dodson, 1991, Vol. 1, p. 55.
38. Dodson, 1991, Vol. 1, p. 43.

10 War on All Fronts

1. Task Force Aboriginal Social Justice, 1994.
2. Job application dated 7 May 1990, Rob Riley personal papers.
3. *Sunday Times*, 2 January 1994.
4. Transcript, HREOC Inquiry into Racist Violence, 1991.
5. Graham, 1989.
6. ALS, 1992–93.
7. ALS, 1990–91, pp. 26–7.
8. ALS, 1991, p. 14.
9. Royal Commission into Aboriginal Deaths in Custody.
10. Riley, 1991.
11. Beresford and Partington, 2003.
12. *Sunday Times*, 13 July 1980.
13. *Daily News*, 13 April 1987.
14. Ibid.
15. Mathews, 1991.
16. *Australian*, 28 February 1990.
17. Cited in Anderson, 1997.
18. Letter dated 19 April 1990, Rob Riley personal papers.
19. Transcript of Evidence, Royal Commission into Aboriginal Deaths in Custody, 30 May 1990.
20. Press release dated 11 July 1990, Rob Riley personal papers.
21. Ibid.
22. Transcript, 12 July 1990.
23. *West Australian*, 2 April 1991.
24. *West Australian*, 11 April 1991.

25. Cited in Patterson and Roth, 2004, p. 55.
26. *West Australian*, 8 May 1991.
27. *Sunday Times*, 5 May 1991.
28. *West Australian*, 11 May 1991.
29. *West Australian*, 9 May 1991.
30. Press release dated 15 May 1991.
31. *West Australian*, 8 June 1991.
32. *West Australian*, 12 June 1984.
33. *West Australian*, 26 June 1991.
34. *West Australian*, 5 August 1991.
35. *West Australian*, 7 August 1991, 8 August 1991.
36. *West Australian*, 2 September 1991.
37. Open letter dated 9 September 1991.
38. *West Australian*, 7 August 1991.
39. *Daily Commercial News*, 22 October 1991.
40. *West Australian*, 23 August 1991.
41. *West Australian*, 21 August 1991.
42. Ibid.
43. Ibid.
44. Select Committee on Youth Affairs (WA), 1992.
45. Ibid., p. 9.
46. Ibid., p. 47.
47. *Bulletin*, 29 October 1991.
48. ALS 1990–91, p. 24.
49. Equal Opportunity Commission, 1990.
50. Transcript, Radio 6WF, 8 August 1990.
51. Laurie, 1991.
52. *West Australian*, 10 September 1991.
53. *West Australian*, 30 January 1992, 8 February 1992.
54. Riley, 1992.
55. *West Australian*, 6 February 1992.
56. Eggleston, 2002.
57. Letter dated 3 August 1992.
58. *West Australian*, 18 June 1992.
59. *West Australian*, 17 June 1992.
60. *West Australian*, 9 November 1992.
61. Letter undated but written just after his marriage break-up. Letter used with the permission of Maxine Chi.
62. Rob Riley personal papers.

11 Mounting Despair

1. See McNally, 2003, for a description of post-traumatic shock disorder.
2. *West Australian*, 15 January 1993.

3. Ibid.
4. *West Australian*, 27 March 1993.
5. *West Australian*, 2 April 1993.
6. *West Australian*, 25 March 1993.
7. Letter dated 7 April 1993, Rob Riley personal papers.
8. *West Australian*, 28 April 1993.
9. Ibid.
10. Mick Dodson, Aboriginal Social Justice Commissioner; Lois O'Donoghue, George Mye, and Gerhardt Pearson from ATSIC; Jean George and Noel Pearson from the Cape York Land Council; Patrick Dodson and Wenten Rubuntja from the Council for Aboriginal Reconciliation; Manul Ritchie and Danny Chapman from the NSW Aboriginal Land Council; Galarrwuy Yunupingu and John Ah Kit from the Northern Land Council; Kunmanara Breadan and David Ross from the Central Land Council; John Watson and Peter Yu from the Kimberley Land Council; Tauto Sansbury and Esther Williams from the South Australia Aboriginal Legal Service; Getano Lui from the Torres Strait Island Coordinating Council; and Rob Riley and Ted Wilkes from the West Australia ALS.
11. Mabo Ministerial Meeting, 1993, Rob Riley personal papers.
12. Tickner, 2001, p. 114.
13. Mabo Ministerial Meeting, 27 April 1993, Rob Riley personal papers.
14. ALS, Executive Meeting, 15–18 June 1993, Executive Officer's Report, Rob Riley personal papers.
15. *West Australian*, 21 June 1993.
16. *West Australian*, 13 May 1993
17. Ibid.
18. *West Australian*, 6 May 1993
19. *West Australian*, 8 May 1993.
20. *West Australian*, 21 June, 14 July 1993.
21. *West Australian*, 14 July 1993.
22. *West Australian*, 21 June 1993.
23. ABC Radio, 'Background Briefing', 13 July 1993.
24. *Australian*, 27 May 1993.
25. *West Australian*, 7 June 1993.
26. ABC Radio 'Background Briefing', 13 July 1993.
27. *West Australian*, 13 July 1993.
28. *West Australian*, 29 May 1993.
29. *West Australian*, 3 June 1993.
30. See Ackermann and DeRubeis, 1991, and Benatell, 2004.
31. Tickner 2001, p. 123.
32. *West Australian*, 2 June 1993.
33. *West Australian*, 23 August 1993.
34. Bennett, 1999, p. 167.
35. *West Australian*, 20 October 1993.

36. Ibid.
37. *West Australian*, 5 November 1993.
38. *West Australian*, 3 November 1993.
39. *West Australian*, 5 November 1993.
40. *West Australian*, 17 March 1995.
41. *West Australian*, 6 August 1993.
42. *Sunday Times*, 2 January 1994.
43. *West Australian*, 25 November 1993.
44. WAAMAA Radio, 'Tribute to Rob Riley', 24 June 1996.
45. *West Australian*, 18 June 1994.
46. *West Australian*, 16 February 1994.
47. ALS Executive Meeting, December 13–15, 1994. Executive Officer's Report, Rob Riley personal papers.
48. ALS, 1994, p. 3.
49. Aboriginal Justice Council, 1995, p. 78.
50. ALS Discussion Paper, undated, 'Replacement of Meal Allowance Scheme', Rob Riley personal papers.
51. ALS, 1994, p. 48.
52. Aboriginal Justice Council, 1995, p. 41.
53. *West Australian*, 'Big Weekend', 11 April 1992.
54. Riley, 1995.
55. Buti, 1999.
56. *West Australian*, 4 October 1994.
57. *West Australian*, 12 April 1995.
58. ALS Executive Meeting December 1994, Executive Officer's Report, Rob Riley personal papers.
59. *West Australian*, 27 December 1994.
60. *West Australian*, 7 September 1994.
61. Cited in Morgan, 2002, p. 80.
62. Cited in Mayman, 1996.
63. Letter dated 11 September 1995, Rob Riley personal papers.
64. *West Australian*, 8 August 1995.
65. Ibid.
66. *West Australian*, 2 August 1995.
67. *West Australian*, 3 August 1995.
68. Mayman, 1995.
69. 'Personal Explanation of the Events of July 12/13 1995', Rob Riley personal papers.
70. Rob's psychiatric report was offered to this project by his family.
71. Ulman and Brothers, 1988
72. Freud, 1981.
73. Hartley and McKee (eds), 1996.
74. Mayman, 1996.
75. *Sunday Times*, 28 April 1995.

Legacy

1. Cited in Keeffe, 2003.
2. International Federation of Chemical, Energy, Mine and General Workers' Unions, 1997.
3. Priest, 2005.
4. See Adams, 1995, Jasper, 1997.
5. *Weekend Australian* Magazine, 19 January 2004.
6. *West Australian*, 10 November 1986.
7. *West Australian*, 'Big Weekend', 11 April 1984.
8. Mansell, 2003.
9. Kauffman, 2003.

Bibliography

Archival Sources

ROB RILEY PERSONAL PAPERS

Aboriginal Legal Service WA, Executive Committee meeting, Executive Officer's reports, 1992–95. Rob Riley personal papers.
Brennan, F. (1985), 'Western Australian Draft Aboriginal Bill as at February 1985', Rob Riley personal papers.
Mabo Ministerial Meeting minutes, 27 April 1993, Rob Riley personal papers.
National Aboriginal Conference, Executive minutes, 1983–84, Rob Riley personal papers.
National Aboriginal Conference WA Branch (1984), 'WA Branch of the National Aboriginal Conference Submission to the Aboriginal Land Inquiry', unpublished, Rob Riley personal papers.
Royal Commission into Aboriginal Deaths in Custody (1990), Rob Riley transcript of evidence, 30 May, Rob Riley personal papers.

RILEY AND DINAH FAMILY PAPERS

Child Welfare Department File, 'Dinah, Robert Samuel'. Used with permission of the Riley family.
Department of Native Affairs file, 'Anna Dinah, née Miller'. Used with the permission of Sam Dinah.
Riley, V. (n.d.) 'Memories of the Past', unpublished.
Rob Riley Memorial, 1996. In possession of the Riley family.

WESTERN AUSTRALIAN STATE ARCHIVES

Aboriginal Legal Service of Western Australia Inc. MN2024 Acc 5622A/4, 5645A.
Department of Native Welfare, ACC 1667 193 1967 Native Matters Pingelly Report on visit to Pingelly by Assistant Community Liaison Officer.
Sister Kate's Children's Home MN957, 3179A/366.

Newspapers/Journals

The Age
The Australian
The Bulletin
Canberra Times
The Daily News
Direct Action
Land Rights News
National Aboriginal Conference, Newsletter, 1981–85.
The National Times
Pastoralists and Graziers Association of W.A. Newsletter, 1984.
The Sunday Times
The Sydney Morning Herald
The West Australian
Western Mail

Official Documents and Reports

Aboriginal Justice Council (1995), *Getting Stronger on Justice, 1995 Monitoring Report of the Justice Council on the Implementation of the Recommendations of the Royal Commission into Aboriginal Deaths in Custody*, Aboriginal Justice Council, Perth.
Aboriginal Legal Service WA (1979), Submission to Inquiry into the Rate of Imprisonment, State Government Printer, Perth.
Aboriginal Legal Service WA (1984), 'The Establishment and Development of the Service', unpublished.
Aboriginal Legal Service WA (1995), *Telling Our Story*, Aboriginal Legal Service of Western Australia, Perth.
Aboriginal Legal Service WA (1996), *After the Removal:, A Submission... to the National Inquiry into Separation of Aboriginal and Torres Strait Islander Children from their Families*, Aboriginal Legal Service of Western Australia, Perth. Prepared by Toni Buti.
Aboriginal Legal Service WA (n.d.), 'Replacement of Meal Allowance Scheme', discussion paper, Rob Riley personal papers.
Aboriginal Legal Service WA (1978–96), *Annual Reports*.

Australian National Opinion Polls (ANOP) (1985), 'Land Rights: Winning Middle Australia, An Attitude and Communications Research Study', ANOP Market Research, Crow's Nest (unpublished).

Australian Press Council (1984), Adjudication No. 198. Adjudicated 28 June 1984.

Commissioner of Native Affairs, *Annual Reports*, 1947–1953, Votes and Proceedings Legislative Assembly, Western Australian Parliament.

Commissioner of Police (1978), *Annual Report*, Votes and Proceedings Legislative Assembly, Western Australian Parliament.

Committee of Inquiry into the Rate of Imprisonment (1981), *Report*, State Government Printer, Perth.

Coombs, H. C. (1984), *The Role of the National Aboriginal Conference*, Australian Government Publishing Service, Canberra.

Court, C. (1974), Liberal Policy 1974–77, Liberal Party WA Division, Perth.

Department of Aboriginal Affairs (1976), *The Role of the National Aboriginal Consultative Committee*, Australian Government Publishing Service, Canberra.

Department for Community Services (1990), 'Aboriginal Participation Project Consultation', unpublished.

Department of Foreign Affairs and Trade (2005), 'Indigenous Communities and the Mining Industry', available on-line.

Dodson, P. (1991), *Royal Commission into Aboriginal Deaths in Custody. Regional Report of Inquiry into Underlying Issues in Western Australia, Vols 1&2*, Australian Government Printing Service, Canberra.

Equal Opportunity Commission (1990), *Discrimination in Government Policies and Practices, Review of Police Practices, Main Report*, Equal Opportunity Commission, Perth.

Greens WA (1993), 'Background Paper. The Greens (WA)'s Current Position on the Native Title Bill 1993', unpublished.

House of Representatives Standing Committee on Aboriginal Affairs (1975), *Second Report*, Australian Government Publishing Service, Canberra.

House of Representatives Standing Committee on Aboriginal Affairs (1980), *Aboriginal Legal Aid*, Australian Government Publishing Service, Canberra.

Human Rights and Equal Opportunity Commission (1991), Inquiry into Racist Violence, transcript of Rob Riley's evidence, obtained from the Commission.

Initial Conference of Commonwealth and State Aboriginal Authorities (1937), *Aboriginal Welfare*, Commonwealth Government Printer.

Kay, E. A. (1978), *Electoral Act Inquiry of 1978*, State Government Printer, Perth.

Laverton Royal Commission (1975–76), *Report*, State Government Printer, Perth.

National Aboriginal Conference (1975), minutes of Field Congress Meeting 19–26 March, Lowth's Hotel, Queensland, May O'Brien Collection, Edith Cowan University.

National Aboriginal Conference (1979), 'Makarrata', available on-line at www.aiatsis.gov.au.

National Aboriginal Conference (1984a), *National Aboriginal Land Rights. Legislation*, Discussion Paper, National Aboriginal Conference, Canberra.

National Aboriginal Conference (1984b), 'National Aboriginal Conference Submission to the Senate Standing Committee on Science, Technology and the Environment. Land Use Inquiry', Rob Riley personal papers.

Office of the Commissioner for Community Relations (1981), *Discrimination Against Aborigines in Western Australia*, Paper No. 18, Australian Government Publishing Service, Canberra.

PDLA (Parliamentary Debates: Legislative Assembly), Western Australia; Commonwealth House of Representatives; Senate, 1979–1993.

Report of the Special Committee on Native Affairs (1958), Votes and Proceedings Vol. 3.

Royal Commission into Aboriginal Affairs (1974), Report, State Government Printer, Perth.

Royal Commission into Aboriginal Deaths in Custody (1991), 'John Peter Pat — John Pat and his Family', Reconciliation and Social Justice Library, available at www.aistlii.edu.au/au/special/rsjilibrary/rciadic/individualism/brm_jpp.

Seaman, P (1984a), *Aboriginal Land Inquiry Discussion Paper*, State Government Printer, Perth.

Seaman, P. (1984b), *The Aboriginal Land Inquiry*, State Government Printer, Perth.

Select Committee on Youth Affairs (1992), *Youth and the Law Discussion Paper No. 3*, Legislative Assembly of Western Australia, Perth.

Senate Select Committee on Aborigines and Torres Strait Islanders (1976), *The Environmental Conditions of Aborigines and Torres Strait Islanders and the Preservation of their Sacred Sites*, Australian Government Publishing Service, Perth.

Senate Select Committee (1989), *Administration of Aboriginal Affairs*, Australian Government Publishing Service, Canberra (includes dissenting report).

Senate Standing Committee on Constitutional and Legal Affairs (1983), *Two Hundred Years Later ... Report on the feasibility of a compact or 'Makarrata' between the Commonwealth and Aboriginal People*, Australian Government Printing Service, Canberra.

Senate Standing Committee on Science, Technology and The Environment (1984), Hearings, 3 October 1984, Hansard.

Special Cabinet Committee on Aboriginal/Police Relations (1984), 'Report to the Minister For Police The Hon. Jeff Carr, M.L.A.', unpublished.

Special Committee on Native Matters (1958), Legislative Assembly of Western Australia, Perth.

Stakeholder's Report (1997), *Rio Tinto Tainted Titan*, available at www.cfmeu.asn.au/mining-energy/policy/rio.

Task Force on Aboriginal Social Justice (1994), *Report of the Task Force*, Government of Western Australia, Perth.

Toohey, Mr Justice (1984), *Seven Years On: Report of Mr Justice Toohey to the Minister for Aboriginal Affairs on the 1976 Aboriginal Land Rights (Northern Territory), and Related Matters*, Australian Government Publishing Service, Perth.

Broadcast Material

Australian Broadcasting Corporation (ABC) (1996), *Telling His Story*, Four Corners.
Australian Broadcasting Corporation (ABC), transcript of radio interviews 1984–1995. Held in AIATSIS Library.
Shaw, A. (Producer) (1996), *Tribute to Rob Riley*, WAAMA Radio, Broadcast, 24 June.

Books/Articles/Theses

'Aborigines will Appeal to UN' (1976), *Identity*, Vol. 2, No 8, April, p. 17.
Ackermann, R. and R. DeRubeis (1991), 'Is Depressive Realism Real?', *Clinical Psychology Review*, Vol. 11, pp. 565–84.
Adams, D. (1995), *Psychology for Peace Activists*, New Haven, Advocate Press (also available at www.culture-of-peace.info/ppa/title-page.).
Anderson, M. (1997), 'The Ratbags of Radio', *West Australian Big Weekend*, 22 November.
Bentall, R. (2004), *Madness Explained: Psychosis and Human Nature*, London, Penguin.
Beresford, Q., and P. Omaji (1998), *Our State of Mind: Racial Planning and the Stolen Generations*, Fremantle Arts Centre Press, Fremantle.
Beresford, Q., and P. Omaji (1996), *Rites of Passage: Aboriginal Youth, Crime and Justice*, Fremantle Arts Centre Press, Fremantle.
Beresford, Q., H. Bekle, H. Phillips, and J. Mulcock (2002), *The Salinity Crisis: Landscapes, Communities and Politics*, University of Western Australia Press, Nedlands.
Beresford, Q. and G. Partington (eds.) (2003), *Reform and Resistance in Aboriginal Education: The Australian Experience*, University of Western Australia Press, Nedlands.
Black, D. W. and A. Peachment (1982), *Values and Votes: The 1980 Western Australian Election*, Western Australian Institute of Technology, Perth.
Bos, J. (1980), 'Background to Noonkanbah', *Nungalinya Occasional Bulletin*, No. 11, Casuarina, Nungalinya College.
Buti, T. (1999), 'The National Inquiry', *James Cook Law Review*, Vol. 6.
Court, Sir C. (1980), 'Premier's Views on Noonkanbah', *The West Australian*, 8 August.
Deloria, V. (1985), *Behind the Trail of Broken Treaties: An Indian Declaration of Independence*, University of Texas Press, Austin.
Eggleston, P. (2002), 'Gaining Aboriginal Community Support for a New Mine: Developing and Making a Contribution to Sustainable Development', *Energy & Resources Law 2002 Conference*, Edinburgh, Scotland. Available on-line at www.ccmm.com/give_documents/IBAConfPaper.pdf
Freud, S. (1981), 'Mourning and Melancholia' in J. Strachey (ed.), *The Standard Edition of the Complete Works of Sigmund Freud*, London.
Gawenda, M. (1984), 'The Oracle', *The Age*, 30 October.

Graham, R. (1989), *Dying Inside*, Allen & Unwin, St Leonards.
Haebich, A. (1982), 'On the inside: Moore River Settlement in the 1930s', in B. Gammage and A. Marcus, *All That Dirt: Australia 1938: An Australian Monograph*, Australian National University, Canberra.
Hagan, J. (1981), 'The NAC: its history, its development, its performance', *Identity*, Vol. 4, No 5, October 1981, pp. 35–6.
Harris, S. (1979), *'It's Coming Yet...': An Aboriginal Treaty within Australia between Australians*, The Aboriginal Treaty Committee, Canberra.
Hartley, J. and A. McKee (1996), *Telling Both Stories: Indigenous Australia and the Media*, Arts Enterprise, Edith Cowan University, Perth.
Hasluck, P. (1988), *Shades of Darkness: Aboriginal Affairs 1925–65*, Melbourne University Press, Carlton.
Hawke, S. and M. Doyle (1980), 'Noonkanbah', *Identity*, Vol. 4 No 1.
Hawke, S. and M. Gallagher (1989), *Noonkanbah: Whose Land, Whose Law*, Fremantle Arts Centre Press, Fremantle.
Homberger, E. and J. Charmley (eds) (1988), *The Troubled Art of Biography*, MacMillan, Basingstoke, UK.
Howard, M. (1981), *Aboriginal Politics in South-Western Australia*, University of Western Australia Press, Nedlands.
Hutchinson, D. (2004), 'Obituary: Frank Ellis Gare', *The Australian*, 23 January.
Ivanitz, M. and K. McPhail (2003), *ATSIC: Autonomy or Accountability?*, Ashgate, Burlington.
Jacobs, P. (1986), '"Science" and veiled assumptions: miscegenation in W.A. 1930–37'. *Australian Aboriginal Studies*, No. 2, pp. 15–23.
Jacobs, P. (1990), *Mister Neville: A Biography*, Fremantle Arts Centre Press, Fremantle.
Jasper, J. (1997), *The Art of Moral Protest: Culture, Biography, and Creativity in Social Movements*, University of Chicago Press, Chicago.
Kauffman, P. (2003), 'Diversity and Indigenous Policy Outcomes: Comparisons Between Four Nations', *International Journal of Diversity in Organisations, Communities and Nations*, Vol. 3A (also available www.jabidogun.cgpublisher.com/product/pub.29/prod.3A.20).
Keeffe, K. (2003), *Paddy's Road: Life Stories of Patrick Dodson*, Aboriginal Studies Press, Canberra.
Kidd, J. (1967), 'Aborigines in East Perth', geography thesis, Graylands Teachers College, Perth.
Koling, E. (1987), *The Noonkanbah Story*, University of Otago Press, Dunedin.
Lange, S. (1981), *Pingelly: Our People, Our Progress*, Pingelly Tourist and Town Beautification Committee.
Laurie, A. (1991), 'Rewriting the script of WA Law', *The Bulletin*, 29 October.
Leaming, J. (1986), '"Nearly White": Assimilation Policies in Practice in Western Australia at Sister Kate's Children's Home from 1933 to 1964', unpublished.
Libby, R. (1989), *Hawke's Law: The Politics of Mining and Aboriginal Land Rights in Australia*, University of Western Australia Press, Nedlands.

Liffman, M. (1985), 'Immigration and racism in the land of the long-weekend', in A. Markus and M.C. Ricklefs, *Surrender Australia: Essays in the study and uses of history*, Allen & Unwin, St Leonards.

McGlade, H. and Purdy, J. (2001), '"... No Jury Will Convict": An Account of Racial Killings in Western Australia', in J. Milroy, J. Host and T. Stannage (eds), *Wordal Studies in Western Australian History*, Centre for Western Australian History, University of Western Australia Press, Nedlands.

Macintyre, S. (2004), *The History Wars*, Melbourne University Press, Melbourne.

McKeich, R. (1969), 'Part-Aboriginal Education', in R. Berndt, (ed), *Thinking About Aboriginal Welfare*, Department of Anthropology, University of Western Australia, Perth.

McNally, R. (2003), *Remembering Trauma*, Harvard University Press, Cambridge, Mass.

Makin, C. F. (1970), 'A Socio-economic Anthropological Survey of People of Aboriginal Descent in the Metropolitan Region of Perth', University of Western Australia, PhD thesis.

Mansell, M. (2003), 'The Decline of the Aboriginal Protest Movement', *Green Left Weekly*, 27 August.

Markus, A. and M.C. Ricklefs (1985), *Surrender Australia: Essays in the study and uses of history*, Allen & Unwin, Sydney.

Mathews, R. (1991), 'Juveniles Involved in Persistent Car Theft', unpublished research paper, Department for Community Services, Perth.

Maushart, S. (1993), *Sort of a Place Like Home: Remembering Moore River*, Fremantle Arts Centre Press, Fremantle.

Mayman, J (1995), 'No life of Riley for homeless Aborigines', *Canberra Times*, 13 August.

Mayman, J. (1996), 'A Fighter's Farewell', *Canberra Times*, 4 May.

Meyers, G. and B. Landau (n.d.), *Governance Structures for Indigenous Australians on and off Native Title Lands*, Indigenous Law Resources, available on-line.

Mickler, S. (1996), *Gambling on the First Race: A Comment on Racism and Talk-Back Radio — 6PR, the TAB, and the WA Government*, Centre for Research in Culture and Communication, Perth.

Morgan, S. (ed.) (2002), *Echoes of the Past: Sister Kate's Home Revisited*, University of Western Australia Press, Nedlands.

Patterson, D. and Roth, J. (2004), *After-Words: Post Holocaust Struggles with Forgiveness, Reconciliation and Justice*, University of Washington Press, Seattle.

Pedersen, H. (1995), *Jandamarra and the Bunuba Resistance*, Magabala Books, Broome.

Purdy, D. (1992), 'Royal Commissions and Omissions: The Royal Commission into Aboriginal Deaths in Custody and the Death of John Pat', *Alternative Law Journal*, Vol. 17, No 1, pp. 42–3.

Reid, G.S. and M.R. Oliver (1982), *The Premiers of Western Australia, 1890–1982*, University of Western Australia Press, Nedlands.

Riley, R (1983a), 'Address to Aboriginal Treaty Support Group of W.A.', unpublished, Rob Riley personal archives.

Riley, R. (1983b), 'Aboriginal Law and Its Importance for Aboriginal People', *Commission on Folk Law and Legal Pluralism*. Papers of the Symposia on Folk Law and Legal Pluralism xi, International Congress of Anthropological and Ethnological Sciences, Vancouver, Canada.

Riley, R. (1984a), 'Aboriginal Land Requirements', in M. Booth and C. London, *Western Australia Its Land and Future. Proceedings of a Seminar Sponsored by ANZUSS WA Division*, Perth.

Riley, R. (1984b), *Racial Discrimination and Land Rights*, Speech to the United Nations Working Group on the Rights of Indigenous Peoples (Rob Riley personal papers).

Riley, R. (1986), 'Reconciliation?' *Wikaru, Journal of the Institute of Applied Aboriginal Studies*, Western Australian College of Advanced Education, Perth.

Riley, R. (1987), 'Robert Riley' in C. Glass and A. Weller (eds), *Us fellas: An Anthology of Aboriginal Writing*, Artlook Books, Perth.

Riley, R. (1991), 'Criminal Justice — An Aboriginal Perspective', address to 'Prison The last Option' Conference, 18–19 October, Perth.

Riley, R. (1992), 'And you wonder why you're black', address to 'The Way Out': National Conference on the Role of Employment, Education and Training for Offenders in the Criminal Justice System, Perth, 9–12 February, Australian Institute of Criminology, Canberra.

Riley, R. (1994), 'Aboriginal Self-determination: Can State Laws Cope?' in C. Fletcher (ed.), *Aboriginal Self-Determination in Australia*, Aboriginal Studies Press, Canberra.

Riley, R. (1995), 'Psychologists and Aboriginal People, From Exclusion to Negotiation', *Address to Australian Psychologists' Society*, Annual Conference, Perth.

Ritter, D. (2002), 'The Fulcrum of Noonkanbah', *Journal of Australian Studies*, no. 75, pp. 51–8.

Rowley, C.D. (1986), *Recovery: The Politics of Aboriginal Reform*, Penguin, Melbourne.

Rowse, T. (2000), *Obliged to be Difficult: Nugget Coombs' Legacy in Indigenous Affairs*, Cambridge University Press.

Sears, D., C. Van Laar, and M. Carrillo (2004), 'Is it Really Racism? The Origins of white Americans' Opposition to Race-Targeted Policies', in J.T. Jost and J. Sidanius, *Political Psychology*, Psychology Press, New York.

Stannage, T. (1985), 'How Blainey Half-won the Land', in A. Markus and M.C. Ricklefs, *Surrender Australia: Essays in the study and uses of history*, Allen & Unwin, St Leonards.

State Library of Western Australia, 1984, *Interview Robert Riley*.

Tickner, R. (2001), *Taking a Stand: Land Rights to Reconciliation*, Allen & Unwin, St Leonards.

Ulman, R. and D. Brothers (1988), *The Shattered Self*, The Analytic Press, London.

Vincent, P. (1983), 'Noonkanbah', in N. Peterson and M. Langton, *Aborigines, Land and Land Rights*, Australian Institute of Aboriginal Studies, Canberra.

Weaver, S. (1983), 'Australian Aboriginal Policy: Aboriginal Pressure Groups or Government Advisory Bodies?', Oceania, Vol. 54, No 1, pp. 1–21.

Whittington, U. (1999), *Sister Kate: A Life Dedicated to Children in Care*, University of Western Australia Press, Nedlands.
Williams, G. (1980), 'The New Black Power', *Daily News*, 28 March 1980.
Winnicott, D. (1957), *Mother and Child*, Basic Books, New York.
Winnicott, D. (1964), *The Child, the Family and the Outside World*, Penguin, London.
Woolf, V. (1939), 'The Art of Biography', *The Atlantic Monthly*, Vol. 163.
Yu, P. (1985), 'N.A.C. ... The End or What?', *Kimberley Land Council Newsletter*, Vol. 5, No 1.

Index

Page references printed in *italics* are to photographs and their captions following the page indicated.

Abdullah, George, 81–2
Abdullah, Jill, 176, 208, 209
Aboriginal Advancement Council, 78
Aboriginal Advancement League, 82
Aboriginal affairs funding, 248–9, 282, 308; Fraser government, 137; Hawke government, 139; land rights public awareness campaign, 154, 157, 177–8, 182; Whitlam government, 79, 83
Aboriginal Affairs Planning Authority Act 1972(WA), 87
Aboriginal and Torres Strait Islander Commission (ATSIC), 215–19, 222–6, 232–6; Coombs' recommendation for model, 160; reason for Rob's appointment as Hand's adviser, 212
Aboriginal and Torres Strait Islander Heritage Act 1984, 161–5, 169–70, 176–7, 198
Aboriginal Child Care Agency, 96–7
Aboriginal deaths in custody, *see* deaths in custody
Aboriginal Development Corporation, 199, 217, 219
Aboriginal flag, 210
Aboriginal governance, *see* Aboriginal and Torres Strait Islander Commission
Aboriginal Heritage Act 1972 (WA), *see* Western Australian *Aboriginal Heritage Act 1972*
Aboriginal history, *see* history
Aboriginal hostels, 70
Aboriginal Hostels Ltd, 217
Aboriginal identity, 63, 82, 173, 255, 299; knowledge of racial background, 39, 48–9, 56, 63, 64; racial classification, 31, 38–9, 173
Aboriginal Justice Council, 308, 310
Aboriginal Land Bill (WA), 190–2
Aboriginal land councils, *see* Kimberley Land Council; Northern Territory land councils
Aboriginal Land Fund Commission, 104
Aboriginal land rights, *see* land rights
Aboriginal Land Rights (Northern Territory) Act 1976, 126, 207
Aboriginal Land Rights Steering Committee, 148, 161, 184, 201
Aboriginal Lands Trust, 191
Aboriginal Legal Services, 79, 83; *see also* Western Australian Aboriginal Legal Service
Aboriginal Medical Service (WA), 79–80
Aboriginal police aides, 116
Aboriginal/Police Relations Committee, 99
Aboriginal policy, *see* government policy
Aboriginal rights, 61, 77–82, 124, 125, 289; Preamble to ATSIC Act, 217, 218–19, 221, 233–4, 235; *see also* government policy; land rights
Aboriginal Rights Council, 78, 82
Aboriginal Treaty, *see* Treaty
Aboriginal Treaty Committee, 131
Aboriginal Treaty Support Group of Western Australia, 139
Aboriginals Ordinance 1918 (NT), 312
Aborigines Act 1905 (WA), 12–13, 27–8, 78
ACTU, 117

Adlide, Geoff, 287, 290
African–Americans, 77
Age newspaper, 188–9, 191
Ah Kit, Jack, 206, 207, 235, *240*
Allawah Grove, 49–50
Amax, 106, 107–8, 109, 112
AMIC, 158, 164–5, 168, 182
ANOP Market Research, 185–6, 194, 286
Anthropological Society of Western Australia, 118
anxiety, *see* depression and anxiety
armed revolution, 137–8
army, 74–6
Asian migration, 167
ASIO, 176
assault, 69; racist bashing, 63; sexual, 47, 130, 231, 281, 311, 312, 316
assimilation, 16–17, 33–56, 61, 67, 173; biological absorption, 22–3, 28, 35; *see also* child removal
Association of Mining and Exploration Companies, 264
ATSIC, *see* Aboriginal and Torres Strait Islander Commission
ATSIC Task Force, 219
Auditor-General, 199
Australian Council of Trade Unions (ACTU), 117
Australian Democrats, 170, 225, 234
Australian history, *see* history
Australian Human Rights Commission, *see* Human Rights (and Equal Opportunity) Commission
Australian Institute of Aboriginal (and Torres Strait Islander) Studies, 217, 219, 221
Australian Institute of Aboriginal Studies, 219
Australian Labor Party, 126, 153, 178, 194–5; Noonkanbah, 139–40; Whitlam government, 79, 122–3; *see also* Hawke, Bob, and Hawke government; Keating, Paul, and Keating government
Australian Labor Party, WA, 90, 101; Kimberley results in 1977 elections, 92, 142; *see also* Burke, Brian, and Burke government; Dowding, Peter; Lawrence, Dr Carmel, and Lawrence government
Australian Mining Industry Council (AMIC), 158, 164–5, 168, 182
Australian (newspaper), 149–51, 190, 292, 332–3
Australian Press Council complaints, 137, 151, 255–6
Australian Rules football, 65, 96, 208, 221
Australian Security Intelligence Organisation (ASIO), 176
autonomy and self-determination, 122–6, 301; ATSIC, 215–19, 223–5, 228, 232–6
awards, *320*, 332
Ayres, Robyn, 308–9
Ayton, Deputy Police Commissioner Les, 269, 318, 320

Badjiman, Warford, 152
Balderstone, Simon, 284
Barnett, Colin, 292
Bartlett, Marie, 91
Bartlett, Professor Richard, 283–4
Barunga Festival, 227–8, *240*
bashings, *see* assault
Baume, Peter, 234
Beaufort St Law Courts, 71–4
Bedford, Jenny, 250
Bell, Duncan, 158
Benn, Greg, 274
Bennett, Aunty Vi, 39–40, 48
Bicentennial celebrations, 200, 214, 215, 234, *240*
Bidyadanga community, 297
Bieundurry, Jimmy, 124
biography and biographical sources, 5–7
biological absorption, 16–17, 22–3, 28, 35
Birch, Reg, 124
birth, 31, 37; Anna Dinah's children, 16, 17, 19, 22, 23, 25; Riley's children, 129, 173
Black Action, 79–81, 92
Black Americans, 77
Blainey, Geoffrey, 167–8, 291
Blurton, Peter, 251, 272
Bonner, Neville, 131
Bradley, Min, 40–1, 42–3, 45, 48
Bray, Commissioner, 25
Brennan, Frank, 190
Bridge, Ernie, 92, 142
Broadribb, Andrew, 182
Broome, 113, 237, 238, 276, 281
Bropho, Robert, 108, 245–6, 247, 274
Bull, Police Commissioner Brian, 269
Bulletin, 159–60, 188
Bunbury, 69
Burke, Brian, and Burke government, 139, 140–2, 171–2, 187, 195, 266; deal with Hawke, 183–4, 187; land rights

legislation, 190–2; land rights public awareness campaign, 154, 156–7, 177; Pat case, 171–2; Rob's letter (1983), 156–7; Seaman Inquiry, 141–2, 149–53, 157–9, 178–84, 190
Burke, Tom, 140
Burr, Max, 163
Busselton, 241, 275, *320*
Buti, Tony, 312
Butler, Eric, 155

Calder 1973 (Canada), 286
Cameron, Edward, 230–1
Cameron, Leadham, 230
Cameron, Rod, 185–6
Canada, 138–9; native title model, 283–4, 285, 286, 331
Canberra Times, advertisements devised by Rob in, 183
Cape York Land Council, 284
Capel, 31, 37
Carpenter, Alan, 292
Carrolup Settlement, 28–9, 71
cars, 176, 240–1, 317, 322; stolen and raced by Aboriginal teenagers, 251–8, 266–7, 269–70
Casey, Dawn, 221, 224, 227, 230, 231, 236
Castan, Ron, 284
Central Land Council, 126, 146, 147, 228, 284
Chamarette, Christabel, 272, 297–8, 300, 301–4
Chamber of Mines, Western Australia, 158–9, 262, 263–4, 292
Chaney, Fred, 110
Charleton, Eric, 274–5
Cherrabun Station, 152
Chi, Maxine, 276–7, 281, 311, 314, 323–4
child care, 96–7
child removal, 3, 35–9, 64, 154, 311–13; Commissioner of Native Affairs' powers, 12; Keating's Redfern Speech, 294; knowledge of family background, 37–8, 42, 45, 47–8, 56; Miller (Dinah), Anna, 11; children of, 23, 24; national inquiry, 2, 311–13, 315–16, 327; Rob, 31, 37–9, 42; *see also* institutionalisation
child runaways, 16, 18
childhood and adolescence, 33–74; Anna Dinah (Miller) and children, 16, 18–24, 27, 28–32

children, *64,* 129, 173, 316, 319, *320*
Chulung, Frank, 127
Civil Liberties Action Committee, 95
civil rights movement, US, 77
Clark, Reverend E.A., 62
Clutterbuck, Sister Kate, *32,* 34, 35–6; *see also* Sister Kate's Children's Home
coach, 96
Colbung, Ken, 221, 224, 318
Collard, Dean, *240*
Collard, Lydia, *320*
Collard, Rhonda, 267–9
colonisation, intergenerational impacts of, 150
commercial radio, 91, 154–5, 224–5, 257–8, 265–6
Commissioner for Community Relations, Canberra, 127–8
Committee to Defend Black Rights, 220
Commonwealth State Conference on Aboriginal Affairs, 22–3
compact, *see* Treaty
compensation, 123, 148, 157–8, 287, 289, 316; Land Fund, 289, 304–5; Western Australian draft native title legislation, 292
Cook, Peter, 101
Coolbaroo Club, 82
Coombs, H.C. 'Nugget,' 131, 192; NAC inquiry, 143, 160–1, 199
cottage system, 36, 43–4
Coulter, John, 233
Court, Sir Charles, and Court government, 88–90, 126, 129; Electoral Act changes proposed by, *80,* 91–4, 142; Noonkanbah, 102–4, 106, 109–18; *Police Act 1982* 54B amendment, 94–6
Court, Richard, and Court government, 282–3, 291–3, 296, 310, 313; native title legislation, 292, 299–301; in opposition, 263
court proceedings, 95–6, 204, 274–5, 317–18, *320; Calder 1973* (Canada), 286; child removal actions, 312, 313; Mabo decision and aftermath, 280–1, 299–301; after Noonkanbah, 117–18; Pat case, 170–1
Crawford, Catherine, 250, 275, 282, 283, 306, 307, 312
Crime (Serious and Repeat Offenders) Sentencing Bill (WA), 269–73
Criminal Law Amendment Bill (WA), 269–73

Cross, K.C., 30
Crowe, Stuart, 326
Curtin University, 76–7, 80; Rob Riley Walk, *320*

Daebritz, Beth, 41–2, 48–9, *64*
Daebritz, Dennis, *64*
Daily News, 63, 109, 252, 257; 'The New Black Power' article, 87–8; photograph of Dicky Skinner at Noonkanbah, *112*, 113; publication of 'White Australia has a Black history' in, 209–10
Dalai Lama, *272*
Daniels, Mr and Mrs, 39, 44, 50, 51, 52–3, 59
Darlot people, 105
Darwin, 207–9
Davies, Ron, 90
Davies, Sandy, 275
death, 1–3, 7, 326, 328; Dinah (Miller), Anna, 11, 27; grave, *320*; suicide note, 1–2, 324, 325
deaths in custody, 143–5, 170–2, 219–20, 230–1; Royal Commission findings, 259–61; *see also* Royal Commission into Aboriginal Deaths in Custody
Department of Aboriginal Affairs, 198–9, 217, 219; Perkins, Charles, 148–9, 200, 201, 203, 213, 214
depression and anxiety, 279–80, 281, 307, 313–14, 322, 323–8; childhood, 34, 45, 58; depressive realism, 295–6; after land rights discussions, 194
Derby, 306, 314–15; Aboriginal Legal Service (ALS) Office, 101–2
Dexter, Barry, 101
Dinah, Albert, 17–22
Dinah, Anna, 9–28, *32*
Dinah, Sam, 9–11, 23–4, 27, 28–31, *32*, 69; childhood, 28–31; first meeting with Rob, 50–1
Dinah, Violet, *see* Riley (Dinah), Violet
Dixon Inquiry, 97–9
Djugerari community, 152
Dodson, Mick, 207, 296, 297, 316
Dodson, Pat, 136, 146–8, 186, 188, 193, 206, 227; ATSIC, 223; boycott of Land Rights Steering Committee meeting, 201; Canberra land rights rally, 189, 190; memories of Rob, 136, 194, 195; Miriuwung Gajerrong Ord River agreement, 331; Royal Commission into Aboriginal Deaths in Custody, 236–41, 244, 259; tribute to Riley, 329
domestic service, 31, 37
Dowding, Peter, 140, 141, 176, 191–2; Aboriginal Legal Service lawyer, 87; Noonkanbah; urgency motion, 110; Premier, 231, 232, 246
drug use, 175, 244, 307
Duffy, Michael, 220

East Perth, 66–8
education, 83, 325, 326; Curtin University bridging course, 76–7, 80; high school, 65–6, 68–9; primary, 46–7, 58
Edwards, Graham, 260
Eggington, Dennis, 221, 240–1, 247, *272*
Eggleston, Peter, 273
elections, 181; National Aboriginal Conference, 125, 126–7, 128–9, 137, 168–9, 204–6; National Aboriginal Consultative Committee, 79, 122; Western Australia, 91–4, 140–1, 142, 183–4; gerrymander, 89–90; Western Australian Aboriginal Legal Service, 247
Electoral Act 1979 (WA), Court government's proposed changes to, *80*, 91–4, 142
Evans, Gareth, 303

Falconer, Police Commissioner Bob, 317–18
family background, knowledge of, 37–8, 42, 45, 47–8, 50–2, 56
family life, 64–6, 69, 320–1; reunion, 33, 34, 47–54, 316; parents' first visit, 34, 49, 50, 316; transition from Sister Kate's, 58–9; when married, 129, 161, 208–9, 241, 250, 275–7, *320*; *see also* Riley, Jeannie
Federation of Land Councils, 145–8, 164, 165, 181, 194, 201, 202
'Federation rules,' 146
Fischer, Frank, 60
Fischer, Tim, 291
Fitzroy Crossing, 104
flag, 210
Foley, Gary, 223, 224
football, 65, 96, 208, 221
Foundations for the Future, 217–19, 224
Fraser, Malcolm, and Fraser government, 123–6, 130–1, 137, 138; Human Rights Commission, 174–5; Noonkanbah, 110, 112; Treaty proposal, 132, 134
funding, *see* Aboriginal Affairs funding

Gadaffi, Colonel, 213–14
Gallagher, Michael, 80–1, 115
Gare, Frank, 101
Geraldton, 171, 230–1
Gnowangerup, 61
'Going Home' conference, 311
Goodall, Steve, 39, 42–3, 44, 45, 48, 73
Gordon, Sue, 36–7, 39–40, 44, 45, 46, 48; memories of Rob, 43, 58, 74
governance, *see* Aboriginal and Torres Strait Islander Commission
government inquiries, *see* royal commissions and committees of inquiry
government policy, 22–3, 31–2, 61, 145; international presentations of, 124–5, 138–9, 174–5; under Whitlam, 79, 122–3; *see also* Fraser, Malcolm; Keating, Paul; Western Australian government policy
Government Railways, 70
Grayden, Bill, 112, 118
Graydon, Karen, 173
Greens, 297–8, 301–4
Greiner, Nick, 186

Hagan, Jim, 124–5
'half-castes,' 12, 13, 15, 18, 127; biological absorption, 16–17, 22–3, 28, 35; *see also* child removal
Hamersley Iron Marandoo project, 261–5, 273–4
Hancock, Lang, 137
Hand, Gerry, 211–12, 214–15, 226–7, 335; ATSIC, 212, 215–19, 222, 224, 225–6, 233–4, 235; visit to Pintubi people, 223; at Barunga Festival, 227–8, 240; deaths in custody, 220, 231; Liberal Party attacks on, 226, 228; memories of Riley, 2, 230, 236; on television, 229; Treaty, 221–2, 228, 234
Hand, Gerry, adviser to, 211–36, 244, 335
Hand, Maree, 227
Harding River Dam, 176–7
Harris, William, 77
Hassell, Bill, 96, 159, 172, 186, 291–2, 296; family property, 174
Hawke, Bob, and Hawke government, 138, 153–4, 156, 176, 183–8, 195, 212–14, 240; *Aboriginal and Torres Strait Islander Heritage Act 1984*, 161–5, 169–70, 176–7, 198; ATSIC, 215, 226, 232, 233–4; Coombs inquiry into NAC, 143, 160–1, 199; land rights principles, 154, 181, 188–9, 190; land rights public awareness campaign, 177–8; Noonkanbah, 117; Rob's attack in National Press Club speech, 166–7; Royal Commission into Aboriginal Deaths in Custody, 220; Treaty, 221–2, 227–8; Uluru handover, 176; *see also* Hand, Gerry; Holding, Clyde
Hawke, Hazel, 176, 227
Hawke, Steve, 101, 106, 118
'Healing Our Spirit' conference, 311
health, 175, 244, 277; *see also* mental health
High Court decisions, 280–1, 301
high schools, 65–6, 68–9
history, 4–5, 167, 291, 332–3; Rob's views on, 132–3; Seaman Inquiry argument, 179; 'White Australia has a Black history' theme, 209–10
Holding, Clyde, 141, 159, 176, 181, 183, 192, 211; *Aboriginal and Torres Strait Islander Heritage Act 1984*, 162, 164–5, 169–70, 198; Aboriginal deaths in custody, 171; Coombs Inquiry, 143, 199; land rights principles, 153–4, 188; land rights public awareness campaign, 154, 172, 182; motor vehicle directive, 174–5; relationship with Rob, 156, 194, 198–203; Seaman Inquiry, 141, 142; Steering Committee on Land Rights, 148–9, 161, 184, 201; UN Human Rights Commission delegation, 174
homelessness, 320–1, 327
Homeswest, 321
Horrocks, Ian, 87, 129, 250, 257, 318; at Noonkanbah, 112–14, 116
hostels, 70
hotels, 128, 144
housing and living conditions, 78, 79–80, 327; Allawah Grove, 49–50; East Perth, 66–8; Katanning, 71; Moore River Settlement, 19–20; Pingelly, 59–61, 62–3; Riley family in West Perth, 52, 53–4
Howard, John, 228, 229, 230, 234, 332–3
Howard government, 325
Human Rights (and Equal Opportunity) Commission, 174–5, 245, 332; Stolen Generations Inquiry, 2, 311–13, 315–16, 327
Human Rights Commission, UN, 124–5, 174–5
Human Rights Medal, 320, 332

identity, *see* Aboriginal identity
immigration, Asian, 167
imprisonment, *see* prisoners

inferiority complex, 47
institutionalisation, 9–32, 238; *see also* reserves; Sister Kate's Children's Home
intelligence agency monitoring, 176
intergenerational impacts of colonisation, 150
International Covenant on Civil and Political Rights, 174–5
international issues of political sensitivity, 200, 213–14
international NAC delegations, 124–5, 138–9, 174–5
interracial marriage, 12, 15, 16–17, 22–3, 35; *see also* 'half-castes'
Isaacs, Robert, 191

Jackson, Reverend Jesse, 189
Jarlmadangah, 314–15
Johnson, Elliott, 232, 259
Johnson, Freddy, 108
Justices of the Peace (JPs), 87
juvenile crime and detention, 249, 250–8, 265–7, 269–73, 310, 313; deaths in custody, 143–5, 170–2; Pingelli, 61–2; Rob's assistance to author's project, 3

Karajini Corporation, 264
Karratha, 113, 170, 176
Katakutu Hostel, 70
Katanning, 18, 29, 71
Kay, Arthur, 93
Keating, Paul, and Keating government, 280–1, 284, 285–91, 294–9, 312; establishment of Stolen Generations Inquiry, 311–13, 315–16; land fund and social justice package negotiations, 301, 304–5; Native Title Bill, 296–9, 301–4
Kerr, Sir John, 124
Kickett, Darryl, 96, 176, 240, *272*
Kimberley, 77, 92, 124, 152, 314–15; *see also* Noonkanbah
Kimberley Land Council, 80–1, 104, 117, 119, 305–7; representatives at native title discussions, 284, 288; *see also* Northern Territory land councils

Land Fund, 289, 304–5
land rights, 133–5, 139–43, 145–61, 166–9, 172–96, 200–3; attempts to discredit, 90, 127, 137–8, 154–6, 178, 181–2, 188; Native Americans, 207; native title and, 285, 286–7; New Rights' views, 168; Northern Territory, 126, 147, *176*, 207; public protests, 72–3, 80–1, *176*, 189–90, 202; Seaman Inquiry, 141–2, 149–53, 157–9, 177, 178–81; *see also* National Press Club speech; sacred sites
Land Rights Forum, 172
land rights legislation, 149, 153–4, 161, 186–8; Western Australia, 190–2
Land Rights Steering Committee, 148–9, 161, 184, 201
Lange, E.O., 61
Laverton, 85–6
law clerk, 71–4
Lawrence, Dr Carmel, and Lawrence government, 283, 307, 310; juvenile crime, 260, 266, 269–73; Marandoo project, 262–3, 273–4
League of Rights, 155–6
Lefroy, Miss, 35, 39, 46–7
legacy, 329–36
legal proceedings, *see* court proceedings
legal rights, *see* Western Australian Aboriginal Legal Service
Legge, Kate, 136
Leitch, Police Commissioner G.O., 90, 112, 144
Liberal/National Coalition, 186–7, 189–90, 325, 332–3; Aboriginal and Torres Strait Islander Heritage Bill, 163–4, 169–70; ATSIC, 225–6, 232–3, 234–5; native title, 291, 302–3; Treaty debate, 229; *see also* Fraser, Malcolm; Western Australian Liberal/National Parties
Libya, 213–14
Link-Up, 311
living conditions, *see* housing and living conditions
Lockyear, Min, 40–1, 42–3, 45, 48
Lucas, Harry, 61
Lynch, Aubrey, 127

Mabo decision (native title), 280–1, 282–307, 331
Makarrata, 133–5
Makarrata report, 133
Malcolm X, 77, 297
Malezer, Les, 146, 162, 170, 203, 205
Mallard, Caitlyn, *320*
Mallard, Jason, *320*
Mallard, Margaret, 127, 138, *144*, 204
mandatory minimum sentencing, 269–73
Mansell, Michael, 198, 213–14, 302, 335
Maori, 267
Marandoo project, 261–5, 273–4

Margetts, Dee, 301–4
marriage, 71, 245, 276–7; Dinah (Miller), Anna, 17–22; interracial, 12, 15, 16–17, 22–3, 35; *see also* 'half-castes'; Riley, Violet and Bill, 49, 59
Martin, Carol, 314–15
Mayman, Jan, 2, 321
MacArthur River mine, 294–6
MacBeath, Commissioner, 25–6, 27
MacDonald, Geoff, 155
MacDonald, Graham, 87, 94, 111, 141–2
MacPhee, Ivan, 108
media and media coverage, 82, 127, 326; Aboriginal Treaty Committee advertisement, 131; anti-land rights campaign, 149–51, 154–5, 158–60, 181–2, 188–9; Howard's *Weekend Australian Magazine* interview, 332–3; juvenile crime reports, 252, 254–8, 265–6; land rights public awareness campaign, 182–3; Mansell affair, 213; Marandoo project, 263–4; McArthur River decision, 294–5; native title, 297, 300; Noonkanbah, 106, 108–9; National Aboriginal Conference UNHRC delegation, 124–5; Pingelly racial tensions 1980, 127; racism in, 91, 137, 155; Rob's arrest and trial for reckless and dangerous driving, 317–18, 320; *see also Daily News; West Australian*
media and media coverage, Rob's use of, 135–6, 138, 182–3, 193–4, 248, 272, 274; ABC *Pressure Point* interview, 198–9; *Aboriginal and Torres Strait Islander Act 1984*, 187; on announcement of NAC's abolition, 202; Australian Press Council complaints, 137, 151, 255–6; after being voted out as NAC Chair, 206–7; in Black Action, 80, 81; Collard case, 268, 269; Hand on television, 229;juvenile crime, 256–8, 270; Pat case, 170–1; leaking allegation, 191; letters to editor, 172, 188–9; native title, 282, 283, 292–3, 296, 300; Noonkanbah, 109; police corruption, 144–5; Seaman Inquiry, 157–8; talkback radio, 91, 155, 254–5, 257–8; *see also* National Press Club speech
Melbourne *Age*, 188–9, 191
mental health, 55, 73, 237, 293; drug use, 175, 244, 307; *see also* depression and anxiety
Merredin, 171
Mickey's Pool, 112, 114–17

Mickler, Steve, 240–1, *272*
Middleton, S.G., 27–8, 32
migration, Asian, 167
Miles, Chris, 226, 229, 234
military service, 74–6
Miller, Anna, 9–28, *32*
Miller, Clem, 25
Miller, Ivan, 16, 18, 19, 21, 25
Miller, Sam, 11, 17–18, 19, 20, 21, 24–5
Miner, Mr and Mrs, 39, 44
Mining Act 1979 (WA), 102, 107
mining industry, 88, 102, 137, 140–1, 168, 192; cultural change in, 330; heritage legislation campaign, 162, 163, 164–5; land rights campaign, 178, 181–2, 188, 212; Marandoo project, 261–5, 273–4; native title, 280, 282–3, 287; campaign against, 284–5, 288, 292, 296; Noonkanbah, 106, 107–8, 109, 112; Court's views, 103–4; Northern Territory, 208, 294–6; Seaman Inquiry, 142, 157, 158–9, 179, 181–3; Treaty debate, 229; Western Desert, 105
Mining Industry Council (AMIC), 158, 164–5, 168, 182
Ministerial Statement *(Foundations for the Future)*, 217–19, 224
'Ministerial Warrant,' 12–13, 22, 27–8
Minson, Kevin, 301
Miriuwung Gajerrong people, 305–7, 331
missions, *see* reserves and missions
Moore River Settlement (Mogumber Mission), 9–28, *32*, 35, 37, 50
Morgan, Hugh, 158, 167–8
Morrison, Edith, 18
Morrison, Jeannie, *see* Riley, Jeannie
Morrison, Jim, *80*
Morrison, Maisie, 71
Morrison, Pat, 240, *272*
Mosely Royal Commission, 19–20
motor vehicles, *see* cars
Mount Barker, 11, 22, 24–6
Muirhead, Jim, 232
Munro, Lyall, senior, 161, 169, 201–2, 204–6

NAIDOC week 1987 celebrations, 209–10
National Aboriginal and Islander Child Care, 311
National Aboriginal and Torres Strait Islander Fund, 299
National Aboriginal Conference (NAC), 101, 121–206, *144*, 334; Aboriginal and

Torres Strait Islander Heritage Bill, 162, 169–70; annual conferences, 130, 132; **1984,** 168–9, 170–1, 172–3; Coombs Inquiry, 143, 160–1, 199; elections, 126–7, 128–9, 137, 168–9, 204–6; finances, 176, 199; international delegations, 124–5, 138–9, 174–5; land rights discussion papers, 148, 149, 161; land rights public awareness campaign, 154–5, 156–7, 182–3; Seaman Inquiry, 142, 149–51; Treaty (Makarrata) proposal, 132, 133–5; Western Australian land rights legislation, 190–2
National Aboriginal Consultative Committee (NACC), 79, 81, 122–3, 145
National Coalition of Aboriginal Organisations, 212–14
National Federation of Land Councils, 145–8, 164, 165, 181, 194, 201, 202
National Party, *see* Liberal/National Coalition
National Press Club speech, 166–7, 177, 184, 186, 187, 193–4; reprinted in *The Canberra Times,* 183
National Reconciliation Convention, 329
national referendum, 61, 78
National Times, 131
Native Administration Act 1936 (WA), 20, 25
Native Americans, 77, 107, 207, 233; Canadian native title model, 283–4, 285, 286, 331
native title, 280–1, 282–307, 331
Native Title Bill, 296–9, 301–4
Native Title Tribunal, 289, 303, 305
Native Union, 77
Neale, Superintendent Arthur J., 18, 19, 20
Neville, A.O., 12, 13–23, 24, 28, 35
New Era Aboriginal Fellowship, 78, 83
New Norcia Catholic Mission, 27
New Right, 167–8
New South Wales, 153
New Zealand, 267
Ngarluma people, 176
Ngurawaana, 240
Nichols, Roy, 125, 137
nicknames, 58, 65
1967 referendum, 61, 78
Nixon, Richard, 233
Noonkanbah, 94, 100–20, 192; Australian Labor Party and, 110, 139–40, 162; National Aboriginal Conference UNHRC delegations, 124–5, 174
North Dandalup, 69

Northam, 155–6
Northern Land Council, 126, 147, 206–9, 228, 284
Northern Territory, 207–9, 294–6, 297, 312
Northern Territory *Aboriginals Ordinance 1918,* 312
Northern Territory land councils, 126, 201, 202, 206–9, 228; Federation of Land Councils, 145–8, 164, 165, 181, 194, 201, 202; as preferred ATSIC model, 216
Northern Territory Land Rights Act 1976, 126, 207

Oakley, Jackie, 58, 68–9, 96–7
O'Brien, Peter, 41, 130, 249, 250, 316, 323; recollections of National Aboriginal Conference, 124, 125, 131, 135–7, 151
O'Donoghue, Lois, 297, 299
Office of the Commissioner for Community Relations, Canberra, 127–8
One Arm Point, 153
O'Neil, Des, 94
O'Neil, Sharon, 221, 226
Ord River, 102, 331
overseas trips, 138–9, 174–5; Hagan mission to UNHRC, 124–5; Mansell, Michael, 213–14

pan-Aboriginality, 81, 119, 145–8
pastoral industry, 77, 162, 163, 280, 287, 288; Noonkanbah, 104, 105, 115
pastoral leases, 113, 157, 179, 297, 299, 303
Pat, John, 143–5, 170–2, 259, 260
Pea Hill, 106, 107
Peace Plan, 289, 290–1, 297, 305
Peacock, Andrew, 170, 186–7, 189–90
Pearson, Noel, 2, 284, 296, 297, 302
Perkins, Charles, 148–9, 200, 201, 203, 213, 214
Perth City Council, 210
Perth Law Courts, 71–4
Perth Modern School, 68–9
Pilbara, 88, 176–7, 330; Marandoo project, 261–5, 273–4; *see also* Noonkanbah
Pingelly, 56, 59–66, 127, 253; Rob's grave, 320
Pingelly High School, 65–6
Pintubi people, 223
police, 68, 85–6, 99, 105, 238, 330; Collard case, 267–9; corruption, 98, 145, 309;

Court's warning to new graduates, 90; meal allowances, 309–10; Noonkanbah, 104, 112, 112, 113, 115–17; Pingelly, 62, 127; Riley's personal dealings with, 72–3, 95–6, 137–8, 317–18, 322; *see also* deaths in custody
Police Act 1892 (WA) 54B amendment, 94–6, 113
Police Union, 260, 261
Porter, James, 163, 169
poverty, *see* housing and living conditions
Preamble to ATSIC Act, 217, 218–19, 221, 233–4, 235
Presbyterian Home, 36
press, *see* media
primary schools, 46–7, 58
prior occupation, 132–3, 134
prisoners, 97–9, 239, 330; Dinah, Albert, 20, 22; National Aboriginal Conference (NAC) declaration, 124; *see also* deaths in custody; juvenile crime and detention
Pryor, Geoff, 221
Pryor, Paul, 230
public awareness campaigns, 154, 156–7, 177–8, 182–3, 185–6, 286
public opinion, 195; ANOP poll, 185–6, 194, 286
public protests, 80–1, 91, *144*, *272*; ASIO at, 176; deaths in custody, 144, *144*, 170–1, 230–1; against Electoral Bill changes, *80*, 92; land rights, 72–3, 80–1, *176*, 189–90, 202; mandatory minimum sentencing laws, 270, 272; Noonkanbah, 94, *112*, 113, 114–18, 119–20; *Police Act 1892 (WA)* 54B amendment, 94–6, 113; 'Rallies for Justice,' 261, 266
public servant, 71–4
Public Service Act 1902 (WA), 72
Public Works Act 1902 (WA), 111–12

Queens Park Primary School, 46–7
Quinn's Rocks, 42

'race debate,' 167–8
racial background, *see* Aboriginal identity
racial classification, 31, 38–9, 173; *see also* 'half-castes'
Racial Discrimination Act 1975, 280, 284, 289, 296, 297, 299; Western Australian legislation to extinguish native title, 300–1
racism and race relations, 31–2, 68, 71–3, 77, 238–40, 333–4; children, 46–7, 63; Court's views on, 102–4; in education, 46–7, 65–6, 69; in electoral system, 91–4; *Foundations for the Future* Ministerial Statement, 217–19; in health services, 79–80; Holding's guiding set of principles, 154; Homeswest, 321; Human Rights and Equal Opportunity Commission inquiry, 245; imprisonment rate, 97–9; juvenile crime, WA, 254–8, 266–7, 269–73; in the media, 91, 137, 155; native title debate, 291–3; New Right, 167–8; Office of the Commissioner for Community Relations report, 127–8; Pingelly, 59–63, 65–6, 127; in science, 13, 16–17, 18; Treaty debate, 228–30; *see also* government policy; history; police
radio talkback, 91, 154–5, 254–5, 257–8, 265–6
rallies, *see* public protests
'Rallies for Justice,' 261, 266
rape, 47, 130, 231, 281, 311, 312, 316
reconciliation, 154, 287, 289, 290, 295, 333
Red Centre Meeting, 284–5, 305
Redfern, 83
Redfern Speech, 286, 294, 295
referendum, 61, 78
Reibling, Fred, 71–3
reserves and missions, 9–32, 49, 62; Carrolup Settlement, 28–9, 71; Moore River Settlement (Mogumber Mission), 9–28, *32*, 35, 37, 50; *see also* Pingelly
revolution, armed, 137–8
Reynolds, Henry, 132
Ridge, Keith, 105
rights, *see* Aboriginal rights
Riley, Bill, 33, 34, 49–50, 59, 64, *64*, 316
Riley, Denise, 64
Riley, Emma, *64*, 173, 319, *320*
Riley, Izayoh, *320*
Riley, Jaymea, 129, 173, 319, *320*
Riley, Jeannie, *64*, 70–1, 74, 76, 84, 208, 221; at Aboriginal Legal Service, 82; birth of children, 129, 173; marriage, 71, 245, 276–7; memories of Rob: Aboriginal Legal Service (ALS), 87; background, talking about, 71; Hand's adviser, 215, 225; theft allegation and aftermath, 73; photo taken at time of Rob's departure for army, *64*, 76
Riley, Lila, 64, *64*
Riley, Megan, *64*, 129, 173, 316, 319, *320*
Riley, Tim, 321

Riley (Dinah), Violet, 10, 49–54, 58, *64*, 69, *320*; childhood and adolescence, 23, 24, 28–32; removal of Rob from, 31, 37–8, 42
Rio Tinto, 261, 330
Rob Riley Walk, *320*
Robinson, Sugar Ray, 169, *176*, 204–5
Roebourne, 113, 143–5, 176, 259
Roelands Mission, 29–31
'Roo Dog,' 65
Ross, David, 284, 297, 298
Roth Royal Commission, 13
Royal Commission into Aboriginal Deaths in Custody, 144, 170–2, 230–2, 243, *272*, 301; establishment, 220; report and recommendations, 258–61; funding after release of, 248–9, 282, 308; implementation in WA, 307–11; Rob's involvement, 236–41, 243–5, 255–6; Underlying Issues report, 244
royal commissions and committees of inquiry, 13, 19–20, 78, 85–6, 266–7; ATSIC Bill, 225–6, 232–3; imprisonment rate, 97–9; Stolen Generations, 2, 311–13, 315–16, 327; *see also* Seaman Inquiry
Rubuntja, Wenton, 228, 287
Ruddock, Philip, 163
runaways, 16, 18
running, 46, 58, 65
Ryder, Joe, 26, 27

sacred sites, 153, 157, 192, 289; Aboriginal and Torres Strait Islander Heritage Act 1984, 161–5, 169–70, 176–7, 198; Aboriginal Heritage Act 1972 (WA), 105, 107; Marandoo project, 261–5, 273–4; Swan Brewery re-development, 246; *see also* Noonkanbah
Sattler, Howard, 154–5, 254–5, 257–8, 265–6, 276
school uniforms, 47
schools, 46–7, 58, 65–6, 68–9
Scott, Evelyn, 123
Seaman Inquiry, 141–2, 149–53, 157–9, 177, 178–84, 190
secondary schools, 65–6, 68–9
segregation, 9–32, 59–63, 77–8; hotels, 128; in sport, 65; *see also* reserves and missions
self-determination, *see* autonomy and self-determination
Senate Select Committee on ATSIC Bill, 225–6, 232–3
Senate Standing Committee on Constitutional and Legal Affairs, 132, 134
sexual assault, 47, 130, 231, 281, 311, 312, 316
Shelly, Tony, 249
Shipton, Roger, *176*, 189–90, 211
Simpson, Bobby and Meg, 42
Sioux nation, 77
Sister Kate's Children's Home, *32*, 33–56, *64*, 71, 276; sexual assault at, 47, 130, 231, 281, 311, 312, 316; *Telling Our Story* book launch, 316–17; transition to family life, 58–9; transition to Pingelly, 56, 63, 65
Skinner, Dicky, 108–9, 111, 112, 113
Skull Creek incident, 85–6
Smith, Howard, 95, 96
Social Darwinism, 13, 16–17, 103, 291
social justice package, 304–5; *see also* compensation
soldier, 74–6
South Australia, 153
sovereignty, 133–4, 148, 149, 216; *see also* autonomy and self-determination
speaking engagements, 253
Steering Committee on Land Rights, 148–9, 161, 184, 201
Stewart, Geoff, 265
Stolen Generations, *see* child removal
Stolen Generations Inquiry, 2, 311–13, 315–16, 327
'Stolen Generations Project' (*Telling Our Story*), 47, 311–12, 316–17
Stone, John, 167–8
suicide, *see* death
Sully, V.H., 29
Swan Brewery re-development, 246

talkback radio, 91, 154–5, 254–5, 257–8, 265–6
Tambling, Grant, 226, 234–5
Taylor, Cheryl, 326
Taylor, Ian, 269
Telling Our Story ('Stolen Generations Project'), 47, 311–12, 316–17
terra nullius, 132, 180, 281
Thomas, Mrs R.G., 16
Tickner, Robert, *272*, 280, 289
Tilmouth, Tracker, 284
Toohey, John, 87
Tozer, J.C., 92
Treaty, 131–5, 217, 221–2, 233, 234,

333; Barunga Statement and aftermath, 227–30

Uluru, 176, *240*
umpires, 96
Underwood, Rufus, 14
United Nations Human Rights Commission, 124–5, 174–5
United Nations Working Group on Indigenous Peoples, 233
United States, 77, 107, 189, 207, 233
Uniting Church of Australia, 101, 115, 117

Vancouver, 138–9
Vincent, Phillip, 91, 101–2, 111, 117, 124
Viner, Ian, 123
voting, *see* elections

Wallwork, Henry, 87
ward of state application, 51–4
Watson, John, 119, 136, 288, 314, 315
Weatherby, Cathcart, 297
Weaver, Sally, 145
Weebo Stones, 105
weight, 175, 244
Well, 153
West, Stewart, 139–40
West Australian, 2, 20, 128, 172, 260; on Court and Court government, 89, 93, 112, 129; Court's article on race relations, 102–4; interview with Rob, 173–4; native title, 299–300, 301; Neville's articles on biological absorption, 16; reporting of juvenile crime, 254, 255–6, 257, 258, 265
West Australian Newspapers Ltd, 41
West Perth, 50, 52, 53–4, 58
Western Australian Aboriginal Advisory Committee, 224
Western Australian *Aboriginal Heritage Act 1972*, 105–6, 107, 110, 157, 179; Marandoo project, 262–5, 273–4
Western Australian Aboriginal Justice Council, 308, 310
Western Australian Aboriginal Land Bill, 190–2
Western Australian Aboriginal Land Inquiry (Seaman Inquiry), 141–2, 149–53, 157–9, 177, 178–84, 190
Western Australian Aboriginal Legal Service (ALS), 82–120, 127, 170, 242–323, 335; Annual Reports, 249, 261, 268; appeals against magistrate and JP decisions campaign, 87; author's meetings with Rob at, 3, 10; Court government electoral law proposals, 93–4; Dixon Inquiry into Rate of Imprisonment, 97–9; High Court action against WA native title extinguishment legislation, 300–1; Miriuwung Gajerrong native title claim, 305–7; Noonkanbah protest, 101–2, 106–9, 111–12, 116, 118; Skull Creek incident, 86; 'Stolen Generations Project' *(Telling Our Story)*, 47, 312–13, 316–17; UN Human Rights Commission delegation representative, 124
Western Australian Aboriginal Medical Service, 79–80
Western Australian Aboriginal/Police Relations Committee, 99
Western Australian Aboriginal Treaty Support Group, Riley's speech to, 139
Western Australian Anthropological Society, 118
Western Australian Chamber of Mines, 158–9, 262, 263–4, 292
Western Australian Child Welfare Department, 37–8, 50, 51–4, 59
Western Australian Country Party, *see* Western Australian Liberal/National Parties
Western Australian Department of Community Services juvenile crime study, 252–3
Western Australian Department of Native Welfare, 11–32, 51–2, 54, 61, 101; Allaway Grove, 49–50; Miss Lefroy's letter to, 35, 46–7; Pingelly, 65–6; relationship with Sister Kate's Children's Home, 35, 36; Rob's file, 37–9; Rob's grandmother's file, 10, 11
Western Australian Equal Opportunity Commission, 268
Western Australian government policy, 77–8; assimilation, 16–17, 33–56, 61, 67, 173; segregation, 9–32, 59–63, 77–8; *see also* Burke, Brian; child removal; Court, Sir Charles; Court, Richard; Lawrence, Dr Carmel; Noonkanbah; Western Australian Department of Native Welfare; Western Australian legislation
Western Australian Government Railways, 70
Western Australian Green senators, 297–8, 301–4

Western Australian House of Assembly, 92; Select Committee on Youth Affairs, 266–7
Western Australian Inquiry into the Rate of Imprisonment, 97–9
Western Australian Issues Unit, RCIADC, 236–41, 255–6
Western Australian legislation, 72, 87, 111–12, 257; Aboriginal control, 12–13, 20, 25, 27–8, 78; electoral law, Court government's proposed changes to, *80*, 91–4, 142; land rights, 190–2; mandatory minimum sentencing, 269–73; mining, 102, 107; native title, 292, 299–301, 302; *Police Act 1892* 54B amendment, 94–6, 113; *see also* Western Australian *Aboriginal Heritage Act 1972*
Western Australian Legislative Council, 274–5
Western Australian Liberal/National Parties, 87, 89–90, 105, 173–4, 263, 274–5; Kimberley, in 1977 elections, 92; *see also* Court, Sir Charles, and Court government; Hassell, Bill
Western Australian Mines Department, 107, 112
Western Australian Museum, 107, 108, 110, 174
Western Australian Parliamentary Special Committee on Native Affairs, 78
Western Australian Police Department, 309–10; *see also* police
Western Australian Police Union, 260, 261
Western Australian royal commissions, *see* royal commissions and committees of inquiry
Western Australian School Teachers Union, 252
Western Australian Trades and Labour Council, 101

Western Desert, 105, 139, 153
'White Australia has a Black history,' 209–10
Whitlam, Gough, *320*
Whitlam government, 79, 122–3
Whittington, Vera, 35, 36
Wilkes, Ted, 62, 66–7, 81, *240*, *320*; Aboriginal Legal Service, 247, 275, 282, 307, 318, 322, 323
Williams, Joy, 313
Wilson (Stolen Generations) Inquiry, 2, 311–13, 315–16, 327
Winch, Joan, 39, 40, 41, 44, 45
Winmar, Alice, 60, 61
Winnicott, Donald, 55
Wrigley, Constable, 26
Wyatt, Brian, 79–81, 90–1, 93, 118, 120, 177
Wyatt, Cedric, 85, 86, 128, 176, 326; at Aboriginal Legal Service, 82–3, 84, 247

X, Malcolm, 77, 297

Yindjibarndi people, 176
youth crime, *see* juvenile crime
Yu, Peter, 68, 117, *144*, 210, 276; native title, 284, 292, 301, 302; Miriuwung Gajerrong claim, 305–7; Noonkanbah, 113, 117, 119; Royal Commission into Aboriginal Deaths in Custody, 237–8, 240, 241
Yu, Peter, as National Aboriginal Conference (NAC) delegate, 138, 140, 141, 143, *144*, 161, 200; 1981 elections, 126–7, 128, 130; Harding River Dam, 177; on moves against Rob's leadership of NAC, 202–3, 204; travel for, 161
Yungngora, *see* Noonkanbah
Yunupingu, Galarrwuy, 206, 223–4, 227, 288